Strand of Jewels

Strand of Jewels

My Teachers' Essential Guidance on Dzogchen:
Heartfelt and Straightforward

bLa ma'i zhal gdams kyi snying po thams cad phyogs gcig
tu btus pa'i snying gtam nor bu'i do shal

Khetsun Sangpo Rinpoche

COMPILED, TRANSLATED, AND INTRODUCED BY
Anne Carolyn Klein (Rigzin Drolma)

Lama Tenzin Samphel, advisor

A DAWN MOUNTAIN RESEARCH
INSTITUTE PUBLICATION

SNOW LION
BOSTON & LONDON
2015

Snow Lion
An imprint of Shambhala Publications, Inc.
Horticultural Hall
300 Massachusetts Avenue
Boston, Massachusetts 02115
www.shambhala.com

9 8 7 6 5 4 3 2 1

First Edition
Printed in the United States of America

♾ This edition is printed on acid-free paper that meets the American National Standards Institute Z39.48 Standard.
♻ Shambhala Publications makes every effort to print on recycled paper. For more information please visit www.shambhala.com.

Distributed in the United States by Penguin Random House LLC
and in Canada by Random House of Canada Ltd

Designed by Gopa & Ted2, Inc.

Library of Congress Cataloging-in-Publication Data

Khetsun Sangpo, Rinbochay, 1920–2009, author.
[Nor bu'i do shal. English]
Strand of jewels: my teachers' essential guidance on dzogchen / Khetsun Sangpo Rinpoche; translated, introduced, and compiled by Anne Carolyn Klein (Rigzin Drolma).—First edition.
pages cm
"A Dawn Mountain Research Institute Publication."
Includes bibliographical references and index.
ISBN 978-1-55939-438-3 (hardback: alk. paper)
1. Rdzogs-chen. I. Klein, Anne C., 1947– II. Title.
BQ7662.4.K46813 2015
294.3'420423—dc23
2014026245

To the real liberation, in every sense,
of all people everywhere

Contents

Long-Life Prayer for Khetsun Sangpo Rinpoche xiii

Acknowledgments xvii

Translator's Introduction xxi

Meeting Khetsun Rinpoche xxxiii

Technical Note xxxix

PART ONE: THE TEXT

HOMAGE AND PROLOGUE 3

1. YOUR ORIGINAL FACE: BASE, PATH, AND FRUITION 7

Brief Explanation of the View 7

The Ordinary Mind: Eighty Conceptions 15

Our Moving Mind: More on the Eighty Conceptions 17

Illusions Laced with Holes 25

Buddhas and Other Beings 31

Realizing the Great Seal 33

2. MINDNATURE: THE GREAT SEAL IN NYINGMA 41

3. PATH: DISTINCTIONS THAT ARE KEY TO DZOGCHEN PRACTICE 53

Distinguishing Mind from Sheer Awareness 53

Distinguishing Mental Functioning from Sublime Knowing 55

Distinguishing Consciousness from Primordial Knowing 55

Distinguishing the Allground from the Sheer Essence Dimension 57

Serene Abiding and Dzogchen 57

The Three Doors of Liberation 61

Special Seeing in Dzogchen Meditation 65

4. FINE POINTS OF PRACTICE 87

Sidetracking and Slipping: Pitfalls on the Path 87

Specifics on Slippage 95

Phases of Practice 101

The Three Buddha Dimensions 103

Epilogue 111

PART TWO: THE ORAL COMMENTARY

HOMAGE AND PROLOGUE 117

5. YOUR ORIGINAL FACE: BASE, PATH, AND FRUITION 121

Brief Explanation of the View 124

The Ordinary Mind: Eighty Conceptions 127

The Seven Conceptions Associated with Obscuration 130

Our Moving Mind: More on the Eighty Conceptions 131

⁝ ***First Meditation*** 134

Illusions Laced with Holes 134

The Forty Conceptions Associated with Desire 136

⋮ ***Second Meditation*** 137

Questions and Responses: Posture, Dzogchen, and Indrabhuti 137

Buddhas and Other Beings 141

Realizing the Great Seal 144

6. MINDNATURE: THE GREAT SEAL IN NYINGMA 149

⋮ ***Third Meditation*** 154

Questions and Responses: The Three Dimensions and the Two Types of Clarity 155

7. PATH: DISTINCTIONS THAT ARE KEY TO DZOGCHEN PRACTICE 159

On Sublime Knowing and Primordial Knowing 159

Distinguishing Mind from Sheer Awareness 160

Distinguishing Mental Functioning from Sublime Knowing 161

Distinguishing Mental Functioning from Primordial Knowing 161

Distinguishing Consciousness from Primordial Knowing 162

Distinguishing the Allground from the Sheer Essence Dimension 163

The All-Inclusive View That Is Dzogchen 164

⋮ ***Fourth Meditation*** 168

Questions and Responses: Distinctions Key to Dzogchen 169

Serene Abiding and Dzogchen 173

Special Seeing in Dzogchen Meditation 176

The Three Doors of Liberation 179

Knowing Your Mind 179

⁝ ***Fifth Meditation*** 182

Questions and Responses:
Serene Abiding, Drowsiness, and Furthering Compassion 182

8. Fine Points of Practice 187

Instructions and Stories 187

Sidetracking and Slipping: Pitfalls on the Path 193

Questions and Responses:
Pitfalls Regarding Emptiness, Tantra, and Dzogchen 199

The Tibetan Context: Different Moves on the Mountain 205

Stories of Great Practitioners 206

Foundations of Dzogchen Practice 209

⁝ ***Sixth Meditation*** 213

Questions and Responses:
Furthering Meditation and Helping Others 213

The Three Buddha Dimensions 231

Epilogue to *Strand of Jewels* 237

Part Three: Khetsun Sangpo Rinpoche: Episodes from a Life of Practice

Khetsun Sangpo Rinpoche: A Life of Practice 243

Khetsun Sangpo Rinpoche: A Brief History in His Own Words 249

Prayer for Khetsun Sangpo Rinpoche's Swift Return 261

Notes 265

English-Tibetan Glossary 293

Tibetan-English Glossary 311

Bibliography of Works Cited 329

Bibliography of Tibetan-Language Works by Khetsun Sangpo Rinpoche 337

Credits 339

Index 341

His Holiness Dudjom Rinpoche's Long Life Prayer for Khetsun Sangpo Rinpoche

ཨོཾ་སྭ་སྟི།

རབ་འབྱམས་སྐྱབས་གནས་རྒྱ་མཚོའི་མཐུ་བྱིན་དང་།
བདག་ཅག་ལྷག་བསམ་དག་པའི་བདེན་སྟོབས་ཀྱིས།
ཐར་ལམ་དེད་དཔོན་དགེ་བའི་བཤེས་གཉེན་མཆོག
སྐུ་ཚེའི་ལྷོན་རྩ་མི་གཡོ་ཡུན་བརྟན་ཤོག

མཁས་པའི་རྣམ་དཔྱོད་ཤེས་བྱའི་སྒྲོ་འདོགས་ཆོད།
བཙུན་པའི་མངོན་རྟགས་གཞན་ཕན་བྱང་སེམས་འབྱོངས།
བཟང་པོའི་བག་ཆགས་ཐེག་མཆོག་རིགས་སུ་སད།
དམ་པའི་སྐྱེས་བུ་ཁྱོད་སྐུ་ཡུན་འཚོ་ཤོག

ཐོས་བསམ་མང་ཉོར་གྱིས་ཐར་འདོད་སྤུད་ལ་མཁས།
བསམ་བྱང་སྒྲོན་མེས་སྙོངས་མུན་གསལ་ལ་བརྩོན།

Long-Life Prayer for Khetsun Sangpo Rinpoche

A Commentary on the Meaning of the Syllables of His Name

COMPOSED BY H. H. DUDJOM RINPOCHE

This long-life prayer indicates the esteem in which Khetsun Sangpo Rinpoche was held by the world-renowned Dudjom Rinpoche and acknowledges the devotion that Khetsun Sangpo Rinpoche himself had for his lifelong mentor. Khetsun Sangpo spent nearly forty years of his life building, administering, and teaching at the Nyingmapa Wish-Fulfilling Center for Study and Practice, the school he started at the behest of His Holiness Dudjom Rinpoche and His Holiness the Dalai Lama. It first opened in Dalhousie, India, then moved to Mussoorie, India, and from there to Boudhanath, Nepal; finally settling where it is today, in Sundarijal, Nepal. This poetic text is now part of the historic record of Rinpoche's life.

OṂ SVĀSTI.
By the truthful force of our pure excellent intention,
By the power and blessings of the infinite ocean of refuge,
May the roots at the tree of your being, guide to liberation and
Excellent spiritual friend, be steadfast and unmoving.
Your skillful (*khey*) discernment has severed all mistaken
undervaluing of knowable things.
The manifest sign of your illlustriousness (*tsun*) is your
pure wish to help others, your compassionate mind of
enlightenment.

སྒོམ་ཉམས་རྟོགས་པའི་ཡེ་ཤེས་མཆོག་ཏུ་བཟང་།
རྣལ་འབྱོར་དཔའ་བོ་ཁྱོད་སྐུ་ཡུན་འཚོ་ཤོག

ཀུན་ཁྱབ་སེམས་ཉིད་མ་བཅོས་སྟོང་དབྱིངས་མཁར།
སྣང་བ་མ་འགགས་རིག་པའི་རྒྱན་དུ་ཤར།
ཟུང་འཇུག་མཉམ་ཉིད་འོད་གསལ་རྡོ་རྗེ་སྒྲོལ།
ཡེ་ཤེས་སླི་པོའི་ངོ་བོར་རྟག་གྱུར་ཅིག

ཅེས་པའང་སྤྱི་འགྱུར་བཤད་སྒྲུབ་འདོད་འཇོ་གླིང་གི་སློབ་ཚོགས་ཐུན་མོང་ནས་བསྐུལ་བ་དོན་ཡོད་པའི་ཕྱིར་དམར་སེར་ཅན་གྱི་དབྱུང་ཟླའི་༢ཡར་ཚེས་༡་ཤར་བ་ན་འཇིག་བྲལ་ཡེ་ཤེས་རྡོ་རྗེ་འགྲོ་འདུལ་པས་བྲིས་པ་ཛ་ཡ་ནྟུ་ས་ཏ་མངྒ་ལཾ།།

Your predispositions for gentle goodness (*zang*) have awakened the supreme Mahayana lineage.
Excellent being, may you live long.

Through the jewel of your rich hearing you are skilled (*khey*) in attracting seekers of liberation.
Through the lamplight of your reflection you are illustrious (*tsun*) in illuminating the darkness of our ignorance.
Through meditation your primordial knowing, experience, and realization are supremely gentle and good (*zang*).
Heroic yogi, may you live long.

In the expansive, empty sky, suffused with uncontrived mindnature,
Visions dawn as ornaments of sheer awareness (*rig pa*) unceasing.
Unification of these is the diamond integration of sameness and clear light.
Essential heart of primordial knowing, may you be so forever.

In response to a request from the students and faculty
of the Nyingma Wish-Fulfilling Center, this was
written as it dawned for the Tamer of Beings,
Jigdrel Yeshe Dorje [Dudjom Rinpoche] on the
first day of the ninth month of the female
fire-snake year, 1977, *jayantu.*

Sarva mangalam.

Acknowledgments

GREAT GRATITUDE to everyone, seen and unseen, who made this text and teachings possible. In roughly chronological order, streams of thanks to the following people:

Khetsun Sangpo Rinpoche, for guidance in the wonders of *Heart Essence, Vast Expanse,* and other treasures for over thirty-five years, all the while unfailingly displaying the profound gentleness and flowing generosity that wisdom holds.

Harvey B. Aronson, Khetsun Sangpo Rinpoche's first Western student, for introducing me to Rinpoche, traveling with me many times to study with him, taking turns on the hot seat translating his teachings—especially the teachings that became this book—helping to organize many of his trips to visit us, and being my partner in so many travels, retreats, and other Dharma endeavors since we met in 1969.

Friends and students of Rinpoche who were core organizers of one or more of Rinpoche's several visits to California from the mid-1980s to 2006, especially those who made possible the 1996 visit during which he taught *Strand of Jewels*: the late Jey Clark (who recorded the oral commentary included here), Nina Egart, Susan Oliver, Steven Goodman, Cate Hutton, Laurie Ludwig, John Pfeiffer, and Larry Shaw.

Christopher Matthew Walker, who suddenly appeared, without prior knowledge of Rinpoche, and volunteered to transcribe most of those teachings.

Rice University for research funds supporting this work, and also for hosting lectures by Khetsun Sangpo Rinpoche, with special thanks to Laura Hsu and the Glasscock School of Continuing Studies at Rice for last-minute hosting of one of Rinpoche's first visits to Houston.

Mark Yurewicz, to my knowledge Rinpoche's last Western student, who transcribed a good portion of Rinpoche's tape-recorded commentary on this text, digitized the recordings to preserve them, and also made the final transfer of Rinpoche's digitized Tibetan text for pubication.

Etienne Bock for inputting the initial edited digital text.

Elizabeth Wallett for copyediting the transcript of Khetsun Sangpo's story of his life.

P. Jeffrey Hopkins for requesting, translating, and recording Rinpoche's autobiographical reflections, and allowing us to incorporate this here.

Yukari Sueyasu, for swift and crucial help in gathering many details of Khetsun Rinpoche's life.

Kangyur Rinpoche Tulku, Jigme Norbu, Rinpoche's grandson and now head of the monastery, for answering questions about Rinpoche's life.

Tsehua Gyal, for meticulous and swift bibliographical research tracing the many quotations in *Strand.*

The Tibetan Buddhist Resource Center and staff, with special thanks to Michael Sheehy for exceptional help with the bibliographical research in the spirit of TBRC's visionary founder, the generous genius, Gene Smith.

Lama Tenzin Samphel, for reviewing with enormous care the English translation and edits of the Tibetan text, including bibliographical details, and for answering waves of questions, some of them more than once, with gracious perspicacity.

Michele Martin for a rigorous penultimate edit, using her meticulous eye for grammar, Tibetan language, and deep knowledge of the traditions discussed here.

Renée Lynn Ford for excellent final coordinating of the bibliography and glossaries that appear at the end of this book.

Shambhala / Snow Lion in general and in particular Emily

Bower for warmly supportive and keen-eyed editing, and Ben Gleason for likewise bringing the project to conclusion with grace.

Nova Spivack for important last-minute suggestions and moral support during late-stage proofing in China.

Justin Kelley for careful final proofing of the Tibetan pages' match with the English.

Jermay Jamsu for crucial final checking of Tibetan text, spelling, and layout. Justin Kelley for careful final proofing, especially of the Tibetan pages' match with the English.

John Canti and Wulstan Fletcher, on behalf of Padmakara, graciously granting permission to use Protector images from their collection.

The Dawn Mountain board, community, staff, and students for providing a profoundly supportive environment in which to invite and host Khetsun Sangpo Rinpoche, Kangyur Tulku Jigme Norbu Rinpoche, and Lama Tenzin Samphel.

Sidney Piburn, the legendary founding editor of Snow Lion, took an early interest in publishing this work, greatly encouraging me with his commitment to a book presentation that would appropriately honor Khetsun Sangpo Rinpoche.

Translator's Introduction

Mindnature itself is a completely perfect Buddha
So don't seek Buddha anywhere else.
—Jigme Lingpa, *Chariot of Omniscience*

From the very first words of his text, it is clear that Khetsun Rinpoche's book and oral commentary on it are animated by his loving gratitude for his teachers and a wish to share their wisdom. The essence of that wisdom, collected and practiced over his long and fruitful life, is the focus of this book, which he describes as "heartfelt and straightforward." In it he distills a lifetime of studying and practicing Dzogchen texts and teachings. The volume you are holding contains Rinpoche's own text, in the original Tibetan and in English translation, as well as his oral commentary on this, embellished by exceptionally rich responses to a wide variety of questions asked by those in attendance when he gave these teachings.

Khetsun Sangpo Rinpoche was almost forty years old when circumstances forced his departure from Tibet. He had spent twelve years studying sutra, tantra, and Dzogchen in a variety of settings, and about six years devoted to retreat. The first two years of his exile in India were also spent in retreat. He was one of a handful of Dzogchen yogis who, having completed scholarly and meditative training in traditional Tibet, went on to an active teaching role in monastic settings in exile, and he also had significant contact with Western practitioners and scholars.

Wherever he taught, Rinpoche always stayed close to the traditional Tibetan idiom and rigor.

This book begins with a translation of Rinpoche's own text, *Strand of Jewels,* followed by his extensive oral commentary on it, including rich responses to questions from Western practitioners. Together, his body of work here is a unique masterpiece. It combines scholarly depth, meditative experience, and rich oral commentary. Many topics covered are of particular interest to experienced practitioners; seeing them in print in a Western language is rare.

This book is not meant just for reading. It is meant to inspire and nourish lifelong practice, fully informed by Dzogchen perspectives and their wider Buddhist context. Therefore, what you will find here, most centrally, are pith instructions to be ripened and recognized through your own experience. These instructions are portals to the kind of continuous and nuanced practice that alone can bring fruition. Reading is only the first step.

The words required to energize practice must be straightforward, meaning frank and based in experience. Speaking frankly means being ready to say whatever is needed to further understanding, so it is straight-talking in that it unflinchingly points out where our errors may lie. "Heartfelt" means that these instructions come from the heart of experience: Rinpoche's teachers' and his own.

Those of us who knew Rinpoche during the last forty years of his life recognize what an extraordinary gesture this work is. Throughout those four decades, he unfailingly declined to speak a word about Dzogchen to anyone who had not completed the foundational practices. As he mentions here, this resulted in his turning away many students. Only practitioners who had completed the practices, or were seriously in the process of doing so, were admitted to the weeklong retreat where these teachings were initially given, at Pema Osel Ling, the late Lama Tharchen's beautiful center near Santa Cruz, California, in 1996. Harvey Aronson and I orally translated Rinpoche's teaching and commentary on his text during that retreat. Some time later, I asked Rinpoche if he wished to see an English translation of this text published. At first he did not. However, over time, Rinpoche became enthusiastically committed to seeing this text made more widely available, and ultimately he determined that even his commentary on it—which contains even more deeply insider teachings than the text itself—should also be published in translation.

Throughout his life and work, as well as in this text, Khetsun Sangpo Rinpoche emphasizes that all followers of Buddhist paths are equally children of the Buddha, and that whatever spiritual path we choose, Buddhist or non-Buddhist, it is important to practice it well while at the same time genuinely respecting the practice of others. All these paths bring benefit. This honoring embrace, and Rinpoche's wish to impart sacred and pith instructions for dedicated practitioners, are central pillars of his work. These pillars are grounded in his deep study of Nyingma and other Buddhist literatures.

Rinpoche's expansive and studied view on the merit of all spiritual teachings harkens back to the great openhearted scholarly figures of the Rimé (*ris med*), or all-inclusive, religious vision, in Tibet. Great masters who studied multiple traditions have been identified throughout Tibetan religious history. In the nineteenth century this panoramic perspective cohered as an important movement, in which Jamgön Kontrul Lodro Thaye and Jamyang Khyense Wangpo, with their masterful compendia of literatures from multiple traditions, were major figures. This universalist-like movement was characterized by an interest in learning from any or all of the Tibetan traditions.

The eighteenth-century Jigme Lingpa, who compiled the *Heart Essence, Vast Expanse* (Longchen Nyingthig) teachings after receiving visions of Longchen Rabjam, is seen as an important forerunner of this movement, especially in view of his historic compilation of the Seventeen Tantras, crucial ancient sources for Dzogchen in Tibet. Khetsun Sangpo Rinpoche, heir to this lineage, reflects in the course of his commentary on the interrelated meanings of Geluk, Kagyu, Sakya, as well as Nyingma sources.

Another striking feature of his work is Khetsun Rinpoche's commitment to furthering both experiential development and the cognitive understanding that helps sustain and make sense of such development. This, and Rinpoche's embracing of the nonsectarian approach just mentioned, means that he cites and discusses a wide range of sources, sutra as well as tantra, along with commentarial material from all four schools of Buddhism in Tibet. We see this especially in his extensive reflections on the harmonious meanings of *Dzogchen* (the Great Completeness), Mahamudra (the Great Seal), and *Madhyamaka* (the Middle Way) (chapters 2 and 5) and in his richly informed synthesis of the fine distinctions central to Dzogchen practice (chapters 3 and 6).

Rinpoche's opening homage is itself a teaching on the centrality of mindnature and lineage. In Dzogchen teachings on mindnature, base, path, and fruition are an important triad around which many texts are structured. Rinpoche's prologue pithily identifies these. From there, *Strand of Jewels* continues with a gentle introduction to reality through the three dimensions of enlightenment: the sheer essence, richly resplendent, and emanation dimensions (*dharmakāya, sambhogakāya,* and *nirmāṇakāya*).

At the most fundamental level of our being, referred to as "the base" (*gzhi*), these three Buddha dimensions reside as essence, nature, and compassionate responsiveness. These dimensions are always present, though not always in manifest form. Longchenpa also mentions them in laying out Dzogchen in his *Precious Treasury of Philosophical Systems.*[1]

Historically speaking, the three may receive their first mention in a verse from the *Pearl Garland Tantra* cited by Longchenpa in his *Treasury of Philosophical Tenets.*[2] There, as in Jigme Lingpa's famous refuge prayer[3] and in Rinpoche's writing here, this triad is an analogue of the three Buddha dimensions. In terms of the basis, the three dimensions are the three inborn qualities of sheer awareness: empty essence, luminous nature, and compassionate responsiveness. On the path, the three are dynamism, playful expression, and ornament. And in the full fruition of practice, they are the actual Buddha dimensions of sheer essence, rich resplendence, and emanation. Practice is able to awaken these qualities because they are already within us. As Nagarjuna's famous teacher, Saraha in a verse cited by Rinpoche, says, "Our one mindnature is the seed of everything." Negative qualities arise from our mindnature as well, but whatever arises, that nature itself remains stainless.

The fourth century Indian scholar-practitioner Asanga describes visions he had of Maitreya Bodhisattva in which he received very precise teachings from him, known as the five books of Maitreya. One of these, the *Sublime Continuum (rGyud bLama, Uttara Tantra)*, as well as Asanga's commentary on it, are an important source for Nyingma interpretations of stainless space (*chos dbyings; dharma dhatu*). Stainless space, also understood as Buddha nature, is described here in terms of three aspects: its luminous clarity, unchanging nature of suchness, and orientation to Buddhahood.[4]

The third aspect, the orientation to Buddhahood, is described by Asanga as twofold: a beginningless lineage, which has always been, and the transformed lineage, which requires one's effort.[5] The first of these is important because knowing we are already a Buddha inspires us to the effort of purifying the afflictions which prevent that Buddhahood from being fully manifest. Thus, Longchenpa writes, it is important to recognize our own quality of stainless space.[6] As Rinpoche's teaching emphasizes, what we seek in practice is not something other than we already are. Rather, we seek (in Longchenpa's words) to become a "Buddha again."

The *Sublime Continuum* states that "the utterly lucid nature of mind is unchanging, like space." Longchenpa cites and builds on this statement by equating stainless space with ultimate truth and primordial wisdom on the bodhisattva path. In doing so, he follows Maitreya's description of *dhatu* as "empty of adventitious stains."[7] When Longchenpa subsequently discusses stainless space in terms of Dzogchen,[8] he again describes it as pure, as well as lucid, spontaneous, and ever present.[9] Rinpoche's comments here help us see the roots and broad significance of this inborn, inviolable purity.

Chapter 1 opens with a distilled discussion of the Dzogchen view, citing several ancient-transmission tantras as well as works by Longchen Rabjam, Saraha, and other great figures from all four traditions.

The genuine view rescues us from error. The genuine view to which Dzogchen refers is mainly a term of experience. It is not simply an idea, as when persons articulate a particular view of society, justice, or global warming. Buddhists acknowledge a wide variety of views: views with extremes, views without extremes, skillful views, clever views, good views, and bad views. All these are views with an object, a point of focus, and are anchored in correct or faulty reasoning. Such views are created by mind. The Dzogchen view is not.

> To view is to mind-stain.
> Stainlessly pure reality is
> Twice free: of viewed and of viewer.
> View itself has no view.
> —Jigme Lingpa, *Chariot of Omniscience*

To have a correct view is to be free from error. Where do these errors come from, according to Dzogchen? Although the base is without error, we ordinary beings perceive it erroneously.

One way of describing this erroneous perception is through the eighty conceptions that perpetuate cyclic existence. Rinpoche draws from the enumeration of these in Aryadeva's third-century work, *Lamp Distilling the Practices: A Commentary on the Meaning of the Five Stages [of the Guhyasamaja Completion Stage]* (*sPyod bsdus sgron ma, Caryamelapakapradipa[pradipa]*). In this way he combines sustained discussion of Dzogchen's view with details from classic and relatively early Indian Mahayana descriptions of error.

Erroneous perception governs our sense of ourselves and our world. This error is largely the work of mind (*sems*) and mental functioning (*yid byed*). Mind is what makes an initial connection to an object, and mental functioning is a more robust, conceptual engagement with it. Mental functioning is central to the types of habits and predispositions that trap us. To better understand the functioning of our mistaken mind, Rinpoche lays out the eighty conceptions that dissolve when the light of wisdom dawns (chapters 1 and 5) and distills the kind of distinctions needed to further contrast ordinary mind with such wisdom (chapters 2 and 6).

The fact that we can navigate the world, that there seems to be so much agreement on how things work, supports our powerful yet erroneous sense that our everyday understanding is enough. We get by. What's the problem? For Buddhism in general, the problem is that we are blind to what we are and to the real truth of everything around us. Therefore, receiving and integrating with a qualified lama's introduction to our mind's naked reality is central to Dzogchen practice. This introduction sets practitioners on course to transcend obscuring error. Instead of being sealed with error, our experience is sealed by reality. And thus there is much interest in precisely identifying that seal, that great *mudra*. Gaining an experientially grounded identification is a vital step for the Dzogchen practitioner. It requires trust and a deep connection between teacher, student, and steadfast practice. Once this identification resonates clearly, it is the basis for all subsequent practice. Slowly it becomes possible to recognize and eventually undo our mistaken mind's beginningless chains of error. Until we are fully wedded to wisdom, we seek to understand this mind well and deploy it optimally. Even though our ordinary mind, being mistaken, always obscures reality, it can also, in Rinpoche's words, take us right to the brink of liberation.

In light of this, Khetsun Rinpoche reviews a range of important teaching lineages in Tibet, especially major Sakya, Kagyu, and Geluk interpretations of Mahamudra, the Great Seal. He also includes the Jonang, Pacifiers, and Severers, and others. In accord with the nonsectarian vision running through his entire work, he carefully reads this material to conclude that all the traditions' identifications of reality, which are not identical, nonetheless accomplish the same great purpose. The breadth of his contemplative reflection, the fruit of a lifetime of careful study and deep practice, then sets the contemplative framework for Rinpoche's discussion of Nyingma.

Guru Rinpoche identifies mindnature as the Great Seal and this identification is central to Nyingma's understanding of Mahamudra. Mindnature is what the lama identifies for the student, and what the student seeks to recognize and make familiar. Rinpoche takes this identification as his gateway to the very heart of Dzogchen practice, unveiling key points that, with time, dedication, and the power of transmission, can undo the otherwise endless cycles precipitated by our eighty conceptions.

In an exceptionally practical and nuanced reflection, meant to support one's own meditation and exploration of mindnature, Rinpoche introduces the subtle discriminations key to such Dzogchen practice. These are essential instructions for seeing the reality that is one's true face. These include an unusually subtle parsing of serene abiding and special seeing; a brief summary of how the three doors to liberation, well known in sutra literature, are complete in Dzogchen; and pithy descriptions of the three phases of serene abiding from a Dzogchen perspective.

Of course, just reading such words will not accomplish much. Anyone oriented toward such discovery will attend to practice and seek out a good relationship with a qualified teacher with whom there is enough mutual trust to discuss the intricacies of practice and the habit-holdings that obstruct it. In this way it becomes possible to give and receive words that illuminate experience. This is how real contact with the teachings can occur, so that our inborn basic awareness—the sheer awareness of primordial wisdom—can know itself. As Guru Rinpoche points out in a verse that closes *Strand*'s second chapter:

> Unless sheer awareness's intrinsic dynamism pours
> forth
> Whatever rests on unclear stability[10]
> Will not give rise to the slightest improvement.
> Therefore, precise and lucid sheer awareness is vital.
> Many meditators understand their meditation very
> little.

The discriminations at the heart of Dzogchen practice are exquisitely subtle and easily missed. It is easy to think of our experience as correct when it is not, to mistake the continuity of an ordinary state with the sublime continuity of real presence. These are the fine discriminations that Khetsun Rinpoche introduces in chapters 3 and 6 and elaborates upon during question-and-answer periods in the retreat. In discussing the special seeing of Dzogchen, the center of chapter 3, Rinpoche offers this mirror for a meditator's experience:

> Once you have seen your own face, there is no way for all abiding and proliferation *not* to be the view, a union of serene abiding and special seeing.

This does not come about through will, striving, or intellectual acuity, even though all of these have roles to play. As the ordinary mind-habits become less powerful and more diluted with wisdom, the path is powered by blessings (literally, "waves of splendor"), rather than by our own push-and-pull mind.

Blessings are of great consequence on the path of Secret Mantra. Rinpoche points this out and then commences a cascade of inspiring and clarifying descriptions of the interplay of serene abiding and special seeing, augmenting this by a three-phase description of how serene abiding feels in the early, middling, and culminating stages of practice.

Such a path involves transforming our relationship to our own thoughts and emotions. Above all it is a process of delivering ourselves from our overwhelmingly addictive habit of fully identifying with whatever we think or feel. Practice slowly dissolves the core experiences of self that form on the basis of these. Finally, the root of all our erroneous and limited experiences of self give way to wisdom. Regarding this, Khetsun Rinpoche cites Gyalwa Lorepa's words:

> A tree's branches and leaves are fully unfurled—
> Cut its root and a billion leaves go dry.

In chapters 4 and 7 Khetsun Rinpoche illuminates the challenges of staying the course and not mistaking error for a path. This caution is crucial, and a priceless boon for practitioners seeking to deepen and stabilize understanding.

Students sometimes wonder why, if reality is so fundamentally simple, we should engage in complex sets of practices, or be required to complete foundational practices, or why we need explanations of any kind, much less as detailed as we find here? Why not just sit and quiet the mind? One is right to contrast the effortful gestures needed as we set out on the path with the utterly simple reality we long to know. Yet, without guidance, training, and enough conceptual scaffolding to counter doubt and build support for sustained commitment, we cannot break out of our ordinary way of seeing things. It is quite impossible. Hence, Khetsun Rinpoche began this work with crucial information about the nature of the trap we are in, and he closes with a reminder that the profound practices core to *Strand of Jewels* must be supported by the foundational practices. In addition, he calls the creation and completion stages of tantra the best friend our Dzogchen practice can have. These, complemented by the guidance of a qualified teacher as well as our own daily practice, are crucial ingredients for successful path-making.

Each day during the retreat, after giving commentary on that session's section of the text, Rinpoche took a generous amount of time to respond to questions. During these sessions, Rinpoche opened up on many topics, especially clarifying points of experience. Some readers might prefer to turn to the commentary before reading the text itself, allowing the text then to serve as a distillation of material you are already in the process of digesting.

May the text, commentary, and on-the-spot question-and-answer sessions included here, as well as central elements of Rinpoche's life story, convey in some small measure the depth and breadth of Rinpoche's scholarly richness as well as the grace and skill he brought to his personal and public conversations.

Meeting Khetsun Rinpoche

An Overview of His Work in the West

IN THE AUTUMN of 1971, I walked down a winding dirt road in Darjeeling. Harvey Aronson and I had just visited the renowned Buddhist master Kangyur Rinpoche. About halfway along, we met a sweetly radiant presence, moving swiftly along the road. It was Khetsun Sangpo Rinpoche, walking up to see his teacher, Kangyur Rinpoche.

This was a second serendipity. The first occurred the previous year, a few days after Khetsun Sangpo Rinpoche returned to India after a full decade in Japan as Dudjom Rinpoche's representative. Harvey spotted him at a tea stall in Sarnath and, after several intriguing conversations, followed him to Dharamsala, where Rinpoche was writing his twelve-volume *Biographical Dictionary of Tibet and Tibetan Buddhism* and working in various scholarly capacities at the newly founded Library of Tibetan Works and Archives. I joined Harvey in India that summer, and by the time we were walking down that Darjeeling road, he had already told me a great deal about Rinpoche. My lighthearted delight and surprise on seeing him face to face was immediate, even before Harvey told me who he was.

I next saw Rinpoche in the predawn dark at Dulles airport outside Washington, D.C., in January 1974. Several of us, including Harvey, Jeffrey Hopkins, and Donald S. Lopez Jr.—who at the time was an undergrad at the University of Virginia—were there to welcome Rinpoche on his first trip to the United States.

Jeffrey had studied extensively with Rinpoche in Dharamsala in 1972. Now, as a professor of religious studies at the University of Virginia, he had invited Rinpoche to teach there.

With Jeffrey translating, Khetsun Rinpoche taught the great classic of the *Heart Essence, Vast* Expanse tradition, Patrul Rinpoche's *Words of My Perfect Teacher,* to more than one hundred students. These lectures became the basis for Rinpoche's first book in English, *Tantric Practice in Nyingma*, translated by Jeffrey, for which I was coeditor. Rinpoche also gave extracurricular instructions to students and townspeople interested in the foundational practices in the tradition known as Heart Essence, Vast Expanse (Longchen Nyingthig).[11] To those of us living in the same house with him, he would charmingly ask after our minds when we were gathered in the kitchen. We spent hours around the table, before, during, and after meals, bemused and giggling at our inability to describe what mind was like or locate it. We found it a delightful way to pass time with Rinpoche. We had no idea what it had to do with Dzogchen.

Gradually we learned more about who Rinpoche was: how he received the *Heart Essence, Vast Expanse* transmission from the great Jetsun Shugseb herself (at Longchenpa's meditation place, Kangri Thogar) and from the eminent recluse Lama Gonpo Rinpoche, and the training he received in sutra and tantra in Tibet; and that he spent several summers in the mountains protecting the area from hail, another specialized training in which he excelled.[12]

Just before he returned to India, Khetsun Rinpoche spent an evening reading and discussing some select few pages from his autobiography to a few of us. He reflected briefly on his experiences in the dark retreat (*mun mtshams*) according to the Essential Black (Yangti Nagpo) cycle, a rare lineage that only he and Trulzhig Rinpoche of Solo Khumbu held at that time. He spoke softly, simply, and modestly. By evening's end, we were thoroughly inspired. How and when could we hear more? That was simple. If we wanted to study further with him, we would complete the foundational practices and learn Tibetan. He would not give such profound instructions through a translator. Fortunately, Jeffrey was teaching Tibetan at the University of Virginia, and also inviting renowned scholars every year, usually handpicked by His Holiness the Dalai Lama, with whom we could begin to read texts in Tibetan and practice conversation.

Still, it was 1977 before we would meet Rinpoche again. Harvey and I traveled to Mussoorie, where Khetsun Sangpo Rinpoche had established his school, the Nyingmapa Wish-Fulfilling Center, now also integrated with the Dudjom Institute, for young Tibetan refugee monks. Despite his already full schedule, Rinpoche taught us at least five or more hours daily for two months.[13] His Tibetan students shared a room in the back of Rinpoche's house. One afternoon Harvey opened the door to have a look. Sixteen-year-old Tenzin Samphel, anticipating the arrival of his schoolmate, was at that moment standing alert inside the doorway, his arm primed with a bucket of water which he energetically emptied toward the approaching footsteps, only to discover with horror the honored American visitor who was now dripping wet.

Decades later Rinpoche told us that Lama Tenzin Samphel seemed to be his very best student. In the 1990s, Lama Tenzin was invited to France, where he taught in Paris at the Bibliothèque Nationale de France and the Sorbonne, as well as at Dudjom Rinpoche's center in Dordogne. He also founded his own center near the beautiful town of Septvaux outside Paris. Rinpoche visited there several times, and I reconnected with Lama Tenzin during one of those visits and also at Rinpoche's monastery in Nepal. Lama Tenzin has been of great help in finalizing this translation during his visits to Houston to teach, at my invitation, at Rice University and Dawn Mountain.

Jeffrey Hopkins also continued to invite Khetsun Rinpoche to the University of Virgina. During one of these visits, Jeffrey requested and received his extensive and very practical commentary on Ju Mipham Rinpoche's *Three Cycles of the Fundamental Mind* (*gNyug sems skor gsum*). The first volume of this work, translated and edited by Jeffrey, is published as *Fundamental Mind: The Nyingma View of the Great Completeness.* More volumes are expected soon.

During another of Rinpoche's visits to Charlottesville, Virginia, Jeffrey had the happy inspiration to conduct an extensive interview with him about his adventurous and challenging life. Jeffrey kindly gave me permission to edit and include that interview, which he translated orally, as part of this volume, so that readers of Rinpoche's own work on Dzogchen could know more about him.

At my invitation Khetsun Rinpoche visited California—which he cheerfully named "the peak of cyclic existence"—in the late eighties when I was teaching at Stanford, and he also came several times to Rice University in Houston, from where he would travel elsewhere in the United States at the invitation of different groups. Over the years he gave many teachings, several of them more than once, including Atisha's *Seven Point Mind Training* (*bLo spyong don bdun ma*), Dudjom Rinpoche's *Mountain Dharma* (*Ri chos*), Patrul Rinpoche's commentary on Garap Dorje's *Three Striking Phrases* (*Tshig gsum gnad brdeg*), and Jigme Lingpa's practice texts on *powa* and severance (*gcod*). He also gave initiation into the Guru Rinpoche and Dakini Yeshe Tsogyal consecrations from the Essential Black cycle and taught a small section from that tradition during a group retreat at the Margaret Austin Center outside Houston, Texas.

During several weekend teachings at the Shambhala Center in Boulder, Colorado. Khetsun Rinpoche taught Mipham Rinpoche's *Abiding, Movement, and Awareness* (*gNas, 'gyu, rig gsum*), and, on his final trip, and for the very first time, a text he told us he had brought out of Tibet and carried with him for over forty years, Yeshe Tsogyal's *Parting Questions for Guru Rinpoche* (*'dri lan Jo mo kar chen 'tsho rgyal gyis zhus lan*). Immediately after this teaching, the town of Boulder was suddenly covered with unseasonable and unprecedentedly heavy hail.

During the last fifteen years of his life, Rinpoche fully established his school, the Nyingma Wish-Fulfilling Center, in Sundarijal, outside Boudhanath, Nepal, and traveled widely to Japan, Europe, and the United States. Students also came from all those places to study with him in Nepal. In 1997, Harvey and I brought a group of our students for a three-week teaching from Khetsun Rinpoche on Longchenpa's *Three Cycles of Natural Liberation* (*Rang grol skor gsum*). Several of us were able to complete retreats on those teachings.[14]

Rinpoche kept a very low profile as a Dzogchen master. Many people, at least until very late in his life, did not know the extent of his practice and the transmissions he held. He taught these very privately to select, dedicated students, relaxing this somewhat only toward the very end of his life, especially for the benefit of students in the West. Until the late 1990s, when he was already over seventy years old, it was not clear that he would ever teach the precious Essential Black to more than five people. Alarmed by this, and keenly grateful for the transmission's power and blessings, Harvey and I begged Rinpoche to extend his teaching of it. In what we thought was a clinching argument, we expressed concern that it might otherwise disappear.

At this Rinpoche just smiled, sweet and easy as always. Wholly untroubled, his relaxed demeanor, gentle gaze, and mellow voice made it clear that, against all our urgent expectations, he did not share our concern. "It does not matter," he said. "It can only be taught when circumstances are right. Whatever happens is fine. The dakinis will take care of it."

During Sagadawa, the Buddha Month, of 2009, Rinpoche conducted a Great Accomplishment *puja* (*gDrub chen*) of the Yangti Nagpo. It was held in the Tamang Monastery by the Great Stupa in Boudhanath, Nepal. Close students from around the world came, including Harvey and me and several of our students from Dawn Mountain who had become close to Rinpoche. The weeklong event closed with a grand feast and long-life ceremony for Rinpoche. He was clearly frail, yet he attended every day, staying in Boudhanath to be close to the proceedings. Always a great storyteller, his frailty seemed banished one evening when he spent two hours relating the intertwined myths and powerful history of the place where we were, the Great Stupa. He emphasized that, as in the past, so today, any wish for good or for ill that one made while circumambulating the stupa would have great power. It was the last discourse we heard from him.

In December of that same year, we received a call from Nepal that Rinpoche was very ill. We arrived a few days later, and had the blessing of one brief *darshan* before his *parinirvana* on December 6, 2009. The prayer for his swift rebirth, composed soon after by His Eminence Dungse Thinley Norbu Rinpoche, was a kind of bookend to the profound prayer that his father wrote for Khetsun Sangpo Rinpoche's long life in 1977.

Technical Note

ERRORS IN THE initial printing of the Tibetan translated as *Strand of Jewels* have been corrected in the digitized Tibetan text created for this volume; endnotes labeled "TEXT EDIT" give the original and what the translator understands to be the correct Tibetan rendering. In the Tibetan text, bracketed numbers 1a, 1b, and so forth indicate the *end* of that page in the original typeset copy from which we are working.

Headings and subheadings were added by the translator to help readers identify core themes, and to indicate correspondence between the text and Rinpoche's commentary on it. For ease of reading, diacritics for Sanskrit names (such as *Nagarjuna*) and terms (such as *dakini*) that are well known to English speakers familiar with Buddhism appear in the glossary only.

Wherever possible, citations are given for works quoted in *Strand*. In most cases the bibliographical reference is to the Tibetan Buddhist Resource Center, giving the TBRC reference number as well as the volume and page numbers of the text in question to help scholars of Tibetan locate the digital version of these texts.

Transliterated Tibetan Wylie and Sanskrit words appear in parentheses. Where one such term is shown, it is Tibetan, unless otherwise indicated; if two appear, the Sanskrit term follows the Tibetan.

Part One

The Text

༄༅། །བླ་མའི་ཞལ་གདམས་ཀྱི་སྙིང་པོ་ཐམས་ཅད་ཕྱོགས་གཅིག་ཏུ་བཏུས་པའི་སྙིང་གཏམ་ནོར་བུའི་དོ་ཤལ་ཞེས་བྱ་བ་བཞུགས་སོ། །

༄༅། །བཀའ་དྲིན་མཚུངས་ཟླ་མ་མཆིས་པ་དཔལ་ལྡན་བླ་མ་དམ་པ་རྣམས་ལ་ཕྱག་འཚལ་ཞིང་སྐྱབས་སུ་མཆིའོ། བདག་གི་རྒྱུད་བྱིན་གྱིས་བརླབ་པར་མཛད་དུ་གསོལ། ཞེས་གསོལ་བ་བཏབ་ནས། འདིར་བརྗོད་པར་བྱ་བ་ནི། ལས་ཅན་སྙིང་གི་བུ་མཆོག་རྣམས་ལ་གྲས་པོ་བདག་གི་སྔོན་གྱི་དམ་པ་གོང་མ་རྣམས་ཀྱི་གསུང་བྱིན་ཅན་ཆོས་སྐུའི་རིང་བསྲེལ་དང་འདྲ་བ་རྣམས་ལས་ཉུང་ཟད་རེ་བཏུས་ཏེ་གསང་བ་ལས་ཀྱང་ཆེས་[1] གསང་བ་གསང་ཆེན་རྫོགས་པ་ཆེན་པོའི་གཞི་ལམ་འབྲས་བུའི་ཆོས་སྐུར་ལམ་བླ་མེད་པར་འཇུག་པར་བྱེད་པའི་ལྷག་པའི་ཆོས་སོ། དེ་ཡང་དང་པོ་གཞིའི་བཞུགས་ཚུལ། ལམ་གྱི་བགྲོད་ཚུལ། འབྲས་བུའི་ཡིན་ལུགས་བཅས་ལ་རིམ་པར་སྦྱར་ཏེ་འཆད་པའི་ཐོག་མར། གཞི་དབུ་མ་བདེན་གཉིས་ཟུང་འཇུག ལམ་དབུ་མ་ཚོགས་གཉིས་ཟུང་འཇུག འབྲས་བུ་དབུ་མ་སྐུ་གཉིས་ཟུང་འཇུག་ཏུ་དབང་གི་ཡེ་ཤེས་ཀྱི་ཐབས་ཁྱད་པར་ཅན་ལ་བརྟེན་ནས་གཞི་ལམ་འབྲས་བུའི་རྣམ་བཞག་མཛད་པ་དེ་ཉིད། གསང་ཆེན་རྫོགས་པ་ཆེན་པོས་ནི། གཉུག་མའི་སེམས་ལྷན་སྐྱེས་འོད་གསལ་གྱི་གནས་ལུགས་ངོ་བོ་ཀ་དག་རང་བཞིན་ལྷུན་གྲུབ་ཐུགས་རྗེ་ཀུན་ཁྱབ་སྟེ། གཞི་དུས་ཀྱི་སྐུ་གསུམ་དང་།

1. TEXT EDIT: 2a.1. *ched* corrected to *ches.* This and all other text edits were checked either with Khetsun Rinpoche himself or, in most cases, with Lama Tenzin Samphel.

Homage and Prologue

SEEKING REFUGE, I bow down to my glorious, excellent lamas and their unparalleled kindness; please bless my mindstream. With this earnest prayer, I begin.

For the supreme heirs of my own heart, this aged practitioner has gathered the splendid, enlightened speech of his own superb teachers. Their words are like sacred, radiant relics of Buddha's sheer essence enlightened dimension (*dharmakāya*).

The Great Completeness teachings on base, path, and fruition are unsurpassed and swift, holding a great secret.[15] These teachings provide supreme entry to the path. We begin here with a stage-by-stage discussion of how the base exists, how the path proceeds, and what their fruition is.

The base is the union of the Middle Way's two truths; the path, a union of the Middle Way's two collections, and the fruition, a union of the Middle Way's two Buddha dimensions.[16]

The Great Seal presents aspects of base, path, and fruition by relying on a special method—namely, the consecrating power of primordial knowing. This itself [is the deep secret described by the Great Completeness].[17] The genuine state (*gnas lugs*)[18] of our innately luminous and most basic mind is primordially pure in essence, spontaneously occurring in nature, and ubiquitous in its compassionate responsiveness. These three (essence, nature, compassionate responsiveness) are the three dimensions of a Buddha's embodiment in the context of the base: sheer essence dimension (*dharmakāya*); richly resplendent dimension (*sambhogakāya*); and emanation dimension (*nirmāṇakāya*).[19]

དེ་ལ་གློ་བུར་དྲི་ལྡན་སྐབས་སེམས་ཅན་དང་གློ་བུར་གྱི་དྲི་མ་དེ་བྲལ་དུས་སུ་དག་པ་གཉིས་
ལྡན་གྱི་སངས་རྒྱས་ཞེས་པའི་རང་ངོའི་ཆོས་ཉིད་ལ་ལྟོས་ཏེ། གཞི་འབྲས་དབྱེར་མེད་རོ་
གཅིག་ཏུ་རྟོགས་ཏེ་སངས་རྒྱས་དང་། དེ་མ་རྟོགས་ཏེ་སེམས་ཅན་ཞེས་པ་དང་། གྲོལ་
འཁྲུལ་གཉིས་མ་མྱོང་བའི་དུས་དེ་ལ་གཞི་དང་། གཞིའི་གནས་ལུགས་འགྱུར་མེད་དོན་གྱི་
ཡེ་ཤེས་ལ་རང་བཞིན་ལྷུན་གྱིས་གྲུབ་པའི་ཡོན་ཏན་མཁྱེན་བརྩེ་ནུས་གསུམ་གྱི་བདག་ཉིད་
ཅན་ངོ་བོ་རང་བཞིན་ཐུགས་རྗེ་གསུམ་ནི་གཞི་དུས་ཀྱི་སྐུ་གསུམ་དང་། དེ་ལ་རང་མདངས་
འགག་པ་མེད་པའི་རྩལ་རོལ་རྒྱན་གསུམ་ནི་ལམ་དུས་ཀྱི་སྐུ་གསུམ་བཞེད་པ་དང་། འབྲས་
དུས་ཀྱི་སྐུ་གསུམ་ནི་ཐེག་ཆེན་གྱི་གཞུང་ལུགས་ཡོངས་ལ་གགས་པའི་ཆོས་ལོངས་སྤྲུལ་
གསུམ་མོ། དེ་ཡང་རྒྱལ་བའི་བཀའ་རབ་འབྱམས་མཐའ་ཡས་པ་ཀུན་གྱི་དགོངས་དོན་སྙིང་
པོ་ནི་འགྲོ་བའི་ཁམས་ལ་བདེ་གཤེགས་སྙིང་པོ་གནས་པ་དེ་ཉིད་རྟོགས་པར་བྱ་བའི་སླད་དུ
ཆོས་ཀྱི་རྣམ་གྲངས་[2] མཐའ་ཡས་པ་གསུངས་མོད་ཀྱི་དེ་ནི་གདུལ་བྱའི་མོས་བློ་དང་སྐལ་བར
འཚམ་པའི་འདུལ་བྱེད་ཀྱི་ཆོས་གདམས་པའི་རྣམ་གྲངས་ཀྱང་དེ་སྙེད་དུ་འབྱུང་བ་ནི་སངས་
རྒྱས་རྣམས་ཀྱི་ཐུགས་རྗེའི་ཕྲིན་ལས་རྨད་དུ་བྱུང་བ་གནོད་མི་ཟ་ན། དེ་ལས་མཆོག་ཏུ་གྱུར
པའི་ཉེ་ལམ་འབྲས་བུ་གསང་སྔགས་རྡོ་རྗེ་ཐེག་པ་ཀུན་གྱི་རྩེ་མོའི་དོན་མཐར་ཐུག་པ་ནི། རང་
སེམས་གཉུག་མའི་གནས་ལུགས་སྐུ་གསུམ་ལྷུན་གྲུབ་ཀྱི་རང་ཞལ་རྗེན་པ་བདེ་བླག་ཏུ
རྟོགས་པར་[3] བྱེད་པའི་ཐབས་མཆོག་དེ་དག་གྲུབ་པའི་དབང་ཕྱུག་རིག་འཛིན་གོང་མ་རྣམས་
ཀྱིས་བགྲོད་པ་གཅིག་པའི་ལམ་པོ་ཆེ་གསང་ཆེན་རྫོགས་པ་ཆེན་པོ་ཞེས་ཉི་ཟླ་ལྟར་ཡོངས་སུ་
གྲགས་པ་

2. TEXT EDIT: *rnam grang* corrected to *rnam grangs.*
3. TEXT EDIT: 3b.3. *blag tu rol par* corrected to *blag tu rtogs par.*

So long as our adventitious defilements are present, we are sentient beings. Once we no longer have any adventitious defilements, we are Buddhas possessed of two purities. We see our own face, reality.

Once we realize that base and fruition are one taste, indivisible, we are called a Buddha. So long as we do not realize this, we are called a sentient being. The state of not experiencing either liberation or delusion is the base. The base's unchanging genuine state, which is actual, primordial knowing,[20] has the threefold nature of intrinsic and spontaneously present omniscience, kindness, and power.

Again, essence, nature, and compassionate responsiveness are the three Buddha dimensions in connection with the base. In tandem with this, the unceasing and intrinsically radiant triad of dynamic display, playful emergence, and ornamentation are regarded as the three Buddha dimensions of the path. Likewise, the triad of sheer essence, richly resplendent, and emanation dimensions, renowned throughout the textual discourse of the Great Vehicle, are the three Buddha dimensions in fruition.

Let us go further and consider the enlightened state. This is the core meaning of all the Majestic One's voluminously infinite words. He spoke limitless and varied teachings in consonance with beings' dispositions so that they might realize the actual state that is the heart of the Blissful Ones. An equal number[21] of doctrinal instructions also came forth as training methods well suited to devoted and fortunate disciples. Beyond any doubt these are astounding and compassionate Buddha activities.

Most excellent among them is the swift fruitional path of Secret Mantra, the vajra vehicle. This is the actual final vehicle whose teachings comprise supreme methods for easily realizing[22] the genuine state of your own most basic mind—the three spontaneously occurring Buddha dimensions[23] that are your own original face. Accomplished great beings of old, the holders of sheer awareness (*rigzin; vidyādhara*) proceeded along this great path, known as a Great Completeness, secret and unique, a path as renowned everywhere as the sun and the moon.

འདི་དག་ལ་རིམ་ས་བཀྲི་བར་བྱེད་པའི་དགོངས་དོན་བླ་ན་མེད་པར་རྟོགས་པར་བྱེད་པ་ལ་ཉེ་བར་མཁོ་བའི་ཐབ་གནད་འདི་ལའང་དོན་རྣམ་པ་གསུམ་གྱི་སྒོ་ནས་སྟོན་པར་བྱེད་པ་ལ། དེ་གང་ཞེ་ན། གཞི་རྟོགས་པ་ཆེན་པོ། ལམ་རྟོགས་པ་ཆེན་པོ། འབྲས་བུ་རྟོགས་པ་ཆེན་པོ་ཞེས་པར་རིམ་གྱིས་ཁྲིད་པར་བྱེད་པ་ལ་གཞི་དངོས་པོ་གཤིས་ཀྱི་གནས་ལུགས་འཁྲུལ་གྲོལ་གཉིས་ཀྱི་སྒོ་ནས་ལྟ་བའི་དོན་མདོར་བསྟན་པ་དང་། ལམ་རྟོགས་པ་ཆེན་པོ་རང་བྱུང་རང་བབས་ཀྱི་གནས་ལུགས་ལ་འཇུག་པར་བྱེད་པ་ལ་ཐོག་མར་ཞི་ལྷག་གཉིས་ཀྱི་སྒོ་ནས་འཇུག་པའི་ཉམས་ལེན་ཇི་ལྟར་བསྒྲོད་པའི་ཚུལ་རྒྱས་པར་བཤད་པ་དང་། འབྲས་བུ་རྟོགས་པ་ཆེན་པོ་དྲི་བྲལ་དོན་གྱི་སངས་རྒྱས་སྐུ་གསུམ་མངོན་དུ་གྱུར་ནས་འགྲོ་བའི་དོན་མཛད་ཚུལ་བཤད་ནས་འགག་བསྡུ་བ་དང་གསུམ་གྱིས་སྟོན་པར་བྱེད་པའི་དང་པོ་ནི། འཁོར་འདས་གང་དུའང་མ་གྲུབ་ཅིང་། ཕྱོགས་དང་རིས་སུ་མ་ཆད་པའི་རང་ངོ་ལ་བདེ་སྡུག་ཡིན་མིན་ཡོད་

1 Your Original Face

Base, Path, and Fruition

THE PROFOUND KEY instructions necessary for complete attainment of the enlightened state, our unsurpassed well-being, are laid out in stages. They are taught by way of three significant topics: first, the great completeness that is the base; second, the great completeness that is the path; and third, the great completeness that is fruition.

In leading us through these one by one, I will succinctly explain the meaning of the view from the perspectives of making and liberating errors in the base, the intrinsic genuine state. And I will explain in detail how you initially proceed with the practices of serene abiding and special seeing in order to enter the self-risen and settled ease of the genuine state, the Great Completeness path. After explaining the fruitional great completeness—namely, how the three genuine and stainless Buddha dimensions, once they become manifest, act to benefit beings—I describe Dzogchen through explanation, refutation, and synopsis.

Brief Explanation of the View

Our original face is established in neither cyclic existence nor nirvana, nor is it oriented in any particular direction. And it is unencumbered by any conventional designation such as "happiness" or "pain," "existence" or "nonexistence," "eternal" or "nil,"

བདག་གཞན་ལ་སོགས་པའི་མིང་འདོགས་ཀྱི་ཐ་སྙད་གང་གིས་ཀྱང་མ་གོས་ཤིང་མ་བསླད་པ་སྤྲོ་བསྐུར་གྱི་མཐའ་དང་བྲལ་བ། ངོ་བོ་ཅིར་ཡང་མ་གྲུབ་པའི་གནད་ཀྱི་རྣམ་པའམ་མཚན་ཉིད་ཅིར་ཡང་འཆར་བའི་གཞིར་གྱུར་པ་ལ་གང་ཤར་དོན་ལ་བདེན་པར་གྲུབ་པ་སྤྱི་ཙམ་མེད་དོ། །སྐྱེ་འགག་གནས་གསུམ་གྱི་མཐའ་དང་བྲལ་བའི་སྟོང་པ་ཆེན་པོ་འདུས་མ་བྱས་པའི་ཆོས་ཀྱི་དབྱིངས་དེ་ཉིད་སྐུ་གསུམ་ལྷུན་གྲུབ་ཀྱི་རང་བཞིན་ཉིད་དུ་ཡེ་ནས་ཡིན་པ་དེ་ལ། གཞི་དངོས་པོ[4]་གཤིས་ཀྱི་གནས་ལུགས་རྫོགས་པ་ཆེན་པོ་ཅེས་བྱ་སྟེ། གསང་སྙིང་ལས། གཞི་རྩ་མེད་པའི་སེམས་ཉིད་འདི། །ཆོས་རྣམས་ཀུན་གྱི་རྩ་བ་ཡིན། ཅེས་གསུངས་པ་དེ་ནི་གང་ཟག་དང་། སངས་རྒྱས་རེ་རེ་ཙམ་གྱི་ཐུགས་རྒྱུད་ལ་ཡོད་པ་ལྟ་བུ་ནི་མ་ཡིན་ཏེ། སྣང་སྲིད་འཁོར་འདས་ཀྱི་ཆོས་ཐམས་ཅད་ལ་ཁྱབ་པ་ཡིན་ཞིང་འདིའི་གནས་ཚུལ་ལམ་ཡིན་ལུགས་རྟོགས་ཤིང་རིག་པ་ན་སངས་རྒྱས་ཞེས་བྱ་བ་དང་། དེ་མ་རྟོགས་མ་རིག་ཅིང་འཁྲུལ་པ་ཤར་བ་ལ་སེམས་ཅན་ཅེས་བྱ་བ་སྟེ་འཁོར་བ་མུ་མཐའ་མེད་པར་འཁྱམས་པའི་གཞི་བྱེད་པའི་ཕྱིར་རོ། །དེས་ན་འཁོར་འདས་ཀྱི་སྤྱི་གཞི་ཞེས་སུ་གགས་པ་སྟེ་དགོངས་པ་ཟང་ཐལ་གྱི་རྒྱུད་ལས། གཞི་གཅིག་ལམ་གཉིས་འབྲས་བུ་གཉིས༔ །རིག་དང་མ་རིག་ཆོ་འཕྲུལ་ཏེ༔[5] དེ་ཉིད་རིག་ན་སངས་རྒྱས་ཏེ༔ མ་རིག་སེམས་ཅན་འཁོར་བར་འཁྱམས༔ ཞེས་དང་།[6] དཔལ་ས་ར་ཧས་ཀྱང་། སེམས་ཉིད་གཅིག་པུ་ཀུན་གྱི་ས་བོན་ཏེ། །གང་ལས་སྲིད་དང་མྱ་ངན་འདས་འཕྲོ་བས།[7] །ཅེས་གསུངས་པ་ལྟར།

4. TEXT EDIT: 4b.4. *gzhis dngos* corrected to *gzhi dngos*.
5. TEXT EDIT: 5a.4. *tsho phrul gyi* corrected to *tsho phrul de*.
6. TEXT EDIT: 5a.5. *zhes* corrected to *zhes dang* because the next lines are also quoted from the same text, the *Gong pa Zang Thal*.
7. TEXT EDIT: 5a.6. *mya ngan das gro bas* corrected to *mya ngan das phro bas*.

"self" or "other." It is uncontaminated, free from the extremes—neither overstated nor underplayed. A key instruction is that its essence is in no way established. Yet, it is the basis for whatever defining characteristics arise. Anything that dawns lacks even a hair's worth of true existence.[24]

The great empty is the unconditioned stainless space; it is free from the three extremes of production, abiding, or cessation. It has forever been the nature of the three spontaneously occurring Buddha dimensions. It is known as the base[25] and it is the genuine state of your own homeground. The *Secret Essence Tantra*[26] says:

> This mindnature, a base without root,
> Is the root of each and every thing.[27]

This is not something that exists only in the mindstream of special people or in Buddhas; it suffuses everything that appears or exists in cyclic existence and nirvana! Whoever realizes and is aware of their own abiding state or way of being is called a Buddha. Whoever does not realize and is unaware of this is called a sentient being, because delusion dawns and becomes the basis for their wandering in circles without end or limit.[28] This is how the renowned general base of cyclic existence and nirvana is described in the *Unimpeded-State Tantra*:[29]

> One base, two paths, two fruitions,
> Knowing and unknowing, a magical display[30]
> When you know this, you are a Buddha
> When you do not know it, you are a sentient being,
> wandering in circles [samsara].[31]

Also, the glorious Saraha said:

> Our one mindnature is the seed of everything
> All existence and nirvana move forth from there.[32]

ངོ་བོ་ཅིག་ལ་སྣང་ཚུལ་ཐ་དད་དེ། རྟོགས་མ་རྟོགས་ཀྱི་ཁྱད་པར་སོ་སོར་སྣང་མོད་ཀྱི། དེ་གཉིས་གང་གི་ཚེ་ནའང་རང་གི་ངོ་བོ་ལ་བཟང་ངན་དང་འཕོ་འགྱུར་སོགས་ཀྱི་སྐྱོན་གྱིས་མ་གོས་པར་གདོད་ནས་སྐུ་གསུམ་དབྱེར་མེད་ཆེན་པོར་གནས་པ་འདི་ལ།[8] ཐུན་མོང་ཐེག་པའི་སྐབས་རྣམས་སུ་འགྱུར་བ་མེད་པའི་ཡོངས་གྲུབ་ཅེས་[9] ཀྱང་བྱ་སྟེ། ཐོག་མའི་གཞིའི་གནས་ལུགས་ཡིན་ནོ། །རང་ཤར་ལས། སེམས་ཅན་གཞི་དང་སངས་རྒྱས་གཞི། །ཁྱད་པར་གཅིག་གི་ཕྱེ་བར་ངེས། ཞེས་པ་དེ་ལྟ་བུའི་གནས་ཚུལ་དེ་རྟོགས་མ་རྟོགས་གཉིས་ཀ་མ་ཡིན་པའི་བཏང་སྙོམས་ལུང་མ་བསྟན་དུ་གནས་པ་དེ་ལ་ཀུན་གཞི་ཞེས་བྱ་སྟེ། རང་ཤར་ལས། ཀུན་གཞི་རྣམ་རྟོག་འཛིན་པ་ལ། །སྣ་ཚོགས་འཕྲུལ་པའི་ཤེས་པས་བསྐྱེད། །ཀུན་གཞི་མ་རིག་དངོས་པོ་ཡིན། །ཀུན་གྱི་གཞི་ཞེས་དེ་ལ་བྱ། །ཞེས་པའི་ཀུན་ནི་མང་ཚིག་[10] དང་། གཞི་ནི་བག་ཆགས་སྣ་ཚོགས་པ་རྟེན་པའི་གཞིར་གནས་པའོ། །རྟེན་བརྟེན་པའི་ཆ་ནས་ཕྱེ་ན། ཀུན་གཞི་ནི་རྟེན། སེམས་ནི་བརྟེན་པར་གསུངས་སོ། །དེས་ན་ངོ་བོ་ལུང་མ་བསྟན་འཁོར་འདས་གཉིས་ཀའི་གཞི་བྱེད་པའི་ཕྱིར་རོ། །ཀུན་གཞི་དེ་ཉིད་ཀྱང་ཅི་ཡང་མེད་པའི་སྟོང་པ་ཕྱང་ཆད་མ་ཡིན་པར་རང་གསལ་གྱི་ཤེས་པ་འགག་པ་མེད་པར་འཆར་རུང་དུ་ཡོད་པ་དེ་ལ་ཀུན་གཞིའི་རྣམ་ཤེས་བྱ་བ་སྟེ། མེ་ལོང་དང་དེའི་དྭངས་ཆ་ལྟ་བུ་འམ་ཡང་ན་རྒྱ་མཚོ་དང་རྒྱ་མཚོའི་ཐ་རླབས་ལྟ་བུའོ།

8. TEXT EDIT: *gnas la di la* corrected to *gnas pa di la*.
9. TEXT EDIT: 5b.2. *yongs grub cis* corrected to *yongs grub ces*.
10. TEXT EDIT: 5b.6. *kun gzhi ni mang tshig* corrected to *kun ni mang tshig*.

In other words, this single essence can appear in many ways.[33] Specific appearances come about in connection with realization and lack of realization, but in either case, your own essence (your primordial base)[34] does not wear the garments of good, bad, change, and so on. From the very first, it has been completely indivisible from the three Buddha dimensions.[35]

In the context of the ordinary vehicles, this means that anything considered thoroughly established[36] is the genuine and abiding state of the primordial base. *Self-Dawning [Tantra]* says:

> Certainly, sentient beings' base and Buddhas' base
> Are categories subordinate to a single distinguishing feature.
> Abiding in a neutral equanimity that
> Neither realizes nor fails to realize this abiding state
> Is called the allground.

The *Self-Dawning [Tantra]* also says:

> Thoughts held on the allground
> Are polluted by various mistaken consciousnesses.
> The allground is unawareness, an impermanent thing
> We call it "the ground of everything."

"All" is a term of plurality.[37] "Ground" indicates it is a base supporting various predispositions. When we distinguish between support and supported, the allground is the support and mind the supported. Hence, a neutral entity acts as the basic ground of both cyclic existence and nirvana.

The allground itself is neither an emptiness nor utter nothingness. Like a mirror with its limpidity or the ocean with its waves, this [allground] is a self-clarifying consciousness capable of ceaseless surfacings, for which we use the term "allground consciousness."[38]

Samsara and nirvana radiate out individually from that single

ཀུན་གཞི་གཅིག་པུ་དེ་ལས་འཁོར་འདས་སོ་སོར་གྱེས་ཚུལ་ཡང་རང་གསལ་གྱི་ཤེས་པ་དེའི་རིག་ཆའམ་[11] ཡེ་ཤེས་ཀྱི་ཆ་ངོ་བོ་སྟོང་ཞིང་རང་བཞིན་གསལ་ལ་དབྱེར་མེད་རིག་པའི་སྙིང་པོ་དེ་ནི་སངས་རྒྱས་ཀྱི་ཡོན་ཏན་དང་ཡང་དག་པའི་ལམ་གྱི་ཆོས་ཐམས་ཅད་ཀྱི་ས་བོན་ནམ་རྒྱུ་ཡིན་པའི་ཕྱིར་ན། སྦྱོར་བ་དོན་གྱི་ཀུན་གཞི་ཡང་ཟེར། བདེ་གཤེགས་སྙིང་པོ་དང་། རང་རིག་ཆོས་སྐུ་ཤེས་རབ་ཀྱི་ཕ་རོལ་ཏུ་ཕྱིན་པ་སྟེ། ཀུན་བྱེད་རྒྱལ་པོ་ལས། ཀྱེ་ང་ནི་མ་བཅོས་ཇི་བཞིན་སྙིང་པོ་ལ། །སྒྲོ་འདོགས་སྐུར་འདེབས་དོན་ལས་ཀུན་འདས་ཏེ། །དུས་གསུམ་རྒྱལ་བ་ང་ལས་བྱུང་བས་ན།[12] །རྒྱལ་བའི་ཡུམ་ཞེས་ངེས་པར་བསྟན་པ་ཡིན། །ཞེས་རང་སེམས་སངས་རྒྱས་ལ་སོགས་མྱ་ངན་ལས་འདས་པའི་ཆོས་ཀྱི་རྣམ་གྲངས་ལས་བཏགས་པའི་མིང་ཐམས་ཅད་འདིར་མཐུན་ཅིང་། རྣལ་འབྱོར་པ་ལམ་ལ་ཞུགས་པ་རྣམས་ཀྱིས་མངོན་སུམ་དུ་བྱ་རྒྱུ་དང་རང་ངོ་སྤྲོད་[13] དགོས་རྒྱུའི་ཡང་སྙིང་འདི་ཡིན་ཏེ། ཀུན་གཞི་ལུང་མ་བསྟན་དེའི་གཏི་མུག་གི་ཆ་ལས་རང་ངོ་རང་གིས་[14] མ་རིག་[15] ཅིང་གནས་ལུགས་མ་རྟོགས་པར་རང་གིས་རང་ཉིད་བསྒྲིབས་པ་དེ་ལ་ལྷན་ཅིག་སྐྱེས་པའི་མ་རིག་པ་ཅེས་ཀྱང་བྱ། ཐོག་མ་མེད་པའི་དུས་ཀྱི་མུན་ཆེན་ཞེས་ཀྱང་བྱ་སྟེ། ཤིང་རྟ་ཆེན་མོའི་ཤོག་ ༣༠༢-༨ ནས་རང་གི་ཡེ་ཤེས་རང་ངོ་མ་ཤེས་པའི་ཆ་ནས། ལྷན་ཅིག་སྐྱེས་པའི་མ་རིག་པ་ཞེས་བྱ། ཞེས་གསུང་ཏེ། འདི་ལ་བརྟེན་ནས་ཉོན་མོངས་པ་དང་འཁྲུལ་རྟོག་མཐའ་དག་འབྱུང་བའི་ཕྱིར་ན་བག་ཆགས་སྣ་ཚོགས་པའི་ཀུན་གཞི་ཞེས་ཀྱང་བྱ། སེམས་ཅན་ཐམས་ཅད་ཀྱི་འཁྲུལ་གཞི་ཡིན་ནོ། །དགོངས་པ་ཟང་ཐལ་ལས།

11. TEXT EDIT: 6a.6. The text's *rig bya* is a misprint of *rig cha*.
12. TEXT EDIT: 6b.3. *byung bas nas* corrected to *byung bas na*.
13. TEXT EDIT: 6b.6. *ngo spros* corrected to *ngo sprod*.
14. TEXT EDIT: 7a.1. Omitted *cha las rang ngo rang gis*. (The scribe mistakenly repeated these words from the previous line.
15. TEXT EDIT: 6b.6. *rang ngo rang gi cha las rang ngo rang gis ma rig* should be *rang ngo rang gis ma rig*.

allground.[39] An intrinsically clear conscious awareness, or factor,[40] of primordial knowing, accesses the indivisibility of emptiness and luminosity, the essence of sheer awareness. And just that is the seed or cause of a Buddha's good qualities and of all attributes associated with a correct path.[41] This is therefore also known as "the actual preparatory allground."[42]

This is the heart of the Blissful Ones and the self-knowing sheer essence dimension, as definitively indicated in the following verse from the *Majestic Creator of Everything*:

> Hear me! I am the uncontrived heart of is-ness
> Beyond overstating or underplaying.
> Past, present, and future Buddhas arise from me[43]
> and so
> I am definitively known as "Mother of the Majesties."[44]

Names such as "your own mind," "Buddha," and so forth, all align in designating the phenomenon of nirvana.[45] This is the essence of what yogis accomplish on the path. It is also the essence of what we need to recognize.[46]

However, due to the factor of ignorance associated with the indeterminate (neutral) allground[47] we remain unaware of our own face[48] and, failing awareness of our genuine abiding state, we obstruct ourselves. This inborn unawareness has greatly obstructed us since time without beginning.[49] [Longchenpa's] *Great Chariot*[50] states,

> From the perspective of not recognizing itself
> Our own primordial knowing is called "inborn
> unawareness."[51]

All our afflictions and delusions occur because of this. Our unawareness is therefore also known as the allground of our various predispositions, the basis of error in all living beings. The *Unimpeded-State Tantra* says:

གཞི་ལ་རིག་པ་མ་ཤར་བས།[16] ཅི་ཡང་དྲན་མེད་ཐོམ་མེ་བ། དེ་ཀ་མ་རིག་འཁྲུལ་པའི་རྒྱུ། ཅེས[17]་གསུངས་ཤིང་བདག་འཛིན་མ་རིག་པ་འདིའི་འཁོར་གྱི་ཚུལ་དུ་ཆགས་པ་བརམ་དང་ བརྗེད་ངེས[18]་ལ་སོགས་པ་གཏི་མུག་ལས་བྱུང་བའི་རྟོག་པ་བདུན་ཡང་ཡོད་དེ། གང་ཞེ་ན། སྤྱོད་བསྡུས་ལས། ཆགས་པ་བརམ་ཞེས་པའང་སྣང་། ༡ མི་གསལ་བ་དང་། ༢ བརྗེད་ངེས[19]་དང་། ༣ འཁྲུལ་པ་དང་། ༤ མི་སྨྲ་བ་དང་། ༥ སྐྱོ་བ་དང་། ༦ ལེ་ལོ་དང་། ༧ ཐེ་ཚོམ་སྟེ། ཐམས་ཅད་གཏི་མུག་གམ་ཐོབ་པ་ལས་བྱུང་བའི་རྟོག་པ་བདུན་པོ་དེ་དག་དགག་གོ་ཞེས་སོ། དེ་ལྟ་བུའི་ན་སྐྱེས་ཀྱི་མ་རིག་པ་དེ་ལས་ང་དང་བདག་ཏུ་འཛིན་པའི་རྣམ་པར་རྟོག་པ་ཤར། བདག་ལ་བརྟེན་ནས་གཞན་དུ་བཟུང་བ་བྱུང་ཞིང་། རང་སྣང་ལ་རང་དུ་མ་ཤེས་པར་ཕྱིའི་ཡུལ་དུ་བཟུང་སྟེ་གཟུང་འཛིན་གྱི་རྟོག་པ་རོམ་ཤེས་པས་འཁྲུལ་པའི་མགོ་རྩོམ་པ་དེ་ལ་ཀུན་ཏུ་བརྟགས་པའི་མ་རིག་པ་ཟེར། ཡིད་ཀྱི་རྣམ་ཤེས་ཀྱང་ཟེར་ཏེ། ཡུལ་སེམས་ཐ་དད་དུ་འཁྲུལ་པའི་སེམས་ཡིན། འདིའི་འཁོར་དུ་ཆགས་དང་ཞེན་པ་ལ་སོགས་པ་འདོད་ཆགས་ལས་བྱུང་བའི་རྟོག་པ་བཞི་བཅུ་རྣམས་བྱུང་སྟེ། སློབ་དཔོན་ཨཱརྱ་དེ་བའི་སྤྱོད་བསྡུས་སྒྲོན་མ་ལས། འདོད་ཆགས་ལས་བྱུང་བའི་རྟོག་པ་བཞི་བཅུ་གང་ཞེ་ན། ༡ ཆགས་པ་དང་། ༢ ཆགས་པ་བརམ་དང་། ༣ ཀུན་ཏུ་ཆགས་པ་དང་། ༤ དགའ་བ་དང་། ༥ དགའ་བ་བརམ་དང་། ༦ ཤིན་ཏུ་དགའ་བ་དང་།

16. TEXT EDIT: 7.a.5–6. *gzhi la ma rig ma shar* corrected to *gzhi la rig pa ma* shar. Khetsun Sangpo Rinpoche commented that this means there is unawareness (*ma rig pa*) in the base. (Oral communication to Harvey Aronson, April 2009, Sunderijal, Nepal.)
17. This is cited from Dudjom Rinpoche's *chos sbyod*, page 325.4.
18. TEXT EDIT: 7b.1. *rjes ngas* corrected to *brjed ngas* (Khetsun Sangpo Rinpoche).
19. TEXT EDIT: 7b.2. *brjed ngas* corrected to *brjed nges*.

> Once awareness fails to dawn in the base[52]
> There is no knowing at all, we are stupefied.
> Exactly that unawareness is the cause of delusion.[53]

The Ordinary Mind: Eighty Conceptions

This unawareness takes self to be [really] existent. It is accompanied by forgetfulness and so forth, the seven conceptual thoughts that arise from an obscuration [known as] mid-level desire.[54] What are these? [Aryadeva's] *Lamp Distilling the Practice*[55] says:

> There appears what is known as "middling desire" (*chags pa bar ma*), which consists of[56] (1) unclarity, (2) forgetfulness,[57] (3) error, (4) intentional speechlessness, (5) discouragement, (6) laziness, and (7) doubt. All the seven thoughts come from delusion or [what the *vaibhāṣika* call] attainment. These cease.[58]

From such inborn unawareness (namely, the obscuration associated with a mind of middling desire) dawns thought holding to I and to self; based on this, we grasp at other. Then, failing to recognize our own display for what it is, we grasp onto external objects.[59]

Failing to recognize that we conceive of subject and object is our key delusion. We call this a "learned unawareness." We also identify it as a mental consciousness, a mind deluded into differentiating objects from itself.[60] This [mental consciousness and mind are] accompanied by attachment, yearning and so forth, the forty thoughts arising from desire,[61] as described by Master Aryadeva in his *Lamp Distilling the Practices*:

> What are the forty thoughts arising from desire?[62] They are (1) attachment, (2) middling attachment, (3) clinging anxiety, (4) joy, (5) middling joy, (6) great joy,

༧ རངས་པ་དང༌། ༨ རབ་ཏུ་མགུ་བ་དང༌། ༩ ངོ་མཚར་བ་དང༌། ༡༠ དགོད་པ་དང༌། ༡༡ ཚིམས་པ་དང༌། ༡༢ འཁྱུད་པ་དང༌། ༡༣ འོ་བྱེད་པ་དང༌། ༡༤ འཇིབ་པ་དང༌། ༡༥ བརྟན་པ་དང༌། ༡༦ བརྩོན་པ་དང༌། ༡༧ ཁེངས་པའམ་ང་རྒྱལ་དང༌། ༡༨ བྱ་བ་དང༌། ༡༩ འགྲོགས་པ་དང༌། ༢༠ སྟོབས་དང༌། ༢༡ དབྲོག་པ་དང༌། ༢༢ སྤྲོ་བ་དང༌། ༢༣ ལྷན་ཅིག་བྱེད་པའི་དགའ་བ་ལ། ནང་གསེས་བཞི།[20] སྦྱོར་བ་དང༌། རབ་བར་མ་དང༌། ཤིན་ཏུ་སྦྱོར་བ་དང༌། ཤིན་ཏུ་དགའ་བ་[21]ལ་སྦྱོར་བ་དང༌། ༢༤ སྡིག་པ་དང༌། ༢༥ རྣམ་པར་སྡིག་པ་དང༌། ༢༦ ཞེ་འགགས་པ་དང༌། ༢༧ དགེ་བ་དང༌། ༢༨ ཚིག་གསལ་བ་དང༌།

༢༩ བདེན་པ་དང༌། ༣༠ མི་བདེན་པ་དང༌། ༣༡ ངེས་པ་དང༌། ༣༢ ཉེ་བར་ལེན་པ་དང༌ ༣༣ སྦྱིན་པ་པོ་དང༌། ༣༤ གཞན་ལ་བསྐུལ་བ་དང༌། ༣༥ དཔའ་བོ་དང༌། ༣༦ ངོ་ཚ་མེད་པ་དང༌།

༣༧ གཡོ་སྒྱུ་དང༌། ༣༨ སྡུག་པ་དང༌། ༣༩ མི་སྲུན་པ་དང༌། ག་གྱུ་ཆེ་བ་སྟེ་ཐབས་དང་འདོད་ཆགས་ལས་བྱུང་བའི་རྟོག་པ་བཞི་བཅུའོ། །ཞེས་གསུངས་སོ། །དེ་ནས་ཡིད་ཀྱི་རྣམ་པར་ཤེས་པ་དེའི་རྩལ་བག་ཆགས་འཁྲུལ་པ་སྣ་ཚོགས་པ་ཤར་ཞིང་རྒྱས་པ་དང༌། དེའི་གྲོགས་སུ་ལས་རླུང་ཁྱབ་བྱེད་ཀྱི་རྐྱེན་དང་ཀུན་གཞི་མ་རིག་པའི་རྒྱུ་སོགས་རྟེན་ཅིང་འབྲེལ་འབྱུང་གི་མཐུ་བརྟས་པའི་དབང་གིས་ལུས་སྣང་སེམས་གསུམ་ཚང་བར་གྲུབ་ཅིང་སྒོ་ལྔའི་དབང་ཤེས་ཀྱི་བྱེ་བྲག་དང་ཚོགས་དྲུག་གི་རྣམ་རྟོག་ཤར་བ་ལ་གཞན་དབང་ཞེས་ཀྱང་བྱ། རྩ་བའི་རླུང་ལྔ་དང༌། ཡན་ལག་གི་རླུང་ལྔ་སོགས་ཀྱི་རྣམ་རྟོག་གི་ཞོན་པ་[22]བྱས་ཤིང་ཞེས་པའི་རྩ་བའི་རླུང་ལྔ་ནི། སྲོག་འཛིན། མེ་མཉམ།

20. TEXT EDIT: 8b.2. *nang gsel gzhi* corrected to *nang gses bzhi.*
21. TEXT EDIT: 8b.2. *shin tu dka ba* corrected to *shin tu dga ba.*
22. TEXT EDIT: 9a.3. *gzhon pa* corrected to *zhon.*

> (7) rapture, (8) exhilaration, (9) embarrassment, (10) laughter, (11) contentment, (12) embrace, (13) kissing, (14) sucking, (15) stability, (16) effort, (17) arrogance or pride, (18) activity, (19) robbery,[63] (20) force, (21) plunder, (22) enthusiasm, (23) inborn joy, regarding which there are the four subdivisions[64] of union, middling union, intense union, and very blissful[65] union, (24) flirting, (25) intense flirting, (26) enmity, (27) virtue, (28) clear speech, (29) truth, (30) untruth, (31) certainty, (32) taking up,[66] (33) giving, (34) exhorting others, (35) heroism, (36) lack of embarrassment, (37) deceit, (38) loveliness, (39) maliciousness, and (40) crookedness. These are the forty thoughts that arise from desire [and have the nature of] method.[67]

Following this, various misleading predispositions which are the dynamic display of this mental consciousness [that grows stronger in dependence on any of the forty desirous thoughts][68] dawn and proliferate. Through the force of the expanding capaciousness of dependent arising, causal conditions consisting of the accompanying pervasive karmic winds, along with [other] causes such as the allground and unawareness, as well as the triad consisting of body, appearing objects, and mind, are fully established.[69] The consciousnesses particular to the five sense doors and the conceptual thoughts belonging to the six collections [of consciousness] dawn. These are called "other-powered."

Our Moving Mind: More on the Eighty Conceptions

The five main winds which are said to form the mount[70] of thoughts associated with the five root and five secondary winds and so forth are the

> (1) life-bearing wind,[71] (2) fire wind, (3) pervasive wind,

ཁྱབ་བྱེད། གྱེན་རྒྱུ། ཐུར་སེལ་གྱི་རླུང་ངོ༌། བྱེད་ལས་ནི། སྲོག་འཛིན་གྱིས་[23] སྲོག་བརྟེན། མེ་མཉམ་གྱིས་མེ་དྲོད་བསྐྱེད། ཁྱབ་བྱེད་ཀྱིས་ལུས་ཉམས་བརྟས། གྱེན་རྒྱུ་དང་ཐུར་སེལ་གྱིས་དབུགས་ཀྱི་འགྲོ་འོང་དང༌། འགྲོ་འདུག་དང་བཤང་གཅི་འཕེན་པའི་བྱ་བ་བྱེད་དོ། དེའང་ཕོ་རླུང་གྱེན་རྒྱུ་སྟོད་ན་གནས། མོ་རླུང་ཐུར་སེལ་སྨད་ན་གནས། མ་ནིང་རླུང་ནི་མཉམ་པར་གནས་སོ། ནང་གི་རླུང་ནི། འབྱུང་ལྔའི་ཁ་དོག་ཅན་ཏེ། ཕུང་པོ་ཁམས་དང་སྐྱེ་མཆེད་གནས་པའི་རྟེན་བྱེད།[24] དུག་ལྔ་ནི་ཡེ་ཤེས་ལྔ། རྒྱུ་འབྲས་ལྷ་བུར་མཆེད་པའི་རྟེན་བྱེད་དོ། གནས་ནི། སྲོག་འཛིན་སྙིང་ག་ན་གནས་ཏེ་སྲོག་གནས་པར་བྱེད། མེ་མཉམ་[25] ལྟོ་བ་ན་གནས་ཏེ་དྲོད་འབེབས་པར་བྱེད། ཁྱབ་བྱེད་ལུས་ཁྱིང་ལ་གནས་ཏེ་ལུས་ཉམས་བརྟས་པར་བྱེད། གྱེན་རྒྱུ་སྟོད་ན་གནས་ཏེ་དབུགས་འབྱུང་རྔུབ་བྱེད། ཐུར་སེལ་སྨད་ན་གནས་ཏེ་འགྲོ་འདུག་དང་ཟག་པ་འདོན་པའི་བྱ་བ་བྱེད། ནང་གི་རླུང་ལྔ་ནི། འབྱུང་ལྔའི་རང་བཞིན་ཏེ། ས་རླུང་སེར། ཆུ་རླུང་དཀར། མེ་རླུང་དམར། རླུང་གི་རླུང་ལྗང་། ནམ་མཁའི་རླུང་མཐིང་ག་སྟེ། བསྒོམ་ཚུལ་གྱི་དབང་དུ་བྱས་ན། དབྱིབས་ཀྱང་རིམ་བཞིན་གྲུ་བཞི། ཟླ་གམ། གྲུ་གསུམ། གཞུའི་དབྱིབས་ལྟ་བུ་དང༌། ཟླུམ་པོའོ།། བྱེད་ལས། ཕུང་ཁམས་སྐྱེ་མཆེད་གནས་པའི་རྟེན་བྱེད།[26] མ་དག་པའི་དུས་སུ་དུག་ལྔ་མཆེད་པའི་གཞི་བྱེད་ལ། ལམ་དུས་སུ་ཟད་པར་གྱི་ཏིང་ངེ་འཛིན་ལ་རྟེན་ནས་རྫུ་འཕྲུལ་གྲུབ་པ་དང༌། དག་པའི་ཡེ་ཤེས་ལྔ་མཆེད་པའི་རྟེན་བྱེད་དོ། དེ་དག་རྒྱུ་ཚུལ་གྱི་དབང་དུ་བྱས་ན། དབྱར་མེ། སྟོན་རླུང་། དགུན་ཆུ།

23. TEXT EDIT: 9a.4. *srog gis* corrected to *srog dzin gyis*.
24. TEXT EDIT: 9b.2. *mchod gnas pa i rten byed* corrected to *mched gnas pa i rten byed*.
25. TEXT EDIT: 9b.3. *mi mnyam* corrected to *me mnyam*.
26. TEXT EDIT: 10a.2 and 10a.3. *mchod pa i rten byed* is corrected to *mched pa i rten byed*.

> (4) upward-moving wind, and (5) downward-voiding wind. As for their activities, the life-bearing wind supports life, the fire wind[72] keeps a person warm, the pervasive wind enhances the body's disposition, the upward-moving and downward-voiding winds foster the coming and going of the breath as well as walking, sitting, and the process of eliminating waste.[73]

Further, the male wind resides in the upper part [of the body], the female wind is found in the lower part [and is downwardly oriented]. The neutral wind abides evenly. The internal winds have the color of the five elements. These winds support the stability of the aggregates, sensory sources, and constituents. The five poisons act as supportive increasers, similar to cause and effect of the five primordial knowings.[74]

As to where they reside, the life-bearing wind dwells in the heart. It makes life stable. The fire wind[75] dwells in the belly and creates heat. The pervasive wind abides everywhere, enhancing the entire body (complexion, strength, and capacity). The upward-moving wind abides in the upper body and facilitates inhalation and exhalation of the breath.

The five internal winds have the nature of the five elements [respectively]: the yellow earth-wind, white water-wind, red fire-wind, the green wind-wind, and the deep blue space-wind. If one considers this in terms of meditation, their shapes, respectively, are (1) square, (2) half-moon, (3) triangular, (4) like the shape of a bow (*gzhu*),[76] and (5) round.

In terms of their functions, these winds support stability in our aggregates, sensory sources, and constituents. Also, in the context of impurity they are a basis for giving rise[77] to the five poisons and, in the context of the path, they support the arising of miraculous [Buddha] activities by relying on meditative stabilization associated with extinguishment. They also then give rise to the five primordial pure wisdoms.[78]

In terms of how these [winds and elements] function, in

དབྱིད་སའི་རླུང་རྒྱུ་བས་དེའི་གཉེན་པོར་གོ་ལོགས་ནས་བསྒོམས་པའམ་ནམ་མཁའི་རླུང་འབབ་ཞིག་གམ། ཡང་ན་ཁམས་ཕྱོད་བསྒོམས་པ་ཡིན་ནོ། །ཡན་ལག་གི་རླུང་ལྔ་ནི། གསུམ་སྐོར་མ། དོད་མ། འཁྱིལ་མ། གཏུམ་མོ། བདུད་འདུལ་མ་ཞེས་པའོ། །ཡང་ལམ་རིམ་ཡེ་ཤེས་སྙིང་པོའི་འགྲེལ་པ་ ༣༥༨-༣ ནས་གསལ་བ་ལྟར་བྱས་ན། རྒྱུ་བ། རྣམ་པར་རྒྱུ། ཡང་དག་རྒྱུ་བ། རབ་ཏུ་རྒྱུ་བ། ངེས་པར་རྒྱུ་བ། དེ་དག་ནི་དབང་པོ་ལྔ་ལ་གནས་ཤིང་བསྐྱེད་པ་སོགས་བྱ་བ་བྱེད། ཞེས་སོ། །དོན་ནི་རང་སྣང་འཁྲུལ་འཛིན་གོམས་པའི་མཐུ་ལས་གྲུབ་པའི་སྣོད་བཅུད་དུ་སྣང་བས་གཞི་རྟེན་དང་ཡུལ་དུ་བྱས་ནས་མཐའ་དག་བསྐྱེད་པའི་ཕྱིར་ན་ཉོན་མོངས་ཅན་གྱི་ཡིད་ཟེར། དབང་པོ་སྒོ་ལྔ་སོ་སོར་རྒྱུ་ཞིང་ཆགས་སོགས་ཀྱི་བྱེད་པོ་ཡིན་པས་ཕྱིར་ན་སྒོ་ལྔའི་རྣམ་པར་ཤེས་པ་ཡང་ཟེར་ལ། འདིའི་འཁོར་དུ་ཆགས་བྲལ་བར་མ་ལ་སོགས་ཞེ་སྡང་ལས་གྱུར་པའི་རྟོག་པ་སུམ་ཅུ་རྩ་གསུམ་ཡང་ཡོད་དོ། ཨཱརྱ་དེ་བའི་སྤྱོད་བསྡུས་ལས། རྣམ་རྟོག་སུམ་ཅུ་རྩ་གསུམ་གང་ཞེ་ན། ༡ འདོད་ཆགས་དང་བྲལ་བ་དང་། ༢ འདོད་ཆགས་དང་བྲལ་བ་བར་མ་དང་། ༣ ཤིན་ཏུ་འདོད་ཆགས་དང་བྲལ་བ་དང་། ༤ ཡིད་ཀྱི་འགྲོ་འོང་དང་། ༥ མྱ་ངན་དང་། ༦ མྱ་ངན་བར་མ་དང་། ༧ ཤིན་ཏུ་མྱ་ངན་དུ་གྱུར་པ་དང་། ༨ ཞི་བ་དང་།

summer the fire-wind [is strongest], in fall the wind-wind, in winter the water-wind, and in spring the earth-wind. Therefore [to create balance,] one meditates on the opposite, which acts as its antidote. [For example, fire is the antidote to the water-element.] Or [one meditates] on the space-wind alone or else as suits one's constitution.[79]

The five secondary winds, which are female[80] [whereas the five main winds are male], are (1) the three cycles of winds, (2) [winds of the] heart-channel desire, (3) spiraling wind,[81] (4) heat-wrath,[82] and (5) subjugating.[83] Also, as it clearly says in [Chog Gyur Lingpa's] *Commentary on the Heart of Primordial Knowing, Stages of the Path:*[84]

> Movement, intense movement, correct movement, exceeding movement, definitive movement:
> These bring about abiding, development and so forth with respect to the five winds, the five sense faculties.

This means that our own display, which we see as vessel and essence, comes about through the force of our being accustomed to holding onto error. Everything develops from our taking [such appearances] as a basic support and object.[85] Therefore, this [mistaken perceiver] is called an afflicted mind.

Individual causes consisting of the five sense-doors are agents of longing, desire, and so forth. Therefore, we also speak of the consciousnesses of the five doors. Accompanying these are the thirty-three conceptual thoughts arising from hatred, such as middling freedom from desire. Aryadeva's *Lamp Distilling the Practices* [86] states:

> What are these thirty-three? They are (1) freedom from desire, (2) middling freedom from desire, (3) great freedom from desire, (4) mental coming and going, (5) painful mind, (6) middling painful mind, (7) extremely painful mind, (8) pacification [of pain],

༩ རྣམ་རྟོག་དང་། ༡༠ འཇིགས་པ་དང་། ༡༡ འཇིགས་པ་བར་མ་དང་། ༡༢ ཤིན་ཏུ་འཇིགས་པ་དང་། ༡༣ སྲེད་པ་དང་། ༡༤ སྲེད་པ་བར་མ་དང་། ༡༥ ཤིན་ཏུ་སྲེད་པ་དང་། ༡༦ ཉེ་བར་ལེན་པ་དང་། ༡༧ མི་དགེ་བ་དང་། ༡༨ བཀྲ་ཤིས་པ་དང་། ༡༩ སྐོམ་པ་དང་། ༢༠ ཚོར་པ་དང་། ༢༡ ཚོར་བ་བར་མ་དང་། ༢༢ ཤིན་ཏུ་བརྩེ་བ་དང་། ༢༣ རིག་པ་པོ་དང་། ༢༤ འཛིན་པའི་གཞི་དང་། ༢༥ སོ་སོར་རྟོག་པ་དང་། ༢༦ ངོ་ཚ་ཤེས་པ་དང་། ༢༧ སྙིང་རྗེ་དང་། ༢༨ བརྩེ་བ་དང་། ༢༩ བརྩེ་བ་བར་མ་དང་། ༣༠ ཤིན་ཏུ་བརྩེ་བ་དང་། ༣༡ དགོས་པ་དང་བཅས་པ་དང་། ༣༢ སྡུད་པ་ཉིད་དང་། ༣༣ ཕྲག་དོགས་ཏེ། ཤེས་རབ་ཀྱི་རང་བཞིན་གྱི་རྟོག་པ་སུམ་ཅུ་རྩ་གསུམ་མོ། །ཞེས་གསུང་པ་དེ་ལྟར་རྩ་བ་བག་ཆགས་སྣ་ཚོགས་པའི་ཀུན་གཞི་དང་། དེའི་ཡན་ལག་རང་བཞིན་བརྒྱད་ཅུའི་རྣམ་རྟོག་རྣམས་ཀྱང་རིམ་གྱིས་མཆེད་ཅིང་འཁྲུལ་པ་ལུ་གུ་རྒྱུད་དུ་གྱུར་པས་འཁོར་བ་མཐའ་མེད་དུ་འཁྱམས་པ་འདི་ནི་མ་རྟོགས་སེམས་ཅན་རྣམས་ཀྱི་འཁྲུལ་ཚུལ་ཡིན་ཏེ། རང་ཤར་ལས། སེམས་ནི་བག་ཆགས་ཀུན་གྱི་གཞི། ལུས་ཅན་རྣམས་ཀྱི་དྲི་མ་ཡིན།། གཟུང་བ་ཡུལ་ལ་འཛིན་པ་སེམས། །དེ་ཕྱིར་འཁོར་བའི་ཆོས་ཉིད་ དོ། །ཞེས་གསུངས་སོ།། དེ་ཡང་རང་བཞིན་བརྒྱད་ཅུའི་རྟོག་པ་གང་ཞེ་ན། སློབ་དཔོན་ཨཱརྻ་དེ་བའི་སྤྱོད་བསྡུས་སྒྲོན་མ་ལས། རང་བཞིན་རྣམ་པ་བརྒྱད་ཅུ་ལས། ཉོན་མོངས་དགུ་བཅུ་རྩ་བརྒྱད་འབྱུང་བ་ལ། ཡང་ལྟ་བ་དྲུག་ཅུ་གཉིས་ལ་སོགས་པ་འབྱུང་བར་འགྱུར་རོ། །ཞེས་དང་། སྒྲོན་གསལ་འགྲེལ་ཏིག་ལས ༦༡-༡༠-༥-༥ འདོད་ཆགས་ལ་སོགས་པ་ནི་ཤེས་རབ་ཀྱི་རང་བཞིན་སུམ་ཅུ་རྩ་གསུམ་གྱི་ཆོས་

> (9) conceptuality, (10) destruction [of conceptions], (11) middling destruction, (12) great destruction, (13) existence, (14) middling existence, (15) great existence, (16) taking up, (17) non-virtue, (18) good fortune, (19) evenness, (20) amazement, (21) middling amazement, (22) great playfulness, (23) awareness, (24) base of grasping, (25) discernment, tenderness, (30) great tenderness, (31) needing, (32) collecting, (33) jealousy. These thirty-three conceptions have the nature of wisdom.

Accordingly, their root is the allground of the various predispositions and their offshoots are the eighty natural conceptions[87] that gradually increase and form a chain of delusion due to which there is endless wandering in cyclic existence. Such is the manner of delusion for unrealized sentient beings. *The Self-Dawning [Tantra]* says:

> Mind, the latency allground,
> Is the stain of embodied ones
> It's a beholder (*gzung*)
> A mind apprehending objects
> And is, therefore,
> The real nature of cyclic existence.[88]

What is the nature of the eighty conceptions? Master Aryadeva's *Lamp Distilling the Practices*[89] says:

> From among the eighty natural [afflicted] conceptions
> Arise ninety-eight afflictions and
> Sixty-two views and so forth also arise.

The *Clear Lamp Commentary* [on Aryadeva's *Lamp Distilling the Practices*] says:

> Desire and so forth, the thirty-three conceptions [arisen from hatred] and possessing the nature of wisdom,

དང་ཐབས་ཀྱི་རང་བཞིན་བཞི་བཅུ་དང་མ་རིག་པའི་རང་བཞིན་བདུན་ཏེ། ཉིན་དང་མཚན་དུ་བརྒྱད་བཅུ་གཉིས་འགྱུར་ནས་བརྒྱ་དྲུག་ཅུར་འགྱུར་པའོ། །དེ་རྣམས་ཀྱང་རང་བཞིན་ཞེས་པ་ནི་བརྒྱ་དྲུག་ཅུར་གྲངས་དང་ལྡན་པའོ། །ཞེས་སོ། །དེ་ཐམས་ཅད་ཀྱང་བདེན་པར་གྲུབ་པ་མེད་པར་སྒྱུ་མ་རྨི་ལམ་ལྟ་བུའི་རང་བཞིན་ལས་མ་འདས་ཏེ། སྒྱུ་མ་ངལ་གསོའི་འགྲེལ་ཆེན་ཤིང་རྟ་བཟང་པོ་ལས། ཅི་སྣང་ཅི་བྱེད་ཅི་བསམ་ཐམས་ཅད་ཀུན་ལམ་ཡིན་པའི་འདུ་ཤེས་མ་བྲལ་བས་བདེན་མེད་འལ་འོལ་བན་བུན་ཕྱད་ཕྱོལ་དང་། སང་སེང་ཁྲལ་ཁྲོལ་འཛིན་མེད་ཆེན་པོར་སྐྱོང་། ཡུལ་གང་དུ་འགྲོ་ཡང་གནས་གང་དུ་འདུག་ཀྱང་། ཟས་ཅི་ལྟ་བུ་ཟ་ཡང་། གཏམ་ཇི་ལྟར་སྨྲ་ཡང་། རྣམ་རྟོག་ཇི་ལྟར་འཕྲོ་ཡང་། སྤྱོད་ལམ་ཇི་ལྟ་བུ་བྱེད་ཀྱང་། སྣང་བ་ཇི་ལྟ་བུ་ཤར་ཡང་། སྐད་ཅིག་དེ་ཉིད་དུ་རྨི་ལམ་དངོས་ཡིན། རྨི་ལམ་གྱི་ངོ་བོ་བདེན་མེད་ཡིན། བདེན་མེད་ཀྱི་ངོ་བོ་འཛིན་མེད་ཡིན། འཛིན་མེད་ཀྱི་ངོ་བོ་འལ་འོལ་ཡིན། འལ་འོལ་གྱི་ངོ་བོ་བན་བུན་ཡིན། བན་བུན་གྱི་ངོ་བོ་ཕྱལ་ཕྱོལ་ཡིན། ཕྱལ་ཕྱོལ་གྱི་ངོ་བོ་སང་སེང་[27]ཡིན། སང་སེང་གི་ངོ་བོ་ཁྲལ་ཁྲོལ་ཡིན། ཐམས་ཅད་མེད་པ་གསལ་སྣང་ཡིན་སྙམ་དུ་མ་ཡེངས་པར་འདུན་པ་རྩེ་གཅིག་གིས་སྦྱང་བར་བྱའོ།

27. TEXT EDIT: 12b.4. *sang se* corrected to *sang seng.*

> together with the forty [conceptions arisen from desire] and possessing the nature of method,[90] plus the seven possessing the nature of unawareness [make eighty]. Eighty by day and eighty by night total one hundred and sixty. Therefore, the full total is one hundred and sixty.

None of these are truly established and none go beyond an illusory or dreamlike nature.

Illusions Laced with Holes

[Longchen Rabjam,] in his *Fine Chariot: A Great Commentary on Putting Illusions to Rest,* says:[91]

> Your ongoing discrimination that all and everything that appears, functions, or is contemplated is a path. Through this you understand all these as lacking an existence that is true. They seem laced with holes, evanescent, fluctuating, pristinely pure like bits of light jingling together—and you are purified into a great release from any holding [to true existence].[92]

Wherever we go, wherever we are, whatever food we eat, whatever conversation we make, whatever thoughts proliferate, whatever activities we take up, and whatever appearances might dawn for us, all these are actually, in that very moment, the stuff of dreams. The essence of dreams is untruth, and there is no holding on to an untrue nature.

The essence of non-holding is being flimsy (*al 'ol*), the essence of being flimsy is flickering (*phyal phyol*), the essence of flickering is haziness (*ban bun*). The essence of haziness is mistlike vanishing (*sang seng*),[93] the essence of mistlike vanishing is evanescence (*khral khrol*). Reflect that everything is a clear appearance of the nonexistent. Practice undistractedly and with single-pointed determination.

ཞེས་གསུངས་པ་ལྟར་སྣང་སྲིད་འཁོར་འདས་ཀྱི་སྡུད་པའི་ཆོས་ཐམས་ཅད་རྨི་ལམ་སྒྱུ་མའི་རང་བཞིན་ཁོ་ན་ཡིན་པར་ཤེས་པའི་སྒོ་ནས་དུས་རྟག་ཏུ་ཡང་དག་པར་མ་ཡེངས་པར་སྐྱོང་བ་ནི་གནད་དམ་པ་སྟེ། དེ་ཉིད་ལས། སྒྱུ་མ་མཁན་བཟང་པོས་ཞུས་པའི་མདོ་ལས། ལས་ཀྱི་སྤྲུལ་པའི་སྒྱུ་མ་ནི། འགྲོ་བ་རིགས་དྲུག་འདི་དག་གོ། །རྐྱེན་གྱིས་[28] སྤྲུལ་པའི་སྒྱུ་མ་ནི། མེ་ལོང་[29] གཟུགས་བརྙན་ལ་སོགས་སོ། ཆོས་ཀྱིས་སྤྲུལ་པའི་སྒྱུ་མ་ནི། ང་ཡི་འཁོར་གྱི་དགེ་སློང་ངོ་། ང་ནི་ཡང་དག་སྒྱུ་མ་སྟེ། འདུས་མ་བྱས་པ་ཆོས་ཀྱི་སྐུ། །ཞེས་གསུངས་པ་ལྟར། སྐྱེ་བ་སྔ་མ་བྱས་ཤིང་བསགས་པའི་ལས་ཀྱིས་སྤྲུལ་པའི་སྒྱུ་མས་ངན་འགྲོ་གསུམ་གྱི་ཚ་གྲང་བཀྲེས་སྐོམས་བླུན་རྨོངས་ཀྱི་སྡུག་བསྔལ་དང་བདེ་འགྲོ་གསུམ་གྱི་འཕོ་ལྟུང་འཐབ་རྩོད་སྐྱེ་རྒ་ན་འཆི་སོགས་ཀྱི་སྡུག་བསྔལ་གྱི་རྣམ་གྲངས་བརྗོད་པར་དཀའ་ལ་ཡུན་རིང་བ་འདི་དག་དང་། རྐྱེན་གྱིས་སྤྲུལ་པའི་སྒྱུ་མ་ནི་མེད་བཞིན་འཁྲུལ་ངོར་སྣང་བ་མེ་ལོང་ནང་གི་གཟུགས་བརྙན་ལྟ་བུ་འདི་དག་དང་། སྒྱུ་མའི་གཉེན་པོར་སྒྱུ་མ་ཆོས་ཀྱིས་སྤྲུལ་པས་བཅོམ་ལྡན་འདས་ཀྱིས་ཀྱང་ངའི་འཁོར་བུམ་པ་བཟང་པོ་ལྟ་བུ་དགེ་སློང་ཤ་རིའི་བུ་དང་། མོང་གལ་གྱི་བུ་ལ་སོགས་པའི་འཁོར་རྣམ་བཞི་འདི་དག་ཏུ་མ་ཟད་སངས་རྒྱས་ཉིད་ཀྱང་སྒྱུ་མ་སྟེ། ཡུམ་ལས། རབ་འབྱོར་ཆོས་ཐམས་ཅད་ནི་སྒྱུ་མ་དང་རྨི་ལམ་ལྟ་བུ་དང་།

28. TEXT EDIT: 13a.2. *rkyen gyi* corrected to *rkyen gyis* to parallel previous line's construction.
29. TEXT EDIT: 13b.1. *mi long* corrected to *me long*.

Likewise, all phenomena that are or could be in samsara or nirvana are only the nature of dreams, of illusions. This is an excellent essential to remember at all times, correctly and without wavering.

The same text (Longchenpa's *Fine Chariot*)[94] cites the *Sutra on the Questions of Bhadra the Magician*:

> Magical illusions issue forth from karma and
> Wander the six realms,
> Illusions issuing forth from causal conditions[95]
> Are reflections in a mirror. And so on!
> Illusions issuing from the dharma are
> My retinue of monks
> I myself am, in fact, an illusion:
> The unconditioned sheer essence dimension.

Because of illusions sent forth by actions done and accumulated in former births, we suffer in the three unfortunate realms—heat and cold, hunger and thirst, stupidity and dullness—and suffer as well in the three fortunate realms from plummeting [to] lower [realms], quarreling, birth, aging, sickness, death, and so on. These sufferings are hard to bear and long lasting.

The illusions issuing forth from causal conditions are like reflections in a mirror,[96] bereft of their own nature. We perceive them due to error. The same is true of illusory phenomena that issue forth from the dharma and function as antidotes to illusion. The Blessed One said that not only is the auspicious vessel of his entourage illusory—the four retinues (male and female monks and lay persons) consisting of Shariputra, Maudgalayana, and so forth—but Buddha is also illusory. This is as stated in [the *Mother Perfection of Wisdom Sutra*]:

> Subhuti [a Hearer renowned for his understanding of emptiness], all phenomena are like illusions, like dreams,

དེ་ལས་ལྷག་པས་སངས་རྒྱས་བཅོམ་ལྡན་འདས་ཀྱང་སྒྱུ་མ་དང་རྨི་ལམ་ལྟ་བུའོ། ཞེས་པ་ལྟར་མདོར་ན་ཅི་བསམ་ཅི་སྣང་མས་ཅད་སྒྱུ་མའི་རང་བཞིན་ལས་མ་འདས་ཏེ་དེ་ཉིད་ལས། སྒྱུ་མའི་ཡུལ་དང་སྒྱུ་མའི་གྲོང་ཁྱེར་དང་། སྒྱུ་མའི་སྐྱེ་བོ་སྒྱུ་མའི་ལོངས་སྤྱོད་དང་། སྒྱུ་མའི་བདེ་སྡུག་སྒྱུ་མའི་སྐྱེ་འཇིགས་[30] དང་། སྒྱུ་མའི་བདེན་རྫུན་ཇི་ལྟར་སྣང་བ་ལྟར། འགྲོ་དྲུག་སྣང་བ་དེ་ལྟར་ཤེས་པར་བྱ། ཞེས་གསུངས་པའི་འགྲོ་བ་དྲུག་པོ་འདི་དག་ནི་སྒྱུ་མ་རྨི་ལམ་ལྟ་བུར་འཁྲུལ་ངོར་སྣང་བ་ཡིན་ནོ། །ཡང་ཀུན་གཞི་ལ་འཁོར་འདས་ཐམས་ཅད་ཀྱི་བག་ཆགས་ས་བོན་གྱི་ཚུལ་དུ་གནས་པའི་མཐུས། རང་གི་ལུས་བརྗོད་བཅས་ཤ་ཁྲག་རགས་པ་དང་རྩ་རླུང་ཐིག་ལེ་དྭངས་སྙིགས་སྣ་ཚོགས་པའི་དངོས་པོ་དང་། ཕྱི་རོལ་དུ་འཁོར་འདས་ཁམས་གསུམ་སྣོད་བཅུད་ཀྱི་དངོས་པོ་ཐམས་ཅད་གཅིག་ལ་གཅིག་བརྟེན་གྱི་ཚུལ་དུ་སྣང་བ་འདི་དག་ཀྱང་དོན་ལ་མེད་བཞིན་དུ་ཀུན་རྫོབ་འཁྲུལ་སྣང་དུ་སྣང་བ་ལ་རྟག་འཛིན་ཨ་འཐས་བདེན་ཞེན་ལ་ཆེས་ཆེར་གོམས་པས་ཁམས་གསུམ་རིགས་དྲུག་གི་བདེ་སྡུག་བཏང་སྙོམས་སོགས་སྣ་ཚོགས་ལ་སྤྱོད་ཅིང་། འཁོར་བའི་རྒྱུ་འབྲས་ཟྲོ་ཆུའི་འཁྲུད་མོ་ལྟ་བུ་ལ་རྟག་ཏུ་འཁོར་བ་ནི་སེམས་ཅན་སྤྱིའི་མཚན་ཉིད་ལས་མ་འདས།

30. TEXT EDIT: 13b.6. *skye dzig* corrected to *skye 'jigs.*

> and even the best among these, the blessed Buddha, is like an illusion, like a dream.

Accordingly, and to put it briefly, none of our thoughts and nothing that appears to us passes beyond the nature of illusion. The same sutra says:

> Illusory places, illusory cities, illusory persons, illusory resources, as well as illusory happiness and suffering, illusory production[97] and destruction, illusory truth and falsity. Understand that just as this is the case with these appearances, so it is also the case with appearances of the six realms.[98]

The six realms described here are like illusions, like dreams. They are perceived in error.

Also, through the force of predispositions dwelling in the all-ground, which are seeds for the whole of cyclic existence and nirvana, there comes to be the materializing of our own bodies—coarse flesh and blood, as well as impermanent phenomena such as our various channels, winds, essential orbs, the pure and the unrefined. Like them, all external things in the three realms of cyclic existence and nirvana, environments and beings, appear by way of one depending on the other.

In fact, these present themselves as mistaken appearances, as conventionalities that lack any [true] nature. However, we are so deeply habituated to orienting toward them as true that we stubbornly hold on to them as permanent! This is how we get involved with the various kinds of suffering, happiness, and neutrality associated with the six types [of rebirths in] the three realms. The cause-and-effect process of cyclic existence is like the rim of a water wheel. We spin continuously but never get beyond the commonplace characteristics of sentient beings.

དེ་ལྟར་ལུ་གུ་རྒྱུད་དུ་འབྲེལ་ཞིང་འཁོར་བར་འཁྱམས་དུས་ཀྱང་ཁམས་བདེ་བར་གཤེགས་པའི་སྙིང་པོའམ་རང་རིག་པའི་ངོ་བོ་ལ་ནི་ངན་དུ་སོང་བའམ་འགྲིབ་པར་འགྱུར་བ་ནི། རྡུལ་ཙམ་ཡང་མེད་དོ། །ཀྱེ་རྒྱུད་བརྟག[31] གཉིས་ལས། སེམས་ཅན་རྣམས་ནི་སངས་རྒྱས་ཉིད། །འོན་ཀྱང་གློ་བུར་དྲི་མས་བསྒྲིབས། །ཅེས་གསུངས་པ་ལྟར་དོན་དམ་པར་ནི་ཡེ་གདོད་མའི་གནས་ལུགས་དེ་སྐུ་གསུམ་དབྱེར་མེད་དུ་ལྷམ་མེ། བར་དུ་འབྲེལ་སྣང་གློ་བུར་གྱི་དྲི་མས་བསྒྲིབས་དུས་ཀྱང་གཤིས་ཀྱི་རང་ངོ་ལ་སྐུ་གསུམ་དུ་ལྷང་ངེ། མཐར་སྒྲིབ་བྱེད་སངས་ནས་མཁྱེན་གཉིས་རྒྱས་པའི་འབྲས་བུ་མངོན་དུ་གྱུར་ཀྱང་སྐུ་གསུམ་དུ་ལྷན་ནེར་བཞུགས་པ་ཉིད་དེ། དེའི་ཕྱིར་ན་འཁྲུལ་རྟོག་མ་རིག་པའི་དྲི་མ་དང་བྲལ་མ་བྲལ་གྱི་ཆ་ལ་འཁྲུལ་གྲོལ་གཉིས་ཀྱི་ཐ་སྙད་བཏགས་པ་ཙམ་སྟེ། རྒྱུད་བླ་མ་ལས། ལྟར་སྔར་བཞིན་ཕྱིས་དེ་བཞིན། འགྱུར་བ་མེད་པའི་ཆོས་ཉིད་དོ། །ཅེས་དང་། ཀུན་བྱེད་རྒྱལ་པོ་ལས། སེམས་ཉིད་ཀུན་ཏུ་བཟང་པོ་ཡི། བཞུགས་ཚུལ་བསྟན་པ་འདི་ལྟ་སྟེ། །བྱང་ཆུབ་སེམས་སུ་བཞུགས་ཙ་ན[32]། །ཆོས་རྣམས་ཀུན་གྱི་སྙིང་པོར་བཞུགས། །དེ་རྟོགས་ཀུན་བྱེད་རྒྱལ་པོ་ཡིན། ཀུན་བྱེད་རྒྱལ་པོར་འགྱུར་བ་མེད། །དེས་ན་འགྱུར་བ་མེད་པར་བསྟན། །ཞེས་གསུངས།

31. TEXT EDIT: 14b.3. *stag* corrected to *brtag*.
32. TEXT EDIT: 15a.3. *bzhugs tsam na* corrected to *bzhugs tsa na*.

Buddhas and Other Beings

Yet, even while wandering around in the unbroken chains of our own delusion, this domain, namely the heart-essence of the Blissful Ones, which is also the essence of our own sheer awareness, has not worsened or been obscured by a single iota. *The Tiger Root Tantra*[99] (*rDza rgyud stag pa*[100]) says:

> Sentient beings are really Buddhas
> Though adventitiously obscured by defilement.

And so we see that, ultimately, from the very beginning, our genuine state is clearly inseparable from the three Buddha dimensions. Even right now, while we are obscured by mistaken appearances due to our adventitious defilements, our own basic face is bright with these three dimensions. Once we purify our obstructions, the fruit, which is an unfolding of the two omniscient knowers, becomes evident. The three Buddha dimensions vividly reside here. All told, error and liberation are just conventions that come about on the basis of whether one does or does not have the stain of mistaken thought, unawareness. As it says in the *Highest Tantra* (*rGyud bla ma*):

> As it was before, so it is thereafter:
> Reality itself does not change.

Also, the *Majestic Creator of Everything* says:

> The all-good mindnature's way of being is taught thus:
> It is there as the mind of enlightenment[101]
> It is there as the essence of everything.
> Realizing it, you are a majestic creator of everything.[102]
> That majestic creator of everything is unchanging
> And is therefore taught as changeless.[103]

དེ་ལྟར་བས་ན་སེམས་ཉིད་གདོད་ནས་དག་པའི་ངོ་བོ་རང་བཞིན་ལྷུན་གྱིས་གྲུབ་ཀྱང་ལྷན་སྐྱེས་མ་རིག་པ་ལ་ཡུལ་རྐྱེན་གྱིས་གློ་བུར་[33] འཁྲུལ་སྣང་གི་དྲི་མ་ཚབ་ཆེན་འདིས་གསེར་ལ་གཡའ་སྐྱེས་པ་བཞིན་རང་ལས་བྱུང་བས་རང་ཉིད་བསྒྲིབས་པ་འདི་སྦྱོང་ཞིང་དག་པར་བྱེད་པའི་ཐབས་ཀྱི་བྱེ་བྲག་སྣ་ཚོགས་པ་གསུངས་ཀྱང་། དོན་གྱི་ངོ་བོ་ནི་དུས་གསུམ་འཕོ་འགྱུར་བྲལ་བའི་རང་བྱུང་གི་ཡེ་ཤེས་མཚན་མའི་སྤྲོས་པས་དབེན་པ་ཆོས་ཉིད་[34] དོན་གྱི་ཡུལ་ལོ། དེས་ན་ལམ་ཐམས་ཅད་ཐབས་ཤེས་གཉིས་ལ་འདུ་བ་ནི་རྒྱལ་བའི་དགོངས་པ་མཐར་ཐུག་པ་ཡིན་ཏེ། གུ་རུ་རིན་པོ་ཆེས། ཐབས་ཤེས་དབྱེར་མེད་ཅེས་ཀྱང་བྱ་སྟེ། འགག་མེད་དྲན་སྣང་གི་ཡེ་ཤེས་ཐབས། དེའི་རང་བཞིན་སྐྱེ་བ་མེད་པ་ཤེས་རབ། ཐབས་ཤེས་གཉིས་མེད་ཀྱི་ཡེ་ཤེས་ཆེན་པོ་དེ་ནི་ཐམས་ཅད་ཀྱི་བཞུགས་ཚུལ་ལོ། ཞེས་དང་། དཔལ་མགོན་ཀླུས། ཉོན་མོངས་དྭ་བས་གཡོགས་པ་ན། སེམས་ཅན་ཞེས་ནི་བརྗོད་པར་བྱེད།།དེ་ཉིད་ཉོན་མོངས་བྲལ་གྱུར་ན། །སངས་རྒྱས་ཞེས་ནི་བརྗོད་པའོ། ཞེས་སོ། །

33. TEXT EDIT: 15a.6. *blo bur* corrected to *glo bur*.
34. TEXT EDIT: 15b.2. *dbyen pa chos nyid* corrected to *dben pa chos nyid*.

As this says, mindnature is from the very beginning pure in essence and spontaneous[104] in nature. Still, when it comes to inborn unawareness, we have serious contaminations and adventitious deluded appearances that come about because of our perception and our circumstances. Like rust on gold, it arises from itself and obstructs itself.

Realizing the Great Seal

Kagyu Words on Wisdom

Although we describe various specific methods for cleansing and purifying [obstructions], their actual essence is the self-risen primordial knowing which, free from any iteration of characteristics, abides without change in the past, present, and future. Being devoid[105] of change, it is the genuine object, reality itself. In this regard, all paths are included in the two, method and wisdom. Such is the final understanding of the Conquerors. Guru Rinpoche said:

> What we call "method" and "wisdom" are indivisible:
> Primordial knowing that heeds ceaseless appearance[106]
> is method[107]
> Its unborn nature is sublime knowing.
> That great primordial knowing—method and wisdom
> undual—
> Is the abiding nature of everything.[108]

The glorious protector Naga [Nagarjuna] said:

> When covered with a web of afflictions
> We are called sentient beings.
> Once we are freed from afflictions
> We are called Buddhas.

དེས་ན་ཕྱག་རྒྱ་ཆེན་པོར་གགས་པ་ལའང་ངོས་འཛིན་ཚུལ་མི་འདྲ་བ་མང་སྟེ། རྒྱ་གར་དུ་ཏེ་ལོ་པ་དང་ན་རོ་པ་སོགས་ནི་ཐབས་ཤེས་གཉིས་ལ་གཙོ་བོར་མཛད་ནས་བདེ་སྟོང་ལྷན་ཅིག་སྐྱེས་པའི་ཡེ་ཤེས་ལ་ཕྱག་རྒྱ་ཆེན་པོར་བཞེད་ཅིང་ཉམས་ལེན་ཀྱང་ཐབས་ལམ་ཁོ་ན་གནད་དུ་བསྟུན། དེའི་རྗེས་འབྲངས་མར་པ་དང་མི་ལ་རས་པ་དང་རས་ཆུང་པ་སོགས་ཀྱང་དེ་ལྟར་མཛད། མི་ཏྲི་པ་དང་དེའི་བླ་མ་རི་ཁྲོད་དབང་ཕྱུག །དེའི་བླ་མ་ས་ར་ཧ་དང་བཅས་པས་ནི་ཤེས་རབ་སྟོང་པ་ཉིད་ལ་གཙོ་བོར་མཛད་དེ་རིག་སྟོང་ཕྱག་རྒྱ་ཆེན་པོའམ་ཨ་མ་ན་སི་ཀ་ར་ཏེ་ཡིད་ལ་མི་བྱེད་པ་ཅེས་བྱ་བ་མ་བཅོས་སོར་བཞག་ཁོ་ནའི་དོན་གྱི་ཡེ་ཤེས་ལ་ཕྱག་རྒྱ་ཆེན་པོར་བཞེད་པའི་ཕྱག་སྲོལ་མར་པ་མི་ལ་ནས་བརྒྱུད་དེ་མཉམ་མེད་དྭགས་པོ་ལྷ་རྗེས་ལྷན་ཅིག་སྐྱེས་སྦྱོར་རྒྱ་ཆེན་སྤེལ་བར་མཛད་ལ། གར་དབང་ཆོས་ཀྱི་གགས་པས་ཡིག་ཆ་ཡང་མཛད། འབྲུག་པ་ཡབ་སྲས་དང་ཁྲིད་པར་ཀྲོད་ཚངས་པ་སོགས་ནི་ཐོལ་སྐྱེས་ཀྱི་ཤེས་པ་ག་མཉམས་པ་ཉིད་ལ་བཞེད་པ་དང་། ཞང་ཚལ་པས་ནི་འོད་གསལ་ལ་བཞེད་པ་དང་། རྗེ་འབྲི་གུང་པས་ནི་རང་རིག་ཉག་ཅིག་ལ་བཞེད། ཀམ་ཚང་པ་ནི་རྒྱུད་སྡེ་ཐམས་ཅད་ཀྱི་མཐར་ཐུག་གི་དགོངས་པ་ཐབས་ཤེས་གཉིས་མེད་ཀྱི་གཉུག་མ་ལྷན་སྐྱེས་ཀྱི་དབྱིངས་སུ་རང་ཤར་སོ་མ་སྣང་རིག་རྗེན་པ་འདི་ཉིད་ལ་ཕྱག་རྒྱ་ཆེན་པོའམ་ལྷག་མཐོང་གི་ངོ་བོར་བཞེད།

The renowned Mahamudra, the Great Seal, is identified in several different ways. For example in India, Tilopa and Naropa named the twofold method and wisdom as most significant and, having done so, taught the inborn primordial knowing of bliss and emptiness as the Great Seal. In terms of their practice also, the path of method itself [for example, the completion stage of channel-wind practices] pierces to the pith.[109] Their disciples Marpa, Milarepa, and Rechung accord with them.

Maitripa and his teacher, Lord Shvari [Rithro Wangchug], together with their Lama, Saraha, take sublime knowing (*shes rab*), which is emptiness, as their main focus.[110] This is the empty sheer awareness, the Great Seal, known as "a mind without doing." This is genuine primordial knowing, uncontrived and simply at rest. Such primordial knowing, which this tradition describes as the Great Seal, is an unparalleled lineage from Milarepa to Dagpo Hlaje (*Dwags po lha rje*), widely known as Gampo-pa, 1059–1153), who composed the *Simultaneously Arisen Union*.[111]

Garwang Chögyi Dragpa[112] wrote texts propagating the practice of simultaneously arisen union.[113] The Drukpa father and heir[114] and, very particularly, the Drukpa Lama Gotsangpa (*rGod tshang pa*)[115] and so forth explain the Great Seal in connection with the swift-sprung (*thol skyes*) [or ageless] consciousness, a term synonymous [with the sheer awareness of Dzogchen].

The Zhang Tshal[116] discuss clear light and the Venerable Drikung discuss seamless self-opening presence.[117] The Kamtshangpa [of the Karma Kagyu lineage] explain that the final intention of all tantras is fundamental primordial knowing, free of any dualistic relationship between method and wisdom. This naked sheer awareness, a sensing into freshness that genuinely and simply dawns into spaciousness right along with [that knowing] is itself the essence of the Great Seal or special seeing.

ས་སྐྱ་པ་རྗེས་འབྲང་རྣམས་ནི་ཕྱག་རྒྱ་ཆེན་པོ་ཅེས་བྱ་བ་དབང་དོན་གྱི་ཡེ་ཤེས་ཉིད་ཡིན་པས་དབང་གལ་ཆེ་བ་ཡིན་བཞེད་དེ། རབ་དབྱེ་ལས་ཀྱང་། ངེས་ཀྱི་ཕྱག་རྒྱ་ཆེན་པོ་ནི། དབང་ལས་བྱུང་བའི་ཡེ་ཤེས་དང་། རིམ་པ་གཉིས་ཀྱི་ཏིང་འཛིན་ལས་འབྱུང་བའི་རང་བྱུང་ཡེ་ཤེས་ཡིན། ཞེས་སོ། མཁས་གྲུབ་ཀོ་བྲག་པ་ནི་སེམས་འབྱུང་གནས་འགྲོ་གསུམ་གྱི་རྩལ་བས་མ་རྙེད་པའི་རང་ངོ་ལ་བཞེད་པ་དང་། ཀུན་མཁྱེན་བུ་སྟོན་ནི་བདེ་གཤེགས་སྙིང་པོ་ལ་བཞེད་ནས་གཞིའི་བཤད་པ་གཙོ་ཆེར་མཛད་པ་དང་། ཇོ་ནང་ཏཱ་ར་ན་ཐ་སོགས་ནི་སེམས་ཀྱི་རྒྱུད་ལ་འབྲས་བུའི་ཡོན་ཏན་མཚན་དཔེ་རྫོགས་པ་ཞིག་ལ་བཞེད་ནས་འབྲས་བུའི་བཤད་པ་གཙོ་བོར་མཛད་པ་དང་། དགེ་ལྡན་པས་ནི། པཎ་ཆེན་བློ་བཟང་ཆོས་རྒྱལ་གྱིས་ཕྱག་ཆེན་རྩ་བ་ལས། ཞི་བྱེད་གཅོད་ཡུལ་རྫོགས་ཆེན་དང་། ཕྱག་རྒྱ་ཆེན་པོ་ལ་སོགས་པ། སོ་སོར་མིང་འདོགས་མང་ན་ཡང་།[35] ངེས་དོན་ལུང་རིག་ལ་མཁས་ཤིང་། ཉམས་མྱོང་ཅན་གྱིས་རྣལ་འབྱོར་པས།།

35. TEXT EDIT: 17a.6. *mang yang* corrected to *mang na yang*.

Sakya Words on Wisdom

For followers of the Sakya, the Great Seal is an empowering consecration (*dbang*), an actual primordial knowing. Empowering consecration is therefore considered very important. *Discriminating the Three Vows* states:[118]

> That which I call the Great Seal,
> Primordial knowing arisen through empowering
> consecration,
> Is the self-risen primordial knowing that
> Comes to be through the two stages of meditative
> stabilization.[119]

Kaydrub Trodragpa (*Khas grub kro brag pa*) teaches that our own face is what we do not find in searching for our mind's place of arising, abiding, and vanishing. The omniscient Budon (*Bu-ston*), having explained the heart essence of the Blissful Ones, mainly emphasized explanations of the base. The Jonangpa Taranatha and so forth, having described the complete signs and marks which are the mindstream's fruitional qualities, emphasized explanations of the fruit.

Gelukpa Words on Wisdom

The Gedunpa (Gelukpa) Panchen Losang Chogyal in the *Root of the Great Seal (Phyag chen rtsa ba)* wrote:

> The Pacifers,[120] the Severers [followers of Machig
> Labdron],
> The Dzogchenpas,
> The Great Seal and so forth—
> Although many different names are given,[121]
> When yogis, skilled in the definitive meaning of
> Scripture, understanding, and practice,

དཔྱད་ན་དགོངས་པ་གཅིག་ཏུ་མཐུན། །ཞེས་དང་། ཚུལ་འདི་དག་ལ་ནི་མཁས་པའི་དབང་པོར་གགས་པ་འགྲོ་བ་མང་པོའི་འདྲེན་པར་རློམ་པ་འགའི་ཡི་གེ་ལའང་ངེས་པ་མ་མཆིས་མོད་འོན་ཀྱང་སྒྲུབ་པ་སྙིང་པོར་མཛད་པའི་དམ་པ་རྣམས་ཁོ་ན་ཐུགས་རྒྱུས་[36] ཆེ་བ་འདུག་སྟེ། ཞེས་གསུངས་པ་དང་།

36. TEXT EDIT: 17b.3. *thugs rgyud* corrected to *thugs rgyus*.

> Investigate, they find a single, harmonious, enlightened state.

Losang Chogyal also wrote:

> When it comes to these systems, even persons well known for their powerful scholarship who boast that they guide many seekers, or who write numerous books, do not have certainty. The excellent ones with accomplishment at their core possess great and intimate familiarity.[122] (Thus, the understanding of those who meditate is far greater than those who concern themselves only with texts.[123])

སྔ་འགྱུར་རྙིང་མ་པ་རྣམས་ནི་གུ་རུ་རིན་པོ་ཆེའི་ཕྱག་ཆེན་ཞལ་གདམས་ལས། སེམས་ཉིད་ཕྱག་རྒྱ་ཆེན་པོ་ཞེས་བྱ་བ་གསལ་སྟོང་གཉིས་སུ་མེད་པའི་ཡེ་ཤེས་ལ་ཟེར་བ་ཡིན། སྣང་སྲིད་འཁོར་འདས་ཀྱི་བསྡུས་པའི་ཆོས་ཐམས་ཅད་དང་པོར་འབྱུང་ཡང་སེམས་ཉིད་ལས་འབྱུང་། ད་ལྟ་ཡང་སེམས་ཉིད་ངང་ལ་གནས། མཐར་ཡང་སེམས་ཉིད་ཀྱི་ཀློང་དུ་ཐིམ་ཕྱིར། ཐམས་ཅད་སེམས་ལས་མ་འདས་སེམས་དེ་ཉིད་བླ་མའི་བྱིན་རླབས་དང་གདམས་ངག་གིས་ཟིན་པས་རང་རིག་རང་ངོ་ཤེས་[37] ནས་མྱ་ངན་ལས་འདས་པའི་ཡོན་ཏན་ཐམས་བསྐྱེད་པའི་གཞི་ཡིན། དེ་ཅིའི་ཕྱིར་ན། སེམས་ཉིད་རང་བཞིན་གདོད་ནས་མ་བཅོས་པ་ཆོས་སྐུ།[38] རང་མདངས་འགག་མེད་དུ་གསལ་བ་ལོངས་སྤྱོད་རྫོགས་སྐུ། རོལ་རྩལ་ཐུགས་རྗེ་ཀུན་ལ་ཁྱབ་པ་སྤྲུལ་པའི་སྐུ། དེ་གསུམ་གདོད་ནས་དབྱེར་མེད་ལྷུན་གྲུབ་ཏུ་བཞུགས་པ་ངོ་བོ་ཉིད་ཀྱི་སྐུ་སྟེ།

37. TEXT EDIT: 18a.1. *rang ngo she* corrected to *rang ngo shes*.
38. TEXT EDIT: 18a.2–3. *gdod nas ma bcos sku* corrected to *gdod nas ma bcos pa chos sku*.

2 Mindnature

The Great Seal in Nyingma

ADDRESSING FOLLOWERS of the ancient transmission, Guru Rinpoche writes in *Great Seal of Heartfelt Advice,*[124]

> Mindnature, called the Great Seal, indicates a primordial knowing that is the nonduality of the clear and the empty. All phenomena included in appearances and possibilities, or cyclic existence and nirvana, arise from mindnature when they initially arise. Everything in the present likewise abides within mindnature and in the end dissolves into the expanse of mindnature.
>
> Nothing lies outside mindnature.[125] When mind itself is conjoined with a lama's blessings and quintessential instruction, the intimate knowing of our own sheer awareness recognizes itself[126] and in this way becomes the basis for the complete unfolding of all the good qualities of nirvana. Why is this? The very being (*rang bzhin*) of mindnature (*sems nyid*) is from the first the uncontrived sheer essence dimension. Its ceaseless, luminous radiance is the rich and joyful resplendent dimension. Its all-pervasive dynamic displays[127] and compassionate responsiveness are the emanation dimension. That these three are from the beginning spontaneously present and indivisible is the full essence dimension (*ngo bo nyid*

དེ་ལྟར་རྟོགས་པས་སངས་རྒྱས་ཀྱི་ཡོན་ཏན་ཐམས་ཅད་ལྷུན་གྲུབ་ཏུ་འབྱུང་བའོ། །ཞེས་དང་། སེམས་ཉིད་ཡེ་གདོད་མ་ནས་སྐྱེ་བ་མེད་པ་ལས། འགག་མེད་དུ་འཁོར་འདས་ཀྱི་ཆོ་འཕྲུལ་སྣ་ཚོགས་ཤར་ཡང་སྐྱེ་མེད་ཀྱི་རོལ་པ་ལས་མ་འདས། དེའི་ཕྱིར་སྣང་བ་ཐམས་ཅད་སྟོང་པ། སྟོང་པའི་རང་མདངས་སྣང་བ་སྟེ་སྣང་སྟོང་གཉིས་སུ་མེད་དོ། །ཅེས་སོགས་དང་། ཡང་དེ་ལས། ཐབས་ཤེས་དབྱེར་མེད་ཅེས་ཀྱང་བྱ་སྟེ། འགག་མེད་དྲན་སྣང་གི་ཡེ་ཤེས་ཐབས། དེའི་རང་བཞིན་སྐྱེ་བ་མེད་པ་ཤེས་རབ། ཐབས་ཤེས་གཉིས་མེད་ཀྱི་ཡེ་ཤེས་ཆེན་པོ་དེ་ནི་ཆོས་ཐམས་ཅད་ཀྱི་བཞུགས་ཚུལ་ལོ། །ཞེས་སོ། །དེས་ན། འཇིག་རྟེན་ཞེན་པ་ལིངས་ཀྱི་བོར། འཁྲུལ་པའི་སྣང་བ་གཤིགས་ཀྱི་བཤིགས། བག་ཆགས་འཛིན་ཞེན་བུན་གྱིས་ཐོང་། ཤེས་པ་རང་སོར་ལྷོད་དེ་གློད། །ཆོས་ཉིད་དང་ལ་ལྷན་གྱི་ཞོག །སངས་རྒྱས་ཀུན་གྱི་མེས་པོ་སེམས། །སེམས་ཀྱི་དེ་ཉིད་རྟོགས་པ་གཅེས། །སུམ་ཅུ་རྩ་བདུན་བྱང་ཆུབ་ཆོས། །ས་བཅུ་ལམ་ལྔ་ཕར་ཕྱིན་དྲུག །སྐུ་གསུམ་སྐུ་ལྔ་ཡེ་ཤེས་ལྔ། །དེ་སོགས་ཆོས་རྣམས་ཐམས་ཅད་ཀུན།

sku; svabhāvikakāya). To realize this is to bring forth the spontaneously present Buddha qualities.

And the same text says:

> Many different magical emanations consisting of cyclic existence and nirvana dawn ceaselessly from our eternally unborn mindnature. Yet, these are nothing but the play of the unborn! Therefore, all that appears is empty and the intrinsic radiance of emptiness shines forth. The appearing and empty are not dual.

Again in the same text:

> In terms of method and wisdom indivisible, the primordial knowing of ceaseless mindfulness and perception is method. Its unborn nature is sublime knowing. The great primordial knowing, a nonduality consisting of method-wisdom, is the steadfast nature of everything.

And also, from the same work by Guru Rinpoche:

> Worldly longing, utterly cast off,
> Deluded perception destroyed and self-disrupted—
> The trap of old tendencies and longings, gradually
> dissolves.
> Consciousness reclines and rests, just where it is.
> Be right there with reality.
> Mind is the ancestor of all Buddhas.
> Realizing mindnature is crucial for
> All thirty-seven elements of enlightenment,[128]
> The ten grounds, five paths, six perfections,
> Three Buddha dimensions, five Buddha dimensions,
> and five primordial knowings,
> For every one of these and more,

སེམས་ཉིད་ཐིག་ལེ་ཉག་གཅིག་གི །གཞི་རྩ་གཅོད་ན་དེ་ལ་འདུས། །ཅེས་གསུངས་སོ།།

དེ་ལྟར་གསང་སྔགས་ཐབས་ཀྱི་ཐེག་ན་གཞི་རྫོགས་པ་ཆེན་པོའི་གནས་ལུགས་ཀྱི་རང་སོ་ཐེན། ལམ་རྫོགས་པ་ཆེན་པོས་འཁྲུལ་རྟོག་གི་དྲི་མ་སྦྱངས། འབྲས་བུ་རྫོགས་པ་ཆེན་པོ་སྐུ་གསུམ་ཡེ་ཤེས་ལྔའི་རྒྱལ་ས་ཐེན་ཏེ་དོན་གཉིས་ལྷུན་གྱི་གྲུབ་པའི་ཕྱིར་སྟེ། མས་ཉིད་ཡེ་གདོད་མ་ནས་ཡོངས་དག་ཆེན་པོར་ལྷུན་གྱིས་གྲུབ་ཅིང་འདས་མ་འོངས་ད་ལྟ་དུས་གསུམ་དུ་སྐྱེ་འགག་གནས་གསུམ་དང་འགྲོ་འོང་གི་སྤྲོས་པ་སོགས་དང་བྲལ་བ་འཁོར་འདས་ལམ་གསུམ་དུ་འཛིན་པའི་དམིགས་མཚན་གྱིས་ཆ་ཙམ་མ་བསླད་པ་ཡོད་མེད་ཡིན་མིན་རྟག་ཆད་བཟང་ངན་མཐོ་དམན་ལ་སོགས་པའི་སྤྲོ་སྐུར་མ་བྱས་པར་སྣང་སྲིད་འཁོར་འདས་ཀྱིས་འདུས་པའི་ཆོས་ཐམས་ཅད་ལ་འགག་སྒྲུབ་སྤོང་ལེན་བསྒྱུར་བཀོད་མ་བྱས་པ་ཡེ་ནས་གནས་པའི་ཚུལ་ལམ་ཡིན་ཚུལ་ཇི་ལྟ་བའི་རང་བཞིན་སྣང་སྟོང་དབྱེར་མེད་དུ་ཁྲིག་གི་གསལ་སྟོང་ཟུང་འཇུག་ཏུ་ཆམ་མེ། འདི་ནི་ལྟ་བའི་དངོས་གཞིར་ཡིན་ལུགས་ཇི་བཞིན་དུ་གདོད་མ་ནས་རང་བྱུང་། དེ་ཉིད་འཁོར་འདས་ཀུན་གྱི་ངོ་བོ་ཡེ་ཁྱབ་ཏུ་གྱུར་པ་འདི་ལས་གཞན་པའི་ལྟ་བ་ཞེས་ཁོལ་བུའམ་དུམ་བུར་རིས་སུ་ཆད་པ་ཞིག་མེད་[39]དེ། དེ་ལྟ་བུ་ཡེ་ནས་ཡིན་ཚུལ་ཤེས་པས་གཉིས་འཛིན་གྱི་བརྫུན་མཚང་རིག་པ་ལ་ལྟ་བ་རྟོགས་པ་ཡང་ཟེར།

39. TEXT EDIT: 19b.5. *zhagi med* corrected to *zhig med*.

> All these are present when you sever the base and
> root of
> Mindnature—an unbounded wholeness.[129]

So it is. If you take up the method of secret mantra, you access your basic abiding condition. This is the base great completeness. The path of great completeness purifies stains of deluded conceptions. The fruition of great completeness holds the majestic ground comprising the three Buddha dimensions and five wisdoms. It is the spontaneous accomplishment of your two great purposes.

Mindnature is from the first a spontaneous and immense purity. It is free from the triad of birth, cessation, and abiding in past, present, or future and free from iterations such as going and coming. It is uncontaminated by even a smidgen of object-grasping characteristics regarding any of the three paths [environment, sense-objects, and body] that lead to cyclic existence or nirvana. Without either overstating by saying "it exists" and "is" or undervaluing by saying "it does not exist " or "it is not," there is also freedom from any other exaggerations and deprecations such as "permanence and annihilation," "good and bad," "high and low." [To speak of mindnature] neither negates nor establishes, neither discards nor adopts, neither casts away nor presents anything that appears or could be—that is, any of the phenomena comprising cyclic existence and nirvana.

From the beginning, your nature is such that whatever appears and whatever is empty are indivisible. This is, quite precisely, a union of clarity and emptiness.

From the first its way of being is self-risen. It is also the actual base, the view, the very essence that suffuses all cyclic existence and nirvana. Nothing we call a "view" can be other than this.[130] To know that this has been its status from the beginning is to understand all hidden faults as well as the falseness of dualism.[131]

Appreciating this vital point is called "realizing the view." We

སེམས་ངོ་མཐོང་བ་ཡང་ཟེར། ཆོས་དོན་རིག་པ་ཡང་ཟེར་སྟེ། དོ་ཧ་མཛོད་ལས། རྟོགས་པར་གྱུར་ན་ཐམས་ཅད་དེ་ཡིན་ཏེ། དེ་ལས་གཞན་ཞིག་སུས་ཀྱང་ཤེས་[40]མི་འགྱུར། ཞེས་དང་། ཀུན་བྱེད་ལས། ཀུན་བྱེད་ང་ཡི་རང་བཞིན་ལ། འཁོར་གྱི་འདོད་པ་རྣམས་ཀྱིས་མིང་བཏགས་པ། ལ་ལས་བྱང་ཆུབ་སེམས་སུ་མིང་ཡང་བཏགས། ལ་ལས་ཆོས་ཀྱི་དབྱིངས་སུ་མིང་ཡང་བཏགས། ལ་ལས་ནམ་མཁའི་ཁམས་སུ་མིང་ཡང་བཏགས། ལ་ལས་རང་བྱུང་ཡེ་ཤེས་མིང་ཡང་བཏགས། ལ་ལས་ཆོས་ཀྱི་སྐུ་རུ་མིང་ཡང་བཏགས།[41] ལ་ལས་ལོངས་སྤྱོད་རྫོགས་སྐུར་མིང་ཡང་བཏགས། ལ་ལས་སྤྲུལ་པའི་སྐུ་རུ་མིང་ཡང་བཏགས། ལ་ལས་སྐུ་གསུང་ཐུགས་སུ་མིང་ཡང་བཏགས། ལ་ལས་ཐམས་ཅད་མཁྱེན་པར་མིང་ཡང་བཏགས། ལ་ལས་ཡེ་ཤེས་གསུམ་དང་བཞིར་ཡང་བཏགས། ལ་ལས་ཡེ་ཤེས་ལྔ་རུ་མིང་ཡང་བཏགས། ཞེས་གསུངས་པ་བཞིན། དོན་ལ་སྣང་སྲིད་འཁོར་འདས་ཐམས་ཅད་སྐུ་གསུམ་གྱི་རོལ་པ་ཡིན་པ་དང་། རང་སེམས་ཉིད་ཀྱང་སྐུ་གསུམ་གྱི་རོལ་པ་ཡིན་པ་དང་། རང་སེམས་ཉིད་ཀྱང་སྐུ་གསུམ་གྱི་རང་བཞིན་ཉིད་དང་། དེ་དག་ཉིད་ཀྱང་དོན་དམ་ཆོས་ཉིད་ཀྱི་དབྱིངས་ལས་འདའ་བ་མེད་ཅིང་། དེ་ཡང་འཁོར་བའི་ཆོས་ཐམས་ཅད་ནི། སེམས་ཀྱི་མཚན་ཉིད་ཀྱི་ཚུལ་དང་། ལམ་གྱི་ཆོས་ཐམས་ཅད་ནི་

40. TEXT EDIT: 19b.6. *sus kyang she* corrected to *sus kyang shes*. The point here is that nothing exists or can be known that is beyond the mind. Realizing mind nature is all-encompassing.

41. TEXT EDIT: 20a.3. *sku ru ming btags* corrected to *ku ru ming yang btags*.

can also call it "seeing the mind which is your original face" and "knowing the principle of phenomena." Further, the *Treasury of Praise*[132] says:

> Once you are realized, everything is there.[133]
> No one ever knows anything other than this.[134]

And the *Majestic Creator of Everything* says:

> I, creator of everything, have a single nature, even though
> [Many] names [for me] are given by those hungry for samsara.
> Some coin the name enlightenment-mind and
> Some, stainless space
> Some, sky-realm
> Some call me the self-risen primordial knowing, and
> Some use the name[135] sheer essence dimension.
> Some speak of the richly resplendent dimension while
> Some refer to emanation dimensions and
> Some talk of body, speech, and exalted mind.
> Some name a knower of everything and
> Some speak also of three or four primordial knowings and
> Some enumerate five primordial knowings.[136]

Accordingly, everything that appears or exists in cyclic existence and samsara is actually the play of the three Buddha dimensions. Our own mindnature is likewise the play of these three dimensions, and this mindnature is also the very nature of the three dimensions. These do not pass beyond the ultimate stainless space that is reality.[137]

Moreover, all the phenomena of cyclic existence bear the defining characteristics of mind, and all phenomena of the path

སེམས་ཀྱི་ཡོན་ཏན་གྱི་རྩལ་དང་། འབྲས་བུའི་ཆོས་ཐམས་ཅད་སེམས་ཀྱི་ནུས་པའི་རྩལ་དུ་ཚང་བ་སྟེ། སེམས་ཉིད་ཁོ་རང་གི་གཤིས་སྐྱེ་མེད་ཆོས་སྐུ། གདངས་འགག་མེད་ལོངས་སྐུ། རྩལ་ཅི་ཡང་འཆར་བ་སྤྲུལ་སྐུ། དེ་གསུམ་ཀྱང་ངོ་བོ་དབྱེར་མེད་དུ་ལྷུན་གྱིས་གྲུབ་ཅིང་། དེ་ལྟར་ཡིན་ལུགས་རང་ངོ་ཤེས་ཤིང་ཐག་ཆོད་པ་ནི་ལྟ་བ་སྐྱོན་མེད་ཕྱིན་ཅི་མ་ལོག་པ་ཡང་དག་པར་རྟོགས་པ་ཅེས་བྱ་སྟེ། གསང་འདུས་ལས། རིན་ཆེན་སེམས་ལས་གཞན་གྱུར་པ། །སངས་རྒྱས་མེད་ཅིང་སེམས་ཅན་མེད། །ཅེས་སོ། །འདི་ལས་གཞན་པའི་ལྟ་བ་མཐའ་དང་བྲལ་མ་བྲལ་མཐོ་ཁྱད་བཟང་ངན་ལ་སོགས་དམིགས་གཏད་ཀྱི་ཚད་མ་དང་བློས་བྱས་ཡིད་དཔྱོད་ཀྱི་རྟོག་པས་བཏགས་པའི་ལྟ་སྒོམ་གང་ཡང་རྫོགས་པ་ཆེན་པོའི་ལྟ་བར་མ་གསུངས་ཏེ། རྣམ་མཁྱེན་ཤིང་རྟ་ལས། ཐག་པ་རྣམས་ཀྱི་ཡིད་དཔྱོད་དང་། །རིག་པ་མངོན་སུམ་ལྟ་བ་གཉིས། །ལྟ་བའི་ཕྱོགས་ནས་འདྲ་གཉིས་པས། །འདྲ་བོ་འདྲ་བོ་ནོར་བ་རེད། །རྫོགས་ཆེན་ཨ་ཏི་ཡོ་ག་ལ། །ལྟ་བ་ཉིད་ལ་བལྟ་རྒྱུ་མེད། །བལྟ་བ་སེམས་ཀྱི་དྲི་མ་ཡིན། །དྲི་མེད་དག་པའི་ཆོས་ཉིད་ལ། །བལྟ་བྱ་བལྟ་བྱེད་གཉིས་དང་བྲལ། །ལྟ་བ་ཉིད་ལ་བལྟ་རྒྱུ་མེད། །ཅི་ཕྱིར་བལྟ་བ་ཡོད་གྱུར་ན། །རིག་པའི་སྒྲོན་མེ་མེད་པར་གྱུར། །ཞེས་དང་།

bear good qualities of mind, while all fruitional phenomena are complete in bearing the power of mind.[138]

Mindnature's own homeground[139] is our unborn sheer essence dimension. Its unceasing radiance[140] is our rich dimension, and the arising of its dynanism in any way at all is our emanation dimension. These three occur spontaneously as an indivisible essence. Thus, to recognize and determine your own way of being is widely recognized as correctly realizing the flawless and unmistaken view. *The Collection of Secrets Tantra*[141] says:

> Other than precious mind
> There are neither Buddhas nor sentient beings.

Views other than this, whether free of extremes or not, whether high or low, good or bad, and so on, any view or meditation whatsoever that is characterized by focusing on an object is constructed by mind or realized through mental analysis. For that very reason it is not considered a view of the Great Completeness.

The Chariot of Omniscience[142] says:

> Two views there are: practice vehicles that analyze and
> Manifest sheer awareness.
> Because these views are somewhat similar
> You may err in thinking them the same.
> In unsurpassed Great Completeness yoga
> There is no view in the view itself.
> To view is to mind-stain.
> Stainlessly pure reality is
> Twice free: of viewed and of viewer.
> View itself has no view
> For if a view existed
> The lamp of sheer awareness would not be there.

གསང་བ་སྙིང་པོའི་རྩ་བ་ལས།[42] དུས་བཞི་ཕྱོགས་བཅུ་གང་ནས་ཀྱང་། གས་པའི་སངས་རྒྱས་བརྙེད་མི་འགྱུར། །སེམས་ཉིད་རྫོགས་པའི་སངས་རྒྱས་ཏེ། སངས་རྒྱས་གཞན་དུ་མ་ཚོལ་ཅིག །ཞེས་གསུངས་སོ། །

42. TEXT EDIT: *yang de las* changed to *gsang ba snying po i rtsa ba*, chap. 12, 16.6, in TBRC Vol. W00EGS1016299-I1CZ5003, pp. 521–86. Vol. *kha* of Longchenpa's *bsung 'bum.* This change is based on the quotation we were able to locate.

The same text[143] says:

> Nowhere among the four times or ten directions
> Will you find a completely perfect Buddha.
> Mindnature itself is a completely perfect Buddha
> So don't seek a Buddha anywhere else.[144]

གཉིས་པ་ལམ་རྫོགས་པ་ཆེན་པོར་དགྲི་ཚུལ་དངོས་ལ། སེམས་དང་རིག་པའི་ཤན་འབྱེད། ཡིད་དང་ཤེས་རབ་ཀྱི་ཤན་འབྱེད། རྣམ་ཤེས་དང་ཡེ་ཤེས་[43]ཀྱི་ཤན་འབྱེད། ཀུན་གཞི་དང་ཆོས་སྐུའི་ཤན་འབྱེད། དང་པོ་སེམས་དང་རིག་པའི་ཤན་འབྱེད་ནི། གཞི་མ་རིག་པ་ལས་རྒྱལ་རྣམ་པར་རྟོག་པ་སྐྱེ་འགག་གི་བདག་ཉིད་ཅན་ནི་སེམས་ཡིན་ལ། གཞི་མངོན་དུ་གྱུར་པ་ལས་སེམས་ཉིད་སྐྱེ་འགག་གནས་གསུམ་དང་བྲལ་བ་རྒྱལ་ཡེ་བབ་ཆེན་པོའི་རང་བཞིན་ནི་རིག་པ་སྟེ། ཕྱི་མ་ལ་གཞིའི་གནས་ལུགས་སམ། ཡིན་ལུགས་ཞེས་པ་ལ། གཞིའི་རིག་པ་དང་། ཆོས་ཉིད་མངོན་བྱེད་ཀྱི་ཤེས་པ་དྭངས་གསལ་སྙོགས་མ་དང་བྲལ་བ་ནི་ལམ་རིག་པ་དེ་གཉིས་ཀ་དུས་འཛོམས་པ་ནི།

43. TEXT EDIT: 21b.4. *yid shes* corrected to *ye shes.*

3 Path

Distinctions That Are Key to Dzogchen Practice

When it comes to actually engaging the Great Completeness path, you need to distinguish your mind experientially from sheer awareness and to distinguish as well your mental functioning from wisdom, your mental consciousness from primordial knowing,[145] and your allground from the sheer essence dimension.

Distinguishing Mind from Sheer Awareness

Mind consists of conceptual displays that are characterized by the production and cessation emerging from a base of unawareness. Mindnature is a direct manifestation from the base itself. Sheer awareness is free of the triad of birth, cessation, and abiding. It is by nature a great primordial and easefully settled dynamism.

Regarding this latter, basic sheer awareness refers to understanding our base's genuine state or way of being. Path sheer awareness is our clear limpid consciousness, free of crassness,[146] to which reality is evident. The joining of these two is our all-suffusing sheer awareness, the Great Completeness. This is the threefold division of sheer awareness.

ཁྱབ་བརྡལ་རིག་པ་རྫོགས་པ་ཆེན་པོ་སྟེ། གསུམ་དུ་དབྱེའོ། །གཉིས་པ་ཡིད་དང་ཤེས་རབ་ཀྱི་ཤན་འབྱེད་ནི། རྣམ་པར་རྟོག་པའི་ཚོ་འཕྲུལ་མཆེད་པའི་སྣང་བ་[44]ཐམས་ཅད་མངོན་དུ་བྱེད་པའི་ཤེས་པ་ལ་ཡིད་དང་། སྣང་བ་མཆེད་པའི་ཡུལ་དྲུག་གོ་མ་འགགས་པ་ལ་ཡིད་ཀྱི་རྣམ་པར་ཤེས་པ་ཞེས་བརྗོད་དོ། །ཤེས་རབ་ལ་ནི་གསུམ་སྟེ། འཁོར་འདས་སྟོང་ཉིད་ཆེན་པོའི་དང་ཚུལ་ཇི་ལྟ་བ་བཞིན་དུ་ཤེས་པ་ལ་གཞིའི་ཤེས་རབ། ཤེས་པ་ཟང་ཀ་རྒྱུ་ཡན་གོ་མ་འགགས་པ་དེ་ཉིད་ངོ་སྤྲོད་པ་ལམ་གྱི་ཤེས་རབ་དེ་ཉིད་དུས་འཛོམས་པ་ལ་ཁྱབ་བྱེད་ཀྱི་ཤེས་རབ་དང་གསུམ་མོ། །གསུམ་པ་རྣམ་ཤེས་དང་ཡེ་ཤེས་[45]ཀྱི་ཤན་འབྱེད་ནི། འདོད་ཡོན་གྱི་སྣང་བ་མཆེད་པའི་[46]སྣང་ཡུལ་གོ་མ་འགགས་པ་ལ་རྣམ་ཤེས་དང་སྣང་བ་ལ་དངོས་པོར་འཛིན་པའི་རྣམ་པར་རྟོག་པ་གཡོས་པ་ནི་ལས་རླུང་ཞེས་ཀྱང་བྱའོ། །ཡིད་ཀྱི་ཤེས་པ་ཕྲ་རག་འཛོམས་པ་ལས་འཁོར་བ་ཡོངས་སུ་གྲུབ་པའོ། །ཆོས་ཉིད་བདེ་གཤེགས་སྙིང་པོའི་དང་ཚུལ་ཇི་ལྟ་བ་བཞིན་དུ་ཤེས་པ་ཇི་ལྟར་མཁྱེན་པའི་ཡེ་ཤེས་ཆོས་ཉིད་དེ་བཞིན་ཉིད་ཀྱི་གནས་ལུགས་མངོན་དུ་བྱེད་པའི་དུས་སུ་ཀུན་ཤེས་ཀུན་རིག་གི་གོ་མ་འགགས་པ་ཇི་སྙེད་པ་གཟིགས་པའི་ཡེ་ཤེས། དེ་གཉིས་མཉམ་དུ་བརྡལ་བ་ལ་ཀ་དག་མཉམ་པ་ཉིད་ཀྱི་ཡེ་ཤེས་སོ། །

44. TEXT EDIT: 22a.4. *mchod pa i snang ba* corrected to *mched pa i snang ba*.
45. TEXT EDIT: 22b.1. *rnam shes dang yid shes* corrected to *rnam shes dang ye shes*.
46. TEXT EDIT: 22b.2. *sang ba mchod* corrected to *snang ba mched*.

Distinguishing Mental Functioning from Sublime Knowing

"Mental functioning" is the name given to a conceptual consciousness for which all[147] conceptual apparitions[148] are evident. "Mental consciousness" [which here refers to all sense consciousnesses] is the name given to [direct knowing of the] unceasing six objects, those appearances presenting [to the senses].[149]

Sublime knowing is threefold. First, the sublime knowing of the base is our understanding how things are while within a state of the great emptiness of cyclic existence and nirvana. Second, sublime knowing of the path is our recognizing the unceasing, unimpeded, uninhibited consciousness. Third, these two coming together is our all-encompassing sublime knowing, fruitional sheer awareness.[150]

Distinguishing Consciousness from Primordial Knowing[151]

This involves an experiential distinction between consciousness[152] and primordial knowing. Your meandering conceptuality, which, in connection with ceaselessly increasing appearances,[153] holds consciousness and appearances to be real, as well as your perception of desirable objects, are associated with what we call "the working winds" (*las rlung*), the wind of karma. All cyclic existence derives from the conglomerate of coarse and subtle mental consciousnesses [based on these winds].[154]

Reality is the Blissful Ones' heart essence. Their knowing wholly accords with what is, a primordial knowing of how things are. When the genuine state, reality just as it is, becomes fully evident, we unceasingly know [the nature of] everything, and we are present to everything [in all its variety] as well. The flowing forth of these two, the primordial knowing that knows how things are and the primordial knowing that knows the varieties of things, is the primordial knowing of originally pure sameness.[155]

བཞི་པ་ཀུན་གཞི་དང་ཆོས་སྐུའི་ཤན་འབྱེད་ལ་གཉིས། ཤན་འབྱེད་དངོས་དང་། དོན་དམ་ཀུན་རྫོབ་གཉིས་སུ་གནས་བསྡུས་པའོ། །དང་པོ་ཤན་འབྱེད་དངོས་ནི། གཞི་དབྱིངས་མ་རིག་པའི་དབང་གི་ལུང་མ་བསྟན་དུ་སོང་བ་ནི་ཀུན་གཞི་སྟེ། དཔེར་ན་གཉིད་ཀྱི་དང་དུ་མི་ལམ་སྣ་ཚོགས་སྣང་བ་ལྟར་དེའི་ངང་ལས་ཀྱི་རླུང་གཡོས་པས་འཁོར་བ་ཀུན་གྱི་གཞི་དང་རྩ་བར་གྱུར་པས་དེ་ལྟར་དུ་བརྗོད་པའོ། །ཆོས་སྐུ་ནི། ཆོས་ཅན་གྱི་སྣང་བ་ཆོས་ཉིད་སྤྲོས་མཐའ་བྲལ་བར་ཧར་སངས་ཀྱི་དང་རྒྱ་ཡན་ཆོས་སྐུའོ། །དེ་ལྟར་ཤན་རྣམས་མཐའ་ཆོད་པར་བྱས་ཏེ། ལྷག་པའི་ཞི་གནས་དང་། ལྷག་པའི་ལྷག་མཐོང་གཉིས་ཀྱི་སྐྱོན་ཡོན་མཉམ་རྗེས་རྣལ་འབྱོར་པས་ལམ་བགྲོད་ཚུལ་སོགས་བསྟན་པ་ནི། དེ་ཡང་སྤྱིར་སྒོམ་པ་ཞེས་པའི་མིང་འཛུག་ལུགས་ནི་མང་ལ། གྲུབ་མཐའ་སོ་སོ་ལ་རང་རང་སྐབས་ཀྱི་བསྒོམ་ཚུལ་ཀྱང་མཐའ་ཡས་ནའང་། འདིར་ནི་སྔར་བཤད་མ་ཐག་པའི་ལྟ་བ་གནས་ལུགས་ཀྱི་དོན་དེ་རྒྱུད་ལ་གོམས་འདྲིས་སུ་བྱ་བ་ལ་སྒོམ་པའི་མིང་དང་ཐ་སྙད་དུ་བཏགས་པ་ཙམ་མ་གཏོགས། དངོས་པོ་ཁ་དོག་དབྱིབས་ཅན་ལྟ་བུ་བློས་བཅོས་ནས་བསྒོམ་པའམ། སེམས་ཀྱི་འགྱུར་དྲན་འཆར་སྣང་བཀག་པའི་བཅོས་མའི་སྟོང་ཉིད་ལྟ་བུ་ཞིག་ཆེད་དུ་བསྒོམ་པ་ནི་གཏན་ནས་མ་ཡིན་ཏེ། རང་སེམས་རང་བབས་བཟོ་མེད་དུ་སྐྱོང་བ་ཁོ་ན་ཡིན་ལ། བྱེ་བྲག་ཏུ་གང་གི་དབང་པོ་དང་བློ་རིགས་སྣ་ཚོགས་པའི་ཕྱིར་ན། ཅིག་འཆར་དབང་པོ་རྣོན་པོ་སྦྱངས་པ་མངོན་གྱུར་དག་ལ་ནི།

Distinguishing the Allground from the Sheer Essence Dimension

The two topics related with distinguishing the allground from the sheer essence dimension are, first, the significant distinctions and, second, summarizing the ultimate and conventional states.

The allground comes about through the power of unawareness, namely, through failure to be aware of basic stainless space. Just as dreams appear during sound sleep, so within the allground state our karmic wind is distracted. Therefore we have the base and root for the whole of cyclic existence. Hence, it is described in this way.

The reality appearing to the subject, a state of sudden clarity free of elaborations and extremes, is the thoroughly open sheer essence dimension.[156]

Serene Abiding and Dzogchen

In light of this, let us consider how to distinguish the faults and good qualities of serene abiding and special seeing. In this way we demonstrate how yogis proceed and so on during meditation sessions and between sessions.

Generally speaking, the term meditation is used in many ways, since each tenet system has its own contextualized style of meditation. These are infinite. However, the meaning of the view just explained, the genuine state, is not included among the terms or conventions of meditation on objects as cultivated in tantra. The meditation we are discussing here does not in any way deploy mental contrivances. It does not take on something which has color and shape [as in tantra], nor is it a meditation intent on connecting a mind tight with mindfulness to a contrived emptiness that stops appearances from arising. We simply maintain our settled ease without actually doing anything.

More specifically, capacities and types of minds vary. When it comes to setting forth the training for those of simultaneous,

ཞི་ལྷག་རིམ་ཅན་དུ་དགྲི་མི་དགོས་པར་ངོ་འཕྲོད་པ་དང་གྲོལ་བ་དུས་མཉམ་དུ་འགྱུར་པ་དག་བྱུང་ན་འང་།[47] གཞན་ཕལ་བ་བདག་འདྲ་བ་དག་ལ་ནི་རིམ་གྱི་ཁྲིད་དགོས་ཏེ། དེ་ཡང་གང་གི་ཞེ་ན། དཀོན་མཆོག་སྤྲིན་ལས། ཞི་གནས་ནི་སེམས་རྩེ་གཅིག་པའོ། །ལྷག་མཐོང་ནི་ཡང་དག་པ་ཇི་ལྟ་བ་བཞིན་དུ་ཆོས་ལ་སོ་སོར་རྟོགས་པའོ།[48] །ཞེས་དང་། བྱེད་ལས་ནི། ཞི་གནས་ཀྱིས་[49] ཉོན་མོངས་འགོ་གནོན་པར་བྱེད་དོ། །ལྷག་མཐོང་གིས་ནི་ཉོན་མོངས་པ་ཡོངས་སུ་སྦྱོངས་བར་བྱེད་དོ། །ཞེས་གསུངས་[50] པ་བཞིན་གཉིས་ཀ་མྱང་འདས་ཀྱི་རྒྱུར་འགྲོ་བ་ཡིན་ནོ། །དབྱེ་བ་ནི་གཉིས་ཏེ། མདོ་དགོངས་པ་ངེས་འགྲེལ་ལས། ཞི་གནས་དང་ལྷག་མཐོང་ནི་གཉིས་ཏེ་ཤེས་རབ་ལས་འབྱུང་བ་དང་། གདམས་ངག་ལས་འབྱུང་བའོ། །དེ་ལ་ཤེས་རབ་ལས་འབྱུང་བ་ནི་མདོ་སྡེ་བཅུ་གཉིས་ཀྱི་ཚིག་ཡིད་ལ་བྱེད་པ་ནི་ཞི་གནས་སོ། །དེའི་དོན་རྟོགས་པ་ནི་ལྷག་མཐོང་ངོ་། ཞེས་གསུངས་པ་ལྟར་མ་ཟད་སྐབས་འདིར་བསྒོམ་ཚུལ་ནི་ལྷག་པའི་ཞི་ལྷག་ཁྱད་པར་ཅན་གྱི་བསྒོམ་ཚུལ་བཤད་པར་བྱ་བའི་ཕྱིར་ཐོག་མར་ཞི་གནས་ཀྱི་རིམ་པ་མཚན་བཅས། སྐུ་རྟེན་ནམ་ཡིག་འབྲུ་ཐིག་ལེ་རླུང་གི་སྦྱོར་བ་སོགས་བསླབ་དགོས་ཅིང་དེ་དག་ལ་ངེས་པ་རྙེད་ནས་སླར་མཚན་མེད་མཆོག་ཞི་གནས་ལ་འཇུག་པར་བྱ་སྟེ། ལྷག་པའི་ཞི་གནས་དངོས་ནི་མཉམ་པར་བཞག་ཐབས་གསུམ་གྱི་སྒོ་ནས་སྟོན་ཏེ། དེ་ཡང་ཕྱི་ནང་གི་ཡུལ་རྐྱེན་གྱི་རྗེས་སུ་སེམས་ཡེངས་པ་མ་ཡིན་པར་ཡེངས་མེད་སོ་མར་བཞག་པ་དང་།

47. TEXT EDIT: 23b.6. *byung med na* corrected to *byung na ang.*
48. TEXT EDIT: 24a.2. *so sor rtog pa* corrected to *so sor rtogs pa.*
49. TEXT EDIT: 24a.3. *gzhi gnas kyi* corrected to *zhi gnas kyis.*
50. TEXT EDIT: 24a.3. *zhe gzungs* corrected to *zhes gsungs.*

or sharp, capacity, there is no need to proceed stage-by-stage through serene abiding and special seeing. Recognition and liberation are simultaneous for such persons. Purification simply arises.[157] Otherwise, ordinary persons like ourselves must proceed serially. Why? The *Cloud of Jewels Sutra*[158] says:

> Serene abiding is a mind one-pointed.
> Special seeing is discerning precisely[159] what really is.
> When it comes to hatred and activities,
> Serene abiding dampens down afflictions.[160]
> Special seeing overcomes afflictions completely.
> As this states, both act as causes for nirvana.[161]

Regarding these two divisions, the *Definitive Commentary on the Enlightened State Sutra*[162] says:

> Each of the two, serene abiding and special seeing, can arise from either sublime knowing or spiritual counsel. Mental engagement, which means recalling well, [without forgetting] the words of the twelve sets of sutras,[163] is serene abiding. Realizing their meaning is special seeing.

In addition to these statements, the "how to" of meditation in this context is explained as a very special serene abiding and special seeing. Therefore, you need initially to train in the stage of serene abiding conjoined with an object on which you focus, using a statue, syllable, bright orbs, or practices of the winds and so forth as a support. Once you have gained certainty in this, you enter into the supreme state of stillness without an object on which you focus.

Actual serene abiding is taught by way of three methods of easeful equilibrium (*mnyam par bzhag thabs*). These are:

1. Resting in unwavering freshness so that your mind does not waver in its attention to any supporting object, outside or in.

དེ་ཡང་དཔལ་ས་ར་ཧ་ནས། བློ་གསུམ་ཧ་ཅང་བསྒྲིམས་དྲག་པས་བཅིངས་པ་མ་ཡིན་པར་རྩོལ་མེད་རང་བབས་ལྷུག་པར་བཞག་པ་དང་། རྣམ་རྟོག་གི་ངོ་བོ་དང་དྲན་རིག་གཉིས་ཡ་བྲལ་ཐ་དད་གཉེན་པོ་བསྟེན་པ་ལྟ་བུ་མ་ཡིན་པར་རང་རིག་རང་གསལ་རང་དྭངས་སུ་བཞག་སྟེ། འདི་གསུམ་ལ་མིང་གི་རྣམ་གྲངས་གཞན་དུ་མ་ཡེངས། མི་བསྒོམ་བཟོ་མེད་ཅེས་ཀྱང་བྱ་ལ། ཐུན་མོང་གི་ཐེག་པར་གསུངས་པའི་རྣམ་པར་ཐར་པའི་སྒོ་གསུམ་ཡང་འདིར་ཚང་སྟེ། སེམས་དེ་ཀ་སྤྲོས་འདས་པའི་བྱ་བྱེད་སོགས་ལ་འདི་བྱས་འདི་བྱུང་གི་རྗེས་གཅོད་མི་བྱ་བ་ནི་རྣམ་པར་ཐར་པའི་སྒོ་མཚན་མ་མེད་པ་ཅེས་བྱ་བ་དང་། དེ་ལྟའི་སེམས་ལ་བློས་བྱས་ཀྱིས་བསྒྱུར་བཀོད་དང་འདི་སྣང་འདི་བྱའི་དགག་སྒྲུབ་མེད་པ་ནི་རྣམ་པར་ཐར་པའི་སྒོ་སྟོང་པ་ཉིད་དང་། མ་འོངས་པར་འདི་དང་འདི་བཞིན་འབྱུང་འགྱུར་གྱི་སྔོན་བསུ་བ་དང་། སྒོམ་ཡོང་དུ་རེ་བ་དང་མི་ཡོང་གི་དོགས་པ་[51] ལྟ་བུའི་འདོད་འདུན་མེད་པ་ནི་རྣམ་པར་ཐར་པ་སྨོན་པ་མེད་པའི་སྒོ་ཞེས་བྱ་ཞིང་། མདོར་བསྡུ་ན། རང་སེམས་རང་བབས་བཅོས་བསླད་མེད་པར་འཇོག་པ་ཉིད་ལ་འདུས་སོ། །དེའི་ངང་ནས་རྣམ་པར་རྟོག་པ་ཅིག་ཁྱུགས་ཀྱི་ཤར་བའི་ཚེ་ན་གང་ཤར་བ་དེ་ལ་རྗེས་འཕྲུད་དུ་མ་སོང་བར་རང་ངོ་ཧྲིག་གི་ཤེས་པར་བྱ་བ་ཁོ་ནས་ཆོག་གི །ཆེད་དུ་བཀག་པའམ། སྒོམ་ལ་རྩུར་བཀུག་པའམ། གཉེན་པོ་གཞན་གྱིས་གཅུན་པ་སོགས་གང་ཡང་མི་བྱ་སྟེ། དེ་དག་གང་བྱས་ཀྱང་སེམས་ཉིད་མ་བཅོས་བཟོ་མེད་སྐྱོང་བའི་གནད་མ་ཡིན་ཅིང་ལམ་གྱི་བྱེ་བྲག་གཞན་ལས་སྣ་ཚོགས་བྱུང་མོད་ཀྱང་འདིའི་སྐབས་སུ་ནི་གང་ཤར་རང་ངོ་ཤེས་པའི་ལམ་ཁོ་ན་ཡིན་པས་ཐབས་གཞན་བཙལ་ན་རྫོགས་པ་ཆེན་པོའི་སྒོམ་དུ་མི་འགྱུར་ཏེ།

51. TEXT EDIT: 25a.5. *mi yong gi dgos pa* corrected to *mi yong gi dogs pa.*

2. Resting at ease in effortless self-settling, without being bound by very tight focusing.
3. Resting in your own presence, your own clarity and limpidity, without relying on any antidote that differentiates or separates the nature of thought from mindful presence.[164] This is not to be confused with other similar-sounding names.[165]

The Three Doors of Liberation

Although referred to as non-meditation and effortless, all three doors to full liberation described in the ordinary vehicle are complete here. Your own mind, not following after past deeds, doers, and so forth, and not following after anything that you did or that occurred in the past, is known as the door to liberation, which is signlessness. As for your mind right now, its not making any mental alterations, that is, neither negating nor establishing appearances and objects, is the door to liberation, which is emptiness. Your mind's not anticipating that such and such will arise in the future, neither desiring nor aspiring that meditation will succeed, nor having any fear that it will not,[166] is known as the door to liberation, which is wishless.

In brief, we are speaking of a mind in settled ease, a mind uncontaminated by artifice. When, within this, a thought briefly arises, you need only be in wide-awake recognition of your own nature, without following after or augmenting what has arisen. You neither block nor urge on your meditation, nor do you exert yourself with some other antidote. Indeed, to engage in any of these would be to miss the key instruction on sustaining mind-nature, uncontrived and without fabrication.

Although the specifics of the path vary, in the present context the only path is the one in which whatever dawns is recognized as your own face. Making effort at other methods is therefore not Dzogchen meditation. Indeed, the glorious Saraha has said:

འགྲོ་རྣམས་བསམ་གཏན་སྩོལ་བས་བསླད། །སྒོམ་རྒྱུ་ཅི་ཡང་མེད་པ་ལ། །ཡེངས་རྒྱུ་སྐད་ཅིག་མི་འདོད་པས། །ཕྱག་རྒྱ་ཆེན་པོའི་བསྒོམ་པ་ཡིན། །ཅེས་གསུངས་ཤིང་། དེ་ལྟར་སེམས་ཀྱི་གནས་ལུགས་ཇི་བཞིན་པའི་ཐོག་ཏུ་མཉམ་པར་བཞག །ཞི་གནས་ཀྱི་ཉམས་གསུམ་པོ་རིམ་པ་བཞིན་དུ་[52] འཆར་བར་འགྱུར་ཏེ། གང་ཞེ་ན། དང་པོར་སེམས་ཆེར་རྒོད་ཅིང་འཕྲོ་བས་རྟོག་པ་སྔར་ལས་ཀྱང་མང་དུ་སོང་བ་ལྟ་བུའི་བར་མཚམས་ཙུང་ཟད་ཙམ་རེ་གནས་པ་ཞིག་འབྱུང་བའི་འཕྲོ་བ་དེ་ལ་སྐྱོན་དུ་མི་བལྟ་སྟེ། སྔོན་ཆད་འཕྲོ་བ་ཤ་སྟག་ཡིན་ཀྱང་ངོས་མ་ཟིན་པ་དེ་འདི་སྐབས་འཕྲོ་གནས་ཀྱི་དབྱེ་བ་ཤེས་པ་ཡིན། ཞི་གནས་དང་པོ་རི་གཟར་གྱི་འབབ་ཆུ་ལྟ་བུ་ཅེས་བྱ། དེ་ལྟར་བསྐྱངས་པས་རྣམ་རྟོག་ཕལ་ཆེར་མགོ་ནོན་ཏེ་འཇམ་ཉལ་གྱི་འགྲོ་ཞིང་ལུས་སེམས་བདེ་འབོལ་གྱི་སོང་བས་བྱ་བྱེད་གཞན་ལ་ཞེན་པ་མི་འདུག་པར་མཉམ་པར་གཞག་ལ་སྤྲོ་ཞིང་། ཐང་རེ་ཙམ་ལས་གཞན་རྟོག་པའི་འགྱུར་འཕྲོ་མེད་པའི་གནས་པ་ཤས་ཆེར་བྱུང་པ་ནི། ཞི་གནས་བར་མ་ཆུ་བོ་དལ་ལ་འབབས་པ་ལྟ་བུ་དང་། སླར་ཡང་རྣམ་གཡེང་[53] མེད་པར་བརྩོན་པས་ཉམས་སུ་བླངས་ན། ལུས་ཀྱི་ཚོར་བའི་ཟུག་རྔུ་གང་ཡང་མེད་པར་བདེ་ཆམ་མེ། སེམས་གསལ་དྭངས་ལ་རྟོག་པ་མེད་པར་ཉིན་མཚན་འདས་པ་མི་ཚོར་ཞིང་ཇི་ཙམ་མཉམ་པར་གཞག་གི་བར་དུ་གཡོ་བ་མེད་ཅིང་རྐྱེན་གྱིས་མི་གནོད་ལ། ཉོན་མོངས་མངོན་གྱུར་ཞི་ཞིང་ཟས་གོས་སོགས་ཀྱི་ཞེན་པ་ཆེར་མི་འབྱུང་བ་དང་། ཟག་བཅས་ཀྱི་མངོན་ཤེས་དང་གསལ་སྣང་གི་ཉམས་ཀྱི་བྱེ་བྲག་སྣ་ཚོགས་འཆར་བ་སོགས་ཐུན་མོང་གི་ཡོན་ཏན་ལྟར་སྣང་བ་དུ་མ་བྱུང་བ་ནི་ཞི་གནས་མཐར་ཐུག་རྒྱ་མཚོར་མི་གཡོ་བ་ལྟ་བུ་ཞེས་བྱ་ཞིང་།

52. TEXT EDIT: 26a.2. *gsum pa rim du* corrected to *gsum pa rim pa bzhin du*.
53. TEXT EDIT: 27b.1. *slar yang rnam yengs* corrected to *slar yang rnam g.yeng*.

Wanderers contaminate meditative stabilization with
effort;
Meditation cannot be caused!
Not welcoming a moment of distraction
Is meditation of the Great Seal.

As you rest in easeful equilibrium in the immediacy of your mind's genuine state, just as it is, the three meditative experiences[167] associated with stillness arise in turn.

Why? At first, your mind is very wild and scattered, making it seem as if you have even more thoughts than before. Next, in the middle phase, there is just a little bit of abiding. Do not see the scattering that emerges as a problem! Previously, even though you experienced nothing but scattering, you did not identify it. Now, however, you are understanding the difference between scattering and stability. At first, your serene abiding is said to be like water rushing down a steep mountain. As you maintain this, your conceptual thoughts are for the most part suppressed. With the onset of a gentle restfulness, your mind and body become a blissful cushion and because of this, without engaging in any other objects or activities, you delight in easeful equilibrium. You are by and large abiding without thought stirring or proliferating, except for very occasionally.[168]

Midstage stillness is like a great water stream flowing onto a flat area. More than that, if you practice undistractedly[169] and with vigor, your body feels serenely blissful without any sense of discomfort. Your mind is limpidly clear and without thought; you do not feel the passage of day or night and remain undistracted for however long you continue in easeful equipoise, unimpaired by any circumstances. All evidence of afflictions is pacified and you have no real interest in the likes of food or clothing. Various instances of meditative experience, such as contaminated clairvoyance and clear appearances, arise and, likewise, a similitude of many ordinary good qualities come to the fore.

The final state of stillness is described as an unmoving ocean.

འདིའི་སྐབས་སུ་བླ་མ་ཉམས་མྱོང་ཅན་དང་མ་ཕྲད་ཅིང་སྙིང་རུས་ཆེ་ལ་ཐོས་པ་ཆུང་བའི་སྒོམ་ཆེན་པ་མང་པོ་ཡོན་ཏན་ལྟར་སྣང་བ་ལ་རློམ་སེམས་སྐྱེ་ཞིང་། སྐྱེ་བོ་དག་གིས་ཀྱང་གྲུབ་ཐོབ་ཏུ་མཐོང་བ་ལ་བརྟེན་ནས་རང་གཞན་མང་པོ་ཕུང་ཉེན་ཡོད་པས་གཟབ་དགོས་སོ། །དེ་ལྟར་ཞི་གནས་ཀྱི་སྒོམ་རྒྱུད་པས་ནི། རྫོགས་པ་ཆེན་པོའི་ལམ་དངོས་གཞིར་རུང་བ་མ་ཡིན་ཀྱང་གཞི་རྟེན་གྱི་ཚུལ་དུ་ངེས་པར་གལ་ཆེ་བར་གསུངས་ཤིང་། དེ་ཡང་གུ་རུ་རིན་པོ་ཆེས། རིག་པའི་རང་རྩལ་མ་ལྷོངས་པར། །གནས་པ་ངར་མེད་སྟོང་ངེ་བ།[54] །ཐོགས་ནི་ཅུང་ཟད་མི་འབྱུང་བས། །རིག་པ་གསལ་ངར་ཐོན་པ་གཅེས། །སྒོམ་མཁན་མང་སྟེ་སྒོམ་ཤེས་ཉུང་། །ཞེས་གསུངས། དེ་ན་དངོས་གཞི་ལྷག་མཐོང་ནི། སེམས་ཀྱི་ངོ་བོ་ལ་དབྱིབས་ཁ་དོག་སོགས་མཚན་མ་དངོས་ཅན་དུ་གྲུབ་མ་གྲུབ་དང་། འབྱུང་གནས་འགྲོ་གསུམ། སྐྱེ་འགག་ཡོད་མེད་རྟག་ཆད་མཐའ་དབུས་ལ་སོགས་ཀྱི་བརྡར་ཤ་བཅད་དེ་ཐེ་ཚོམ་གྱི་ཕུ་ཐག་མ་ཆོད་ན་ལྟ་བ་ཡིན་ལུགས་ཀྱི་ཐོག་ཏུ་མི་ཕེབས། དེ་མ་ཕེབས་ན་སྒོམ་པ་རང་བབས་རང་འགྲོས་ཀྱི་སྐྱོང་ཚུལ་མི་ཤེས། དེ་མ་ཤེས་ཚེ་ཞི་གནས་བླུན་རྨོངས་དང་སྡུག་བཙིར་སེམས་འཛིན་གྱི་སྙིང་རུས་ཇི་ཙམ་བྱས་ཀྱང་

54. TEXT EDIT: 27a.2. *gnas pa ngar med steng ngo bo* should probably be *gnas pa ngar med stong nge ba.*

At this point, many great meditators who are not in contact with an experienced lama and who make great effort but have heard little, can develop pride in their similitude of good qualities. Other people also see them as siddhas. This becomes a source of grave danger to oneself and many others, so you need to take care.

Thus, in and of itself, stillness meditation is neither a basis for nor an actual path of the Great Completeness. However, we definitely consider it a very important method for providing a base and a support. Moreover, as Guru Rinpoche has said:

> When sheer awareness's intrinsic dynamism lets loose,
> Whatever rests on unclear stability[170]
> Will not give rise to the slightest improvement.
> Therefore, precise and lucid sheer awareness is vital.
> Many meditators understand their meditation very
> little.

Special Seeing in Dzogchen Meditation

Here, we come to special seeing, the actual basis. Examine the essence of your mind. Does it have, for example, color? Does it have shape? Does it have real characteristics or not? Examine in fine detail the three states of arising, abiding, and cessation as you explore whether your mind arises and ceases or not; whether your mind is eternal or nothing at all; whether it has edges, a center, and so forth.

If, after doing this, your doubts are not completely eliminated, then you have not fully settled into the view, the way things are. If you have not settled there, you do not understand the method for maintaining meditation through a naturally flowing ease and letting be.

So long as you do not understand this, your state in stillness is dull and undiscerning. No matter how much effort you make, no matter how relentlessly you grasp onto your mind, you do

ཁམས་གསུམ་འཁོར་བའི་རྒྱུ་འབྲས་ལས་མ་འདས་པས་དེས་ན་བླ་མ་མཚན་ལྡན་གྱི་དྲུང་དུ་སློབ་འདོགས་ལེགས་པར་བཅད་ཅིང་། ཁྱད་པར་གསང་སྔགས་བྱིན་རླབས་ཁོ་ན་གཙོ་ཆེ་བས་ལམ་ཡིན་པའི་ཕྱིར་ན་མོས་གུས་གསོལ་འདེབས་ལ་འབད་པས་བརྒྱུད་པའི་བྱིན་རླབས་ཀྱི་རྟོགས་པ་འཕོ་ཐབས་ལ་འབུང་། དེ་ལྟར་བྱས་ཚེ་རང་གི་རིག་པ་ཡེ་གདོད་མ་ནས་ཆོས་སྐུའི་ངོ་བོར་ལྷུན་གྲུབ་ཏུ་ཡོད་པའི་ཚུལ་སྔར་ལྟ་བའི་སྐབས་སུ་བཤད་པ་བཞིན། མངོན་སུམ་རྟོག་བྲལ་གྱི་ཡེ་ཤེས་ཡོད་མེད་ཡིན་མིན་[55] རྟག་ཆད་གང་གི་ཡང་མཐར་མ་ལྷུང་ཤིང་། གསལ་རིག་བསམ་བརྗོད་ལས་འདས་པར་ཉམས་སུ་མྱོང་ཞིང་ཤེས་ཀྱང་དཔེས་མཚོན་དུ་མེད་ལ་ཚིག་གིས་བརྗོད་ཐབས་ཟད་པ། རང་བྱུང་རང་གསལ་དུ་ཧྲིག་གེ་བ་འདི་ལ་ལྷག་མཐོང་ཞེས་མིང་དུ་བཏགས་མོད་ཀྱི། འདི་ཉིད་དང་པོ་[56]སོ་སོ་སྐྱེ་བོའི་དུས་ནས་རང་དང་འདུ་འབྲལ་སྐད་ཅིག་མེད་ཀྱང་གདམས་ངག་དང་བྱིན་རླབས་ཀྱིས་མ་ཟིན་པས་ངོ་མ་ཤེས། བར་དུ་ཞི་གནས་ལ་མཉམ་པར་གཞག་མཁན་ནམ་གནས་མི་གནས་བལྟ་མཁན་སོགས་ཐམས་ཅད་ཁོ་རང་ཡིན་ཀྱང་རང་གིས་རང་མ་མཐོང་བ་ལྟ་བུར་གྱུར་པ་སྟེ། ཐ་མལ་པའི་དུས་ཀྱི་རྣམ་རྟོག་ལུ་གུ་བརྒྱུད་དུ་འཁྲོ་བ་དེ་ཉིད་ཀྱིས་རང་ངོ་སྒྲིབ་པ་ཡིན་ནོ། འོན་ཀྱང་ཞི་གནས་ཀྱི་གནས་སྐབས་ཙམ་དུ་ཉོན་མོངས་མགོ་ནོན་ནས་བདེ་གསལ་མི་རྟོག་པའི་ཉམས་ལ་ཡེངས་ནས་ལྷག་མཐོང་བདག་མེད་རྟོགས་པའི་ཤེས་རབ། བློ་བྲལ་རྗེན་པའི་རང་ངོ་མ་རིག་ན་གནས་ཆ་རྐྱང་པར་སོང་བས་བྱང་ཆུབ་ཀྱི་རྒྱུ་རུ་མི་འགྲོ་བ་ཡིན་ཞིང་། རང་ངོ་མཐོང་ཕྱིན་ཆད་ནི། གནས་འགྱུ་ཐམས་ཅད་ཞི་ལྷག་ཟུང་འཇུག་གི་ལྟ་བར་མ་གྱུར་པ་ཅི་ཡང་མེད།

55. TEXT EDIT: 28a.1. *yod yin min* corrected to *yod med yin min*.
56. TEXT EDIT: 28a.3. *nyid dngos po* corrected to *'di nyid dang po*.

not pass beyond the cause-and-effect processes associated with samsara's three realms. Therefore, dispel these excesses well in the presence of a fully qualified lama.

In particular, because Secret Mantra is a path in which blessings are so important, artfully endeavor in your devotion and prayer; be diligent in methods furthering your realization of lineage blessings. Proceed as explained earlier in terms of the view: your own sheer awareness exists primordially as the spontaneously occurring sheer essence dimension. This is primordial knowing, direct and thought-free, falling neither to an extreme of existence nor nonexistence, neither being nor nonbeing,[171] permanence nor annihilation.

In that case, you experience clear sheer awareness beyond thought or description. Your understanding cannot be demonstrated through examples; descriptions are for naught. Your self-risen, intrinsically luminous alertness is known as special seeing. Even though we give it this name, it has been there for as long as you have been an ordinary being.[172] You have never been apart from it for a single instant, nor have you ever created a connection with it. However, when we fail to connect with blessings of Secret Mantra, it initially goes unrecognized.[173]

In the middle phase, your serene abiding is like equipoise. Although the observer of stability or instability and the like is just [your own sheer awareness], you do not see sheer awareness itself. For, so long as you are an ordinary being, your proliferating train of conceptual thoughts obscures your own face.

However, even when your afflictions have simply been suppressed by your serene abiding, once you get distracted by meditative experiences of bliss, clarity, or nonconceptuality, you need special seeing. You need the special seeing that realizes emptiness—that recognizes your own face, mind-free and utterly naked. The mere fact of your stillness does not serve as a cause for enlightenment. Once you have seen your own face, there is no way for all abiding and proliferation not to be the view, a union of serene abiding and special seeing.

རྒྱལ་བ་ལོ་རས་པས། ཚོགས་དྲུག་ཡུལ་དུ་ཅི་ཤར་ཡང་། །ཡིད་ཀྱི་འཛིན་པ་མ་ཞུགས་ན། ཐམས་ཅད་རང་སྣང་རང་གྲོལ་ཡིན། །དབྱེར་མེད་རྟོགས་སམ་སྒོམ་ཆེན[57]་ཀུན། །ཞེས་དང་། ཕྱག་ཆེན་མན་ངག་ལས། རྟོག་པ་དྲི་མའི་རྒྱུ་དེ་དྭངས་སུ་རྒྱུག །སྣང་བ་དགག་སྒྲུབ་མི་བྱ་རང་སོར་ཞོག། །དེས་ན་ལྗོན་ཤིང་ཡལ་ག་ལོ་འདབ་རྒྱས། །རྩ་བཅད་ཡལ་ག་ལོ་འདབ་ཁྲི་འབུམ་སྐམ། །དཔེར་ན་བསྐལ་སྟོང་བསགས་པའི་མུན་པ་ཡང་། །སྒྲོན་མེ་གཅིག་གིས་མུན་པའི་ཚོགས་རྣམས་སེལ། །དེ་བཞིན་རང་སེམས་འོད་གསལ་སྐད་ཅིག་གིས། །བསྐལ་པར་བསགས་པའི་སྡིག་སྒྲིབ་མ་ལུས་སེལ། །དཔེར་ན་ནམ་མཁའི་དཀྱིལ་ནི་བརྟགས་བྱས་ན། །མཐའ་དང་དབུས་སུ་འཛིན་པ་འགག་པར་འགྱུར། །དེ་བཞིན་སེམས་ཀྱི་སེམས་ལ་བརྟགས་བྱས་ན། །རྣམ་རྟོག་ཚོགས་འགག་རྟོག་མེད་གནས་གྱུར་ནས། །བླ་མེད་བྱང་ཆུབ་སེམས་ཀྱི་རང་བཞིན་མཐོང་། །ཞེས་གསུངས་སོ། །དེ་ཡང་སྤྱི་ལྟར་ན། རྣམ་རྟོག་རང་སར་ཞི་ནས་སེམས་བདེ་གསལ་མི་རྟོག་གི་ངང་དུ་གནས་པའི་ཞི་གནས། སེམས་ཀྱི་ངོ་བོ་རང་གསལ་ཡུལ་མེད་སྒྲོ་སྐུར་དང་བྲལ་བ་རྗེན་ནེ་ལྷང་ངེར་མཐོང་བ་ནི་ལྷག་མཐོང་། ཅེས་སོ། ཡང་རྣམ་རྟོག་འཕྲོ་འདུ་བྲལ་བ་ཞི་གནས།

57. TEXT EDIT: 28b.5. *rtogs bsam sgom chen* = *rtogs sam sgom chen*.

Gyalwa Lorepa[174] said:

> When, no matter what is dawning for the six senses,
> Mental grasping is not present
> Everything is self-appearing, self-liberated:
> Realization, inseparable from great meditation.[175]

And [Gyalwa Lorepa's] *Essential Instructions on the Great Seal*[176] says:

> The water defiled by conception becomes clear,
> Appearances, neither negated nor established, abide as they are.
> A tree's branches and leaves are fully unfurled—
> Cut its root and a billion leaves go dry.
> Just as massive darkness, settled in
> For a thousand eons and longer,
> Is dispelled by a single lamp,
> So a single moment of your mind's luminosity
> Dispels defilements and obstructions settled there for eons.
> Just as when you search out the center of the sky,
> You quit reaching for its periphery and midpoint,
> So, once your mind searches out your mind,
> Masses of concepts cease; you dwell stably without thought.
> Having done so, you see the nature of highest enlightenment.

Further, in general we say that once conceptual thoughts are pacified on their own ground, your mind abides in a state of bliss, clarity, or nonconceptuality. This is serene abiding. Special seeing is nakedly seeing your intrinsically clear mindnature, free of any focal object and without adding or subtracting anything. Freedom from the expansion or contraction of thought is

འགྱུ་བ་རང་ངོ་ཤེས་པ་ལྷག་མཐོང་། ཞེས་སོགས་མང་ཡང་དོན་ལ་ནི་གང་སྣང་ཅི་ཤར་ཐམས་ཅད་ཞི་ལྷག་དབྱེར་མེད་ཡོ་ན་ལས་མ་འདས་ཏེ། གནས་པ་དང་འགྱུ་བ་ནི་སེམས་ཡོ་རང་གཅིག་པུའི་རོལ་པ་ལས་མ་འདས་[58] དེ་གཉིས་གང་གི་ཚེ་ཡང་ངོ་ཤེས་ན་ལྷག་མཐོང་གི་རང་བཞིན་ཉིད་དང་། ཕྱི་རོལ་གྱི་ཚོགས་དྲུག་གི་སྣང་བ་གང་ཨ་འཐས་ཀྱི་ཞེན་པ་མ་ཞུགས་པ་ནི་ཞི་གནས། འཆར་སྒོ་འགག་མེད་དུ་སྣང་བ་ལྷག་མཐོང་སྟེ། སྣང་ཐོག་ཏུ་ཞི་ལྷག་ཟུང་འཇུག་ཚང་། རྣམ་རྟོག་ལྷོངས་[59] ཀྱི་ཤར་ཚེ་ངོ་ཧྲིག་གེར་ཤེས་པར་བྱེད་པ་ཞི་གནས། དེ་ཉིད་རང་སེམས་གློ་བྲལ་རྗེན་པར་གྲོལ་བ་ལྷག་མཐོང་སྟེ། རྣམ་རྟོག་ན་ཡང་ཞི་ལྷག་ཟུང་འཇུག་ཚང་[60] ཉོན་མོངས་པ་ཤིན་ཏུ་དྲག་པོ་ཞིག་སྐྱེས་པའི་ཚེ་ནའང་། དེའི་རྗེས་སུ་ཨ་འཐས་མ་སོང་བར་རང་ངོ་ལ་བལྟ་བ་ནི་ཞི་གནས། བལྟ་མཁན་གྱི་རིག་པ་དང་བལྟ་བྱའི་ཉོན་མོངས་སོ་སོར་མ་གྲུབ་པའི་གསལ་སྟོང་རྗེན་པ་ནི་ལྷག་མཐོང་སྟེ། ཉོན་མོངས་ཀྱི་ཐོག་ཏུ་ཡང་ཞི་ལྷག་ཟུང་འཇུག་ཚང་བ་སྟེ། མདོར་ན་སེམས་ཉིད་རང་གི་ངོ་བོ་ལ་ནི་གནས་འགྱུ་འཕྲོ་འདུ་བཟང་ངན་དུ་གྲུབ་པ་མེད་ཅིང་དེ་དག་གི་སྣང་བ་རྣམས་ནི་རོལ་རྩལ་ལས་འགག་མེད་ཀྱི་འཆར་ཚུལ་ཙམ་མོ། །ཞེས་དང་།[61] རྫོགས་ཆེན་པ་ཨ་བུ་ཧྲལ་པོའི་སྙིང་གཏམ་ལས་ཀྱང་། སྟོང་ཉིད་ཆོས་སྐུ་ཞེས་བྱ་བ། བླ་མ་གྲུབ་ཐོབ་ཐམས་ཅད་ཀྱི་ཐུགས་དམ། དུས་གསུམ་སངས་རྒྱས་ཐམས་ཅད་ཀྱི་དགོངས་པ། ཡི་དམ་ཐམས་ཅད་ཀྱི་སྲོག་རྩ། མཁའ་འགྲོ་ཐམས་ཅད་ཀྱི་སྙིང་ཁྲག །ཆོས་སྐྱོང་ཐམས་ཅད་ཀྱི་བརྟེན་གནས། མོ་རྒྱུད་ཐམས་ཅད་ཀྱི་ཉིང་ཁུ། གསང་སྔགས་རིགས་སྔགས་ཐམས་ཅད་ཀྱི་ཡང་བཅུད།

58. TEXT EDIT: 29b.3–4. *rol pa das ma das* corrected to *rol pa las ma das*.
59. TEXT EDIT: 29b.6. *lhangs* corrected to *lhongs*.
60. TEXT EDIT: 30a.1. *gzung jug yang* = *zung 'jug tshang*. That is, even though thoughts remain, serene abiding and special seeing are complete. (Comment from Lama Tenzin Samphel, October 24, 2013, Houston.)
61. TEXT EDIT: 30a.5. *Zhes* has been excised, as it does not signify an identifiable quotation at this point, though it closes the phrase beginning *Yang rnam rtog* (29b.2).

serene abiding; the movement that is recognition of your own face is special seeing.[177]

There are many such statements. The point is that whatever appears and however it dawns does not pass beyond the sheer inseparability of serene abiding and special seeing. Such stillness and seeing do not pass beyond being the play of your very own mind.[178] Your recognition of these two [serene abiding and special seeing] is the very nature of special seeing.[179]

Not remaining fixedly attracted to any external object that appears to the six senses is stillness. The ceaseless appearance of sensory impressions [within this fixation-free stillness] is special seeing.[180] Immediately on [the sense objects'] appearing, your union of stillness and special seeing is complete. To know with precise alertness the eruption[181] of thoughts right when they dawn is stillness. That itself, liberated into a mind nakedly free of mind-ness (*sems blo bral*), is special seeing. Moreover, even when thoughts are present, your union of stillness and special seeing is complete.[182]

Should a very strong affliction occur, your not fixedly following after it but rather looking it right in the face is stillness. Your naked empty clarity in which neither observing awareness nor observed afflictions are individually established, is special seeing. In brief, when it comes to your mindnature's own essence, neither abiding nor movement, neither expansion nor contraction, are established as good or bad. They simply appear, unceasing arisings from dynamic playfulness (*rol rtsal*).[183]

Also, in *Heartfelt Instructions*, the Dzogchen practitioner Abu Hralpo (Patrul Rinpoche) writes:[184]

> We call emptiness the sheer essence dimension, excellent heart of all accomplished lamas, enlightened state of all Buddhas of the three times, life channel of each *yidam*, heart blood of every dakini, and support of all Dharma protectors. This is the essential essence of all mother tantras, vital elixir of all Secret Mantra lineage holders, the

ཕྱག་རྫོགས་དབུ་གསུམ་གཅིག་ཏུ་བསྟན་པ། ཆོས་སྐུ་རང་སེམས་བྱེར་མེད་ངོ་སྤྲོད་པ་གཅིག་ཤེས་ཀུན་གྲོལ། གཅིག་ཆོག་རྒྱལ་པོ། ཆོས་ཉིད་ཕྱག་རྒྱ་ཆེན་པོ། ནང་རྟོགས་ན་ནང་སངས་རྒྱས། ནུབ་རྟོགས་ན་ནུབ་སངས་རྒྱས། ཞེས་བྱ་བ། མིང་ཆེ་ལ་དོན་ཆེ་བ། འདི་ཉིད་ནི། རང་སེམས་སྟོང་པ་མ་བཅོས་རང་ཤར་ཐོག་ཏུ་བཞག་པ་རང་ལ་ཟེར་བ་ཡིན་ནོ། །རྣལ་འབྱོར་པོ་མོ་རྣམས་ཀྱིས་ཡང་དག་པའི་ལྟ་བ་མ་ནོར་བ་ཞིག་རྟོགས་པར་བྱེད་ན། སེམས་མ་བཅོས་སྟོང་པའི་ངང་དུ་གསལ་ལྷང་ངེར་ཞོག །སེམས་འདུག་ན་འདུག་པའི་ཐོག་ཏུ་མ་བཅོས་པར་ཞོག །མི་དྲན་ན་མི་དྲན་པའི་ཐོག་ཏུ་མ་བཅོས་པར་ཞོག །མདོར་ན་སེམས་མ་བཅོས་གང་ཤར་ཐོག་ཏུ་ཞོག །བཅས་བཅོས་དགག་སྒྲུབ་གང་ཡང་མ་བྱེད། ཅི་བྱུང་ན་ཐོག་ཏུ་མ་བཅོས་པར་ཞོག །རང་སེམས་ཕྱུར་ལ་མ་བཞག །བསྒོམ་རྒྱུ་ཕར་ལ་མ་བཙལ། སྒོམ་བྱེད་མཁན་སེམས་པོ་རང་གི་ཐོག་ཏུ་ཞོག །རང་སེམས་བཙལ་བས་མི་རྙེད་སེམས་ཉིད་ཡེ་ནས་སྟོང་། བཙལ་ཡང་མི་དགོས་བཙལ་མཁན་དེ་ཉིད་ཡིན། བཙལ་མཁན་པོ་རང་གི་ཐོག་ཏུ་མ་ཡེངས་པར་ཞོག །ཞེས་གསུངས་པ་དང་། རྫོགས་ཆེན་ངོ་སྤྲོད་སྐལ་ལྡན་སྙིང་ནོར་ལས་ཀྱང་། རྗེ་བའི་བླ་མ་དང་ཨོ་རྒྱན་པདྨ་དབྱེར་མེད་ལ་གསོལ་བ་དྲག་ཏུ་བཏབ། མཐར་ཕྱུགས་ཡིད་བསྲེས་ཏེ་མཉམ་པར་བཞག །

> unified teaching of Mahamudra, Dzgochen, and Madhyamaka, all three.
>
> Once you recognize that the sheer essence dimension is inseperable from your own mind, this one understanding liberates everything. This alone is sufficient. Just reality is the Great Seal. If you realize this in the morning, you are a Buddha that very morning. Realize it in the evening, and you are a Buddha that same evening. These are all magnificent appellations, their meaning also magnificent.

Just this names your own mind: empty, uncontrived, self-dawning, alighting on that state right then and there. May male and female yogis flawlessly realize the correct view. May they be vividly clear within an uncontrived and empty mind.

Once mind is there, right in the immediacy of it being there, let mind be uncontrived. When there is forgetfulness, right in the immediacy of forgetfulness, let mind be uncontrived. In brief, whatever is dawning, be right there with an uncontrived mind. Do not involve yourself with stopping, or starting, or with any modification whatsoever. Whatever arises, stay uncontrivedly right with that arising. Don't reel your mind in, don't cast around for an object of meditation out there. Be right there with the meditator, your very own mind. Unfound when sought, your own mind is primordially empty mindnature. Seeking also is unnecessary; the seeker—yourself—is that [which one is seeking]. Unwaveringly remain right with that very seeker.

[Dudjom Rinpoche's] *Introducing Dzogchen, a Heart Jewel for the Fortunate* also states:[185]

> Pray intently to your root lama, inseparable from
> Ogyen Lotus Born.
> In the end, that exalted heart-mind infuses your mind;
> rest in evenness;

དེ་ལྟར་བཞག་དུས་རིག་པ་སྟོང་གསལ་དེའི་ངང་དུ་ཡུན་རིང་མི་གནས་པ། སེམས་ཚབ་ཚུབ། ཟང་ཟིང་། ཐང་ཐིང་། སྤྲེའུ་འདྲ་བ་ཞིག་ལངས་ནས་འོང་། དེ་སེམས་ངོ་མ་དེ་རེད། རྣམ་རྟོག་ཟེར་བ་དེ་རེད། ཁོའི་རྗེས་སུ་ཤོར་ན་རྣམ་རྟོག་འདིས་མི་དྲན་[62] བསམ་པ་དང་། མི་དགོས་བསམ་པ། མི་བྱེད་བསམ་པ་ནི་གཅིག་ཀྱང་མེད། སྔར་ཡང་འཁོར་བའི་རྒྱ་མཚོའི་ནང་དུ་ནག་ཐིམ་གྱིས་ཁོས་འཕངས་པ་ཡིན། ཕྱིན་ཆད་ཀྱང་འཕེན་ཐག་ཆོད་རེད། དེ་ནི་རྣམ་རྟོག་འཁྲུལ་པ་ནག་འཐྲུམས་འདི་དང་མཚམས་བཅད་ན་དགའ། མཚམས་ཆོད་དུས་རིག་པ་ཁོ་ཅི་འདྲ་ཞིག་འདུག་ཟེར་ན། སྟོང་སང་ངེ་། ཧ་ཆེད་དེ། ཡངས་གྲོལ་ལེ། བདེ་ལྷང་ངེ་། དངོས་པོའི་མཚན་མ་ཅན་དུ་གྲུབ་མ་མྱོང་བ། འཁོར་འདས་ཐམས་ཅད་ལ་མ་ཁྱབ་པ་མེད་པ། ཡེ་ནས་རང་དང་ལྷན་སྐྱེས་སྐྱེས་པ་ནས་བྲལ་མ་མྱོང་བ། བྱ་རྩོལ་བློ་ཡུལ་ལས་འདས་པ་ཞིག་འདུག་གོ་ཞེས་གསུངས་པ་དང་། རྒན་མོ་མཛུབ་བཙུགས་ཀྱི་གདམས་ངག་ལས་ཀྱང་།

62. TEXT EDIT: 31b.3. *rnam rtog di mi dran* corrected to *rnam rtog 'dis mi dran*.

As you rest, your empty, clear, and sheer awareness does not
Long remain. Your mind is racing.
It's a helter-skelter arrow of maliciousness, just plain foul, and
Vaulting about like a monkey.
This is what your mind is actually like.
These are what we call "thoughts."
If you go along with them, then
Exactly because of such conceptualizing,
You have no reflective remembering
And no thought, not one, of any limits on what you are doing![186]

In the past, I, too, was propelled by erroneous conceptions,[187]
Fading into blackness in the ocean of cyclic existence.
That this plunging will continue is for sure.
So better set a limit to
Erroneous thoughts, this dark meandering.

Do you wonder what sheer awareness is like once this limit is set?
It is an utterly vivid emptiness,
A state of no doing,
A spacious immensity and clarified bliss
Free from experiencing anything as defined by its particulars.
There is nothing in all of cyclic existence and nirvana that it does not embrace.
It's primordially inborn, never apart,
Transcending effort and objects of mind.[188]

Also, in *Quintessential Advice: Simplified Pointing-Out Instructions, as for an Old Woman*[189] [Guru Rinpoche] writes:

ད་ཆོས་ཉིད་ཀྱི་དོན་དང་སངས་རྒྱས་ཀྱི་དགོངས་པ་བླ་མའི་གདམས་ངག་ཚིག་གསུམ་ལ༔ ཕྱི་གཟུང་[63] བའི་ཡུལ་དག་པས་སྣང་བར་རང་སར་གྲོལ༔ ནང་འཛིན་པའི་སེམས་དག་པས་འཛིན་མེད་ཀྱི་རིག་པ་རང་སར་གྲོལ༔ བར་འོད་གསལ་ཉམས་དགའ་བས་རང་ངོ་རང་གིས་ཤེས་པའོ༔ འདི་ལ་ཕྱི་གཟུངས་བའི་ཡུལ་ཇི་ལྟར་དག་ན༔[64] རྣམ་རྟོག་རང་གིས་མ་བསླད་པར་རང་གསལ་དུ་སྣང་བ་འདི་ལ་བཞག་པས༔ ཡུམ་སྣང་ལ་འཛིན་པ་མ་ཞུགས་པས་སྣང་བ་གང་སྣང་ཡང་དོན་དུ་བདེན་པའམ་དངོས་པོར་མི་འཛིན་ཏེ༔ སྣང་བ་གང་ཡིན་ན༔ ས་རྡོ་རི་བྲག༔ རྩི་ཤིང་ནགས་ཚལ་ཁྱིམ་དང་མཁར༔ ནོར་དང་རྫས༔ དག་དང་གཉེན༔ སྤུན་དང་གྲོགས༔ བུ་དང་ཆུང་མ༔ ཕྱོ་དང་བུ་མོ༔ དེ་དག་ལ་སོགས་པ་གང་ལ་ཡང་བདག་པའི་བློ་མ་ཞུགས་པས་སྣང་ཡང་དོན་དུ་མི་འཛིན་གང་ལའང་ཞེན་པ་མེད་པས་ཕྱི་གཟུང་བའི་ཡུལ་དག་པ་བྱ་བ་ཡིན༔ ཡུལ་དག་ཟེར་ནས་སྣང་བ་མེད་ནས་མི་འགྲོ་སྟེ་ཞེན་པ་དང་འཛིན་པ་གསལ་ལ་སྟོང་པ་དཔེ་མེ་ལོང་གི་གཟུགས་བརྙན་འདྲ་སྟེ༔ དེ་སྣང་ཡང་གཟུང་རྒྱུ་མེད་པ་སྟོང་པ་ལྟར་སྣང་བ་རང་སར་སྟོང་པ་ལ་བྱའོ། །ནང་འཛིན་པའི་སེམས་དག་པས་འཛིན་མེད་ཀྱི་རིག་པ་རང་སར་གྲོལ་བའི་མན་ངག༔ སེམས་ལ་རྣམ་རྟོག་དང་འགྱུ་བྱེད་ཀྱི་དྲན་པ་དང་༔ དུག་ལྔ་གང་སྐྱེས་ཀྱང་དྲན་པ་དེ་བློས་མ་བཟུང་བས༔ འགྱུ་བ་རང་

63. TEXT EDIT: 32a.4. *spyi gzungs* corrected to *sphyi gzung*.
64. TEXT EDIT: 32a.5–b.1. The citation from Guru Rinpoche continues; hence tersar indicators were added to these lines as well.

There are three phases to a lama's key instructions on reality's meaning and a Buddha's enlightened state: First, when we purify external objects,[190] appearances are freed right where they are. Next, when we purify our internal grasping mind, we are right there freed into ungrasping sheer awareness. Then, in that space, delighting in sheer radiance, we know our own face![191]

Given all this, once you purify external objects just as they are, your thoughts appear clearly without polluting themselves. In staying with that, you do not grasp anything that appears, which means that even right when it is showing itself you won't hang onto any appearance whatsoever as true in import or as a thing.

After all, whatever might appear—earth, stone, rock precipices, greenery, thick forests, groves, households or castles, wealth or property, enemies or friends, relatives or companions, men or women,[192] all these and more, whatever they may be, are not grasped as real, even right while they are appearing.[193] Because the mind of selfhood is not present, you don't grasp at it or feel an attraction to things as real. Therefore, external objects are purified [in the sense that you do not grasp at them or take them to be real]. Having determined them to be pure objects, and given that nothing is appearing [as real] you do not regard them as such. Longing and grasping are dispelled. They are empty, like reflections in a mirror.

Even though something appears, there is no cause for grasping. What appears as empty is taken to be empty right on its own ground. Because your internal grasping mind is cleared away, your ungrasping sheer awareness is freed on its own ground. This is a key instruction![194] Regarding mind, even when you have conceptual thought, or awareness of movement, or awareness that the five poisons have come about, your mind does not hang onto them. Therefore, movement itself proceeds

སངས་སུ་འགྲོ་སྐྱེ་འགྱུ་བྱེད་ཀྱི་རྐྱེན་གྱིས་[65] མ་གོས་པའོ། །ནང་དྲི་མ་མེད་ཟེར་ནས་སེམས་ས་རྡོ་ལྟར་འགྲོ་བ་མ་ཡིན་ཏེ༔ རིག་པ་ལ་རྟོག་པའི་དྲི་མ་མི་འཛག་པ་ལ་ཟེར་བ་ཡིན༔ དཔེར་ན་རིན་ཆེན་གླིང་དུ་ཕྱིན་པ་དང་འདྲ་སྟེ༔ རིན་ཆེན་གསེར་གྱི་གླིང་ན་ས་རྡོའི་མིང་ཡང་མེད༔ དེ་བཞིན་དུ་དྲན་རིག་ཡེ་ཤེས་སུ་གྲོལ་ཙ་ན་རྣམ་རྟོག་གི་མིང་ཡང་མེད་དོ༔ བར་འོད་གསལ་ཉམས་དགའ་བས་རང་ངོར་རང་གིས་ཤེས་པའི་མན་ངག་ནི༔ ཉམས་སུ་བླང་བའི་དུས་སུ་རང་གི་ཤེས་པ་རིག་པ་དྲི་མ་མེད་པ་གསལ་ལེ༔ སེང་ངེ༔ ཧྲིག་གེ་བ་ཆོས་ཉིད་རང་བྱུང་གི་ཡེ་ཤེས་དེ་རྒྱུད་ལ་ཉམས་སུ་བླངས་པས་བདེ་བ་གསལ་བ་མི་རྟོག་པ་ལ་ཞེན་འཛིན་དང་བློ་ཡིས་མ་བསླད་པའི་ཉམས་ཤིག་འོང་བས་དེ་སངས་རྒྱས་ཀྱི་དགོངས་པ་ཡིན་ཏེ༔ རིག་པ་རང་ངོ་རང་གི་ཤེས་པས་དཔེར་ན་རང་གི་མ་ཡིན་ལ་མར་བསྒོམ་མི་དགོས༔ མ་ཡིན་སྒོམ་པའི་རྟོག་པ་གང་ཡང་མི་འཆར་རོ༔ དེ་བཞིན་དུ་རང་གི་རིག་པ་ཆོས་ཉིད་ཡིན་པར་ངོ་ཤེས་པའི་དུས་ན༔ འཁོར་བའི་ཆོས་ཐམས་ཅད་ཆོས་ཉིད་ཡིན་སྒོམ་པ་མི་དགོས་ཏེ༔ མ་བསྒོམ་ཀྱང་ཆོས་ཉིད་ཀྱི་དོན་དང་མི་འབྲལ་བས་མ་བསྒོམ་པའི་བསྒོམ་པ་བྱ་བ་ཡིན༔ ཆོས་ཐམས་ཅད་རང་བཞིན་མེད་པ་དེ་ཆོས་ཀྱི་མ༔ རང་བཞིན་མེད་པ་ཤེས་པ་དེ་ཆོས་ཀྱི་བུ༔ རིག་པ་ཆོས་ཉིད་ཀྱི་དབྱིངས་སུ་ངོས་འཛིན་པས་རང་ངོ་རང་གིས་ཤེས་པ་བྱ་བ་ཡིན་ནོ་གསུངས༔

ཞེས་དང་༔

65. TEXT EDIT: 33a.2. *skyen gyi* corrected to *rkyen gyis.*

to awakening without the causal condition, movement, bearing any blemish.[195]

We have said that there is no stain within. Yet mind does not become like earth or stone. Rather, when it comes to sheer awareness, thought-stains are inoperative, like coming upon an island made of jewels and gold, where not even the name "stone" is present. Similarly, when mindful presence (*dran rig*) is liberated into primordial knowing, not even the name "conceptual thought" is present.

Here is the quintessential instruction for recognizing your own face through the blissful experience of clear light in the bardo: practice maintaining in your mindstream the clarity that is your own stainless knowing, your sheer awareness, the limpid and wide-awake nature itself—self-risen primordial knowing. Your practice then becomes unstained by longing for or grasping after bliss, clarity, or nonconceptuality, or by mind. Thus it is a Buddha's enlightened state.

Sheer awareness knows its own face. You don't cultivate this knowing in meditation any more than you cultivate an ability to recognize your mother; no thought arises that she's not [your mother, so cultivating recognition is unecessary]. Likewise, once you recognize that your own sheer awareness is reality, you don't need to think about all the phenomena of cyclic existence being reality. Even without meditation, you are inseparable from the fact that is reality. Therefore, this is a case of non-meditating meditation. The naturalness of all phenomena is the mother of phenomena. Your knowing this naturalness is the child of phenomena. Through recognizing sheer awareness as stainless space, reality, you will know your own face.

རྒན་མོ་མཛུབ་བཙུགས་ཀྱི་གདམས་ངག་ལས་ཀྱང་། ཅོན་ཅིག་རྒས་པོ་རང་གི་རིག་པ་བྱང་ཆུབ་ཀྱི་སེམས་འདི་ལ་ལྟོས་ཤིག༔ གཟུགས་དང་ཁ་དོག་ཏུ་གྲུབ་པ་མེད༔ ཕྱོགས་དང་རིས་སུ་གྲུབ་པ་མེད༔ མཐའ་དང་དབུས་སུ་གྲུབ་པ་མེད༔ དང་པོ་བྱུང་ས་མེད་དེ་སྟོང་༔ བར་དུ་གནས་ས་མེད་དེ་སྟོང་༔ མཐའ་མར་འགྲོ་བ་མེད་དེ་སྟོང་༔ སྟོང་པ་ཅི་ཡང་མ་གྲུབ་པ༔ གསལ་ལ་དྭངས་པ་གཅིག་ཏུ་འདུག་པ་[66] དེ་མཐོང་ནས་ངོ་ཤེས་ན་རང་ངོ་རང་གི་ཤེས་པ་ཡིན༔ སེམས་ཀྱི་དེ་ཉིད་མཐོང་བ་ཡིན༔ དངོས་པོ་དོན་གྱི་གནས་ལུགས་གཏན་ལ་ཕེབས་པ་ཡིན༔ ཤེས་བྱའི་སྒྲོ་འདོགས་ཆོད་པ་ཡིན༔ རིག་པ་བྱང་ཆུབ་ཀྱི་སེམས་དེ་དངོས་པོ་ཅིར་ཡང་མ་གྲུབ་པས༔ རང་བྱུང་རང་ལ་གནས་པས༔ གཞན་ནས་བཙལ་དུ་མེད་པས༔ ཆོས་ཉིད་ཀྱི་དོན་རྟོགས་པར་སླ་བས༔ ཆོས་ཉིད་དོན་གཟུང་འཛིན་དངོས་པོར་མ་གྲུབ༔ རྟག་ཆད་ཀྱི་མཐའ་ལས་འདས༔ ཅེས་གསུངས་སོ། །དེས་ན་རྟག་ཆད་ཀྱི་མཐའ་ཐམས་ཅད་དང་བྲལ་བ་རིག་སྟོང་རྗེན་པ་གསལ་ལེ། ཧྲིག་གེ་བ། འདི་ཉིད་ཀྱི་ངོ་བོ་སྟོང་པ་ཆོས་སྐུ། རང་བཞིན་གསལ་བ་ལོངས་སྐུ། ཐུགས་རྗེ་ཀུན་ཁྱབ་སྤྲུལ་སྐུའི་རང་བཞིན་ཅན་འདི་ཉིད། རྫོགས་ཆེན་སྐལ་ལྡན་སྙིང་ནོར་དུ། རང་ངོ་ཤེས་དུས་ཅི་འདྲ་ཞིག་འདུག་ཟེར་ན།

66. TEXT EDIT: 34a.4. *gdug* corrected to *'dug*.

Also,

> Although this is a quintessential pointing-out instruction for an old woman,
> Old man, you listen!
> Look into your own sheer awareness.
> Your mind of enlightenment
> Is not comprised of form or color,
> Not inclined in any direction, not leaning,
> Not organized around limit or center.
> There's no place where it first arises—empty.
> No place where it abides thereafter—empty.
> No place to which it finally goes—empty.
>
> Its being empty is not established in any way:
> Clear and limpid, it's an abiding wholeness.[196]
> To see and recognize it is
> Knowing your own face and[197]
> Seeing your mindnature,
> Settles the genuine state of things,
> Severing superimpositions onto familiar objects.
> Because sheer awareness, enlightenment mind, is not
> Some thing in any way established, it is
> Self-risen, abiding in itself, and thus
> Not to be sought anywhere else.
> Reality's meaning is easy to realize.
> Reality's meaning is not some object to be grasped;
> It's beyond extremes of the eternal and the nil.[198]

And so it is. Sheer awareness is empty, bare, clear, and right here. It is wide awake, free of any extremes of the eternal or the nil. Its empty essence is the sheer essence dimension of enlightenment. Its clear nature is the richly resplendent dimension. And its all-suffusing love is the nature of the emanation dimension.

Perhaps you wonder, "What's it like, knowing your own face?"

རང་རིག་རང་ངོ་ཤེས་ཀྱང་བརྗོད་མི་ཤེས་པ་ལྐུགས་པའི་རྨི་ལམ་ལྟ་བུ། སྐྱོང་མཁན་རང་དང་བསྐྱངས་རྒྱུའི་རིག་པ་གཉིས་སོ་སོར་འབྱེད་མི་ཤེས་པ་ཞིག་འདུག །དེ་ལྟ་བུའི་རིག་པ་ཀློང་ཡངས་ཆེན་པོའི་ཐོག་ཏུ་རང་བབས་སུ་རྗེན་ནེ་བཞག་ཙ་ན།[67] ཕྱར་སྐད་ཅིག་ཙམ་ཡང་སྡོད་མི་ཐུབ་པའི་མི་དྲན་དགུ་དྲན་མི་བྱེད་དགུ་བྱེད་རྣམ་རྟོག་ཕུང་ཀྲན་ཁོ་ལ་ཅི་བྱེད་འདི་བྱེད་མེད་པར་རིག་པ་སྤྲིན་བྲལ་ནམ་མཁའ་ལྟ་བུའི་ཀློང་དུ་རྣམ་རྟོག་འབྱུ་བ་ཡལ་ཤོར། འཕྱོར་ཤོར། ཞིག་ཤོར་ནས་རྣམ་རྟོག་ཁོའི་དབང་ཤེད་ཐམས་ཅད་རིག་པ་ལ་ཤོར། རིག་པ་རང་གནས་ཆོས་སྐུའི་ཡེ་ཤེས་རྗེན་ལྷང་ངེར་གདའོ། འོ་ན་དེ་ལྟ་བུའི་རིག་པ་དེ་ཕྱུས་ངོ་སྤྲོད། ཐག་གང་ལ་གཅོད། གདེངས་ཇི་ལྟར་འཆའ་ཟེར་ན། རིག་པ་དང་པོ་བླ་མས་ངོ་སྤྲོད་པས་རང་ངོ་རང་གི་ཤེས་ནས་ངོ་རང་ཐོག་ཏུ་འཕྲོད། འཁོར་འདས་ཀྱི་ཆོས་ཇི་ལྟར་སྣང་ཡང་རིག་པ་རང་གི་རྩལ་ལས་མ་འདས་པར་ཤེས་པས་ཐག་རིག་པ་གཅིག་ཐོག་ཏུ་ཆོད། རྣམ་རྟོག་གང་ཤར་ཐམས་ཅད་རྒྱ་མཚོའི་ཐ་རླབས་རྒྱ་མཚོ་ལ་ཐིམ་པ་ལྟར། རིག་པ་རང་གི་ཐོག་ཏུ་ཡལ་འགྲོ་བས་ན་གདེང་གྲོལ་ཐོག་ཏུ་བཅས་པས།[68] བསྒོམ་བྱ་སྒོམ་བྱེད་ལས་འདས་པ་སྒོམ་འཛིན་གྱི་བློ་དང་བྲལ་བ་ཞིག་གདའོ། འོ་དེ་འདྲ་ཡིན་ན་མ་བསྒོམས་ཀྱང་ཆོག་འདུག་མོད་ཟེར་ན། འོ་དེ་འདྲ་ག་ལ་ཡིན། རིག་པ་ངོ་ཤེས་པ་ཙམ་གྱིས་[69]གྲོལ་བའི་ས་ལ་སླེབས་པ་མིན། ངེད་རང་ཚོ་ཚོ་རབས་ཐོགས་མེད་ནས་འཁྲུལ་པའི་བག་ཆགས་ཀྱིས་སྦྲུབས་སུ་འཐུམ། ཕྱར་ནས་དབར་རྣམ་རྟོག་ཁོའི་སྐྱུག་འོག་ཏུ་མི་ཚེ་འཕྱོལ། འཆི་དུས་གར་འགྲོ་འདིར་འགྲོ་མེད་པར་ལས་ཀྱི་རྗེས་སུ་འབྲངས་ནས་སྡུག་བསྔལ་མྱོང་དགོས་པ་རེད། དེས་ན་ད་ལྟ་རིག་པ་ངོ་འཕྲོད་པ་དེའི་རྒྱུན་བསྐྱངས་ནས་བསྒོམ་དགོས་པ་ཡིན། ཀུན་མཁྱེན་ཆེན་པོས། རང་ངོ་འཕྲོད་ཀྱང་གོམས་འདྲིས་མ་བཏང་ན།

67. TEXT EDIT: 34b.6. *bzhag co na* corrected to *bzhag tsa na.*

68. TEXT EDIT: 35a.4. *thog tu chod* corrected to *thog tu bcas.* The three phrases here are almost identical to the famous three statements of Garab Dorje: *Ngo rang thog tu sprad*; *Thag gcig thog dug cad*; and *gDengs grol thog du 'cha.*

69. TEXT EDIT: 35b.1. *tsam gyi* corrected to *tsam gyis.*

Even when your self-knowing sheer awareness knows its own face, it cannot express this, like a dumb person's dream. There is no distinguishing the sustainer itself from the sheer awareness being sustained. In the same way, as soon as[199] naked sheer awareness settles itself into the immense expanse, its archenemy, your conceptual thoughts, which can think or do anything, cannot remain even for another moment. Without doing anything, fleeting thoughts vanish, sliding into the expanse like a sky freed of clouds. Scattered and gone. Having fallen apart and slipped away, all your sense consciousnesses associated with such thoughts vanish into sheer awareness.

Sheer awareness is called the vividly naked primordial knowing of the self-sustaining essential Buddha dimension. By whom is such a sheer awareness recognized? What decision do you make? How do you gain confidence?

Sheer awareness itself is definitive.[200] All your dawning thoughts are like waves dissolving into their ocean. Because of your full confidence that this is definitive in terms of liberation, your mind is freed from grasping onto meditation. You have transcended any sense that the meditator is a subject or that meditation is an object.

Perhaps now you are wondering whether you could just as well skip meditation? But how could that be! Mere recognition of sheer awareness does not take you to the ground of liberation.[201] From beginningless time until now we have been encased, all wrapped up, due to our erroneous predispositions. From then until now, we have been buried under the excrement of our own thoughts. As such, we made it to a human lifetime. When we die, where do we go? Helplessly trailing our karma, we inevitably experience suffering.

Therefore, once we have identified sheer awareness, it is vital for us to meditate, protecting our mindstream. The omniscient one [Longchenpa] says:

> Even once you have identified your nature, unless you

རྣམ་རྟོག་དགས་ཁྱེར་གཡུལ་ངོའི་བུ་ཆུང་འདྲ། ཞེས་གསུངས། སྤྱིར་སྒོམ་པ་ཞེས་པ་འདི། རང་བབས་གཉུག་མའི་དྲན་པས་རྒྱུན་སྐྱོངས་ཏེ་རིག་པ་ཡེངས་མེད་འཛིན་མེད་དུ་བཞག་ནས་གཉུག་མའི་གཤིས་སུ་གོམས་འདྲིས་གཏོང་བ་འདི་ལ་ཟེར། གོམས་འདྲིས་གཏོང་ཚུལ་ཡང་སྒོམ་པའི་ཚེ་རྣམ་རྟོག་ཤར་ནའང་ཤར་དུ་ཆུག་དག་རུ་བལྟ་མི་དགོས་ཤར་གྲོལ་དུ་གློད། མ་ཤར་ན་ཨེ་འཆར་བསམ་མི་དགོས། མ་འཆར་བའི་ཐོག་ཏུ་ཞོག །ལར་སྒོམ་གྱི་ཚེ་རྣམ་རྟོག་རགས་པ་ཞིག་ཐོལ་གྱིས་ཤར་བྱུང་ན། དེ་ངོས་ཟིན་སླ་མོད། རྣམ་རྟོག་ཕྲ་མོ་འགའ་ཙམ་ཤར་ཟིན་ཡང་བར་དུ་ཧ་མ་གོ་བ་ཞིག་ཡོད། དེ་ལ་རྣམ་རྟོག་འོག་འགྱུ་ཟེར། འདིས་སྒོམ་གྱི་འཇབ་རྐུན་བྱེད་འོང་བས་དྲན་པས་རྒྱང་སོ་འཛུག་པ་གལ་ཆེ། དྲན་པའི་རྒྱུན་འདི་ཟ་ཉལ་འགྲོ་འདུག་མཉམ་རྗེས་གང་གི་སྐབས་སུའང་ཡོད་པ་ཞིག་བྱུང་ན་དེ་ག་རང་ཡིན། སློབ་དཔོན་ཆེན་པོས། བརྒྱ་བཤད་སྟོང་དུ་ལབ་ཀྱང་གོ་བ་གཅིག །གཅིག་ཤེས་ཀུན་གྲོལ་རང་རིག་རང་ངོ་སྐྱོང་། ཞེས་གསུངས། ཡང་སྐྱེས་མཆོག་ཨ་བུས་ཀྱང་། སྒོམ་ཆེན་པོ་མོ་ལ་ལས། སེམས་ངོ་ཤེས་རྒྱུ་མ་རེད་བསམ་ནས་སྡུག་སྡེ་མཆིམ་ཤར་ཤར་འབབ་ནས་འོང་སྟེ། སྡུག་མི་དགོས། མི་ཤེས་རྒྱུ་ཅི་ཡང་མེད། སེམས་དེ་ཤེས་རྒྱུ་མ་རེད་བསམ་མཁན་པོ་རང་གི་ཐོག་ཏུ་ཞོག་དང་དེ་རང་ཡིན་གསུངས་སོ། །ཡང་དེ་ལས། སེམས་པོ་རང་ཅི་དྲན་བྱུང་ཡང་། བྱུང་ཐོག་ཏུ་མ་བཅོས་པར་ལྷོད་དེ་མ་ཡེངས་པར་སྐྱོང་དང་ཆོག །བདེ་མོ་སླ་མོ་ཤུགས་ལ་འོང་བ་ཡིན་གསུངས་པ་བཞིན་སྐྱོང་དགོས་པ་ཡིན་ནོ། །

> gain familiarity with it, you are like a small child in a battlefield. You get carried off by the enemy—that is, by conceptual thoughts.[202]

In general what we call meditation means maintaining continuity through being mindful of a basic and very natural settling.[203] With your sustained continuity of this, sheer awareness remains undistracted and free of grasping. This is called "gaining familiarization with your most basic intrinsic condition."

Also, gaining familiarization does not involve methods in which a thought about to dawn is seen as an enemy. When it comes to dawning, you are relaxed. If nothing dawns, you need not wonder whether anything is about to arise. If something does arise, just let be. Also there is this: coarse thoughts are easily recognized when they suddenly pop up in meditation. However, when only subtle thoughts are dawning, and until you actually notice them, we say you have a conceptual undercurrent. Because such sneaky thieves of meditation do arrive, we consider it very important to spy out their entry with mindfulness. Once you have continuous mindfulness at all times—eating, sleeping, walking, or standing, as well as during easeful equipoise and its aftermath—that is as it should be.

One time, several great male and female meditators were in acute distress, bursting into tears because they felt they had no way to recognize their mind. The supreme Abu (Patrul Rinpoche) told them, "You have no need for worry. There is no reason at all for failing to understand. Your mind is not something to understand. Just let the thinker be right there in itself."[204] He also said,

> No matter what reflection comes to mind
> Whatever arises, just continue in unfraught simplicity,
> Unwavering ease in undistraction.
> That is sufficient. Comfort, ease, come naturally.
> As we say, sustained continuity is crucial.[205]

དེ་ནི་སྐྱོན་དང་གོལ་སའི་བྱེ་བྲག་ཅུང་ཟད་འཆད་དེ། སྤྱིར་མཉམ་གཞག་སྐྱོང་ཚུལ་མ་ཤེས་པའི་ནོར་བ་དང་། བྱེ་བྲག་ཏུ་གོལ་ས་དང་ཤོར་སའི་རྣམ་གྲངས་དེ་དག་གི་སྐྱོན་བསལ་བཤད་པ་ལ་གཉིས་སོ། །དང་པོ་ནི། དེ་ཡང་ཕྱག་རྫོགས་སམ་ཞི་གཅོད་སོགས་སྒོམ་གྱི་མན་ངག་ཟབ་རྒྱས་མཐའ་ཡས་པ་ཀུན་གྱི་དགོངས་པའི་གནད་གཅིག་ཏུ་མཐུན་པར་རང་སེམས་མ་བཅོས་པར་འཛོག་པ་ཉིད་ཡིན་ཀྱང་། གང་ཟག་སོ་སོའི་བློ་ཚུལ་གྱི་དབང་གི་སྣ་ཚོགས་ཞིག་སྣང་མོད་དེ། དེ་ལས་སྒོམ་ཆེན་འགའ་ག་ནི། ཚོགས་དྲུག་གི་སྣང་བ་ཕྲ་རགས་ཐམས་ཅད་འགགས་པའི་ཤེས་པ་རྟོག་མེད་ཁོ་ན་ལ་སྒོམ་དུ་འཛིན་པ་གདའ་སྟེ། འདི་ནི་ཞི་གནས་སྟོང་[70] པོར་གོལ་བ་དང་། འགའ་ཞིག་གི་དྲན་རིག་གིས་མ་ཟིན་པའི་གཏི་མུག་ལུང་མ་བསྟན་ལ་སྒོམ་བརྟན་པོ་རུ་རློམ། ལ་ལ་ནི་སེམས་གསལ་སེང་བ་དང་བདེ་ལྷན་ནེ་བ་དང་སྟོང་ཆམ་མེ་བ་སོགས་ལ་སྒོམ་དུ་འཛིན་སྟེ་ཉམས་ལ་ཞེན། ལ་ལས་རྟོག་པ་སྔ་མ་འགགས་ནས་ཕྱི་མ་མ་སྐྱེ་བའི་བར་གྱི་ཤེས་པ་ཧད་པོ་ཁོ་ན་དགོས་པར་འདོད་དེ་སྒོམ་དུམ་བུ་ཆད། ཡང་ལ་ལས་ནི་སེམས་ཉིད་ཆོས་སྐུ་ཡིན་ནོ། སྟོང་པ་ཡིན་ནོ།

70. TEXT EDIT: *steng* corrected to *stong.*

4 Fine Points of Practice

Sidetracking and Slipping: Pitfalls on the Path

Now we come to a brief, detailed explanation of possible errors and places one might go astray. In general, there is the error of not understanding how to maintain an even placement of mind. More specifically, there are various points at which one might slip away [from the intended path]. I will elucidate clearly the faults associated with these two.

As for the first, just being in your own uncontrived mind is consistent with the single quintessential instruction that is the enlightened intent of all the limitless, profound, and vast essential meditations in Dzogchen, Mahamudra, Pacification,[206] Severance, and so forth. Nevertheless, it indeed seems to be the case that individuals vary in their capacity for understanding. Some are very fine meditators but [erroneously] take meditation to be simply a state of nonconceptuality—a cessation of all coarse and subtle appearances to the six collections of consciousness. But this is just an empty state of serene abiding.[207] It is a deviation in terms of serene abiding.

Others take pride in an obscured neutral state conjoined neither with mindfulness nor sheer awareness. Still others take meditation to be a clear, vivid mind, or a naturally relaxed bliss, or a serene emptiness, and they long for such meditative experience.

Yet others hold that one need only relax one's consciousness after the previous concept has ceased and before the next one arises.[208] For some, mindnature is the sheer reality dimension, [merely] empty. Being wedded to the idea that "there is

ངོས་བཟུང་མེད་དོ་སྙམ་པ་སོགས་ཡོད་ལ་བཙངས་པ་དང་། དེ་བཞིན་དུ་ཐམས་ཅད་བདེན་པར་མ་གྲུབ་པའོ། །སྒྱུ་མ་ལྟ་བུའོ། ནམ་མཁའ་ལྟ་བུའོ་སྙམ་པ་ལ་སོགས་པའི་འཛིན་སྟངས་ལ་སྒོམ་དུ་འདོད་པ་ནི་བློས་བྱས་ཡིད་དཔྱོད་ཀྱི་མཐར་ལྟུང་། འགའ་ཞིག་ནི་གང་དྲན་ཅི་ཤར་ཐམས་ཅད་སྒོམ་གྱི་རང་བཞིན་ཡིན་ཟེར་ནས། རྣམ་རྟོག་ཐ་མལ་གྱི་དབང་དུ་བཏང་བས་སྨྱོན་པར་གོལ། གཞན་དག་ཕལ་ཆེར་ནི་འགྱུ་བ་ལ་སྐྱོན་དུ་བལྟ་ཞིང་དགག་པ་དང་། འགྱུ་བ་དེ་རྩུར་བཀུག་ནས་སྒོམ་ལ་འཛོག་པར་འདོད་ཅིང་། འཛུར་དྲན་དམ་པོས་སྤྱུག་འཆོར་དུ་འཆིངས་བར་བྱེད་པ་སོགས་ཏེ། མདོར་ན་སེམས་ཉིད་འདི་གནས་སམ། འགྱུ་འམ། རྣམ་རྟོག་དང་ཉོན་མོངས་སུ་གོར་རེ་འདུག་གམ། བདེ་གསལ་མི་རྟོག་གང་རུང་དུ་ལྷན་ནེར་འདུག་གམ། གང་ལྟར་སྣང་ཀྱང་དེ་ཀའི་ཐོག་ཏུ་བཟོ་བཅོས་སྤྱོང་བསྒྱུར་མི་དགོས་པར་གཉུག་མ་ལྷན་སྐྱེས་ཀྱི་རང་འགྲོས་བསྐྱངས་ཤེས་པ་ནི་ཤིན་ཏུ་དཀོན་པར་མཆིས་ན། ངོས་དོན་གྱི་མདོ་རྒྱུད་དང་། གྲུབ་ཐོབ་བརྒྱུད་པའི་བཀའ་འབུམ་མན་ངག་ཁྲིད་ཡིག་སོགས་ཀྱི་དགོངས་པ་དངོས་བསྟན་དང་། མཐུན་པའི་ཉམས་ལེན་སྐྱོན་མེད་ཞིག་དགོས་པར་སྣང་ངོ་། །ཞེས་མཁས་མཆོག་རྩེ་ལེ་སྣ་ཚོགས་རང་གྲོལ་གྱིས་གསུངས། དེ་བཞིན་ཀུན་མཁྱེན་ཆེན་པོས་[71]ཀྱང་། དེང་སང་གི་བསམ་གཏན་པ་ཁ་ཅིག །ད་ལྟའི་རིག་པ་འོག་འགྱུ་འཕྲང་[72]གསུམ་པོ་འདི་སྒྲིབ་གྲོལ་ཡིན་པས། གང་ཤར་ཅི་འགྱུས་སེམས་སུ་ངོ་ཤེས་ན་དེས་ཆོག་ཅེས་སྐྱེ་འགག་གནས་སུ་འདེབས་པ་རྣམས་ཀྱང་།

71. TEXT EDIT: 38a.5. *chos po* corrected to *chen po*.

72. TEXT EDIT: 38a.6. *'phreng* corrected to *'phrang*. Each of these imperils practice because if you do not recognize it you will fall into error. Khetsun Rinpoche notes that there are really two obstacles: (1) a failure to be aware of the true nature of the arising, abiding, and cessation of these subtle conceptions, and (2) at the same time thinking one is free from all proliferations. Therefore, if no matter what appears, we recognize it as our own mind, this is sufficient. See the oral commentary for further discussion.

nothing to be recognized" binds the mind and fails to establish the truth of everything as it is.[209] To maintain that meditation means holding to thoughts such as "it is like an illusion" or "it is like space," itself falls to the extreme of engaging your mind in mental analysis.

Other practitioners fall under the power of ordinary thought, believing that whatever they think and whatsoever dawns is the nature of meditation. This makes additional sidetracks likely; for example, seeing movement as erroneous and stopping it or, having brought on movement, asserting that one is set in meditation. These persons also get tied up in an unpleasantly tight mindfulness. And so on.

In brief, when you know how to sustain the spontaneous unfolding of your inborn and basic nature, then no matter how your mindnature shapes up, whether in abiding or movement, whether in concepts or afflictions, it becomes vivid as either bliss, clarity, or nonconceptuality.[210] It's a rare person who can sustain the intrinsic and basic continuity of consciousness without falling into error by fixing, dispatching, or shifting, no matter what state the mind is in.

The actual teaching is the enlightened state as presented in definitive sutras, tantras, and the one hundred thousand vibrant words of *siddha* transmission, quintessential precepts, instructional texts, and so forth. Obviously, what we need is a faultless practice that accords with these, as was stated by the supreme scholar Tsele Natsok Rangdrol.[211]

Likewise, the omniscient [Longchen Rabjam][212] also states:

> Some practitioners of meditative stabilization say that because the sheer awareness we have right now is triply free,[213] recognizing as mind whatsoever dawns or stirs is sufficient. They even busy themselves by enumerating [their thoughts'] arising and cessation.[214]
>
> Yet, all these methods involve mental grasping. Therefore [this kind of erroneous practice] is as different from

གནས་ལུགས་ཀྱི་དོན་དང་གནམ་ས་བས་ཀྱང་རིང་བ་ཡིན་ནོ། །ཡང་སྨུན་པ་ཅན་ཁ་ཅིག །ཟང་ཐལ་ཆིག་རྫོགས་འབྲེལ་ཐག་ཆོད་པ་ཡི། ས་ལེ་ཧྲིག་གེ་བར་མཚམས་ངོས་བཟུང་ནས། དོན་མཐོང་འདོད་"པས་དོན་མེད་ཕྱིན་ཅི་ལོག །ཡང་ཁ་ཅིག །ད་ལྟའི་ཤེས་པ་ཟང་ཐལ་ཆིག་རྫོགས་ཀྱི་ངོ་བོ་རྗེན་པ་འདི་ལ། སྐད་ཅིག་གང་ཤར་འབྲེལ་ཐག་ཆད་དེ་བར་མེད་ཧ་རེ་བ་གང་དུའང་མ་གྲུབ་པ་དེ་དོན་རང་བྱུང་གི་ཡེ་ཤེས་ཡིན་པས། དེའི་ངང་ལ་འགྲོ་གནས་ཅི་བྱུང་ཡང་ས་ལེ་ཧྲིག་གེ་ཉམས་སུ་ལེན་པ་ཡང་ཡིད་ཆེས་པའི་རྒྱུད་ལུང་དངོས་ནི་མེད། གཞན་དག་དེའིར་མདར་ཟློག་ནས་ངེས་ཤེས་བྱེད་དེ་སྔན་རྒྱུད་ཡིན་ཡང་དོན་དང་མ་འབྲེལ་བས་ཕྱིན་ཅི་ལོག་ཏུ་སྣང་ངོ། །ཅིའི་ཕྱིར་ཞེ་ན། སྐད་ཅིག་ཡུད་ཙམ་ངོས་གཟུང་འགྱུར་བའི་ཕྱིར། སྔ་ཕྱི་སྒོམ་མིན་བར་དེར་སུ་ཡིས་བཅུག །དེ་འདྲའི་ལམ་ངན་མདོ་རྒྱུད་དང་འགལ་བས། ཐར་པ་འདོད་ན་རིང་དུ་སྤང་བར་བྱ། མ་འགགས་མ་སྐྱེས་ངོས་བཟུང་བའི་བར་དེར་བསྒོམ་དུ་འགའ་ཞིག་གིས་བཅུག་པ་མེད་དེ། དེ་གསུམ་རིག་པ་མཚུངས་ན་བླང་དོར་གཉིས་བྱེད་པའང་མདོ་རྒྱུད་དང་འགལ་བས་སང་བྱ་ཁོ་ནའོ། །ཡང་ཁ་ཅིག་གིས། རབ་ཀྱིས་སོར་བཞག་[73]འབྲིང་གིས་

73. TEXT EDIT: The cited text says *sor bzhugs*, but Rinpoche's *sor bzhag* seems more correct.

[actually recognizing] your genuine state as earth is from sky.

Additionally, some obscured people are convinced that limpid clarity alone includes everything.[215] They believe that identifying this [limpidity] as the interstitial luminosity [between one thought and the next] constitutes seeing the meaning. Therefore [their practice] is pointless and erroneous.

When it comes to the naked essence of right-now consciousness or the limpidity it includes, some surmise that any manner of nonestablishment associated with the gap in a linked chain of whatever [thoughts] dawn at any particular moment is what is meant by self-risen primordial knowing.[216] In that state, your mind either proliferates or simply abides. Whichever occurs, they say, just practice brilliancy and vivid awakeness. But the actual tantras and scriptures in which we have confidence do not support this.

Others, having heard about this, [think that] resolving this definitely is the oral tradition. But since this [point] is not connected with the actual meaning, it appears to be erroneous. Why? Because only a single fleeting moment is being identified[217] [as sheer awareness].[218]

When there is neither prior nor subsequent meditation, who puts the middle there? Such an unworthy path contradicts sutra as well as tantra, so if you desire liberation, banish it to the distance. Do not enter into some meditation on an in-between state that you identify as unborn and unceasing. If those three [the former, in-between, and latter moment] are the equivalent of sheer awareness, then there are subdivisions regarding what we take up and abandon. This contradicts sutra and tantra.

And again someone says: "The most gifted [practitioner] lets be.[219] The middling practitioner sustains

ངང་ལ་བསྐྱངས།[74] ཐ་མས་སོ་སོར་རྟུལ་སྦྱངས་ཞེས་སྨྲ་བ། སྨུན་པའི་བློ་ཅན་སྟོན་མེད་གླང་ཆེན་ཞིག །གང་ཡང་ཡིད་ལ་མི་བྱེད་པ་དེ་གཅིག་པུས་ཆོག་སྟེ། བྱས་པ་ལན་པ་ཡིན། དེས་ན་རབ་ཀྱིས་ད་ལྟའི་ཤེས་པ་རང་སོར་ཐ་མལ་དུ་བཞག །འབྲིང་གི་སྐྱོན་ཕྱི་ནས་ས་ལེ་ཧྲིག་གེའི་ངང་ལ་བསྒོམ་པས་ཕྱིས་འཆར། ཐ་མས་འགྱུ་བའམ་གནས་པ་གང་རུང་གཅིག་ནས་བསྐྱངས་པས། ཕྱིས་འབྲིང་དང་རབ་ཏུ་འགྱུར་ཞེས་སྨུན་པ་ཅན་དག་སྨྲའོ། །གཤིས་ལ་དེ་གསུམ་གང་གནས་པ་ཡིན། མི་གནས་པ་བསྒོམས་ནས་གཟོད་གནས་སུ་རེ་ན་མི་སྲིད་དེ། སྲོལ་བ་ནག་པོ་ལས་གཞན་དུ་མི་འགྱུར་བ་བཞིན་ནོ། །སོར་གཞག་ཀྱང་རབ་མ་ཡིན་ཏེ། འཁོར་བ་བརྒྱུད་དུས་དེ་འབའ་ཞིག་ཡོད་པ་ལས་འཁོར་བ་དང་། ཐ་མལ་པ་ཡང་གྲོལ་བར་རིགས་པ་དང་། བཞག་བྱ་འཇོག་བྱེད་འགལ་བས་མ་གྲུབ་པ་དང་། གཏི་མུག་ལུང་མ་བསྟན་ལ་སྒོམ་དུ་རེ་བ་ཁྱོད་ལ་ཆོས་ཀྱི་སྐལ་བ་མེད་པ་ཞིག་སྟེ། ཕྱི་རོལ་བས་ཀྱང་དེ་སྐད་མི་སྨྲ་བས། སྟོན་མེད་པའི་གཉིས་འཐུང་འགྱིང་བ་ཞིག་གོ །ལམ་ཡང་དག་པར་ཚོགས་གཉིས་ཐབས་ཤེས་སུ་འབྲེལ་དགོས་ན་དེ་མེད་པས་བསྟན་པ་འདི་ལས་ཕྱི་རོལ་དུ་གྱུར་པ་སྟེ་བྱང་ཆུབ་འདོད་ན་དེ་ལས་བཟློག་དགོས་པར་ཤེས་པས། མདོ་རྒྱུད་གཟིགས་ལ་སྦྱོངས་ཤིག །ཅེས་གདམས་པ་ཡིན་ནོ། །ཞེས་གསུངས།

74. TEXT EDIT: 39a.4. *ngang bskyangs* corrected to *ngang la bskyangs*.

the state (*ngang bskyangs*[220]). And the least practitioner trains in dynamism."[221]

Such an elephantine obscured mind is unprecedented! Simply not having any mental application is sufficient. Doing is an error. Therefore, the most gifted practitioner leaves the profoundly ordinary[222] as it is, a consciousness of the now. The middling practitioner's faults will eventually be erased as meditation dawns within a state of vivid clarity, purifying obscurations. The least practitioners will sustain understanding of movement and abiding, gradually becoming like the middling and the best. Therefore, in the future, these obscured ones will be known as middling or superior.

When it comes to their home ground, the abiding state of any of these three practitioners is a nonabiding state. Primordial abiding could never come about through meditation on a nonabiding state, just as coal's blackness will never change into anything else.

Simply letting be is not ideal so long as one is merely in cyclic existence. Why? Because what is required is that you get free of cyclic existence and the merely ordinary. Since being in place and placing are contradictory, they are not established.[223] You who place hope in an obscured or neutral meditation do not have a fortunate lot when it comes to the teaching. Even Outsiders do not make such claims. This is one unprecedentedly snooty elephant!

The correct path necessarily combines the two collections, method and wisdom. Without them, you remain outside the teaching. Know that you must turn away from this [kind of error] if you seek enlightenment. Therefore, when it comes to fathoming sutra and tantra avoid [these faults].[224] Such is our advice.

དེ་བཞིན་དུ་རྩེ་ལེ་སྣ་ཚོགས་རང་གྲོལ་གྱིས་ཀྱང་། བྱེ་བྲག་ཏུ་གོལ་ས་དང་ཤོར་སའི་དབྱེ་བ་ནི། དེ་ཡང་མཉམ་གཞག་གི་སྐབས་སུ་བདེ་གསལ་མི་རྟོག་གསུམ་གང་རུང་གི་ཉམས་ལ་ཞེན་ན་འདོད་ཁམས། གཟུགས་ཁམས། གཟུགས་མེད་ཁམས་དང་གསུམ་དུ་སྐྱེ་བའི་རྒྱུ་བྱེད་ལ། དེ་དག་ཏུ་སྐྱེས་ནས་ཚེ་ཚད་རྫོགས་པ་དང་སླར་ཡང་ངན་སོང་དུ་ལྟུང་བ་ལས་སངས་རྒྱས་ཀྱི་ལམ་དུ་མི་འགྱུར་ཞིང་། དེ་ཚུལ་ཞིབ་ཏུ་དབྱེ་ཚེ་བྱེ་བྲག་ཏུ་སྙོམས་འཇུག་གི་བསམ་གཏན་དགུ་ཡོད་དེ། མཛོད་ཆེན་རྣམས་དང་ཤིང་རྟ་རྣམ་གཉིས་སོགས་ལ་གཟིགས། ད་ནི་ཤོར་བ་བརྒྱད་ཀྱི་རྣམ་གྲངས་སྟོན་ཏེ། དེ་ཡང་སེམས་ཉིད་རྣམ་ཀུན་མཆོག་ལྡན་སྣང་སྟོང་ཟུང་འཇུག་རྒྱུ་འབྲས་རྟེན་འབྲེལ་འགག་མེད་དུ་མི་རྟོགས་པར།[75] སྟོང་པ་[76]བལྟ་ལ་འབྱམས་པ་ནི་སྟོང་ཉིད་གཤིས་ལ་ཡེ་ཤོར་དུ་སོང་བ་ཞེས་བྱ་བ་ཡིན་པས་དེའི་སྐྱོན་རིག་པར་བྱ་ཞིང་། དེ་བཞིན་དུ་སྒོམ་ལ་ཞུགས་ནས་དོན་ཚུལ་ཙམ་གོ་ཡང་། ཉམས་མྱོང་རྒྱུད་ལ་མ་སྐྱེས་ཤིང་། སྐྱེས་པ་དག་ཀྱང་བཟོད་དེ།

75. TEXT EDIT: 40b.2. *mi rtog par* corrected to *mi rtogs par.* This accords with Khetsun Rinpoche's own oral commentary.
76. TEXT EDIT: *pha* seems to be a scribal error and is omitted here.

Specifics on Slippage

In a similar vein, Tsele Natsok Rangdrol also very precisely distinguishes sidetracking venues and slippery places (*shor sa*). For him, too, if during easeful equipoise you become attracted to any one of the three meditative experiences of bliss, clarity, or nonconceptuality, you are creating causes for birth in the desire, form, or formless realm [respectively]. Once born in these, your life span reaches completion and you plunge again into a negative rebirth. That's all! So this does not become a Buddhist path.

When we name the relevant categories precisely, there are nine states of meditative absorption.[225] For these see [Longchenpa's] great Seven Treasuries and [Jigme Lingpa's] Two Chariots, and so forth.[226]

Calming practices are described in great detail in texts on meditative stabilization, often in terms of the nine states of serene abiding (*sems gnas dgu*). The Dzogchen view is not much related with the nine levels leading to the calm of serene abiding or the nine cycles associated with easeful equipoise. Also, as we have said, their purpose is to push down or suppress afflictions. But calming practices do not cut them at the root, so that once conditions are ripe, the afflictions return. Cutting afflictions from the root requires the wisdom that realizes emptiness.

The teachings enumerate eight places of slippage. Without realizing[227] that mindnature exists in every direction as an unceasing interplay of cause and effect, a union of appearance and emptiness, you meander in emptiness.[228] This is known as a primordial slippage into emptiness in relation to the home ground. We need to understand the fault in doing so. [That is, due to thinking that emptiness is far away, you do not realize that mindnature is here and everywhere, and in this way you slip away from emptiness in relation to your home ground.]

Likewise, once having entered into meditation and then understanding the meaning a bit, either experience does not arise in your mindstream or, if it does, and you discuss it, intent

གཞན་ལ་ཆོག་འཆད་ཤེས་ཀྱང་དོན་རང་གི་རྒྱུད་ལ་མེད་པ་དེ་ལ། གཤིས་ཐྲང་ཤོར་ཞེས་
བྱའོ། །ཡང་། ད་ལྟ་དགོས་རྒྱུ་འདི་ལམ་ཡིན་ལ། ཕྱིས་ནས་འབྲས་བུ་གཞན་ཞིག་ཐོབ་
རྒྱུར་འདོད་པ་ལ། ལམ་གྱི་ཡེ་ཤོར་ཟེར་ལ། རང་སེམས་ཐ་མལ་ཤེས་པ་སྐྱོངས་བ་འདིས་
གོ་མི་ཆོད་པར་བློས་བྱས་ཀྱི་སྒོམ་བཟང་བཟང་པོར་འདོད་པ་ཅིག་ལོགས་སུ་འཚོལ་བ་ལ།
ལམ་གྱི་ཐྲང་ཤོར་ཞེས་བྱ། ཡང་། ཉོན་མོངས་ལྟ་བུ་སྐྱེས་པའི་ཚེ་དེའི་རང་ངོ་ལམ་ཁྱེར་མི་
ཤེས་པར་ཐེག་པ་འོག་མ་ལྟར་ཐབས་གཞན་ཞིག་བསྒོམ་པ་ནི། གཉེན་པོའི་ཡེ་ཤོར་[77] ཟེར།
རྣམ་རྟོག་ལྟ་བུ་གང་སྐྱེས་ལམ་དུ་ཁྱེར་མ་ཤེས་པར། སྐྱོན་དེ་བཀག་པའམ། བཤིག་ནས་
སྒོམ་ལ་ཕབ་དགོས་ན། གཉེན་པོའི་ཐྲང་ཤོར་དུ་གོལ་བ་ཟེར། སེམས་ཉིད་ཡེ་སྟོང་རྩ་བྲལ་
གྱི་ཡིན་ཚུལ་མ་གོ་བར་རང་བཞིན་མ་གྲུབ་པའོ། །སྟོང་ཉིད་དུ་སྒྱུར་པའོ་སྙམ་པ་ལ་སོགས་
བློས་བཅོས་པ་དང་། ཉེ་ཚེ་བའི་སྟོང་པ་སྟོང་སོགས་སྟོང་ཉིད་རྒྱས་འདེབས་སུ་ཡེ་ཤོར་དང་།
སྔོན་མ་རྣམ་རྟོག་གི་རྗེས་སུ་འབྲེང་ནས་ཡེངས་སོ། །ད་སླར་ལེགས་པར་བསྒོམ་མོ་སྙམ་པའི་
རྟོག་པ་ཁོ་རང་འཁྲོ་འཁྲུད་པའི་ངང་ལ་སོང་བའམ། དྲན་རིག་མེད་ཀྱང་ཡོད་དོ་སྙམ་པ་སོགས་
རྒྱས་འདེབས་ཐྲལ་ཤོར་ཟེར་རོ། །མདོར་ན་གནས་ལུགས་ཀྱི་རང་མཚང་མ་རིག་ཅིང་ཡིན་
ལུགས་ཀྱི་སྒྲོ་འདོགས་མ་ཆོད་པའི་གནད་ཀྱི། སྒོམ་འདྲ་མིན་དུ་ཤོར་བའི་རིགས་འདི་དག་
དང་། གཞན་ཡང་སྣ་ཚོགས་འབྱུང་ཉེན་ཡོད[78]

77. TEXT EDIT: 41a.3. *ye shos* corrected to *ye shor.*
78. TEXT EDIT: 41b.3. *nyin yod* corrected to *nyen yod.*

on how to express this in words to others, the significance is not there in your mindstream. We call this the pitfall of slipping away from the home ground.[229]

What we need now is the path. Regarding this, your wanting to obtain at some future time a fruit that is other [than your own nature] is called a primordial slippage in terms of the primordial in the context of the path. Seeking to improve your mind-made meditation without being capable of sustaining the continuity of your own mind—your profoundly ordinary [sheer awareness]—is called slipping into a danger zone with regard to the path.

Further, when something like afflictions develop, unless you understand how to bring their very essence to the path, your meditation will involve some other method, such as practices from the lower vehicles. This is called a primordial sliding[230] toward an antidote. Unless you know how to draw any rising thought to the path again, that fault is disruptive. After whatever conceptual thought that has developed either disappears or is disrupted, you [feel you] need to [re]settle into meditation. This is known as slipping into the danger zone of the antidote.

Unless you understand that your primordially empty mindnature is wholly unfettered, its nature is not established [for you]. Thinking "it is empty" and so on is a mental contrivance, a partial emptiness and the like. It constitutes a primordial slippage into attaching the emptiness label. Then, after following your prior train of thought, you are distracted.[231] Just thinking "This meditation is well done" brings you into a swamplike, proliferating expanse [of thought]. Or, even though you lack mindful presence, you feel you have it, and so on. Such occurrences are called slipping into the danger zone of labels or enumerations. In brief, unless you know your shortcomings as they relate to how it really is, and unless you cut away your superimposition onto what is actually there, you slipslide into something unrelated to meditation consistent with such key instructions.

These are some of the ways [in which we slip away from the path] and there are others as well. These kinds of hazards[232] mean

ལ་འདྲ་མིན་གྱི་སྒོམ་ལ་ཇི་ཙམ་འབུངས་ཀྱང་དལ་བ་དོན་མེད་དང་འགའ་ཞིག་གིས་ནི་གནས་ངན་ལེན་གྱི་རྒྱུ་རྐྱེན་བྱེས་པས། དེས་ན་སྒོམ་མ་ནོར་བ་གལ་ཆེའོ། །གཞན་ཡང་འགའ་ཞིག་གིས་སེམས་རྟོག་མེད་བྱིང་རྨུགས་ལ་ཞི་གནས་སུ་འཛིན་པ་དང་། རྟོག་པས་བརྟགས་དཔྱད་ལ་ལྷག་མཐོང་དུ་བསྒོམ་པ་དང་། ཨ་འཐས་འཇུར་འཛིན་ལ་དྲན་པར་འདོད་པ་དང་། བཏང་སྒོམ་ལུང་མ་བསྟན་ལ་བཅོས་མིན་དུ་ནོར་བ་དང་། གནས་ལུགས་ཀྱི་རང་ཞལ་མ་མཐོང་བའི་ཐ་མལ་པའི་ཤེས་པ་ཕལ་དང་བཟོ་བཅོས་མེད་པའི་གཉུག་མ་ཐ་མལ་ཤེས་པ་གཉིས་ནོར་བ་དང་། ཉིང་དེ་འཛིན་བཟང་ཞེན་ནམ། ཟག་བཅས་ཀྱི་བདེ་བ་ཙམ་ལ་ཟུག་རྔུ་མེད་པ་རང་བཞིན་མཆོག་གི་བདེ་བར་འདོད་པ་དང་། གནས་ལུགས་ཡུལ་མེད་རང་ངོ་ཤེས་པའི་རིས་པ་མ་རྙེད་པར་སྣང་ཡུལ་ལ་ཞེན་འཛིན་ཞུགས་པ་དང་ཡུལ་མེད་འཛིན་པ་བྲལ་བའི་རང་གསལ་འགག་མེད་གཉིས་ནོར་བ་དང་། གསལ་ཆ་འགགས་པའི་གཏི་མུག་ལ་མི་རྟོག་ཡེ་ཤེས་སུ་ནོར་བ་སོགས་མདོར་བསྡུ་ན། ནོར་འཁྲུལ་འདྲ་མིན་ཤོར་གོལ་གྱི་རིགས་མཐའ་དག་འབྱུང་བའི་རྒྱུ་ནི། དང་པོར་ཚོགས་གསོགས་སྒྲིབ་སྦྱོང་གི་མན་ངག་གཟབ་ཤོས་སྔོན་འགྲོ་ལ་གནད་དུ་མ་བསྟུན་པས་རྐྱེན་གྱི་ལས་ངན་གྱི་སྒྲིབ་པ་མ་དག་པ་དང་། བླ་མའི་བྱིན་རླབས་ཀྱི་རླན་གྱིས་མ་འཕྲུལ་བས་རང་རྒྱུད་ཐ་རྒོད་རེང་པ་དང་། དངོས་གཞིའི་སྒྲོ་འདོགས་ཐམས་ཅད་སེམས་ཐོག་ཏུ་ཐག་མ་ཆོད་པས་ཁ་ཆོས་ཚིག་འབྲུམས་སུ་ཤོར་བ་དང་ཐ་མར་ཉམ་ལེན་རྒྱུད་ལ་མ་ཁེལ་བས་ཆོས་མིན་

that no matter how you exert yourself in a meditation which is not as it should be, you simply tire yourself out to no avail. Some people even develop causes and conditions for bad rebirths. Therefore, it is very important not to err in your meditation.

Further, continuing our summary of errors, some practitioners take a heavy, murky nonconceptual mind to be serene abiding and boast that conceptual analysis is special seeing. Some consider an ongoing tight grasping to be mindfulness. Some err [in believing that] neutral equanimity is uncontrived, while others confuse their common ordinary consciousness, which does not see the actual face of how things are, with the most basic uncontrived, profoundly ordinary consciousness.

And there are those who err in longing for good meditative stabilization or in considering a mere contaminated happiness to be the supreme bliss naturally free of uneasiness. And again, without having found definitive recognition of the unobjectified genuine state, some confuse longing or grasping for perceivable objects with the unceasing intrinsic luminosity that is free from grasping and has no object. Or people confuse murkiness, a state of mind wherein clarity ceases, with nonconceptual primordial knowing! In brief, different types of error and deludedness (*nor 'phrul*) cause a variety of sidetracks and slippages to occur.

They come about, first of all, because of not energetically probing the numerous key instructions of the foundational practices. These are the most precise, key instructions for accumulating the collections [of merit and wisdom] and purifying obstructions.

In this way, you fail to purify negative karmic obstructions that function as causal conditions. Also, rather than being suffused with the moisture of your lama's waves of blessing, your mindstream congeals, becoming hard and uncultivated. Because your [rigid] mind lacks conviction regarding all the superimpositions associated with the main body [of practice], you slip into meandering onslaughts of dharma platitudes. And finally, because your mindstream remains unaffected by dharma, you are

འཇིག་རྟེན་མིན་གྱི་བར་སྲིད་དུ་འཁྲུམས་པས་གཟབ་པར་འཚོལ་དགོས་པའི་སྙིང་པོ་འཁོར་ལོ་བཅུ་པའི་མདོ་ལས། ལས་ཀྱི་རྣམ་སྨིན་རྒྱུ་འབྲས་མི་འདོད་པ། དེ་ནི་མུ་སྟེགས་ཆད་པར་སྨྲ་བ་སྟེ། ཤི་མ་ཐག་ཏུ་མནར་མེད་དམྱལ་བར་སྐྱེས། འདི་ནི་གཞན་ཕུང་རང་ཡང་རླག་པར་བྱེད། ཅེས་གསུངས་པ་ལྟ་བུའོ། །བོགས་འདོན་ལམ་འཁྱེར། དེ་ཡང་སྤྱིར་གསང་སྔགས་ཀྱི་ལམ་ཕལ་མོ་ཆེ་ལས་སྤྱོད་པའི་རྣམ་གྲངས་ནི། སྤྲོས་བཅས། སྤྲོས་མེད། ཤིན་ཏུ་སྤྲོས་མེད་དང་། གསང་སྤྱོད། ཚོགས་སྤྱོད། རིག་པ་བརྟུལ་ཞུགས་ཀྱི་སྤྱོད་པ། །ཕྱོགས་ལས་རྣམ་རྒྱལ་གྱི་སྤྱོད་པ་སོགས་མང་ཡང་[79] ཕལ་ཆེར་བསྐྱེད་རྫོགས་ཐུན་མོང་གི་བོགས་འདོན་ཤས་ཆེ་ཡང་། འདིར་ནི་གཙུག་མ་བློ་བྲལ་གྱི་རང་འགྲོས་སྐྱོང་བ་ཀུན་ཏུ་བཟང་པོའི་སྤྱོད་པ་ཁོ་ན་གཅེས་ཏེ། དེ་ལ་ཡང་དང་པོར་སྔོན་འགྲོ་ཚོགས་བསགས་སྒྲིབ་སྦྱོང་དང་བྱིན་རླབས་འཇུག་ཐབས་ཀྱི་རིམ་པ་བླ་མའི་རྣལ་འབྱོར་སོགས་གཙོ་བོ་ཡིན་ཏེ། འདིའི་སྐབས་སུ་ཡང་ཚེ་འདིའི་བྱ་བྱེད་འཇིག་རྟེན་ཆོས་བརྒྱད་ཀྱི་དྲི་མ་གང་གིས་ཀྱང་མ་བསླད་ཅིང་། རང་སེམས་རང་ལ་མི་ཁྲེལ་བའི་ཉམས་ལེན་གྱི་སྤྱོད་པ་ཀུན་ཏུ་བཟང་པོ་ལ་འབད་པར་བྱའོ། བར་དུ་དངོས་གཞི་ལྟ་སྒོམ་གྱི་བརྟར་ཤ་གཅོད་ཅིང་རང་རིག་གཏན་ལ་འབེབས་པའི་དུས་སུ་ཡང་བློ་མང་གི་གཟེར་མགོ་ནང་ནས་

79. TEXT EDIT: 43a.2. *yang yang* corrected to *mang yang*.

neither a practitioner nor a worldly being. So please be careful. It's important.

As it says in [the] *Ten Essential Teachings [Sutra]:*

> Not accepting the ripening of actions, cause and effect,
> Those who espoused nihilism
> Are born in the hell of endless torment immediately
> after their death.
> This is disastrous for you, and for others too.[233]

Phases of Practice

Furthermore, the Secret Mantra path is, broadly speaking, a framework for activities that can be either elaborate, not so elaborate, or very simple. This includes secret activities, group activities, activities for taming and for entering into self-knowing sheer awareness.

There are also activities such as the conduct of a conqueror[234] and the usual kind of progress in the stages of creation and completion, [or increasing the] factors of wisdom. Sustaining your own unfolding, the most basic state, free of ordinary mind is the activity of Samantabhadra. That alone is essential.

To initiate the path, foundational practices (*sngon 'gro*) are crucial. These practices include many stages, such as gathering the collections [of merit and wisdom], purifying obstructions, and methods for bringing in blessings, for which Guru Yoga is central.[235] Moreover, in doing these, you are not contaminated by any of the stains of object and agent or the eight worldly concerns. Practice diligently so that you are not ashamed when you reflect on yourself. Persevere in connection with Samantabhadra.

In the middle phase, [the stages of creation and completion][236] with yidam meditation as one of your main practices, you make a finely considered discrimination regarding view and meditation. Once you have settled into self-knowing presence you hammer down like nailheads[237] your multiple mind-sets and

བརྡུང་ལ་སྒྲོ་འདོགས་ཀྱི་སླེམ་ཐག་སེམས་ཐོག་ཏུ་ལེགས་པར་བཅད། གཅིག་ཤེས་ཀུན་ལ་མཁས་ཤིང་ཀུན་ཤེས་གཅིག་ཏུ་གྲོལ་བའི་སྤྱོད་པ་ཀུན་ཏུ་བཟང་པོ་ལ་འབྱུངས། མཐར་ཉམས་ལེན་གྱི་བོགས་འདོན་པར་བྱེད་པའི་ཐབས་ཀྱི་སྤྱོད་པའི་བྱེ་བྲག་ཀྱང་། གཞུང་དང་མན་ངག་རྣམས་ནས་སྨྲ་ཚོགས་འབྱུང་མོད་ཀྱི་འོན་ཀྱང་འགགས་སྙིང་པོར་དྲིལ་ཏེ་བཤད་ན། འཇིག་རྟེན་གྱི་འཁྲི་བ་ཐད་ཀྱིས་བཅད་དེ། མི་མེད་ལུང་སྟོང་དབེན་པའི་རི་ཁྲོད་འགྲིམ་པ་རི་དྭགས་རྨས་མ་ལྟ་བུའི་སྤྱོད་པ་དང་། རྐྱེན་ངན་ལ་ཡ་ང་བག་ཚ་མེད་པ་སེང་གེ་རི་སྒྱུལ་བརྙེགས་པ་ལྟ་བུའི་སྤྱོད་པ་དང་། འདོད་ཡོན་ལ་ཆགས་ཞེན་མེད་པ་བར་སྣང་གི་རླུང་ལྟ་བུའི་སྤྱོད་པ་དང་། ཆོས་བརྒྱད་འགག་སྒྲུབ་ཀྱི་འཁྲིས་མི་འཛུག་པ་སྨྱོན་པ་ལྟ་བུའི་སྤྱོད་པ་དང་། རང་སེམས་ཀྱི་རང་འགྲོས་ཁ་ཡན་དུ་སྐྱོངས་པ་ལས་གཞན་པའི་ཁ་འཛིན་གྱི་ཐག་པས་མི་བཅིངས་བ་ནམ་མཁའ་ལ་མདུང་བསྐོར་བ་ལྟ་བུའི་སྤྱོད་པ་རྣམས་ལ་སྦྱད་ཅིང་ཡེངས་འཁྲུལ་རྣམ་གཡེང་རེ་དོགས་ཀྱི་འཆིངས་བ་བཅད། རྟགས་མཚན་ཉམས་རྟོགས་དངོས་གྲུབ་སོགས་ཡོང་བར་འདོད་པའི་ཁོང་མཚང་སྦྱུ་ཙམ་ཞུགས་ཀྱང་གནས་ལུགས་ཆོས་སྐུའི་རང་ཞལ་སྒྲིབ་བྱེད་འབའ་ཞིག་ཡིན་པས། བཟོ་མེད་གཤིས་ཀྱི་འདུག་ཚུལ་སྐྱོང་བ་ཁོ་ན་དྲིལ་བ་ནི་ལམ་ཁྱེར་གྱི་སྤྱོད་པ་ཀུན་ཏུ་བཟང་པོ་མཆོག་ཏུ་གྱུར་པ་དང་། གནས་སྐབས་སུ་རྐྱེན་གྱི་བྱེ་བྲག་ལྟར་སྣང་བའི་རྣམ་རྟོག །ཉོན་མོངས། སྡུག་བསྔལ། འཇིགས་སྐྲག ན་ཚ་འཆི་བ་དང་བཅས་པ་གང་བྱུང་ཡང་གཉེན་པོ་འམ། ཕན་ཐབས་གཞན་ལ་མི་རེ་མི་ལྟོས་པར། གནས་ལུགས་སྐྱོང་བ་ནི་དགོས་དོན་ཐམས་ཅད་ཀྱི་རྒྱལ་པོ་ཡིན་པས། འདི་ལྟ་བུ་ཉམས་སུ་ལེན་ནུས་པའི་རྣལ་འབྱོར་དེ་ནི།

cut away superimpositions which bring on doubt.[238] You apply yourself to Samantabhadra-style conduct whereby in knowing one thing you are skilled in all. And, knowing everything, you are liberated into a single unified wholeness.

Finally, there are certainly many varied details regarding skillful methods for enhancing practice found in texts and quintessential instructions. Yet, when you go straight to the heart of the matter you completely sever the coiled entanglements of cyclic existence. You conduct yourself like that wounded deer wandering among the mountain peaks in empty, uninhabited lands (with no thought except how to return home).[239] You also conduct yourself like a lion fearlessly roaming the mountains, and like the wind in space, without any penchant or attachment for desirable goods. You conduct yourself with the mind of a mad person, engaging neither in desisting from nor accomplishing the eight worldly acts. You also conduct yourself like a lance whirling in space, giving free rein to the natural unfolding of your own mind, which is now no longer tied down with the rope of hanging on to others. And you sever the bonds of mistaken meandering in hope and in fear.

Should you retain even a hair's worth of internal weakness—a desire for signs, for meditative experience, realization, actual accomplishments and so forth—this will only obstruct your natural state, the actual face of your sheer essence dimension.

The Three Buddha Dimensions

Therefore, immerse yourself wholly in the ongoing way of being, sustaining your uncontrived home ground. This is the supreme conduct of Samantabhadra. Fleeting conditions, emblematic of conceptual thinking, which may appear as specific instances of afflictions, suffering, panic, or illness and death, will now all function as antidotes. Sustaining your genuine state, without depending on any other person or method, is the sovereign of all purpose and significance. Therefore, yogis capable of such

འཁོར་འདས་སྣང་སྲིད་ཀུན་ལ་རང་དབང་བསྒྱུར་ཐུབ་པའི་ཕྱིར་ན། བར་ཆད་ཀྱི་གཡུལ་དང་བྲལ། དངོས་གྲུབ་ཀྱི་མཚོ་ཆེན་ཇོ་ལ། སྒྲིབ་གཉིས་ཀྱི་མུན་པ་སངས། གྲུབ་རྟགས་ཀྱི་ཉི་མ་ཤར། སངས་རྒྱས་རང་སེམས་ནས་རྙེས། གཞན་གྱི་གཏེར་ཁ་ཕྱེ་བ་ཆོས་ཉིད་ཡིན་ཀྱང་། གཅིག་ཆོག་གི་ནོར་བུ་ལག་ཏུ་ལེན་པ་དེ་ཐང་ལ་བསྒྱུར་ནས། བྱིས་པ་འཇའ་མཚོན་གྱི་རྗེས་སློགས་པ་ལྟ་བུའམ་འདི་བྱེད་འདི་བཟང་གི་དཀོར་ལ་ཡེངས་པ་འདི་ནི་སྙིང་པོ་གང་ཡང་མེད་དེ། ཨོ་རྒྱན་རིན་པོ་ཆེས། ཆོས་ཀྱི་རྩ་བ་མ་གཅོད་སེམས་ཀྱི་རྩ་བ་ཆོད། སེམས་ཀྱི་རྩ་བ་ཆོད་ན་གཅིག་ཤེས་ཀུན་གྲོལ་འགྱུར། སེམས་ཀྱི་རྩ་བ་མ་ཆོད་ཀུན་ཤེས་གཅིག་སྡུག་འགྱུར། ཞེས་གསུངས། གང་ལྟར་ཡང་སྒོམ་སྒྲུབ་མཐར་ཕྱིན་ནས་རྟོགས་པས་ཡང་སངས་རྒྱས་བས་གདམས་ངག་དག་སྙིང་རུས་གཉིས་ལྡན་གྱི་འབྲས་བུ་སྐུ་གསུམ་ཡེ་ཤེས་ལྷ་ལྡན་མི་ཟད་རྒྱན་གྱི་འཁོར་ལོ་ལོངས་སྤྱོད་རྫོགས་སྐུའི་ཡོན་ཏན་ཁ་སྦྱོར་ཡན་ལག་བདུན་དང་། དབང་ཕྱུག་བརྒྱད་སོགས་འབྲས་བུའི་ཡོན་ཏན་རྣམས་ལ་ལོངས་སུ་སྤྱོད་ཐུབ་པའི་སྙིང་རུས་ཕྱིན་ཅི་ལོག་ཏུ་མ་སོང་བར་འཚོལ་ལོ་ཞེས་ཞུ་རྒྱུ་ཡིན་ནོ། །དེ་ཡང་ཁ་སྦྱོར་ཡན་ལག་བདུན་ནི། ༡ འོག་མིན་ཆེན་པོ་ལྷུན་གྲུབ་སྟུག་པོ་བཀོད་པ་ན་ལོངས་སྤྱོད་ཆེན་པོ་དང་། ༢ ཁ་སྦྱོར་བ་དང་། ༣ བདེ་ཆེན་དང་། ༤ རང་བཞིན་མེད་པ་དང་། ༥ སྙིང་རྗེས་ཡོངས་སུ་གང་བ་དང་། ༦ རྒྱུན་མི་ཆད་པ་དང་། ༧ འགོག་པ་མེད་པའོ། ཡང་དབང་ཕྱུག་བརྒྱད་ནི། ༡ སྐུ་གང་ལ་གང་འདུལ་རྣམ་པ་ཐམས་ཅད་དང་ལྡན་པ་ནི་སྐུའི་དབང་ཕྱུག་དང་།

practice, able to bring all of cyclic existence and nirvana—everything that appears and exits—under their power, are free from any interference. Great oceans of feats burst forth while the rising sun of accomplishment and realization clears away all darkness associated with the two obstructions. Buddhahood is discovered in your own mind! Reality opens other treasures. Taking into your hand this jewel, which is sufficient for everything, and tossing it on the ground is like children running after rainbows. Distractions, such as "I will do this" or "this is good" are utterly essenceless. The great Precious One from Ogyen said:

> Don't sever the root of Dharma.
> Sever the root of your mind.
> Once you've severed your mind's root,
> This understanding alone frees up everything.
> If you don't sever your mind's root
> Understanding everything is nothing but suffering.[240]

Without fail, once you have accomplished your meditation you are a Buddha again on account of this realization. Therefore, I beseech you to have the courage and unerring perseverance of a resplendent dimension sage when it comes to the seven good qualities of complete union. This dimension is the inextinguishable ornamentation possessed by the three Buddha dimensions [on the path] and the five primordial knowings. This dimension also includes the fruit of quintessential instructions associated with the twofold purification, and it includes also the good qualities that are the fruit of mastering the eight ordinary siddhis.

Moreover, the seven aspects of complete union are[241] (1) great resplendence of the richly adorned highest pure land, (2) union, (3) great bliss, (4) lack of self-nature, and (5) being completely filled with compassion that is (6) uninterrupted and (7) unceasing.

Also, the eight masterly qualities are (1) body mastery, gaining whatever type of body, in all its aspects, is needed for taming

༢ གང་འདུལ་ཆོས་བསྐོར་རྒྱུན་མི་ཆད་པ་ནི་གསུང་གི་དབང་ཕྱུག་དང་། ༣ རྟོག་མེད་
ཐུགས་རྗེར་མངའ་བ་ནི་ཐུགས་ཀྱི་དབང་ཕྱུག་དང་། ༤ རྫུ་འཕྲུལ་ཐོགས་པ་མེད་པ་ནི། རྫུ་
འཕྲུལ་གྱི་དབང་ཕྱུག་དང་། ༥ འཁོར་འདས་མཉམ་པ་ཉིད་དུ་རོ་གཅིག་ཏུ་མངོན་པར་བྱང་
ཆུབ་པ་ནི་ཀུན་འགྲོའི་དབང་ཕྱུག་དང་། ༦ རི་རབ་ཀྱི་རྡུལ་གྱི་གྲངས་དང་མཉམ་པའི་ལྷ་
མོས་འདོད་ཡོན་གྱིས་མཆོད་ཀྱང་འདོད་པས་གོས་པ་མེད་པ་ནི་འདོད་པའི་དབང་ཕྱུག་དང་།
༧ ཡིད་བཞིན་གྱི་ནོར་བུ་ལྟ་བུར་འགྲོ་བའི་རེ་འདོད་ཡིད་མཐུན་དུ་སྐོང་བས་ཅི་འདོད་བསྐྱེད་
པའི་དབང་ཕྱུག་དང་། ༨ འོག་མིན་ཆོས་དབྱིངས་ཕོ་བྲང་ན་ཁམས་གསུམ་ཆོས་ཀྱི་རྒྱལ་
པོར་རྟག་ཏུ་བཞུགས་པ་ནི་གནས་ཀྱི་དབང་ཕྱུག་གོ །དེ་ཡང་གཙོ་བོ་ལོངས་སྐུའི་ཡོན་ཏན་གྱི་
རྣམ་གྲངས་ཡིན་ནོ། །སོགས་ལོངས་ནས་ཐུན་མོང་གི་དངོས་གྲུབ་གྲུབ་པ་བརྒྱད་ནི། མཁའ་
སྤྱོད་རལ་གྲི་རིལ་ལུ་དང་། རྐང་མགྱོགས་བུམ་པ་གནོད་སྦྱིན་ཁོལ། བཅུད་ལེན་དང་ནི་
མིག་སྨན་ནོ། །ཞེས་པའོ། ༡ མཁའ་སྤྱོད་ནི། མི་འཆི་བར་ནམ་མཁར་གནས་ནུས་
པའོ། ༢ །རལ་གྲི་ནི། དེས་དག་དཔུང་འཇོམས་ནུས་སོ། ༣ །རྐང་མགྱོགས་ནི།
མཆིལ་ལྷམ་གྲུབ་སྟེ་གྱོན་པས་ཡུད་ཙམ་ལ་རྒྱ་མཚོའི་མཐའ་འཁོར་བའོ། ༤ བུམ་པ་ནི་
དེའི་ནང་དུ་ཟས་ནོར་གོས་ལ་སོགས་པ་ཡོ་བྱད་ཟད་མི་ཤེས་པ་འབྱུང་ངོ་། ༥ །རིལ་ལུ་ནི་
སྨན་འགའ་ཞིག་བསྒྲུབ་པ་དེ་ལག་ཏུ་ཐོགས་པས་ལུས་མི་སྣང་པའོ། ༦ །གནོད་སྦྱིན་གྱི་
ཁོལ་པོ་ནི། དེས་བྲན་བྱེད་པས་ཅི་བསྒོ་བ་སྒྲུབ་ཅིང་མི་འབུམ་གྱི་ལས་ཉིན་གཅིག་ལ་འགྲུབ་
པའོ། ༧ །བཅུད་ལེན་ནི་ཚེ་ཉི་ཟླ་དང་མཉམ། ལྡང་བ་ཤིང་བལ་ལས་ཡང་བའོ། ༨ །མིག་
སྨན་ནི། མིག་ལ་བྱུག་པས་ས་འོག་གི་གཏེར་ལ་སོགས་པ་མཐོང་བའོ། །སྤྲུལ་པའི་སྐུ་ནི།
ཆོས་ལོངས་གཉིས་ཀྱི་རྣམ་པར་འཕྲུལ་པ་བསམ་ཡས་ཀྱི་

anyone; (2) speech mastery, uninterrupted turning of the doctrine wheel for whatsoever training; (3) heart-mind mastery, nonconceptual compassion, (4) magical display mastery, unobstructed magical display; (5) all-suffusing mastery, enlightenment in which one taste, the sameness of samsara and nirvana, are fully evident; (6) mastery of desire, goodness equal to the grains of sand in Mount Meru, offering desirable things without the clothing of desire; (7) wish-fulfillment mastery, granting satisfaction like a wish-fulfilling jewel in accord with beings' hopes and desires; and (8) mastery of place, abiding continuously as a Dharma master of the three realms in the highest stainless space.

Further, regarding enumerations of the main qualities of the richly resplendent dimension, the expression "and so forth," above, includes eight accomplishments which are the ordinary siddhis: (1) flying through space, (2) the sword, (3) the pills, (4) being swift of foot, (5) possessing a gifting vessel, (6) enslaving *yakshas* [harmful deities], (7) subsisting on eating only essence, and (8) eye medicine.

"Flying through the sky" means you can remain in space until you die. With the sword, you can conquer a hostile army. The swift legs are boots that, when you wear them, allow you to circle the ocean in a fleeting moment. Inside the vessel are inexhaustible supplies of food, wealth, garments, and so forth. The special pills [the order here different than in list above] [mean] assembling certain medicines that, when you hold them in your hand, make you invisible. By enslaving yakshas, whatever you command will be done; the work of a hundred thousand people is accomplished in a single day. "Eating only essence" means your life will be long, equal to the sun and the moon. When you walk, your body will be lighter than cotton. By rubbing the eye medicine on your eyes, you can see treasures and the like underground. [This concludes discussion of eight ordinary siddhis; it also completes this discussion of the sambhogakāya.]

As for the emanation dimension, inconceivable emanations of the essential and richly resplendent Buddha dimensions

གདུལ་བྱ་འགྲོ་བའི་ཆུ་སྣོད་ཇི་སྙེད་པར་འདུལ་བྱེད་སྤྲུལ་པའི་ཟླ་སྣང་དེ་སྙེད་དུ་འབྱུང་བ་སྟེ། བཟོ་དང་། སྐྱེ་བ་དང་། མཆོག་སྤྲུལ་བྱང་ཆུབ་སེམས་དཔའ་ལ་སོགས་པ་གང་ལ་གང་འདུལ་གྱི་སྤྲུལ་པའི་བཀོད་པ་རབ་འབྱམས་མཐའ་ཡས་པར་འབྱུང་བ་ནི་སངས་རྒྱས་རྣམས་ཀྱི་སྐུ་གསུང་ཐུགས་ཀྱི་གསང་བ་མི་ཟད་རྒྱན་གྱི་འཁོར་ལོ་ཞེས་བྱ་བ་ཡིན་ནོ། །འགགས་བསྡུ་བའི་ཚུལ་གྱི་བཤད་པ་ནི། ཀུན་བྱེད་རྒྱལ་པོ་ལས། ཀྱེ་སེམས་དཔའ་ཆེན་པོ་ཉོན་ཅིག །ང་ཡི་རང་བཞིན་འདི་ལྟ་སྟེ། ཡོད་ནི་གཅིག་ལས་མེད་པ་སྟེ། །བསྟན་ནི་རྣམ་པ་གཉིས་སུ་བསྟན། །བྱུང་ནི་ཐེག་པ་རིམ་དགུར་བྱུང་། །འདུས་ནི་རྫོགས་པ་ཆེན་པོར་འདུས། །ཁྱབ་ནི་སྣོད་བཅུད་ཀུན་ལ་ཁྱབ། །བྱུང་ནི་སྣང་སྲིད་ཀུན་ཏུ་བྱུང་། །བསྟན་དུ་མཚན་མའི་དངོས་པོ་མེད། །མཐོང་དུ་དམིགས་པའི་ཡུལ་དང་བྲལ། །ཞེས་གསུངས་པ་ནི། ཡོད་ནི་ཆོས་སྐུ་ཐིག་ལེ་ཉག་གཅིག་ལས་མེད་ནའང་། གདུལ་བྱའི་དབང་གི་གཟུགས་སྐུ་རྣམ་གཉིས་བསྟན་ནས་རིགས་ཅན་གསུམ་གྱི་གདུལ་བྱ་བློ་རབ་འབྲིང་མཐའ་གསུམ་རེ་བྱུང་བས་གདུལ་བྱེད་ཀྱི་གཉེན་པོའང་ཐེག་པ་རིམ་པ་གསུམ་མམ་ལམ་དགུར་སྣང་རུང་རྒྱ་མཚོ་ཆེན་པོ་ལ་ཆུ་ཕྲན་ཀུན་བསྡུ་བ་བཞིན་རྫོགས་པ་ཆེན་པོའི་ཀློང་དུ་འདུ་བར་མ་ཟད་འཁོར་འདས་ཀྱི་བརྟན་གཡོ་ཀུན་ལ་རང་བཞིན་སྟོང་པ་ཉིད་ཀྱིས་མ་ཁྱབ་པ་མེད་པ་དེ་ལྟར་ཡང་

come forth in as many moon-appearances of training emanations as there are water vessels of trainees, giving rise to a limitless expanse of display emanations who use whatever techniques are required for training. These emanations are categorized as (1) created, (2) born, or (3) the supreme emanation dimensions. They refer to bodhisattvas, and so forth, known as the wheels of inextinguishable ornamentation—the Buddhas' secret body, speech, and mind, training beings according to their needs.

A summarizing explanation is found in *Majestic Creator of Everything*:

> O
> Listen Great Being!
> My nature is like this:
> What exists is nothing but a oneness.
> "The teaching" is the twofold teaching
> "Arising" is its arising as nine ascending vehicles
> "Gathering" is their gathering into a great completeness
> "Suffusion" is suffusion of all vessels and essences
> "Surfacing" is the coming forth of all appearances and
>   possibilities.
> No actual thing with signs to be shown.[242]
> Free of any place where an object can be seen.[243]

What exists is nothing other than the sheer essence dimension, unbounded wholeness. Also, as we have seen, there are the two form Buddha dimensions whose purpose is to train beings.

Accordingly, there are three categories of trainees: those of sharp, middling, and lesser minds. Just as all rivers stream into the great ocean, it is appropriate for path-vehicles to have three or nine stages that are also antidotes for these trainees. Likewise, [all such paths] are included in the expanse of Dzogchen, the Great Completeness. All the stable[244] and mobile phenomena of cyclic existence and nirvana are unfailingly permeated by their nature of emptiness. Likewise, even though nothing exists with

བེམ་པོ་རང་རྒྱུད་ལྟར་མཚན་མའི་དངོས་པོར་བསྟན་དུ་མེད་པས་ཆུ་བུར་མིག་གི་སྤྱོད་ཡུལ་ལམ་ཀུན་རྫོབ་བློའི་དམིགས་བསམ་ལས་འདས་པའི་གླུ་དག་ཙན་ནོ། ཡང་དེ་ལས། སེམས་ཉིད་ཀུན་ཏུ་བཟང་པོ་ཡི། །བཞུགས་ཚུལ་བསྟན་པ་འདི་ལྟ་སྟེ། །བྱང་ཆུབ་སེམས་སུ་བཞུགས་ཙམ་ན། །ཆོས་རྣམས་ཀུན་གྱི་སྙིང་པོར་བཞུགས། །གཟུང་འཛིན་བྲལ་ལ་འགྱུར་བ་མེད།། ལོངས་སྤྱོད་རྫོགས་སྐུར་བཞུགས་ཙམ་ན། །འདོད་པའི་ཡོན་ཏན་ལྔ་ལྡན་པས། །འདོད་པ་ཕུན་སུམ་ཚོགས་པར་བཞུགས། །སྤྲུལ་པའི་སྐུ་རུ་བཞུགས་ཙམ་ན། གང་གི་འདུལ་བའི་དུས་ཙམ་ན། །གང་ལ་གང་དགོས་སྐུ་སྤྲུལ་ནས། །དགོས་པ་ཕུན་སུམ་ཚོགས་པར་བཞུགས། །ཞེས་པའི་སྐུ་གསུམ་ངོ་བོ་གཅིག་ཡིན་ཀྱང་གདུལ་བྱའི་མོས་དབང་དང་མཛད་པའི་ཕྲིན་ལས་ཀྱིས་དེ་ལྟར་དུ་སྣང་བ་ཡིན་ནོ། །ཡང་དེ་ལས། མི་རྟོག་མཉམ་པ་དེ་ཉིད་ལས།། སྐྱེ་བ་མེད་པའི་ཆོས་སྐུ་བྱུང་། །རང་གི་ངོ་བོ་དེ་ཉིད་ལས། །འདོད་པའི་ལོངས་སྤྱོད་རྫོགས་སྐུ་བྱུང་། །ཐུགས་རྗེ་བྱང་ཆུབ་ཆེན་པོ་ལས། །སྤྲུལ་པས་འགྲོ་བའི་དོན་མཛད་བྱུང་། །

[true] characteristics or as materially self-existent, objects in the water-filled eye's domain and objects conceived by an obscured mind have a naturalness that is inconceivable.

Also, the same text *The Majestic Creator of Everything* says:

> This teaches how
> Mindnature, Samantabhadra, resides:
> Simply residing in enlightenment mind
> Is residing at the heart of all things,
> Free of being subject or object and free of change.
> Simply residing as a resplendent dimension Buddha
> Means possessing the five desirable characteristics, and
> hence
> You reside as an assembly of sublime desirables.
> Simply residing as an emanation dimension Buddha
> And, right when anyone needs to be tamed,
> Emanating whatever body is needed for that,
> Means you reside as a collective of sublime necessity.[245]

Epilogue

Although the three Buddha dimensions described here are indeed a single unity, their appearance accords with the aspiration, capacity, and activities of those to be tamed. The same text says:

> From a nonconceptual state of sameness
> Arises the unborn sheer essence dimension.
> From that, its own very essence,
> Arises the richly resplendent dimension of the desirable, and
> From [its] responsive love, which is great
> enlightenment,
> Come forth emanation dimensions, acting to benefit
> beings.[246]

ཞེས་པའང་། སྐྱེ་མེད་ཆོས་སྐུ། འགག་མེད་ལོངས་སྐུ། ཐུགས་རྗེ་སྤྲུལ་པའི་འགྲོ་དོན་མཛད་ཚུལ་བསྟན་པ་ཡིན་ནོ། །སླར་སྨྲས་པ། ཆོས་སྐུ་སྐྱེ་མེད་མཁའ་ལྟར་དག་པ་ལ། ལོངས་སྐུ་འགགས་མེད་དོ་མཚར་སྣང་བའི་དཔལ། ལས་སྨོན་མཐུ་ཡིས་གདུལ་བྱའི་པད་མཚོ་རུ། སྣ་མང་རྒྱུ་སྐར་[80] ཚོགས་བཞིན་རྟག་ཏུ་སྣང་། །སྐལ་བཟང་ལས་ཅན་སྐྱེས་བུའི་སྤྱན་རས་ཀྱིས། །རྣམ་དཔྱོད་[81] ཤེས་བྱའི་ཆོས་ཀྱི་དེ་ཉིད་གཟིགས། །མཁྱེན་རབ་འདབ་སྟོང་བཀྲ་བའི་ཡོན་ཏན་གྱིས། །སངས་རྟོགས་འབྲས་བུའི་སྙན་གགས་ས་གསུམ་ཁྱབ། །ཅེས་པའང་རྨོངས་ཀྲན་མཁས་བཙུན་བཟང་པོར་འབོད་པས་ཕ་སེའི་རྗེ་དོན་ས་ཕོངས་ནགས་ཚལ་སྤུག་པོའི་དོར་ཡངས་པའི་བསམ་གཏན་གྱི་ཁང་བཟང་ག་ལ་ཕ་དེར། ཕྱི་ལོ་ ༡༩༩༣ - ༨ - ༦ བཟང་པོར་བྲིས་པ་འདིས་ཀྱང་རང་གཞན་ཀུན་ལ་སྨན་པའི་རྒྱུར་གྱུར་ཅིག། ||

80. TEXT EDIT: 48b.2. *sgar* corrected to *skar*.
81. TEXT EDIT: 48b.2. *rnam gcod* corrected to *rnam dpyod*.

So it is said. This indicates the unborn sheer essence dimension, the unceasing richly resplendent dimension, and the loving emanation dimension, which acts to benefit beings.

Again, it is put forth:

> In disciples' Lotus Lake, by the power of karma and prayer
> The unborn sheer essence dimension, pure as space, and
> The unceasing rich and joyful dimension, astounding in its splendor;
> Are continuously appearing like multitudes of stars,[247]
> To the eyes of persons with fortunate karma
> Who very precisely[248] see
> The real nature of all that can be known.
>
> Like a thousand shining lotus petals,
> Their excellent qualities of keen discernment and
> Widely renowned fruition of their accomplishment and realization,
> Suffuses the three realms.[249]

Written by the obscured, gray, old grandfather
known as Khetsun Sangpo in the region of Dordogne
among the great black forests, in the house of meditation,
August 6, 1993.
Despite being written by Sangpo,
may it be a natural medicine for everyone.

Part Two

The Oral Commentary

Homage and Prologue[250]

THE LIFE we have right now is precious beyond measure. Whatever you do, please take care of it and use it well.

With this in mind, and because you requested it, I am offering you this teaching retreat on the ninth of the nine paths of practice, the peak of all vehicles that is known as Dzogchen, the Great Completeness, and also simply as Ati, meaning "the highest."

The Dzogchen path is at once easy and not easy. It is easy because, if we endeavor with body, speech, and mind, it is not far away. It is also easy because all you need do is uncover your mind's real nature. And it is easy because, as soon as you recognize that nature, you are a Buddha. Finally, it is easy because it is very accessible to anyone with auspicious karma. Still, nobody says that the Dzogchen path is easy for everyone. It is easy for people who can simply recognize their own sheer essence dimension. It is not easy for people with a lot of defilements.

The Old Translation school known as Nyingma offers a presentation of nine vehicles and divides this into three segments: outer sutra paths, inner tantra paths, and secret highest tantric paths. The three sutra vehicles consist of hearers, solitary realizers, and bodhisattvas. Their vehicles are causal paths. The three inner paths are action, performance, and yoga tantra. The three secret paths of power and initiation are the great, high, and utmost or highest paths (*maha, anu,* and *ati*). These are a lama's supreme quintessential instructions.

Strand of Jewels is my collection of the inconceivable and quintessential key instructions I received from my teachers.

It contains not only the essential teachings of one profoundly kind lama, but the genuine essence of many lamas' quintessential instructions, which I have gathered here in one place for my heart disciples. Though I myself, Khetsun Sangpo, am an ordinary person, these essential instructions are very special.

Each piece of guidance is a jewel, and my collection of them here is a strand of jewels. Coming from the heart of experience, it is heartfelt. And it is straightforward because it does not aim to flatter but indicates very clearly where you or other practitioners may be in error, and how to undo those errors. Just like the famous wish-fulfilling jewel that allows anyone who sees it, if the situation is genuinely ripe, to reap whatever they seek, so it is with these instructions. Our purpose is the state of Buddhahood and these very special teachings, like wish-granting jewels, make it possible to fulfill all our wishes.

In this life, our body depends on the kindness of our mother and father. No gift from a friend can compare with this body or with the kindness we receive from our parents. But not even this compares with the kindness that our lama extends over many lifetimes. For us to connect with a lama and listen to teachings in this life is a very special opportunity. Even if we don't have much by way of wealth or resources, we can feel deep satisfaction when we recognize that we have met a lama who can help us overcome whatever obstructs our vision and that through depending on this lama we can come to a correct way of being. This is a very promising situation.

Therefore, I begin *Strand of Jewels* by honoring my teachers' kindness, which I describe as splendid. Why? A lama actually has two kinds of splendor. One is the sheer essence dimension, the completion of the lama's own purpose and functioning. The other is the emanation dimension, a vehicle for helping others. These are the lama's two splendors.

The Tibetan word *lama* translates the Sanskrit word *guru.* The first part of the word, *la* (*bla*) refers to the life of the teachings, and also what brings them to life. We access Buddha Shakyamuni's teachings through the lama's speech. Unless we meet a lama, the teaching does not come to life for us, it has no power. Thus, we have this word *la*. And *ma* is "mother" in the sense that the lama, our teacher, has a potent sense of compassionate concern for us and all beings, just like the compassionate concern a mother has for her child.

Why do we bow down to the excellent lama? Our bow indicates the lama's sacred excellence as someone who speaks, expresses, and teaches the excellent Dharma. Dharma is a sacred excellence because it enables us to cut through or sever all afflictions. In this way, the Tibetan word for "dharma," *chö* (*chos*), also means "to cut or sever"—that is, *jö* (*gcod*). Dharma's main purpose is to sever afflictions. A lama has done this, and is therefore excellent.

My homage here refers not just to one lama but to excellent lamas. Why the plural? Because we do not speak only of the lama before our eyes, but of the entire lineage of lamas beginning with Samantabhadra, the dimension of sheer essence, followed by Vajrasattva, the richly resplendent dimension, and Garab Dorje, the emanation dimension, then Shri Singha, and down through all the lineage lamas to our own lamas. They are like an unbroken strand of beads. Hence, we pay respects to many lamas.

In bowing to the excellent, splendid lamas whose kindness is unequalled, we take the highest part of our body, our head, and bring it down to the lowest part of the lama's body, the feet, and to the ground. What does this signify? We offer up our pride. In doing so, we seek to diminish our afflictions, both the afflictive obstructions that prevent liberation and the more subtle obstructions to omniscience. These block us from attaining Buddhahood. And as we bow we make a prayer: "May I accomplish the unsurpassed state of Buddhahood. This is my prayer as I offer homage to you."

And then the text says "I take refuge in the lamas." This is a conventional refuge oriented toward ultimate refuge. Ultimate refuge means that by relying on the unsurpassed kindness of our teachers and practicing what they teach us, we become able to separate from our defilements. Having done so, we can't help but arrive at the unsurpassed state of Buddhahood. Until we accomplish the ultimate refuge, we engage in conventional refuge by, for example, accumulating one hundred thousand prostrations.

Having paid homage in this way, I then request the lama to bless my mindstream. My mind holds many erroneous views, and I fall under their power. I am like a blazing fire. As a result, I will be born in a lower rebirth; there is no other possible outcome. Therefore I ask for the lama's compassion and blessing to pour down on me like a waterfall, extinguishing all my afflictions so that my mind is at peace, tamed, no longer unruly.

What follows is an explanation for my heart children, those excellent heirs with the karmic connection to gather a little of the enduring quality of the sheer essence dimension. Such is the talk that will come from this aged one's excellent former teachers and their quintessential instructions.

5 Your Original Face

Base, Path, and Fruition

THE UNCHANGING NATURE of your own mind is its abiding state. This is your most basic mind. And right there with it are the three spontaneously occurring dimensions of enlightenment: the sheer essence dimension, or dharmakāya, is emptiness; the richly resplendent dimension, or sambhogakāya, is unceasing luminosity; and the emanation dimension, or nirmāṇakāya, is Buddha's special activities for the sake of living beings. All these qualities are spontaneously, automatically, and completely present. You do not have to make or fabricate them.

When you see and understand your own naked face, which is emptiness, you are a Buddha. So long as you do not understand it, you are a sentient being. Why is it so vital to understand your real nature? Because your own real and excellent qualities are spontaneously present there. Once you directly and nakedly see these sheer essence dimension qualities, there arises the playful emergence of the richly resplendent dimension. This supreme of all methods is accomplished with ease!

This is the path traversed by all great holders of sheer awareness: the *rigzin,* the great adepts, or *mahasiddhas*. We call this extraordinary path "the very secret Great Perfection." It is as widely revered as our sun and moon. We call it "secret" because not everyone is a vessel for it. Unless you have the appropriate karma, it is not a teaching for you.

On this path, you proceed by degrees. Its stage-by-stage

instructions center on three principles: the base, the path, and the fruition. Each one of these is a great completeness and that is part of why it is such an accessible path, easily understood and easily accomplished.

The three dimensions of enlightenment are all present in the base, path, and fruition. In the context of the base, the three dimensions are essence, nature, and compassionate responsiveness. In the context of the path, they are dynamic display, playful emergence, and ornamentation. In the context of the fruition, they are the three Buddha dimensions of sheer essence, rich resplendence, and emanation. In short, these three dimensions suffuse base, path, and fruition. It it worth repeating that so long as we are mistaken regarding the base, we are a sentient being. When we liberate that error, we are an enlightened Buddha.

Now that we have briefly indicated the significance of the three dimensions of enlightenment in base, path and fruition, we focus on these three in the context of the base, the first topic explained in *Strand of Jewels.*

The abiding state of the base is the sheer essence dimension. From the perspective of this dimension, Buddhahood is utterly unchanging. Its base, path, and fruition are of one taste and undifferentiated. Still, when adventitious defilements obscure our real nature, like clouds over the sun, we are a sentient being. The moment clouds disperse, the sun shines forth.

Likewise, when we separate from our defilements, the Buddhahood of the two purities can arise. The primordial and ever-present Buddha is the first purity, and the Buddhahood that arises upon the dispersal or purification of defilements is the second purity. This position is characteristic of Nyingma Dzogchen.

To speak of the two purities takes into account the presence, right now, of your own unchanging Buddhahood and also acknowledges the Buddhahood that emerges only once your adventitious afflictions are purified. The abiding state of the base that does not change is the actual primordial knowing, which we could also call our original, sheer awareness. That beginningless wisdom's nature is the spontaneous presence of the three great qualities of omniscience, kindness, and power associated with the three dimensions of enlightenment. These manifest only at Buddhahood.

Our unceasing and intrinsic clarity is associated with the triad of dynamism, playful emergence, and ornamentation. As mentioned, these are the three dimensions of enlightenment at the time of the path. They become fully manifest at the time of fruition.

The sheer essence dimension of the base[251] is empty of any kind of appearance, which means it is free of any stain.[252] Still, just as things can appear in the sky, so there can be appearance, because this empty base is also a base for the arising of appearances. Its capacity for appearances is called its "dynamism of display."[253]

We can also say that the dynamism of display is associated with the sheer essence dimension; the playful emergence with the richly resplendent dimension; and the further activity of these appearances, known as ornaments, with the emanation dimension. These engage in actually relating with and helping living beings.

Again, though we speak of the three dimensions of enlightenment in terms of the path, these dimensions are not fully evident until the time of fruition. Dzogchen's explanation of the enlightenment dimensions wholly accords with the explanations in all the great Mahayana texts. Yet here path and the fruition are utterly of one taste, indivisible. Until we realize this, we are sentient beings; once we realize it, we are Buddhas.

The base in this context is the basis of everything; it is a state of emptiness, unconditioned in nature. The occasion of the base itself is when we are neither with nor without realization, neither a Buddha nor a sentient being. Neither liberation nor mistakenness has occurred.

All of Buddha's vast teachings discuss the empty state, essence of the Blissful Ones, which exists in the mindstream of every living being. Buddha spoke these limitless doctrines for the sake of our realizing this very state—the enlightened state, essential heart of the Blissful Ones. This was taught in precise accordance with the level of his fortunate disciples and trainees. In this way, for the sake of living beings, many different kinds of teachings arose, as well as the Buddha's inconceivable miraculous activities.

The path of Great Completeness is the abiding state that is self-risen and naturally settled. This state, in no way fabricated by our conventional mind, is our actual condition. In order to enter this abiding state of great completeness, we engage in practices of serene abiding and special seeing. There are extensive explanations of these as methods for moving along the path.

The fruitional great completeness is a full manifestation of the three Buddha dimensions, wholly free from defilement. This is when a Buddha of the two purities becomes manifest. Once these three dimensions manifest, we engage in many kinds of beneficial activities.

In short, in the following pages we explain and explore the abiding state of the base, the way of liberation of the path, and attainment of fruition.

The base is unstained, but the allground obscures. When we get caught in it, we fail to identify our ongoing, uninterrupted abiding state.[254] In this sense we are obscured and unaware. This allground is a grasper. It is neutral and dull. As Dzogchen practitioners, we seek to counter this allground by focusing on our sheer essence dimension.

An easy way to understand the allground is to think of it as the ground of all error. In fact, a synonym for it is "error base."[255] If you cultivate the allground, you develop more obscuration and error. Dzogchen meditation does away with the obscuring allground, bringing forth qualities absent from it, especially clarity and awareness.

Brief Explanation of the View

Factors such as clarity and awareness come to the fore when a lama identifies the view for us. In receiving this identification, we gain the possibility of maintaining continuous awareness, remaining in the view with a clear and sharp mind. This is how we overcome the obscuring allground. Most simply, sheer awareness is an antidote to the allground.

To free ourselves from the obscuring allground, we must distinguish it from our sheer essence dimension. That is our practice. As we learn to distinguish the unawareness characterizing the allground from the sheer essence dimension, we discover that the allground is neutral. The sheer essence dimension is not neutral. All omniscient wisdom is present there. Whereas the allground is a place of ignorance, sheer essence dimension is a state of wisdom.

We also distinguish between allground and allground consciousness.[256] For the Mind Only school, the allground consciousness is merely neutral and lacks clarity. Here, however, in Dzogchen, the allground consciousness, as distinct from the allground, is illuminating, unstoppable as sunlight. It is [both] mind (*sems*) and mental functioning (*yid byed*).[257] Mental functioning is what identifies objects as "I" and "mine."

Mind is the allground consciousness.[258] In this context, "mental functioning" (*yid*), which arises from the allground consciousness, is a stronger term than "mind" (*sems*).

Thus, again, in Dzogchen meditation we counter our allground obscuration; we focus on the sheer essence dimension, seeking clear presence. Such meditation becomes possible when a lama identifies the view for us. Once we recognize the view, it becomes possible to maintain continuous awareness of it with a clear, sharp mind. This is how we leave the obscuring allground behind.

Even though nothing is truly established, even though there is nothing there to hold, we grasp. This is how we operate. There is not one iota's worth of something that you could actually point to or which, if you analyzed carefully, you could actually find. In other words, nothing *truly* exists. Nonetheless, our experience of things as truly existent does exist. This means there is a great difference between how things are and how they appear to us. Likewise, in dreams things appear, even though there is nothing to hold on to, and in fact nothing like that object is really there at all. If you close your eyes you may temporarily see some sort of appearance. But if you actually try to point it out, you can't find it.

Despite this, we hold very strongly to things as permanent and we develop great attachment to things we conceive of as true. Based on that holding, the six realms and the beings in them arise throughout our beginningless time as sentient beings. We have grown accustomed to apprehending things this way. We have endless familiarity with our misconstrued sense that these things are real.

The five sense-doors are agents of this yearning attraction we all have to the things that seem real when they appear to our eyes, ears, and other senses. In pointing this out, *Strand of Jewels* brings our attention to how people not yet ennobled by awakening to direct experience inevitably grasp and conceptualize objects of the senses. Such misperception is one among the seven types of mind classified in the study of minds and knowers (*blo rig*).[259]

It is astonishing that you can't really point to what it is you are grasping. You try to point at it, and it isn't there. At the same time you have feelings, you have these experiences, there is something. It is not that the things you see do not exist at all. Anything available to the senses, or any experience we might describe, is not one bit different in status from a dream. The essence of a dream is that something which is not really there, which is not truly established, nonetheless appears to us. None of it is something we can get our hands on. And there is nothing to point the mind at.

We need to realize that this is the case for all living beings. And once we get this, grasping dissolves. Such is the perspective of the ultimate state, the perspective of sheer awareness.

In practicing the Soaring Path (*thögel*), you may see appearances inside rainbow orbs. But these are not truly established appearances. You may see a pillar, you may see a pot, but these cannot perform the functions of pillar or pot; they are just appearances. It's like drawings on butter: these images are not functioning things, nothing substantial is there, and certainly nothing for you to put your hands on. Yet we hold very strongly to things as real or permanent. It is clear that we develop great attachment to what we conceive of as true. Since time without beginning we have been accustomed to this mistaken way of regarding everything. All six realms and all the beings in them arise because of this. It is not that what we see does not exist at all. But we don't know its reality. Such is the mistaken path of all ordinary beings.

In failing to recognize the reality of our own mind, we remain unaware of our own sheer awareness, our basic awareness. Blind to our mind's real nature, we are obscured even from realizing that we are obscured! This self-obscuration is our inborn unawareness. Because it has existed forever, it is also known as a great beginningless darkness. This is what Longchenpa refers to when he says in *Great Chariot*:

> From the perspective of not recognizing itself
> Our own primordial knowing is called "inborn unawareness."[260]

Because of this failure of our awareness, we wander about as confused, ordinary beings.

The Ordinary Mind: Eighty Conceptions

Our grasping mind comprises eighty types of conceptions. Aryadeva lists these in his *Lamp Distilling the Practices*. Thirty-three of these are connected with hatred, forty with desire, and seven with obscuration. The thirty-three associated with hatred have the nature of wisdom, the forty associated with desire have the nature of skillful means, and the final seven have the nature of ignorance. All are related with suffering. The greater, middling, and lesser forms of hatred, desire, and obscuration are what draw us from one life to the next. These three sets of conceptions are paralleled by greater, middling, and lesser vanquishing of them. When suffering decreases, we are at peace.

Longchen Rabjam's *Fine Chariot*[261] mentions delusion in the context of the *Sutra on the Questions of Bhadra the Magician*. How did our illusions come to be? What provokes them into existence? Unwholesome actions from our past lead to emanations and illusions associated with painful places of rebirth. All suffering in the hell, hungry ghost, and animal realms comes from our prior negative actions. All inhabitants of the six realms are emanations of predispositions associated with karma. All are illusory insofar as they depend on a chain of actions and prior existences.

Seven days before they die, gods see that, after such a long period of enormous pleasure, they are about to fall into a low and painful rebirth; seeing this, they suffer more than those in the hell realms. Demigods suffer constant battle. Humans suffer from birth, old age, sickness, and death, as well as the three kinds of suffering—the suffering of pain, the suffering of change, and the pervasiveness of pain. Even though all this is unbearable, we have to experience it as long as we continue accumulating karma, or actions.

Anything arising from causes and conditions is illusory, just like reflections in a mirror are illusory. They are not actually there. Even though it looks as if they are. This is what Longchenpa refers to when he cites the *Sutra on the Questions of Bhadra the Magician*:[262]

> Magical illusions issue forth from karma and
> Wander the six realms,
> Illusions issuing forth from causal conditions[263]
> Are reflections in a mirror. And so on!

Buddha, the glorious one, is like an illusion, like a dream. Buddha's disciples, who emanate from the sheer essence dimension, are also like illusions. Likewise with the monks Shariputra and Maudgalayana and all others who emanate by the power of the dharma and who are like auspicious vessels—you reach inside, and whatever you want comes into your hand. Not only this but, as it states in the *Mother Perfection of Wisdom Sutra*, all phenomena are like illusions, like dreams.

Whatever we think, whatever we see, is illusory. There is nothing beyond that. Everything throughout all of the six realms of existence is an illusion: cities of illusions, illusory beings taking illusory enjoyment, whose pleasure and pain are all illusory, whose creation and destruction are likewise illusory. Nothing here is real. It is all a lie.

The teachings of Dharma are also an illusion. However, this illusory Dharma is the antidote to our illusory delusion.

It is important to realize that our entire experience of all six realms, the whole of cyclic existence, is based on erroneous perception. We are deluded by everything that appears to us. These things that appear are illusory and dreamlike, nothing more.

In addition to coming to grips with this, we want to recognize that our own allground holds seeds for both samsara and nirvana. Samsara's three realms—the desire, form, and formless realms—are a containing vessel and we living beings are its essential contents. Each relies on the other. There is not one iota of ultimate existence to any of this. All are conventional appearances that conceal ultimate reality from us and give rise to conceptions about them. These conceptions have their source in the various predispositions held in the allground. If the allground had form, these conceptions would be its limbs. In short, our eighty conceptions are a chain of error. They multiply and increase as one link leads to another.

The Dzogchen tantra known as *Open Presence Naturally Dawning* describes the allground as the basis of all the predispositions that obscure every embodied being. We see what seem to be external objects and then grasp at them. This sets in motion the whole of cyclic existence. Because of this chain of errors we wander without end.

Not a single one of our 80 conceptions has true or inherent existence. Our afflictions and wrong views arise from them. It is the nature of these 80 to arise both day and night. When we take the daytime 80 conceptions as one category, and the nighttime 80 as another, they become 160. As Aryadeva mentions, all our 98 afflictions and 62 wrong views arise from this, every one of them empty of any inherent existence. They too are like illusion and dreams.

The Seven Conceptions Associated with Obscuration

As practitioners, we seek to cease the seven conceptions associated with obscuration. "Obscuration" is a term found in many texts; a synonym for it used by the Exemplifiers (*Vaibhāṣika*) is "obtainer," meaning that we have obtained and sustained this ignorance from time without beginning, right up to this moment. The Exemplifiers use the term "obtainer" for what most texts refer to as "obscuration." They are the only ones who use the term this way.

All afflictions and erroneous misconceptions, including the seven conceptions, arise from our inborn ignorance. This ignorance is always with us. All mistaken minds, mistaken appearances, all types of predispositions on the allground, arise from this failure of recognition. This nonrecognition is the basis for error in all living beings. Such unawareness is inborn. Because of it, we hold as "me" something that is not "me." Based on it, we take objects to be external, even though there really are no external objects. Would you not be mistaken in thinking that your shadow is altogether separate from your body? Mistaken appearances arise and we are lulled into affirming them. *The Unimpeded-State Tantra*[264] says:

> Once awareness fails to dawn in the basis[265]
> There is no knowing at all, we are stupefied.
> That very unawareness is the cause of delusion.[266]

Desire, hatred, and ignorance come about based on this unawareness, this holding to self. All the seven thoughts associated with obscuration, the mind of attainment, are to cease.

These are the seven conceptual thoughts listed in Aryadeva's *Lamp Distilling the Practices*; together they comprise what is known as middling desire:[267] (1) unclear appearance, (2) forgetfulness, (3) error, (4) intentional speechlessness, (5) discouragement, (6) laziness, and (7) doubt.

"Middling desire" refers to a relatively dull, or midrange, type of desire. "Unclear appearance" means that the mind is not clear. "Forgetfulness" is, for example, speaking and then forgetting what we said; in other words, our mind is not steady. "Error" means thinking that what is, is not, or that something which is not, actually is. This refers especially to the mistaken appearances that come about through not realizing actuality, the error that keeps us in cyclic existence. In this way, we are like bees in a bottle, unable to get free until our errors cease.

When we contemplate just the abiding state of emptiness and nothing else—no appearances such as color or shape—we have a meditative stabilization of cessation. Through such contemplation, all mistaken appearances, all errors whatsoever, are ceased.

Once all defilements are extinguished our five pure wisdoms dawn, making it possible to manifest the magical displays that arise due to certain inner energies.

Our Moving Mind: More on the Eighty Conceptions

The energy currents that flow through our body vary with the seasons. In summer, the chief wind we experience is hot, a fire-wind; in fall, a wind-wind; in winter, a water-wind; and in spring, there is an earth-wind. Overall, wind-currents function to support and maintain continuity of our five aggregates, our twelve constituents, and our eighteen sensory sources. They also provide a basis for increase of the five poisons during the afflicted phase of our existence.

Mistaken appearances arise due to these currents, and the five sense powers [eye, ear, nose, tongue, body] arise in dependence on mistaken appearances. Based on this, we grasp at appearances, and this grasping causes conceptions to arise. This is how things are set up with the vessel, meaning the external world that is our base, and its essence, the beings who depend on that base. Together, these become a catalyst for the development of all sorts of conceptions. The agent of these conceptions is the afflicted mind, seventh of the eight collections of consciousness [the five sense consciousnesses, mental consciousness, afflicted mind, and allground consciousness].

If your energies get out of kilter with the seasons, then in summer instead of a heat-wind you might experience a water-wind. The water-currents of winter act as an antidote to the heat or fire-currents of summer and, similarly, the fire-currents are an antidote to the water-currents. There are meditation practices in which you use the various wind energies appropriate to the seasons and engage their antidote. So one can meditate that such and such a wind, which needs something else as an antidote, is arising. In general, what's best is to meditate using the energy associated with space.[268] Or you can meditate on the wind-currents most harmonious with your own body.

While on the path, these winds, or currents, function as the basis for establishing the magical display that is the Buddha. This occurs based on a meditative state known as the meditative stabilization of extinguishment.

Our tradition also describes five secondary winds: movement, intense movement, correct movement, exceeding movement, and definitive movement.[269] These are mentioned in the commentary on *Heart of Wisdom: Stages on the Path*.[270] Where do these five winds abide? In the five sense faculties. With the arising of these five winds, the five faculties can operate by moving toward their particular objects and in this way give rise to the five sense consciousnesses, also called the consciousnesses of the five doors, which then hold to these objects. We thus distinguish between sense faculty, or power (*dbang po*), and a sense consciousness (*dbang shes*), a classic Buddhist distinction.

The important point here is that mistaken appearances arise via these winds. The five sense powers arise in dependence on those mistaken appearances. Our grasping at such sensory appearance brings about conceptions. This is how it works.

Even though this grasping is powerful, it is malleable. It is not like stone. You can't really point at it. You try, and it's not there. But at the same time, as we have already noticed, you have feelings, you have experiences. The words Dzogchen uses to describe this situation are onomatopoetic words, literally words of transformation, because just the sound of them provokes understanding. Such words, like *dong sang nge*, symbolically express and also embody what they describe. It is almost as if the sound is more important than the translation, which is difficult in any case. The sound is just how they are.

Wherever we go, wherever we sit, whatever we eat, whatever conversations we have, whatever conceptions proliferate, however we engage in activities, everything that appears to our senses is, in that very moment, just like a dream. None of it really, truly exists. There is not one moment of a truly established phenomenon. Just glimmering and glammering.

Please practice to realize that nothing of what so clearly appears to your senses is substantially established. It is important to explore whatever differences you find among things that appear to you when you close your eyes, things that appear to you in dream, and things that appear to your senses when you are awake with your eyes open.

The understanding we seek cannot be had from books. Meditation is vital. We must reflect and explore. This may not be easy, since we are so accustomed to holding onto this so-called reality, even though there is nothing real out there whatsoever.

Every phenomenon in cyclic existence, every possible appearance to our senses, is merely the nature of dream and illusion. We need to meditate on this continuously, unwaveringly, without falling away from understanding how things are. As practitioners, it is vital for us to maintain continuity in our meditation. This is an essential piece of advice on practice.

First Meditation

Let us practice this for five minutes. Please meditate in the sevenfold posture as you are able. Investigate what difference there is between those times when your mind focuses on external objects, on images that come when your eyes are closed, or in dreamtime. This is a very important topic for meditation. In what way do these three differ?

Our mind experiences appearances, but the appearances we experience are not really there. Some sort of clear sensory object occurs, but ultimately it does not exist. Practice, please, to fully recognize that not one of these sensory appearances is substantially established.

Illusions Laced with Holes

When it comes to the base, not even a hair's worth of inherent existence can be found. Earlier in *Strand of Jewels* we cited a passage from the *Majestic Creator of Everything*:[271]

> Past, present, and future Buddhas arise from me,
> and so
> I am definitively known as "Mother of the Majesties."

"Mother" refers to the perfection of wisdom and also to the profound emptiness. "Mother" and "emptiness" name the source from which all ordinary livng beings and all Buddhas arise. To say "I am definitively known" means this is most definitely true.

All Buddhas are born from emptiness. Once we abandon our mistaken mind and access the unmistaken reality of how things are, we encounter our beginningless Buddhaness. This original state of having been a Buddha forever is the essence of the Blissful Ones, the Sugatas. It is a quality that suffuses everything. And so the *Majestic Creator of Everything* exalts reality, the Buddha dimension that is sheer essence. Likewise, as noted in *Strand,* Longchenpa's *Fine Chariot* cites the *Sutra on the Questions of Bhadra the Magician*:[272]

> Illusions sent forth by the dharma are
> My retinue of monks.
> I myself am, in fact, an illusion:
> The unconditioned sheer essence dimension.

Don't feel that Buddhas are off to one side somewhere while we sentient beings are somewhere else. If we look to essence, we find that no matter how intently we seek or analyze, nothing can be found that is established.

We tend to have two kinds of errors regarding what really is. Either we superimpose something that does not exist, overstating the situation, or we detract from and underplay or undervalue what does exist. The first is like taking something small and making more of it than warranted. The second is like saying of an excellent person, "There's nothing good about him." The worst kind of detraction is to say that the excellent Buddha lacks any good qualities or that there is no cause and effect. This is a huge understating of what actually is. It is important to understand that the sheer essence dimension is beyond either of these.

Buddhas, bodhisattvas, hearers, and solitary realizers have all reached the ennobling path of seeing reality. Such yogis proceed along the grounds and the paths and manifestly recognize their own face, the essence that is the reality of their own mind. To know this is also to recognize the state of primordial Buddhahood in oneself.

Tibetans have a famous story about a monkey and a lion. Monkey decides he wants to get the better of Lion and says, "Oh, Lion, do you have bodhicitta? Do you have the loving and compassionate intention to gain enlightenment for the benefit of everyone?" Lion replies: "No one has more of it than me. I am king of the animals, and I have better bodhicitta than anyone." Monkey responds, "I can show you someone with greater bodhicitta than you." "Oh, really?" snarls Lion. "Show me."

Monkey leads Lion to the edge of a large water tank. "Come, see." Lion trots over to have a look. Gazing into the tank he sees an appalling creature with big hair and huge visage. He has never before seen such a face—has never seen himself and so does not know how to recognize his own face. The face he sees looks terrifying to him. He growls, and the lion in the tank growls back. It goes back and forth like this with the lion and his reflection both growling, until Lion becomes so enraged he leaps in to attack the lion in the tank and, of course, he drowns there.

The lion, failing to recognize himself, was deceived by a sight he could not identify. Already in error, he becomes increasingly involved, his grasping escalating in intensity. He grasps at what he thinks is external, when it is really just himself. As a result of this error, he jumps into the water and dies.

This is also our situation. We too do not recognize ourselves. As a result, we fall into a subject-and-object kind of perception. "Subject" refers to our six internal consciousnesses and "object" to the six objects of those consciousnesses: forms, sounds, smells, tastes, tangible objects, and objects of mind. And we become very involved with those apparently external things.

The Forty Conceptions Associated with Desire

There are forty conceptions, which arise in connection with our desire for these apparently external things, as discussed by the master Aryadeva, in his *Condensed Trainings.*[273] Not recognizing our own face is the starting point of all such error. It leads to an acquired and artificial type of ignorance, compounding the inborn ignorance we already have. Innate and acquired ignorance are mental consciousnesses that see subject and object as separate. In this way, our minds go awry. We begin to desire the things we misconstrue as external.

Second Meditation

As before, take up the sevenfold posture with your hands folded. Since we are in the context of Dzogchen, you may also use the sheer essence dimension posture. Either is fine. In the sheer essence dimension posture, in the manner of Longchen Rabjam, your hands are placed like this over the knees as you press each thumb against the bottom of that hand's ring finger. This pressure is a means for blocking the doorway of the afflictions. Along with this posture, take up the sheer essence dimension gaze, your eyes looking upward just a little above the horizon.

Relax your mouth, allowing it to be a little bit open because karmic winds enter through the nose. The wisdom wind enters through the mouth.

In this posture, please maintain the continuity of the empty and the clear.

Questions and Responses: Posture, Dzogchen, and Indrabhuti

QUESTION: Can you give us further advice on how to sit?

RESPONSE: When you touch your thumb to the base of your third finger, don't hold tightly or press on it. No grasping. We are not forcing our posture, either. It is the same with the mind, nothing is knotted up. Such a tight posture or gesture is not comfortably sustainable for a long time. Just as the mind settles itself out, so it is with the body.

QUESTION: Can you give a little more background on the use of different postures in Dzogchen?
RESPONSE: There are several different postures that can be used, including some associated especially with the Soaring Forth practice. Generally, in Dzogchen meditation we use the sheer essence dimension posture with our eyes gazing up into space. It gets this name because it is the best of all postures and because of where it takes you. After all, how could one possibly claim that the sheer essence dimension itself has a certain form or way of gazing? The sheer essence dimension has no posture at all! How could it when it is beyond all thought and all aspects? As the name suggests however, this posture orients or leads you to the actual sheer essence dimension.

In practicing the Soaring Path, you receive initiation into the dynamism of sheer awareness. Then you can receive teachings on postures appropriate to this practice, which have names like "lion" and "elephant." How could there be any such animal in the sheer essence or resplendent dimensions of the enlightened state? Absurd! But postures are given these names because they enhance your channels and facilitate particular states of realization.

Your body's channels are something like the wood that supports a house. Within those channels flow currents of wind. Subtle orbs ride those currents. Completion Stage practice is a way to train in relation to channels, currents, and orbs. Also, there are specific places in the body where dakinis are said to dwell, as enumerated in the *Chakrasamvara Tantra*. Other descriptions speak of tens of thousands of *arhats* in our body. We also describe peaceful and wrathful deities in the body.

Most briefly, our consciousnesses ride on currents and it is very, very important to have a practice that helps cease the karmic winds and develops the wisdom winds—that is, which allows the wisdom wind to enter the central channel. This takes considerable training. All the quintessential instructions regarding such training are part of this completion phase.

In the creation phase, you arise in the aspect of a Buddha, and in the completion phase you dissolve that meditation until you reach a state of emptiness which you then maintain in meditation. These are all essential principles regarding this extremely vast topic.

QUESTION: The Dzogchen path is described as very easy but I find it extremely difficult to maintain continuity, to understand the sheer essence dimension, to discern the mistaken mind.

RESPONSE: No one says Dzogchen is always easy! And yet, as we have said, if you persist, if you recognize your real nature, and if you have the karma for it, it can be very easy. It's not easy for everyone.

The story of Indrabhuti from *The Collection of Secrets Tantra* (*gSang 'dus; Guhya samāja Tantra*) speaks to this question of ease. Indrabhuti lived in Uddiyana, the Ogyen Dakini Land west of India. As he strolled along the roof of his palace one day, he happened to see Buddha and many arhats flying through the sky. "Unusual," he mused, "I never saw a flock of golden birds here before." He asked his ministers whether, in all their experience of India, they had ever seen such birds. "Those were no birds," they told him. "You saw Shakyamuni and his students' emanations!"

Indrabhuti was inspired. "If this is what Buddha's students are like, then I must meet Buddha, no matter what." He queried Indian merchants in the marketplace, "How can I meet Shakyamuni Buddha and his disciples, the arhats?" They countered immediately, "Oh precious king, Shakyamuni Buddha is very far away, and the road there is difficult and dangerous. You cannot go. But if you want to meet him, clean a receiving area very well, prepare excellent food as offering, light some incense, and pray to see him. Shakyamuni Buddha is omniscient and will arrive through his own magical display. That's how you will meet him."

Early next morning, the king swept his palace roof until it shone. He prepared the best food, donned brand-new clothing, and prayed that for the sake of all sentient beings he might meet Shakyamuni. No sooner had his prayer concluded than golden birdlike beings appeared in the sky. Maybe a thousand of them. Maudgalayana, Shariputra, as well as the arhats and all Buddha's disciples were there. They arrived as a group and identified themselves. With each one the king thought, "This is not yet Shakyamuni Buddha, this is not yet Shakyamuni Buddha." Finally Shakyamuni himself appeared and King Indrabhuti bowed to him. Buddha said, "You have offered this wonderful food. You have made fine preparations and invited me here. What would you like to ask?"

"Please teach me your teaching."

"Become a monk and I will teach you."

"I can't become a monk. I would like to become a Buddha right in the midst of my activities."

Recognizing that Indrabhuti was capable of Mahayana motivation and of practicing Secret Mantra, Buddha transformed himself and his retinue of arhats into the main deities of the *Collection of Secrets Tantra*. Immediately all the arhats became tenth-stage bodhisattvas and Buddha initiated Indrabhuti into the *Collection of Secrets*.

Prior to this initiation, Indrabhuti was an ordinary person just like we are. The moment his consecration was complete, Indrabhuti's and Buddha Shakyamuni's state of realization became one and the same. This happened in a single moment. Clearly, Indrabhuti was capable of instantaneous enlightenment. There has never been anyone else like him in the world, as we read in many texts. Other practitioners in the Dzogchen lineage, like ourselves, come to realization gradually. Therefore, it is critical that we endeavor powerfully in our practice. If we simply sit back and let go, we will not achieve the highest accomplishment possible for us.

Indrabhuti was an ordinary being with hugely openhearted and confident devotion. Buddha had tremendous capability. Their confidence and capability in combination made it possible for Indrabhuti to become a Buddha in an instant. The Dzogchen path was indeed easy for him. It is also easy for us because, after all, we have the enlightened sheer essence dimension which is merely covered up for the time being. We have both a mistaken and unmistaken mind. Our six sense consciousnesses are like limbs of our mistaken mind. Once a lama identifies the unmistaken mind of reality for us and we maintain continuity of practice regarding it, we can complete the path rather quickly, especially in comparison with the sutra path, which takes three countless eons.

Yet it also makes sense to describe the Dzogchen path as rather difficult. It's difficult in that we need to make effort; we need to receive initiations and instructions and maintain our commitments. If we do not, we can plunge directly into hell, and that's rather difficult.

In brief, we cannot say that the Dzogchen path in general is either easy or difficult. It is in some sense difficult, and in some sense easy. It depends very much on the karmic connection you have with its teachings. You can look at your own situation and decide this for yourself. If you can understand what is being taught, then indeed it is very, very easy. This ease depends on you and no one else.

Bodhicitta is the foundation of our practice. It is where we begin. We train in its aspiration, in the motivation that whatever we do, we do it to help all beings everywhere. Next, we maintain a state of nondistraction. At the end we transfer and share the merit of whatever good we have done. We pray that our aspiration to benefit all beings will be actualized.

Buddhas and Other Beings

Strand of Jewels[274] cites this verse from the *Second Tiger Root Tantra*:[275]

Sentient beings are really Buddhas
But adventitiously obscured by defilement.

All beings are primordially Buddhas, although Buddhahood is obscured by afflictive obstructions and obstructions to omniscience. In actuality, and from the very beginning, your abiding state as a sentient being is no different from that of the three Buddha dimensions. Your mindnature does not change one iota from the mindnature you have as a sentient being to the mindnature you have when you become a Buddha. Even right now, while we are obscured by adventitious defilements, we have the nature of these three Buddha dimensions. If we were to look right at our own state, we would discover these three dimensions. Once we can see them, it is very clear.

The fruition of eradicating the two obstructions is full manifestation of the three Buddha dimensions. Since you have always been a Buddha, you are a Buddha even when your adventitious defilements obscure this. As we have said, the difference between sentient beings and Buddhas lies solely in whether or not we remain connected to our defilements. A sentient being is someone who is mistaken. A Buddha is someone who is liberated. The *Highest Tantra*[276] underscores this point:

As it was before, so it is thereafter
Reality itself does not change.

In other words, even as sentient beings, our abiding state of reality is present. It is precisely this that manifests as a Buddha and as the three Buddha dimensions. The three dimensions also have been there from the beginning. As stated in the *Majestic Creator of Everything*:[277]

The all-good mindnature's way of being is taught thus:
It is there in the mind of enlightenment[278]
It is there as the essence of everything.

> Realizing it, you are a majestic creator of everything.[279]
> That majestic creator of everything is unchanging
> And is therefore taught as changeless.[280]

The actual reality of any living being's mind is all good. "All Good" is the literal meaning of Samantabhadra, who is the sheer essence dimension Buddha, and whose nature is pure goodness. This Samantabhadra is also enlightenment mind, the abiding state of all things, the heart essence of everything that exists.

To realize the sheer essence dimension, Samantabhadra, is to know the majestic creator of all things. To understand this is to understand the abiding state of all things. That majestic creator does not change. The sheer essence dimension is the primordially present, unchanging and utterly abiding state of everything. When you are a sentient being it is there, when you are a Buddha it is there, fully manifest. The sheer essence dimension itself does not change. This means that your mindnature does not change.

And your mindnature, your sheer essence dimension, is primordially pure. It has been pure forever, from time without beginning. This purity is the essence, the unchanging nature, of the sheer essence dimension. It cannot be defiled. There was never a time when it was impure. However, our inborn ignorance covers and obscures it. What is this inborn ignorance? It is nothing other than our grasping at self. This grasping obscures and then, due to a variety of causes and conditions—for example, the presence of sensory objects—the happenstance of mistaken appearances arises. These adventitious appearances are the defilements overlaying your pure sheer essence dimension. Your sheer essence dimension is like the sun and your adventitious defilements are like clouds covering and temporarily obscuring it from sight.

To put this a little differently, your sheer essence dimension is like pure gold, your adventitious defilements are like rust that covers it. Just like clouds forming in the sky, like rust emerging from gold, like smoke rising from fire, defilements occur in the sheer essence dimension. In every case, what comes forth is self-risen and obscuring. Fortunately, we have many ways of clearing away these obscuring obstructions.[281]

It is important to keep reminding ourselves that the sheer essence dimension is free of change. Its past, present, and future are the same. So what arises? Your self-originated primordial knowing, a natural sheer awareness. Utterly simple, this presence is free from any complexity, elaboration or mental proliferation. It is the key principle, the real nature of everything.

All our practice involves clearing away defilements that temporarily obscure our sheer essence dimension. All practices are included in method and wisdom. Together, method and wisdom have an enormous capacity to overcome such defilements. The sheer essence dimension they obscure is the majestic Buddhas' own final state of understanding.

Guru Rinpoche also taught the indivisibility of method and wisdom. Method is your ceaseless presence to your own real nature. In short, the method is primordial knowing. The unborn nature of primordial knowing is wisdom.

Realizing the Great Seal

Method and wisdom are an indivisible union. We call this union "the great primordial knowing." It is the abiding state of everything. The splendid and superior Nagarjuna teaches that the network of our afflictions—desire, hatred, ignorance, pride, and jealousy—is like a piece of woven cloth with space between warp and woof of the weave.[282] This net covers our real nature. So long as that cover is there, we are a sentient being. Once you doff that garment and are no longer wearing these interwoven afflictions, you are a Buddha. Many great figures of India and Tibet have made this point.

The Great Seal, Mahamudra, is practiced in the lineage that begins in India with Tilopa and then moved to Tibet with

Marpa and Milarepa, where it became very widespread through their great example.

Tilopa and his student Naropa, the great siddhas of India, taught that method and wisdom are central. They identified the primordial knowing of inborn bliss and emptiness as the Great Seal and mainly emphasized the essential method path. These practices were also set forward by their students, the translator Marpa and his famous student Milarepa, as well as Milarepa's own foremost student, Rechungpa. Marpa also studied with the Indian teacher Maitripa whose teacher was Lama Lord Shvari Rithro Wangchug, and who studied with Nagarjuna's teacher, Saraha.

They all consider wisdom, which is emptiness, to be key, and so here emptiness itself gets the name "wisdom." The Great Seal means making this wisdom-emptiness primary in practice and in teaching.

Highest Yoga Tantra is another way of setting forth this practice. Its emphasis is on emptiness as not made by one's mind, and on mind itself as free of directional bias, uncontrived, and fresh. Therefore we simply let it be, just as it is. This is the Great Seal.

Garwang Chögyi Dragpa, also known as Gonpo Dorje,[283] was a student of the translator Marpa and a prolific writer as well as a great yogi in the Drukpa Kagyu lineage. [Another great Kagyu master] Gotsangpa, also known as Lama Gonpo Dorje,[284] identified the practice of first recognizing the luminosity of one's own mind and then relying on the method of maintaining continuous presence to that empty luminosity, remaining so from one moment to the next without coming under the power of thought. He identified luminosity united with emptiness as the Great Seal.

The founder of the Drikung Kagyu school of Tibetan Buddhism, Jigten Gonpo (1143–1217),[285] identified seamless self-mirroring, or self-knowing sheer awareness, as the Great Seal.

The Kamtshang of the Karma Kagyu lineage, associated with the Karmapas, identified primordial knowing as knowing the unduality of method and wisdom to be the final enlightened state of all of sutras and tantras. This primordial knowing is authentic and inborn. It does not change. The Kamtshang identified the final enlightened intent of all tantras as a naked sheer awareness, a sensing of naturalness self-dawning within the stainless space of one's most basic inborn primordial knowing. This wisdom itself is, again, a nondual union of method and wisdom. Stainless space is the empty abiding state. Naked appearance and awareness rise in this domain without any kind of artifice. The Kamtshang call this the Great Seal; some also describe this as the essence of special seeing.

Great scholars associated with the Sakya tradition in Tibet identified attaining an actual wisdom initiation as most important to the Great Seal. What does initiation accomplish? It ripens our mindstream, allowing our self-risen primordial knowing to come forth. [Sakya Pandita] discusses this in his great treatise, *Precisely Discriminating the Three Vows:*[286]

> That which I call the Great Seal,
> Primordial knowing arisen through empowering
> consecration,
> Is the self-risen primordial knowing that
> Comes to be through the two stages of meditative
> stabilization.

This self-risen primordial knowing comes forth through practicing meditative stabilization in connection with the creation and completion stages of tantra.

Kaydrub Trodragpa, also a very great scholar, identified the Great Seal as the emptiness we come upon when we search for the mind's place of arising, abiding, and ceasing. Looking for these three and not finding them brings one to emptiness. Looking at the face of that emptiness is what he called the Great Seal.

The omniscient Budon is also very famous in Tibet. He emphasized the heart-essence of the Sugatas, the Blissful Ones, as most significant. And he wrote many commentaries on this.

The Jonangpa Taranatha, a Tibetan scholar of great repute, took as most central a discussion of the qualities one possesses due to primordially being a Buddha: he emphasized the qualities present in the fully qualified, fully manifest enlightened state. More specifically, he described two kinds of omniscience: that which knows the varieties of phenomena and that which knows their emptiness. Whereas Budon emphasized the source of Buddhahood, the Jonangpa gave greater emphasis to Buddhahood as fruition. One emphasizes the state of the basis, and the other the fruit.

Among the Gandenpas (the Gelukpas) was a great scholar known as Panchen Losang Chogyal, also widely known by his full name, Losang Chogyi Gyaltsen.[287] He was the Fourth Panchen Lama, identified by the Fifth Dalai Lama. In his outstanding work, *Root of the Great Seal*,[288] he writes:

> The Pacifers,[289] the Severers (followers of Machig Labdron),
> The Dzogchenpas, the Great Seal and so forth—
> Although these many different names are given[290]
> When yogis skilled in the definitive meaning of
> Scripture, understanding, and practice
> Investigate, they find a single, harmonious, enlightened state.

Thus, Losang Chogyi Gyaltsen emphasizes that although many different names are used in the various schools, there is one final realization for all of them. This is true whether we speak of the meditation stages taught by the Pacifier school associated with Padampa Sangye, or of the Severance practice associated with Machig Labdron, or of Dzogchen, the Great Completeness, or the Great Seal of the Kagyus. This can be ascertained by those skilled in scripture. Losang Chogyi Gyaltsen further explains that practitioners who have trained in reasoning and scriptures and who also have meditative experience will all reach the final space of realization.

Looking further into the teachings of Panchen Losang Chogyi Gyaltsen, we come to a statement that emphasizes the import of meditation over scholarship. He writes that when we compare those who have studied "how to" books with practitioners poor in book learning but steeped in real experience of the view, the latter are superior. Those who pride themselves on being great scholars may be very famous, may have written a whole lot of texts, and may see themselves as great lamas leading multitudes of students. However, the texts they have written are neither particularly good nor definitive. Only practitioners of the excellent essence with the actual meaning in their heart and mindstream gain realization.

6 Mindnature

The Great Seal in Nyingma

THERE ARE TWO main periods of Buddhist transmission to Tibet. The ancient, or Nyingma, transmission came first, followed by the new schools that began with Atisha and the translator Rinchen Sangpo. I focus here on practice in the Nyingma tradition. Guru Rinpoche, central to practitioners in this tradition, writes in the *Great Seal of Heartfelt Advice* (*Phyag chen zhal gdams*):[291]

> Mindnature, called the Great Seal, refers to the primordial knowing that is a nonduality of clarity and emptiness. All phenomena that do, or could, appear in cyclic existence and nirvana arise initially from mindnature. Presently occurring phenomena also abide within mindnature and, in the end, they likewise dissolve into mindnature's expanse.

Nyingma's identification of the Great Seal is the view described here by Guru Rinpoche. The wisdom which is a unity of clarity and emptiness is also known as the Great Seal. This includes everything that occurs, appears, or exists in cyclic existence and it includes as well the bliss that is related with the Noble One's realization.

Describing mindnature, the natural condition of mind, as the Great Seal, means that primordial knowing is the unity of emptiness and clarity. What clearly appears is empty. Everything that exists, in whatever time or place—indeed the whole of cyclic existence and nirvana—arises in mindnature.

When we explore this, we find that these existing things abide within mindnature right now. Exploring this further, we see that all appearances, all phenomena, simply dissolve into the ground that is mindnature. No exceptions. There is nothing not connected with mind in this way. No thing is separate from, or other than, mindnature. Nothing passes beyond this.

Identifying the Great Seal means identifying your own face, your own sheer awareness or basic awareness. This is mindnature. We recognize our face through the lama's blessings and special instructions. These together allow us to identify the genuine nature of our mind.

Mere identification is not enough for liberation! You need to become thoroughly familiar with it. After all, from beginningless time until now we all have collected a very thick covering of erroneous predispositions. We have been in bondage to multifarious conceptions. Recognition of our nature frees us.[292]

In this way, the lama's identification becomes the basis for all the good qualities associated with passing beyond suffering. Why? Your mindnature has forever been wholly uncontrived. Its nature is the dimension of sheer essence, the dharmakāya. Its unceasing display, its natural radiance, is your mindnature's unceasing and intrinsic luminosity, the utterly resplendent dimension of enlightenment, the sambhogakāya.

We spoke also of dynamism, display, and compassionate responsiveness. Like dynamism and display, this responsiveness extends everywhere to all living beings. It comprises the compassionate Buddha activities that arise in response to the needs of sentient beings. These three—dynamism, display, and compassionate responsiveness—are associated with the emanation dimension of enlightenment, the nirmāṇakāya.

These three dimensions of enlightenment have forever been indivisible and spontaneous. Their being so is the essential natural dimension of enlightenment, the svabhāvavikakāya. If we understand well the triad of dynamism, display, and compassionate responsiveness, and also understand the four dimensions of a Buddha's enlightenment, we understand that all Buddha qualities arise spontaneously. You don't make them emerge; they simply rise forth.

Sometimes we speak of the production, abiding, and cessation of a mistaken mind, but the mind's real nature is not like this. Since time without beginning, mindnature is utterly unproduced, unborn. If you ask whether or not this unproduced mindnature ever ceases, the answer is no. It is utterly ceaseless. Even though it's unborn, all cyclic existence and nirvana arise from its magical displays. These appearances are nothing more than the play of the unproduced. All appearances are empty, an inviolable unity of appearance and emptiness, the natural radiance of the source from which they appear.

Another statement by Guru Rinpoche from the same text is also mentioned in *Strand:*[293]

> In terms of method and wisdom indivisible, the primordial knowing of ceaseless mindfulness and perception is method. Its unborn nature is wisdom. The great primordial knowing, a nonduality consisting of method-wisdom, is the steadfast nature of everything.

In this context, the indivisibility of method and wisdom is the Great Seal. What is this? It consists of recognizing mind as the formless sheer essence dimension. Such primordial knowing is method; its unborn nature is wisdom. This great primordial knowing of the utter indivisibility of method and wisdom is the way of being, the abiding state, of everything that exists.

Guru Rinpoche teaches that mind's real nature, the mind that is reality, is unborn. Being unborn means it neither arises nor ceases. The mistaken mind, however, does arise and cease. Our mistaken mind has birth, old age, sickness, and so forth.

Our unobstructed clarity is like a pane of glass. Sunlight passes right through. All appearances throughout the whole of samsara and nirvana are magical manifestations. From our perspective, it looks like something is arising or appearing. But once we explore, we find that every single appearance to our senses occurs within the sheer essence dimension. This enlightened dimension has no production whatsoever. We therefore want to distinguish between how things look to us and how they actually are. They look like they are findable. But if you actually go and look for that thing which seemed so definitely to arise, if you try to find exactly what is its place of arising, abiding, and cessation, you will not find it. Rather, you can come upon a reality that does not have any such three places associated with it. Everything appearing to your mind or senses is empty. These appearances are the dynamism of emptiness. This is the indissoluble unduality of emptiness and appearance to which Guru Rinpoche referred.

Deep understanding of this overcomes all our attachment to everything. As a result, mistaken appearances and our attraction to them, which are based on our habit patterns, are eradicated. Our consciousness relaxes and takes rest in its own uncontrived naturalness. We simply remain within the reality that is emptiness. Mind is the mother and father of us all, the mother and father of all Buddhas. Realizing the real nature of our own minds is of utmost importance.

The thirty-seven limbs of enlightenment, beginning with the four types of mindfulness, are one important way of identifying the qualities of enlightenment. Whether we look into these, or whether we reflect on the ten grounds and five paths, or the six perfections, the fruition of all of them is the five wisdoms. And the nature of every wisdom is the abiding state of mind, our own mindnature, known also by the Dzogchen term "unbounded wholeness."

The purpose of our meditation is to identify reality and then maintain authentic mindfulness: a natural, self-settled mindfulness. This mindfulness is different from the tight mindfulness that is an activity of the mistaken mind. Sometimes we do need to call on this tight, mindfulness—for example, when multiple thoughts are streaming through us.[294] But we also need to understand that tight mindfulness is different from the natural awareness intrinsic to reality.

Understanding the abiding state—the base, the great completeness—is like an infirm person walking with the support of a cane. This understanding supports us in understanding all other teachings. Yet this is not our central point here. Our point is that we can realize this Dzogchen view without depending on other views.[295]

For example, a child who has been taught and led by the hand can then run wildly as much as she wishes. She is independent. This becomes our relationship to the Dzogchen view, to the base. Your ability to support yourself through this base is your great completeness. If you can support yourself without wobbling in connection with how things are, you can purify your defilements and mistaken conceptions moment by moment.

We practice within the three expanses of our great completeness. As this path purifies all mistaken conceptions moment by moment, we experience fruition—that is, the three enlightenment dimensions and the five primordial knowings become fully evident to us. In this way our own ultimate welfare—our full enlightenment—and the ultimate welfare of all other beings is spontaneously complete.

Your mindnature has forever been pure. Its great purity occurs spontaneously. It has never had any kind of obscuration or stain on it. In the past, the future, and right now, it is free from birth, abiding and ceasing. It is also free of elaboration or movement, any coming or going. It is likewise not contaminated in any way whatever, nor possessed of any graspable characteristic. Throughout the whole of the three realms of cyclic existence and the entirety of nirvana, there is nothing to grasp.

This natural and abiding state of mind cannot be characterized as either existent or nonexistent, external or annihilated, good or bad, high or low. Though some systems of thought will describe it in these ways, it is actually beyond all description. Without exaggerating or undervaluing our mind's abiding state by attributing characteristics to it, we see that there is nothing whatever to be done. None of the myriad appearances in cyclic existence or nirvana require us to do anything in relation to them. There is nothing to stop, nothing to set up. We don't need to abandon or transform them. It is not like exchanging a red shirt for a white one. The path forever remains as it has always been. Its nature of being an indivisible union of appearance and emptiness does not alter.

This emptiness, this abiding state, has always existed in just the same way. It is neither created nor contrived, but ever self-risen. This has always been the essence that suffuses the entirety of cyclic existence and nirvana. And it is a panoramic view, not partial or limited in any way. There is no edge to it, and nothing beyond.

There is nothing beyond because everything is already included! Nothing has been left out. Like the ocean, it contains everything, and everything dissolves back into it. When we understand this well, we overcome every type of dualism and also realize that our view is utterly free of all the deceptions that are associated with duality. This is what we call a robust realization. Realizing the view well, seeing the face of your own mind, and knowing the meaning of phenomena are different names for the same thing.

Third Meditation

Sit as before, and meditate on your mind's abiding state: on that which, when you search, you do not find. This is the empty and the clear. When you see this, remain present to it without interruption. Once you understand this deeply, you will understand all systems of tenets. So please continue in this state, maintaining awareness of the emptiness within which all views are included.

Questions and Responses: The Three Dimensions and the Two Types of Clarity

Question: Can you tell us more about the relationship connecting the three dimensions of enlightenment?
Response: When the sheer essence dimension is completely evident, your own welfare is complete. The two aspects of the form body, the resplendent and emanation dimensions, are to benefit others. These dimensions come about through your merit.

The resplendent and emanation dimensions are naturally and spontaneously inseparable from the sheer essence dimension. The emanation dimension is like a light that extends wherever there is someone with the karma and capacity to benefit from its activities. The moon doesn't appear in one body of water and not another; it is reflected wherever clear water exists. But where there is no water, no reflection can occur. The exact expression of the moon's image depends very much on how clean and still the water is, or how big the water-vessel might be. Appropriate circumstances are needed for the reflection to arise and these same circumstances also impact what kind of reflection is seen. In this way, we need to be an appropriate vessel to receive the ministrations of the emanations. Variations occur based on the karma and reverence of those benefitted. But it is not the moon that changes. From the emantions' own perspective, they are equally ready to help everyone, everywhere.

Question: What is the relationship of ultimate reality to the objects of our senses and to the nature of our own mind?
Response: Everything has its origin in ultimate reality. Nowhere else. Whatever now abides is present in the unconditioned nature that is the reality of mind. Where do all these phenomena of cyclic existence and nirvana ultimately go? Like clouds vanishing into the sky, they dissolve into empty stainless space, the basic field of being that is mind's own reality, or emptiness. Nothing is beyond this.

All the good qualities associated with nirvana arise from recognizing your own face. This in turn comes about through receiving the lama's blessings in your mindstream and through truly taking to heart the lama's excellent instructions. The mind's true nature is the ground from which all good qualities of Buddhahood arise. They have no other place of origin. Your mindnature has always been Buddha, eternally free of artifice. It is the dimension of sheer essence. Bringing all this to the point of genuine realization allows you to experience all Buddha qualities as spontaneously present within you.

Clarity's unceasing dynamism is the Buddha dimension of rich resplendence. This dimension's dynamic display, the activities that come forth in response to the needs of all living beings, is the emanation dimension. It includes the capacity to act as well as a responsive compassion embracing all living beings.

These three dimensions of enlightenment—the sheer essence dimension, the richly resplendent dimension, and the emanation dimension—have been present and inseparable from time immemorial. Their having this nature is called the natural Buddha dimension, the fourth dimension of enlightenment.

QUESTION: Can you say more about the types of clarity needed in meditation?

RESPONSE: There are two types of clarity, so the matter is a little complex. There is the clarity associated with ordinary mind and there is the clarity associated with sheer awareness. The ordinary mind's clarity doesn't help at all with primordial knowing. But primordial knowing can dawn very easily and quickly on the basis of the clear light associated with sheer awareness. To understand this kind of clarity, meditation is essential.

The two types of clarity are very different. The clarity associated with the real nature of mind (*sems kyi chos nyid*) is beyond saying either "it's clear" or "it's not clear." It is beyond any elaboration and, most significantly, beyond any holding (*'dzin pa*) that identifies something as either clear or unclear—that is, in making some kind of judgment about it. Such clarity is associated only with the final view. We do not have it until then. The other kind of clarity comes through the practice of serene abiding. It does not require ultimate understanding.

In other words, the first comes about only through the final view. The second clarity is not conjoined with understanding the view and is associated with a certain degree of grasping in that there is a sense of "this is clearer than before." This sense can be very subtle, but is usually present.

QUESTION: How are clarity, playful emergence, and self-embracing compassionate responsiveness related to each other?
RESPONSE: These three terms refer to developing the capacity of a Buddha. "Clarity" (*gsal ba*) in particular refers to a type of unmanifest power. Playful emergence (*rol ba*) refers to the manifestation of that power. Responsive compassion (*thugs rjes*) refers to the completion of the three qualities of knowledge, kindness, and power that are all fully present in such compassion. And in this context, all-encompassing compassionate responsiveness also refers to a quality that extends or responds equally to everyone, everywhere. You have no sense that some beings are close and others distant; you make no distinction at all in your attitude toward beings.

We have already noted that your mistaken mind and the actual nature of your mind are very different. It is essential to settle this difference completely, and then to experience it. This is not just a question of analysis. Experiential understanding of this is key to Dzogchen practice.

7 Path

Distinctions That Are Key to Dzogchen Practice

WHAT IS MINDNATURE? You must meditate on this again and again, and bring your realization of sheer awareness to it. Until you come to a clear and definitive sense of the distinction between conceptual mind and sheer awareness, your understanding doesn't amount to much. Specifically, you need to understand, through your meditation, what the mistaken mind is. And you need to know, through your meditation, what sheer awareness of reality is. You must see that these have completely different features, completely different qualities. Until you really and experientially know this difference, the correct Dzogchen view will not be realized.

On Sublime Knowing and Primordial Knowing

Sutra speaks of the sublime knowing (*shes rab*), or wisdom, that comes through hearing, contemplation, and meditation. In this sense, wisdom is a factor of awareness. When awareness ripens, sutra calls it wisdom. Tantra speaks of sheer awareness or *rig pa* [with a different meaning than the dualistic knowing indicated by the sutra sense of *rig pa*]. With ripening, this is a source of liberation, for it matures into the actual Buddha dimension of sheer essence. We can also say that primordial knowing, or wisdom (*ye shes*) is the full ripeness of sublime knowing. Neither mistaken mind, nor our ordinary mental functioning through the six consciousnesses, is ever a cause of liberation.

Sublime knowing leads to omniscience, whereas ordinary mental functioning is associated with attachment. Ordinary mind leads to repeated cycling in samsara, whereas wisdom leads to liberation from it.

Distinguishing Mind from Sheer Awareness

Most important of all is gaining an experiential distinction between mind and the recognition or awareness that is sheer awareness. What is ordinary mistaken mind? It is characterized by the deludedness of the allground, by a failure of awareness. In short, it is ignorance. Innumerable conceptions, some of pleasure, some of pain, continuously arise due to our own failure of awareness. The arising and ceasing of different conceptual thoughts characterizes our ordinary mind. Knowing this helps us understand what mind is.

Sheer awareness is an unceasing factor of knowing. It has neither arising, cessation, nor abiding. It has a dynamism that is also a state of being primordially settled, ever at ease. This is because mindnature is basically a manifestation of the basis.[296] Just as it is the nature of mistaken mind to have thoughts that arise, abide, and cease, it is the nature of sheer awareness to be free from this triad.

Mindnature itself is not a realizer: it is the natural condition or nature. The realization of the abiding state of the base (*gzhi'i gnas lugs*) is sheer awareness. When mindnature becomes evident to you, this is the essence of sheer awareness (*rig pa'i ngo bo*). So we can say that when you realize mindnature, sheer awareness is there. The abiding state of the basis (*gzhi'i gnas lugs*) is synonymous with the real nature of mind (*sems gyi chos nyid*) and with mind's abiding state (*gnas lugs*). It is the mind's aspect of abiding (*sems gyi gnas cha*).[297]

The sheer awareness associated with the base (*gzhi'i rig pa*) is aware of reality and has the nature of reality. Utterly clear, it is the sheer awareness of reality. The limpid clarity that occurs on the path is called the "path sheer awareness." This is like a lake bottom becoming clearly visible when all sediment has settled.

When you combine path sheer awareness—the limpid, unobstructed awareness in which the nature of reality is fully evident—with the abiding state of sheer awareness in the context of the base, you have the all-inclusive sheer awareness that is the Dzogchen view. In this way we distinguish the sheer awareness of base, path, and all-inclusive fruition. This has been an analytical presentation of those three.

Distinguishing Mental Functioning from Sublime Knowing

We distinguish between mental functioning and sublime knowing by considering a very subtle type of mental functioning. This subtle mind manifests all the magical emanations known as appearances and conceptions, creating them unceasingly and without obstruction, just as space is the unobstructed place where sun, stars, and planets appear, and where airplanes fly back and forth.

When we understand this mind's real nature we have sublime knowing, but in general we do not understand this. Mental functioning is easily confused with sublime knowing, but they are not the same. Sublime knowing knows how things are. Such knowing takes place within the great emptiness that is the nature of both cyclic existence and nirvana. This is called the sublime knowing of the basis (*gzhi'i shes rab*). This is the first of the triad of the sublime knowings of base, path, and fruition.

Distinguishing Mental Functioning from Primordial Knowing

Likewise, we can distinguish between mistaken mental functioning [which in this context is not different from mind (*sems*)][298] and sheer awareness (*rig pa*). Mental functioning and primordial knowing are like water and milk. So long as they are mixed together, it is difficult to tell them apart. It is said that only swans are able to separate milk and water. We need to be swan-like in distinguishing our mistaken mind from sheer awareness.

Distinguishing Consciousness from Primordial Knowing

In addition to distinguishing between mistaken mind and sheer awareness, we need to recognize the distinction between consciousness and primordial knowing. Consciousness refers to our five sense consciousnesses—eye, ear, nose, tongue, and body consciousness—and to our mental consciousness. These are coarse consciousnesses that do not interfere with each other. For example, you can hear music while gazing at a lake.

Our reactions to the objects of our senses are associated with the karmic currents that move through our body. When we like what we encounter, we tend to develop desire for it; when we don't like it, we tend toward distaste. These and other thoughts are continuously produced. We combine this coarse type of mental functioning, our mental consciousness, with more subtle mental functioning. All of cyclic existence comes forth from the combination of coarse and subtle mental functioning.

All six consciousnesses, including our mental consciousness, are coarse consciousnesses, and all of them cease simultaneously. When they cease, another, more subtle, mental consciousness continues, together with the predispositions it carries. This is the subtle mind, which takes you right to the boundary of ultimate realization. It remains even when the six coarse consciousnesses have ceased.

Primordial knowing is the wisdom that occurs after all six consciousnesses are ceased.[299] This primordial knowing is the full ripening of sublime knowing. In saying this I am not so much articulating a method of meditation as describing what occurs on the path. Although the sensing is more subtle now, all sense perception remains. We see form, hear sound, and so on, but it is subtler.

In the intermediate state, the bardo between death and rebirth, we feel that we have a body, and that we can feel, think, and hear. Although we do not have any physical body, we do have a mental body and we do experience sense perception on the basis of that.

There are many debates and texts on this topic, and you can end up in a good deal of confusion if you don't sort it out. The Mind Only school speaks of an intrinsically clear and self-aware sheer awareness (*rang rig rang gsal*) which they consider ultimate. However, from the perspective of Madhyamaka, and certainly of Dzogchen, this is not ultimate. It is certainly not the sheer awareness of which Dzogchen speaks. It is, however, their way of naming the second type of more subtle mental consciousness.

Distinguishing the Allground from the Sheer Essence Dimension

Another essential distinction is between allground and sheer essence dimension. The allground is the basis or resting place of all [ordinary] consciousnesses. It is neutral, and it remains with us until we reach the tenth bodhisattva ground. On the last three grounds, the subtle obstructions obscuring the allground are not afflictions but are only latent residues of prior tendencies. Once you attain the adamantine or vajra-like meditative stabilization of the tenth ground, at that point, once these are cleared away, the allground is finished and the dimension of sheer essence shines forth.

Unlike the allground, the sheer essence dimension is not neutral. It is omniscient and without stain. All factors of knowing, caring, and capacity are present within this dimension, just as they are absent in the allground.

Prāsangikas do not accept the allground, so they do not describe the sheer essence dimension as appearing once stains and predispositions are removed from it. Still, there is much discussion in the tantras about this process.

The All-Inclusive View That Is Dzogchen

Once we realize the nature of reality, all views are included; nothing more need be realized. We see in *Treasury of Praise* (*Doha mDzod*):[300]

Once you are realized, everything is there.[301]

No one ever knows anything other than this.[302]

Once we recognize mind's nature, we realize the actual state of everything. As the *Majestic Creator of Everything*[303] says:

> I, creator of everything, have a single nature, even
> though
> [Many] names are given by those hungry for samsara:
>
> Some coin the name enlightenment-mind and
> Some, stainless space
> Some name a knower of everything and
> Some also name three or four primordial knowings and
> Some enumerate five primordial knowings.

The majestic creator, lord of all activity, is surrounded by the five lineage emanations of the sheer essence dimension. Their various names are synonymous, all pointing to this dimension. Some use the words "stainless space," while others speak of the expanse of space or self-risen primordial knowing. Others use terms such as sheer essence dimension, richly resplendent dimension, or emanation dimension. Still others speak of the body, speech, and mind of the Buddhas, while others mention omniscience or list the three, four, or five primordial knowings. Such words are used according to the speaker's inclination, but their referent is the same. The view, reality itself, includes them all.

In fact, everything you encounter in either cyclic existence or nirvana is the play of the three Buddha dimensions, your own mind's ultimate nature. Except for being covered by the two obscurations, the nature of your mind is none other than these three dimensions of enlightenment. From the ultimate perspective, there's nothing whatever outside the expanse of reality. Everything without exception in cyclic existence derives from the mistaken mind; all aspects of the path derive from good qualities of mind. This means we are all Buddhas from time immemorial. But this is not manifest. Why? Because our innate Buddhahood is covered by the afflictive obstructions, desire and hatred and ignorance, and by their predispositions which, though not afflicted, still stand in the way of omniscience.

To whatever extent we can separate our real nature from these obstructions while on the path, good qualities start emerging. Still, until we arrive at the boundary of realizing the nature of reality fully, these good qualities continue to be expressions of our mistaken mind. Yes, the very path itself is our mistaken mind expressing itself in positive qualities. This remains true so long as we have not yet arrived at a full realization of reality. When we do, all the innate qualities of our Buddha dimensions' primordial knowing shine forth.

Because the sheer essence dimension does not change, it is not accurate to say that its qualities increase as we move along the path. And we are not saying that. Rather, we recall the familiar example of clouds obstructing the sky or clothing covering the naked body. As these are removed, sky and body become more visible. Likewise, our qualities become increasingly visible on the path.

Candrakirti, in his *Entrance to the Middle Way*, comments on Nagarjuna's statement that unless we rely on the conventional, we cannot realize the ultimate. Accordingly, we depend on the conventions of ground and path. As we move along the path, we become increasingly separate from the afflictions and predispositions that obstruct omniscience.

Having considered the base and path, let us look into the

fruition of practice. What good qualities can arise through this path? In fruition, your mind has real capacity and power. We noted already that, although we speak of cause and effect with respect to the ordinary mistaken mind, we do not speak of cause and effect in respect of the mind's real nature. The objects of our senses are effects, related with our mistaken mind. Yet, this mistaken mind is capable of taking us right to the brink of liberation.

Mind's ultimate nature is the unborn sheer essence dimension, the base. Another way to say this is that the abiding state of mindnature is unborn. The quality of being unborn is a property of the sheer essence dimension. Within it are unobstructed and unceasing manifestations, the rich and joyful resplendent dimension.

Similarly, sheer radiance is a property of this rich dimension. All three dimensions are the same in essence; all are spontaneously present and manifest inseparably.

It is important to distinguish the mistaken mind from its actual state of being and to identify the three Buddha dimensions in connection with the Dzogchen view. We do this by recognizing our mindnature. When we experientially recognize how these dimensions relate with one another, we realize the unmistaken view. In terms of our ultimate mind, we are Buddha. It all comes back to the mind.

If it weren't for mind, there would be no phenomena whatsoever. And without our innate Buddha state we would have no capacity for Buddhahood. Other than our precious mind, there is no Buddha, nor anything else either. All mistaken phenomena manifest from here. And the essence or nature of mistaken phenomena, including the mistaken mind, is no different from reality itself. We are never separate from this.

All conceptual views have targets created by mind and derived through reasoning, through ideas. They do not bring us into the nature of reality, which is not constructed by mind. Conceptual views neither arrive at nor include Dzogchen. "View" in the context of Dzogchen is not about words or description, nor anything constructed by the mind. This view is beyond mind. It is the nature of reality. Other perspectives or ways of being in the world are not called Dzogchen.

Jigme Lingpa's *Chariot of Omniscience*[304] says:

> Two views there are: vehicles that analyze and
> Fully evident sheer awareness.
> Because these views are partly similar,
> One may err in thinking them the same.

Here we see that there are two kinds of views. Views based on analysis are expressed in the various vehicles' description of the stages of the path. The view itself is fully evident sheer awareness. The word "view" is the same in both cases, but to think these are similar is a great mistake. Dzogchen view is not simply an analytical perspective. Its view is beyond all fixation, free of any target to which we might direct our mind. Its view pertains to inconceivable mind free of any fixedness, free of all extremes, and pacified of all elaborations. No wonder Jigme Lingpa says that in this view there is nothing to be viewed!

In this way, views arrived at solely by means of analysis are like stains on the mind. The inexpressible nature of reality, your own mindnature, is completely free of such stains, lacking either anything to be seen or a seer. The view being emptiness, there is nothing to see. If there were something to see, then the lamp, which is one's own sheer awareness, would continually come under the power of the afflictions [because you would remain in a dualistic framework of mental functioning].[305] The same text[306] says,

> Nowhere among the four times or ten directions
> Will you find a completely perfect Buddha;
> Mindnature itself is a completely perfect Buddha
> So don't seek Buddha anywhere else.[307]

The four times are the past, present, future, and a time that is out of time, a timeless time. If during any of those times you search in all the ten directions, you will not find a complete enlightened

Buddha. The empty nature of reality, the empty nature of your mind, is Buddhahood. There is nowhere else to look.

Thus we must experientially distinguish between mind on the one hand and sheer awareness on the other. We must also distinguish experientially between mental functioning, which is another word for mind, and primordial knowing. The primordial knowing of the path is free of conceptuality. It is naked, endless, vast, and unhindered. Mind is not.

To know, just as it is, the essential heart, reality, the actual state of the Blissful Ones, is our primordial knowing. Of the two types of omniscient wisdoms, this one knows how things are, their real nature; the other knows the various things that exist. When these two wisdoms become manifest, there is no obstruction whatever to our knowing. These two are the primordial knowing of primordially pure sameness. This is the final understanding that occurs when you have completely abandoned any kind of obscuration.

Again, primordial knowing (*ye shes*) is the full ripening of sublime knowing (*shes rab*) and it occurs when we have finally clarified our mental consciousness of all obstructions. Then primordial knowing knows everything. At present, we know only a few things. These two types of omniscience are the fruition of actually distinguishing between consciousness and primordial knowing. When we speak of knowing everything, we refer to the primordial knowing that is the omniscient consciousness that sees how things are. A sheer awareness of everything (*kun rig*) is the primordial knowing that sees what things are.

Fourth Meditation

Please meditate without any distraction, one-pointedly.

Questions and Responses: Distinctions Key to Dzogchen

QUESTION: Would you explain further about the difference between the allground and sheer essence dimension?

RESPONSE: We distinguish between the allground and the sheer essence dimension in two stages: first, we discuss the distinctions, and then we discriminate between the ultimate and the conventional.

The base allground is an ignorance that obscures stainless space. This ground itself is ignorance, an unawareness, a state of neutrality in which stainless space is itself [conflated with] the allground.[308]

To call the allground neutral means it can't be ascertained as either virtuous or nonvirtuous. In being an empty expanse, it seems similar to the sheer essence dimension, but it is actually very distinct from the sheer essence dimension because it is obscured by the power of ignorance—most specifically, by factors of obscuration and dullness.

Many dreams come to us in sleep and similarly many different karmic currents move about in the allground. These currents are cooperative conditions for the arising of everything that occurs in cyclic existence. The allground itself is the basis and root of all things in cyclic existence, and the currents within it bring us into cyclic existence.

The sheer essence dimension is completely free from all iterations of conventional appearances and their particular characteristics. It is free from all extremes. Clear and unimpeded, it is inexpressible. Nor is there anything about it that makes it possible to say, "It is like that." In making this distinction, it is essential that you overcome all doubt. Doubt is the worst kind of interference to the correct Dzogchen view. You must vanquish and pass beyond it.

QUESTION: Since the sheer essence dimension is altogether pure, where do afflictions come from?
RESPONSE: They are entirely adventitious. Look at the clear blue sky. Where do the clouds come from? The sheer essence dimension has been an enlightened Buddha since beginningless time. Much like putting up dark glass, which then covers and hides everything on the other side, the fully enlightened becomes obstructed. You can say that obstructions come from the mind, from experience. But we do not say that the sheer essence dimension is the base of the afflictions. Obstructions are the base of the afflictions. The sheer essence dimension is beyond mind. How could it collect defilements?

QUESTION: What is the relationship of the sheer essence dimension to the allground?
RESPONSE: As we have seen, the essence of the sheer essence dimension is stainless. The allground is the ground, or support, for all our mistaken consciousnesses. It is a neutral entity, neither pure nor impure, whereas the dimension of sheer essence is pure from the beginning.

The allground is like a deep sleep, a not knowing. It is also like poison, whereas sheer essence dimension is like medicine. Here, poison is a metaphor for our afflictions. The different vehicles deal with the poison of our afflictions in their own way. Hearers avoid them. Solitary realizers and bodhisattvas apply antidotes to them—for example, the meditation of emptiness. Some of these antidotes might even have a poisonous aspect but can function as medicine. In tantra, you learn to use the energy of the poison itself, much as peacocks are said to eat food poisonous to humans and transform it into medicinal nourishment for their bodies.

Again, the allground and the sheer essence dimension are different. We have already said that the allground is neutral, and you might think that the sheer essence dimension is also neutral because it has the nature of emptiness. But it is not neutral.

Whereas the allground is associated with drowsiness and obscuration, the sheer essence dimension is characterized by the ability to know all phenomena as they are. So, these two have quite a different way of being.

QUESTION: Where does the allground come from?
RESPONSE: The causes and conditions of karma have been in operation since beginningless time. We can't point to a time when they began, much as we can't say whether the chicken or the egg came first. It's a beginningless process. The same can be said about the process of naming. We cannot really say when something first got its name. It is just the nature of things for things to get named. You could never point to the time when the term "water" first came into existence, for example.

Or we can look at it this way. When you study, sometimes you understand well and sometimes you don't. Your understanding is possible because of reality, the nature of things. Without it, your learning would be impossible. Yet misunderstanding also occurs. Those two both exist, the mistaken or obstructed aspect of reality as well as the clear reality. If there were no such reality, then when you got rid of obstructions, there would be nothing left.

In the sutras, Buddha identifies the many adventitious minds that occur. Because of these different types of error, different vehicles are taught. Through study of scripture, reasoned analysis, and practice we seek to arrive at the unbounded wholeness that is beyond all states of mind.

QUESTION: If an ordinary person studies something of which they have no prior experience, do you say that such experience is absent in the sheer essence dimension?
RESPONSE: Let us remember that this dimension is beyond mind. How could it have either experience or afflictions? In terms of our mind, we need to pay attention well, maintain mindfulness, and so on. We have to use the mistaken mind's attention and mindfulness to take us across the samsaric ocean

of the six migrations. We have to rely on it until the time of full realization. Our dimension of sheer essence, however, is primordial knowing, beyond memory or mindfulness.

This means that for the time being we have to pay attention and remember things. This worldly memory, the mistaken mind's memory, can take us to the other shore, once we are there, it can be abandoned. But we need to take it to the end of our path. Once we get to dry land, we can walk, we can ride, we can even fly in a plane. Until then, we must use mindfulness and memory as a method. We have to use the three wisdoms, which come through hearing, contemplation, and meditation. This is all based on the mistaken mind, yet we do have to use it.

QUESTION: What is the difference between the two obstructions?

RESPONSE: They are as different as earth and sky. The first are manifestly afflictive; they are coarse consciousnesses of the desire, anger, pride, and so forth with which we are now involved and on the basis of which we create all sorts of bad karma. This is why they are called afflictive obstructions. They are heavy barriers to liberation. The obstructions to omniscience are not themselves afflictions, but the residue of such coarse afflictions.

Afflictive obstructions are like musk in a cup. Musk is so potent that even after you've emptied the cup, its scent remains for a long, long time. Likewise, even after we've overcome obstructions that are afflictions, a subtle scent of the tendencies toward desire, hatred, and the like obstructs our full omniscience even though these desires are not actually manifest.

Likewise in the dream state, even though we do not see actual objects, we seem to see them. Dream appearances come not because an object is there but because of the power of predispositions present in the allground, the power of our familiarity with those objects. Similarly, even when you attain liberation and are free of all manifest afflictions, something remains that prevents you from omniscience.

In brief, we must overcome our afflictive obstructions first and then go on to the more subtle obstructions to omniscience. Different schools explain this in different ways. Maitreya's *Ornament of Clear Realization* is an important source detailing the categories of afflictions and the stages by which they are removed.[309] As it is said:

> Wisdom is threefold. First, wisdom of the base is understanding how things are within a state of the great emptiness of cyclic existence and nirvana. Second, the wisdom of the path is recognizing the unceasing, unimpeded uninhibited knowing. Third, these two coming together comprises the all-encompassing wisdom, fruitional sheer awareness.[310]

This refers to sheer awareness free of conceptuality, also described as a clear openness, a nakedness without end, extremely vast, free of any hindrance. This vast and naked awareness is what we are identifying. It is the path wisdom. When you combine [the base and path wisdoms] you have the all-encompassing wisdom.

Serene Abiding and Dzogchen

Serene abiding in Dzogchen does not simply mean that your state is stable and the like. It means you are united with wisdom, the sublime knowing that realizes emptiness. This is how practitioners proceed along the path.

Meditation is defined in quite different ways by different systems and different scholars. Here when we speak of meditation we mean gaining familiarity with the abiding state of the sheer essence dimension, the final view. Any meditation that refers to a set of reflections, or to focusing on an object fabricated by the mind, is not the actual view and not the practice we are discussing. "Meditation" here means wholly uncontrived. If you are making effort to get appearances to cease, or to stop certain types of mental activity, this is not at all what we are talking about. Our meditation is simply the steadfast continuity of the unmade, self-settled, abiding state of your own mind. To speak of the various types of ordinary consciousnesses, of mind and awareness, is a topic for the lower vehicles, not for Dzogchen.

A person with sharp faculties can realize this mindnature instantly, like Indrabhuti did. As soon as Indrabhuti's nature was identified for him, as soon as he received the fourth initiation, he manifested full Buddhahood. He did not need to be led along the path, or move through the stages of serenity and seeing. Probably there is no one like Indrabhuti in this respect.

Indrabhuti surely had already practiced a great deal in the past. Just as real familiarity allows you to recognize someone even after a long time apart, so Indrabhuti had a past familiarity that made this instant liberation possible. Other people gain familiarity with their nature over a long period of time, forget it, and then in a later lifetime become accustomed to it again and experience enlightenment. Indrabhuti had no need for such re-familiarization. Ordinary persons like ourselves, however, need to be led through the stages of the path as indicated in the *Cloud of Jewels Sutra*.

Serene abiding is a one-pointed settling. Special seeing is knowing the real nature of things. The specific function of stillness is to submerge (literally, to "push down the head of") afflictions so they do not impinge on you. The function of the wisdom that realizes selflessness is to purify these afflictions completely.

Serene abiding and special seeing are causes that proceed to nirvana. *The Definitive Commentary on the Enlightened State Sutra* explains that these can arise from sublime knowing or from sage and effective instruction.

The insight that comes from studying the twelve divisions of sutra is the special seeing that arises from wisdom. Serene abiding can also arise through analyzing the twelve divisions of the Sutra

Collection. Because some wisdom is involved in this analysis, the calm state that results is said to arise in dependence on wisdom. The very subtle understanding of the meaning that results from such analysis is a special seeing arisen from wisdom.

In addition to these, there is a very particular kind of stillness that we can also call "serene abiding,"[311] which is our focus in this section. First, you cultivate serene abiding in connection with a particular object on which you focus your mind: for example, a statue of the Buddha, one of the arhats, Guru Rinpoche, or your own root lama. Or you may take as your object the white letter AH, or a round orb. Or you might focus on your breath, as we learn in mind-training practices, breathing in and breathing out while counting to twenty-one without distraction. All these are practices associated with an object. By practicing in this way you quickly arrive at serene abiding.

Once we are well accustomed to this kind of practice, meaning that we have gained a specific and very definite state, we can begin a calming practice without any object of focus. This is considered a superb and very special way of cultivating stillness. How do you cultivate this object-less calm, this serenity? You practice with no object whatsoever, only a serene abiding.

This type of meditative stabilization is described in terms of three methods. We begin by entering equipoise, a state in which the mind is fresh and does not wander or follow after any internal or external object. We remain in a state utterly free of mental meandering. If your mind does wander off to anything inside or outside, you do not yet have stillness.

You will not experience your abiding state if your body, speech (or energy), and mind are overly tight. Tightness is like binding yourself with rope and pulling on the ends of it to make a knot! This creates an unnatural situation. Rather, allow your mind to settle without effort. Free of any strain, your mind settles out naturally. This is the second method for cultivating this superb state of stillness, a serene abiding.

In the third method, we do not apply any antidote when thoughts arise. We invite a state of rest, settling within the self-knowing presence of our intrinsic clarity. We abide in this, free from wandering, tight effort, or reliance on antidotes. These three phrases are synonyms for what comes to you through this practice—you find yourself free from distraction, in a state of meditation free of effort, and abiding without any contrivance. These are three ways of describing the same practice.[312] We consider this a calm state because knowing occurs through the power of serene abiding, not through the force of special seeing's discrimination.

In brief, if the simple state of your abiding is very strong, you have serene abiding. If your factor of clarity is very strong, you have special seeing. The union of these in equal measure is the special seeing of emptiness. Your special seeing is therefore a union of the undifferentiated, naked, and empty clarity of the seer, which is sheer awareness, with the seen, the empty afflictions. Right in connection with your afflictions, your serene abiding and special seeing are complete.

Special Seeing in Dzogchen Meditation

In Dzogchen meditation we seek to recognize that whatever arises is a manifestation of reality. Knowing that appearances are the nature of reality, we simply let them arise. We do not take up any other method, because doing anything other than just allowing thoughts to arise within this recognition would not be actual Dzogchen. We simply maintain continuity of that sheer awareness to reality.

The glorious Saraha taught that anyone who contaminates their meditative stabilization with effort, who does anything to set up their meditation or in any way moves from their continuous presence to reality, is not practicing correctly. To waver or come under the power of thought is incorrect practice. To contaminate practice with effort by working to set up causes or conditions so that meditation will be a certain way is not our true practice. When we are not involved in this way, when we do not wander from awareness of reality, this indeed is meditation of the Great Seal. We simply remain in an uncontrived abiding state of mind. This is important. Anyone who does this will eventually have some or all of the three meditative experiences of bliss, clarity, and emptiness.

For someone new to meditation, there seem to be many, many thoughts. You may think, "Oh dear, my meditation is terrible. These thoughts are overwhelming!" This thought itself can be a distraction. Don't worry. Thoughts are always coming and going; no one can count them. The difference is that now we recognize their actual condition. This is good. Before we began to meditate, we were unaware of the constant downpour of thoughts. Now we clearly see how they are constantly raining upon us.

What is it like when you are a beginner at this? Your thoughts stream like water down a mountainside. Then, as you continue to practice, your rushing stream of thoughts grows gentler. Its power decreases. A blissful pliancy suffuses your mind and body. You want to give up all activities and do nothing but meditate.

It can also happen that from time to time you seem to have no thoughts at all. Once in a while, some kind of ideation emerges, but otherwise you are in a nonconceptual state. Your mind is empty. This is a middling kind of abiding. Your mind now is like water settled in a flat place. It stays where you place it.

If you continue to maintain your practice, bliss can arise. You simply remain in the clear and empty. You don't feel your body in the usual way at all. There is no movement of thought, and you experience great bliss. Thoughts may come, but they do not harm your meditation. You have no attachment. All afflictions related to food or clothing subside. Manifest desire, hatred, and the like are wholly pacified. You are completely content. In addition, because of your stability, you may have what we call "tainted clairvoyance." Many kinds of meditative experiences can arise at this time, good and bad. Various ordinary good qualities may arise. You have completed the cultivation of serene abiding. Your mind, replete with these good qualities, is like a calm ocean. Achieving this ultimate calm brings with it the possibility of great error, the greatest possible danger to your practice. At this point it is crucial that you meet with a qualified lama who has real experience of practice.

When practitioners meet with such a qualified and experienced lama, they can develop the actual wisdom that realizes selflessness. Otherwise, if you simply continue in stillness, pride can develop. Quite a bit of pride. Perhaps you have studied some, but at this point you still have very little understanding. Nonetheless, you think "I'm accomplished, I'm a siddha." Just because you have a little clairvoyance, you feel "This is it!"

Be careful about this. Genuinely careful. It is a place of danger for you as a practitioner. It is also dangerous for people who encounter you. Some may feel yes, this practitioner has clairvoyance and all kinds of wonderful qualities; this person is a refuge for me. In this way, both the yogi and the person seeking refuge are deceived. The result will not be good. So we need to be very, very careful. Such a practitioner has not yet accomplished the siddhi that is a union of serene abiding and special seeing.

This person, capable of clairvoyance and all kinds of supernatural displays, has not yet entered the actual Dzogchen path. No matter how much you maintain and cultivate calm, this itself will not give rise to the wisdom that realizes emptiness. Still, calm is the basis for Dzogchen practice and we cannot do without it. Clarity and sharpness are essential. At the same time, Guru Rinpoche warned that we must not confuse this calm state of serene abiding for self-luminous, sheer awareness.

In brief, if abiding is especially strong, it is serene abiding. If clarity is very strong, it is special seeing. The reason we consider the former a state of stillness is because seeing occurs through the power of being calm, not through the force of special seeing's discrimination. The union of calm and insight is the special seeing of emptiness. Recognizing the undifferentiated, naked, and empty clarity of seer and the seen, of sheer awareness and the afflictions, is special seeing.

The Three Doors of Liberation

The three doors of liberation described in the common vehicle, based on the *Ornament of Clear Realization*, are complete in Dzogchen. Your mind's freedom from following after thoughts of the past is identified here as the characterless, or signless, door of liberation. The lack of any mental fabrication, of anything made up by a mind involved with refuting this or proving that, is the door of liberation known as emptiness. Being free from thinking about what might happen in the future—especially from hoping that this or that will come about due to your meditation—or thinking that your meditation isn't going well—in short, the lack of any desire or aspiration associated with meditation—is the door of liberation known as wishlessness.

In these ways we practice without artifice or contrivance. When a thought comes up, we don't go out to meet it and we don't hold on to it. We find that it dissolves on its own. We simply maintain continuity within the view of our own emptiness. When we effortfully try to prevent thought from arising, when we feel disgruntled or distracted, thinking about how thoughts are arising, our meditation is incorrect. Likewise, applying an antidote, like developing love when hatred arises, is not correct practice here. To get involved in any way with a sense that "I'm distracted, now I've got to fix things" means we are no longer in the uncontrived, unfabricated continuity of the mindnature.

Knowing Your Mind

Though many meditate, very few do it correctly. One-pointed focusing does not yield the wisdom that realizes emptiness. It does not bring about special seeing. For this we must look into the mind's essence, its way of being. Can you find shape or color there? Anything at all?

And so we carefully investigate the arising, abiding, and vanishing of our own mind. Next, we look into whether it is produced or ceases. We do this to the point where we have no doubt whatsoever. We want to become utterly clear about the status of our own mind, absolutely certain that it does not in any way truly exist. Once we come to that conclusion, we see that our mind is without existence or nonexistence: it is not characterized by permanence or annihilation; it has neither edge nor center.

Until we fully abandon doubt regarding this, we cannot get to the actual Dzogchen view. So long as we harbor doubt, we cannot leave behind all bias toward permanence or impermanence. So you must gain certainty that the basis of all qualities is neither existent nor nonexistent, neither eternal nor annihilated, nor associated with any boundary or core.

Until you settle this well and digest it deeply, you will not find it possible to enter the self-settled, self-liberated state. You will not know the natural, spontaneous quality of your own mind, or its self-piloting and naturally settled nature. And you will not have the correct Dzogchen view.

Again, merely continuing in obscured delusions of serene abiding won't yield understanding. You are simply tightening up and activating your mistaken mind. This does not take you beyond the causes leading to residence in any of the three realms of cyclic existence. It does not bring forth enlightenment. Therefore, it is crucial, and most fortunate, to meet with a qualified lama who can lead you to the correct view.

And most important in the context of Secret Mantra is that you receive blessings and empowering consecration from the lama. Also extremely important is that you maintain genuine respect for your lama and pray for the success of your practice. In these ways you can invite the descent through your crown and into yourself the entire lineage of blessings from Samantabhadra down to your own lama. Maintaining such respect and prayers enables you to identify and recognize your own sheer awareness, primordially and spontaneously present in the sheer essence dimension of enlightenment. It is not that something new occurs—your sheer awareness has always been there—but now you are able to recognize it.

Along with this realization dawns an understanding of all commentaries you have received and all explanations with which you are familiar. Teachings you received previously meet with your recognition now. You have ascertained the view. Now that the sheer essence dimension is evident to you, you realize that this is the view. Therefore it is vital for you to ascertain the view and then to practice and, finally, to understand how consonant these are.

Our clarity and presence cannot be conceived of or expressed, but can definitely be experienced. This experience is not conveyed through words or signs; all words are extinguished in the face of it. Such wisdom develops in your being, in your mindstream, through meditation practice.

Our self-risen sheer awareness and intrinsic clarity are unchanging. We name them special seeing, the keen knowing that realizes emptiness. Our mind's reality is intrinsically present. Not for a single moment are we ever apart from it. Why, then, do we not understand it? Because afflictions obscure our nature. No one can understand this nature without receiving a good identification of reality and quintessential instructions, as well as blessings and empowerment from a qualified lama. It's the blessings of the lineage that open understanding.

As we cultivate calm, our mind's reality is present already. Our unawareness of it is like not seeing your own eyes with your eyes. For ordinary people, the chain links of thought rising one after the other obscure their own real nature. Even if these people remain in a calm state, feeling the meditative experiences of bliss, clarity and nonconceptuality, they can in no way experience the wisdom that realizes emptiness.

With strong serene abiding comes a very special pliancy and

bliss. You don't want to do anything else. You don't want to work or to study; you'd rather just stay in this state. But this alone does not produce the understanding associated with special seeing—namely, knowing the actual state of your own mind as empty and clear. This factor of stability needs to be disrupted. When water pours down a mountainside, it strikes against the stones, which break its flow. This makes the water fresh and very good to drink.

Fifth Meditation

For all the reasons we have discussed, if you become attached to meditative experiences of bliss, and so forth, there is no way to access real knowing of emptiness. It is good, in this particular context, to break up your meditation, to disturb your attachment. This opens the opportunity for realization of emptiness. At this point you need to break apart your factor of stability. So please meditate this way.

Questions and Responses: Serene abiding, Drowsiness, and Furthering Compassion

Question: What is the relationship between serene abiding and special seeing, and how do these relate to Dzogchen?
Response: When you meditate within the Dzogchen view, you are not overpowered by sloth, agitation, or excitement. Your mind is stable. This is important, because to whatever degree you lack stability of mind, you come under the power of conceptions. Stability is the calming, or stilling, aspect of your practice. It allows you to stay with insight uninterruptedly and for a long time. If you can sustain that, realization will slowly emerge and the view comes very easily. This is the profound view of emptiness, seeing into the abiding state of how things really are.

To really develop this, we need empowerment from a lama. We need to understand and experience this emptiness utterly free of elaborations. Realizing this is special seeing. This emptiness free of elaborations is the view of Madhyamaka and of Dzogchen. Both require an understanding of emptiness, which is a lack of true existence.

QUESTION: What can I do about sleepiness in meditation?
RESPONSE: Give out a long sound of "haaaaaaaaa" and, along with this, give your body a pretty good shake. Or sometimes vocalize a strong *phat* and shake your body. You can do these when you are alone. There is some question about doing this with others around, although if they are also sleepy, you might be helping them! And if they are meditators there is no problem at all. It's just that people who don't know anything about meditation might think you're a bit daft for calling out *phat,* shaking, and so on. Drowsiness occurs when your mind is too withdrawn inside. So it can also be helpful to send your mind out to the far distance. And if that doesn't help, go to sleep.

QUESTION: What is the relationship between compassion and loving responsiveness (*snying rje* and *thugs rjes*)? Both are usually translated as "compassion."
RESPONSE: The first refers to the ordinary compassion that human and animal parents have for their offspring. Ordinary beings' compassion differs in compass and strength from that of bodhisattvas, because a bodhisattva's compassion is directed at all beings.

Besides differing in strength, these two also differ in terms of their object, a difference that depends on the context. In Dzogchen, we talk about the time or context of the basis; we also understand that sheer awareness is empty in essence, limpid in nature, and all-embracing in its loving responsiveness. This loving and ubiquitous compassionate responsiveness relates to the emanation dimension of enlightenment. Such responsiveness is utterly without partiality. It is strong and only comes about through compassion. Someone quite familiar with Dzogchen, a well-practiced person who has read a great deal, would immediately connect the word *thgus rje* with the phrase "essence, nature, and compassionate responsiveness." Others encounter this word and immediately think of the bodhisattva of compassion, Chenrezi, great compassion. It really depends on context, and unless the context is specified, there is no definite answer. There is no end to the commentary I might give here.

This loving and all-pervasive responsiveness is a spontaneous presence, a special heart. Among bodhisattvas, love is a special mind that doesn't differentiate among beings. It is pure and simple, a spontaneously continuous wish to help and never to harm. This wanting to help extends to all living beings. It is an ongoing wish to help them, even if they are your enemies. This is quite an unusual state of mind. Even when enemies are trying to hurt you, you care for them. This is the significance of saying that your responsiveness extends everywhere, to everyone, without bias. These qualities are all present in the context of the basis, but not yet evident. When you are an ordinary human being, they are covered over by afflictions.

QUESTION: Please speak about the relationship of the fifty-one mental factors to compassion.

RESPONSE: When we speak of the fifty-one mental factors, which include compassion, we are talking about the mistaken mind. Loving responsiveness is associated with reality.

The aspiration to gain enlightenment for the benefit of all is like deciding to go somewhere. It involves developing and maintaining this aspiration. Actual engagement in the process of attaining enlightenment is like getting up and moving, as when a bodhisattva actually engages a bodhisattva's deeds. This is the sutra system's way of describing bodhicitta.

For Dzogchen, both aspirational and active bodhicittas are associated with a mistaken mind, although it is a wholesome mistaken mind. Until we gain certainty regarding the inconceivable nature of reality, this is difficult to understand. When I had doubts about this, my own teacher, Geshe Sogyal Rinpoche,[313] gave me a quintessential instruction. He told me that the beginningless nature of reality is like the sun. Unawareness, or ignorance, is like the sun with clouds over it. It's not that the sun gets stronger or weaker because of the clouds. Its power remains the same.

Gaining certainty and realization on this comes down to whether or not we have purified obstructions to it. Meditation based on hearing and thinking is how we remove those obstructions. That and praying to lamas allows our sun to come forward with clarity. It is extremely hard to understand what we are saying here without that sort of experience.

8 Fine Points of Practice

Instructions and Stories

Highest tantra gives teachings on the naturally abiding lineage described as unchanging, without past or future. This lineage is ongoing, definitive, and always pure. It neither improves nor deteriorates. Nine widely accepted metaphors describe it as something pure and merely covered over. Contrary to this, there is also a mistaken way of describing Buddhahood as arising in dependence on causes and conditions. Dzogchen does not say this.

Once your lama identifies your mindnature for you, whether your mind is stable or proliferates out to objects, you see everything within a union of serene abiding and special seeing.

The great Kagyu master Gyalwa Lorepa (*rGyal ba Lorepa*, 1187–1250), composer of many texts, was identified as a *tulku* of Guru Rinpoche. He was an incomparably great adept, a mahasiddha, practitioner of both Mahamudra and Dzogchen. He said that if we grasp any object of any of the six consciousnesses, we are not practicing. When we don't grasp, appearances are self-appearing and self-liberating. We don't hold them as good or bad. They become free, like a knotted snake that just unwinds itself. In this way, we realize our inseparable unity with our own nature.

Some think that once you are realized, all appearances are liberated. Dawning and liberation, however, are simultaneous. If an appearance was *followed* by its liberation, the two could not be inseparable. Conceptions obscure mindnature, just like water obscured by sediment floating in it. When you simply let water be in its own transparency, you can clearly see bugs and whatever else is there. Effort at making appearances arise or cease is like stirring a river bottom. You only muddy things up. The stirred-up dirt, like exerting any degree of mental effort, obscures. Our thoughts are stains on our mindnature. Let it become transparent.

Our recognition that neither sheer awareness nor the afflictions obstructing it are truly established is special seeing. This seer is naked, clear and empty. The special seeing that knows this is itself a clear emptiness, a nakedness of mind. Seen and seer are not separate, for both are clear and both are empty. They are not different. And it is special seeing's place to understand that they are not separate. This is how special seeing and serene abiding are unified. This is how we can carry afflictions to the path.

Appearances are merely the playful display of sheer awareness. No matter how they abide, change, or proliferate, no matter how very good or very bad they are, not one of them is truly established.

When we say appearances have been purified, we do not mean everything becomes empty like the sky. We mean that within an emptiness of attachment, clear and empty objects arise in space, just like objects appearing in a mirror. We cannot hold or grasp those objects, even though they appear. They are on their own empty ground, and they themselves are empty.

At this point, the grasping mind has been purified. It is free from all holding. And now we come to the most essential point: Liberation of grasping occurs right in its own place. Once mind is purified, there is no grasping. Afflictions are liberated. Right in the presence of afflictions, the stillness that is serene abiding and special seeing are complete. As we said in *Strand of Jewels:*[314]

> Not remaining fixedly attracted to any external object that appears to the six senses is stillness. The ceaseless appearance of sensory impressions [within this fixation-free stillness] is special seeing.[315] Immediately on [the

> sense objects'] appearing, your union of stillness and special seeing is complete. To know with precise alertness the eruption[316] of thoughts right when they dawn is stillness. That itself, liberated into a mind nakedly free of mind-ness (*sems blo bral*), is special seeing. Moreover, even when thoughts are present, your union of stillness and special seeing is complete.[317]

And also from *Strand:*[318]

> Even without meditation, you are inseparable from the fact that is reality. Therefore, this is a case of non-meditating meditation. The naturelessness of all phenomena is the mother of phenomena. Your knowing this naturelessness is the child of phenomena. Through recognizing sheer awareness as a stainless space that is reality, you will know your own face.

So long as we do not come to appearances with a sense of "I," what we see are pure appearances. If we do not create the thought of I or mine with respect to anything that appears to our senses, these are pure appearances.

Objects appearing to the senses include such things as earth, stone, mountain, cave, forest, houses, enemies, friends, sons, daughters, male, female, and so forth. When we encounter our child within a sense of "my child," "my daughter," we are mistakenly construing an inherent or truly existent child and a truly existent parent, though neither are there. Yet, all these can appear to us without our constructing them as truly established or real. We can experience them without attachment, free of grasping, and also without the yearning that is a subtler form of grasping.

Again, to say that appearances have been purified does not mean everything becomes empty like space. Rather, things appear in full clarity within emptiness, free from attachment and grasping. You don't grasp at them, even though they vividly appear, because your mind within has been purified of holding. There is only endless purity. Likewise, you cannot hold or grasp objects appearing in a mirror, they are on their own empty ground. This is a quintessential instruction about the liberation of sheer awareness, right in its own place.

Being free of grasping with respect to your mind means that no matter what is occurring, pleasant memories or poisonous afflictions, you are not holding on to them. These arise through some sort of causes and conditions, but they cannot harm. In the face of sheer awareness, even the five poisons bring no harm. How could they? They are clarified in their own place. Right where they are. When these are absent, external objects are purified of being held.

We have already mentioned the example of obstructions being like dirt or rust that obscures gold. When we grasp at what appears to us, the six kinds of sense objects obscure pure appearances, as do our multitudinous thoughts, but only so long as we have not dissipated grasping and yearnings. We have mentioned this already; here I am giving a little more detail about how this process works.

Once you recognize that your own sheer awareness is reality, you also understand the nature of all the phenomena in cyclic existence. Their nature is the same. Knowing the nature of all phenomena, resting in their emptiness, is the mother emptiness, the primordial luminosity. Knowing your own mindnature is the child luminosity. Even without meditating, you are never separate from this reality. As we have said, through recognizing sheer awareness as reality, stainless space, you will know your own face.

Some meditators understand their practice as cultivating an aware presence in present time. However, what actually happens is that they fall under the power of a subtle stream of conceptions. This happens when we fail to be aware [not just of the presence of thoughts but] of the true nature of the arising, abiding, and cessation of these subtle conceptions.[319]

Practitioners may have a very subtle experience of clarity and mistake this for the naked and complete clarity. However, a subtle mind together with its predispositions remains. The predispositions now are very subtle indeed, for once they are no longer associated with the mistaken mind, they are no longer coarse. These are subtle predispositions.

This means that you can be in clear, vivid continuity, and your experience may be quite stable and ongoing, but this is not the actual Great Completeness, not the actual Dzogchen view. Subtle predispositions persist right up until the tenth bodhisattva ground. At that time we have a very subtle mind associated with predispositions that does in fact have clarity and continuity. But some practitioners make friends with the clarity and knowing associated with subtle predispositions. They practice on the basis of that experience, thinking they are following a lineage of oral transmission, when actually they are not. This is not supported by any textual transmission. What they are doing is the antithesis of what they imagine.

It's not hard to see how this happens. Discriminating between this state and the correct Dzogchen view is challenging, since clarity and continuity are present in both. Again, extremely subtle predispositions can remain right along with a state endowed with clarity and continuity. A practitioner with very subtle experience of clarity and continuity can mistake this for completely naked clarity.

This is actually quite a tricky situation. As we know, clarity and continuity are very significant for the Dzogchen view. Still, what we have here is a mistaken mind associated with the all-ground. What is needed at this time is the authentic, or most basic, naturally settled mindfulness. Because such a state is free of effort, it can be maintained continuously. Remaining within this natural mindfulness, not straying from sheer awareness, is a practice known as "mind-holding." But there is no grasping in this. You remain in this self-settled unwavering state, free of grasping, maintaining the continuity. This is meditation.

By meditating in this way you become accustomed to your

most fundamental basic state and maintain continuity with it. Due to your deep familiarity, you need not consider any thoughts to be your enemy, even when they do arise. You remain relaxed and unwavering.

When thoughts do not arise, you need not do anything to bring them on. Remain settled in that lack of arising. As your meditation continues, you will be able to recognize coarse thoughts right away, though subtle thoughts may still go unrecognized. This is called coming under the power of thought. It interferes with meditation. Lest this occur, it is very important to have mindfulness and awareness spying out whether thoughts are coming or not. Otherwise, just like an unseen thief can carry off your goods, thoughts you don't see can steal your meditation.

Meditation goes well when you can maintain continuity of awareness at all times, wherever and whatever you are doing—whether eating, sleeping, walking about, sitting in easeful equipoise, or afterward. The great master Guru Rinpoche said that "though there are hundreds and thousands of explanations, there is only one thing to be understood"—the profound meaning, the real nature of your mind. Once you understand this, everything is liberated. You then maintain your self-aware presence, your own face.

Patrul Rinpoche spoke about a great female meditator who felt her meditation was not going well, and she became very sad. Yet, her sadness was unwarranted. There was nothing she had failed to understand. If you maintain continuity with respect just to the feeling that your meditation is not going well, or any other feeling that occurs, understanding arises. As Patrul Rinpoche says, "Whatever appears or whatever thoughts arise, just maintain the continuity of mindfulness and awareness and your meditation will go well."

When we practice in this way, meditation becomes easy, flows well. And in fact we need that kind of continuity. It is essential to maintain the continuity of your practice once you have identified sheer awareness.

What kinds of faults arise when you do not practice in this way? What kinds of good qualities arise when you do? This is our next topic.

Sidetracking and Slipping: Pitfalls on the Path

Errors are danger points in our practice. In general, error comes about because we can't maintain continuity in our meditative stabilization. Here we consider in some detail the sidetracks and pitfalls that can arise.

"Sidetracking" is taking a wrong turn in an unprofitable direction. "Slipping" is landing in the pit of some particular error.

We have noted many types of profound meditation, including Padampa Sangye's Pacifying meditation, Machig Labdron's Severance as well as the Great Seal and the Great Completeness. Their essential point is the same: remain in an uncontrived state.

Some longtime practitioners say that the thing to do in meditation is to cease appearances to all six consciousnesses, thus stopping both coarse and subtle consciousnesses. This is in no way correct, because one can have strong stability without any knowing. It is a pitfall.

Another error, made even by very experienced meditators, is failing to maintain mindfulness and awareness of actual sheer awareness. Instead, one spends time in an obscured neutral state without any understanding, all the while feeling quite proud and accomplished because of the stability one experiences.

Some have meditative experiences of great clarity, others experience bliss, while still others have a sense of just emptiness. They become attached to these experiences. Yet these are just meditative experiences that occur due to serene abiding. They do not engage the actual view.

Some say that good meditation requires us to cease past thoughts, avoid giving rise to new ones, and remain in a state where there is no memory, no understanding. They consider this a sign of good practice, but it is very far from what we are seeking. Still others, not understanding the inexpressible and abiding state of things, think that some other kind of mindnature is the sheer essence dimension. They mentally create what they think is the nature of mind, but this is just a contrived mental experience that they mistake for the natural sheer essence dimension.

We have been reflecting on Dzogchen's quintessential instructions for clearing away obstructions and afflictions, as well as on sidetracking and slippages. We come now to a statement by Longchen Rabjam cited in *Strand of Jewels:*[320]

> Even once you have identified your nature, unless you gain familiarity with it, you are like a small child in a battlefield, carried off by the enemy—that is, by conceptual thoughts.

Some meditators [correctly] understand their practice as a state of sheer awareness, but are overpowered by a subtle stream of conceptions. They are unaware of the true nature of these subtle conceptions' arising, abiding, and ceasing, yet they regard themselves as free of all proliferation. But they are mistaken about this, and they are also mistaken regarding the nature of emptiness. Being "free of proliferation" is, as we saw in the discussion of Madhyamaka, a synonym for emptiness. In Dzogchen, however, the supreme practice is to identify the actual [empty] face of whatever arises in your mind.

Other meditators count the number of thoughts that arise and cease: "Now the first one is arising, now it is ceasing, here comes the second, now that one has ceased," and so on. That is also mistaken because it involves grasping. A grasping mind and the actual way of being are as different from each other as earth and sky.

Still other practitioners take a continuous and all-embracing state of extreme clarity and transparency as completeness. However, they discriminate between such clarity on the one hand and the way things really are on the other. In this way they [erroneously] construct a relationship [of difference] between sheer awareness and unimpeded clarity. They do have meditative experience of transparent clarity; their mistake is to understand this as different from the mind's own nature, which itself is clear and continuous. To put this another way, they create a false separation between sheer awareness and meditative experiences [such as clarity], thinking these are separate. They want to understand the meaning of Dzogchen, but they have gone down a sidetrack with respect to understanding the real nature of things.

[Some say that sheer awareness is what occurs between thoughts.] They suggest there is a sequence, like two consecutive finger snaps with silence in between, in which they locate presence. As if sheer awareness is only in the middle, between two thoughts! In effect, they are saying that while there is no sheer awareness in the first snap—that is, in an initial thought—sheer awareness *is* present in the gap between this first thought and the second one, and that once the second thought arrives, there is again no sheer awareness! How could we say that sheer awareness is there in the second moment but not the first or the third? Or that it is just in the present and not in the past and not in the future? How can we suggest that the great all-inclusive state of sheer awareness is only this in-between moment? To those who make such claims, Longchen Rabjam responds that this perspective is completely contrary to all sutras and tantras associated with Dzogchen.

Sheer awareness is continuous. There are no rifts in it. It existed before, it continues now and in the future. The stream of reality is unbroken. To say that it didn't exist in the past yet exists in the present and will not exist in the future is missing the point. If you wish to be liberated you should move far away from this sort of view.

According to the Great Completeness view, sheer awareness is unborn and unceasing. Don't be someone who thinks it just exists in the middle of two moments! This contradicts both sutra and tantra. Give up this misguided view.

There also are some who say that excellent Dzogchen practitioners simply settle into an uncontrived state, whereas middling practitioners maintain continuity within, and that the least of Dzogchen practitioners cultivate dynamism. There is no basis for such division.

When your lama identifies your mindnature, the unborn sheer essence dimension, there is no threefold typology of excellent, middling, and lesser. There can be no divisions in this birthless dimension, so anything that has divisions is not the sheer essence dimension. To think of a hierarchically arranged sheer essence dimension means there has been no identification; you haven't arrived at anything and the Dzogchen view is not complete. This kind of view is altogether obscured, a completely new beast, an unprecedented kind of elephantine arrogance.[321]

We can refute this error more extensively as well: If supreme practitioners simply experience their mind as uncontrivedly settled, then ordinary people who have never had any sort of identification of mindnature would all become Buddhas just by quieting and settling the mind. This does not occur.

As for the middling practitioners described here, such a person might think, "I am going to continue practicing now [and in this sense cultivate continuity]. That way, I will have continuity in the future." But they are holding to thoughts of the future, what it will be like when they have clarity and continuity at that time. As we noted already, practitioners have to distinguish the continuity and clarity associated with their predispositions from the continuity and clarity associated with Dzogchen. These practitioners are holding to a sense that "clarity and continuity will arise in the future." They focus on what this future will hold, rather than understanding what is present in their mind right now. And since they are not meditating correctly in the present, they don't have the cause for having that kind of effect in the future.

Others say that the lowest practitioners simply follow along with whatever occurs in the mind, whether it is changing or abiding, and just maintain continuity in that way. They maintain the state of abiding peacefully so that in the future they will be elevated to the ranks of middling and excellent practitioners. Those who say such are completely obscured.

In short, the entire theory of the three types of practitioners misses the point. How can any of these three be abiding with respect to the basis, the foundation of Dzogchen? They cannot. Without a correct identification in the beginning it cannot be identified in the future. Unless we genuinely recognize the reality that is sheer awareness, what positive result can we expect? These meditators are hoping for something to arise in the future even though they are not in the genuine state in the present. This is not how it happens. Poison that you mistake for medicine remains poison. No matter how much you wash charcoal, you cannot make it white. Likewise, as long as you meditate in connection with a mistaken mind, you cannot convert it into an unmistaken mind. This is a pitfall to avoid.

Going along with whatever arises is also a pitfall. All of us now in cyclic existence are doing exactly that. This slipping is a kind of letting go, but not the actual uncontrived state. If we were in an actual state of uncontrived settling, we would be Buddhas without anything further required. This, however, is just slipping along, unaccompanied by greater understanding. It is the deluded meditation of an ordinary person in a neutral state. You have great hope for your Dharma practice, but it does not bring you any positive result.

Non-Buddhists who are either eternalists or nihilists don't discuss such deviations and pitfalls. These identifications of error are unique to Buddhist practice. To practice the path correctly, we need to accumulate both the object-oriented collection of merit and the objectless collection of wisdom. Unless we unify these two collections, we remain outside Buddha's teachings. If you seek the enlightenment of Buddhahood, you must rely on the sutras, tantras, and commentaries and steer away from all the deviations and pitfalls we have just discussed. All of this is a reflection on what Longchen Rabjam stated about these errors. Tsele Natsok Rangdrol's position, also mentioned in *Strand of Jewels*, is similar.

Let me further summarize what is essential regarding the slipping that causes us to deviate from the path.

It may happen that, while within a state of easeful equipoise, and because you are in a state of serene abiding, you have classic meditative experiences of bliss, clarity, or nonconceptuality. You become attached to this. Your attachment is a contaminated experience that can act as a cause for rebirth in one of the three higher realms of samsara. Your attachment to bliss can cause birth in the desire realm; your attachment to clarity can attract you to the form realm; and your attachment to nonconceptuality can lead to the formless realm. Once your karma for rebirth in that particular realm is exhausted, you will take yet another rebirth, at which time you could fall into a quite negative situation with no possibility of following any Buddhist path whatever.

According to Madhyamaka, emptiness is free from any kind of position or directionality. How does emptiness relate to the things appearing to our senses? Is it something that you newly mix in or add on to some sensory object? Not at all. There is a complete union of emptiness and appearance. All appearances are empty. Wherever you look, north, south, east, or west, emptiness is always present. There is no new union to be made of emptiness and appearances. They are forever united. This is what we have to realize to move beyond the desire realm, concentrations and absorptions comprising cyclic existence.

Slipping occurs when we do not understand how things that are part of a causal process, and dependently originated, relate to emptiness. Or when we imagine that emptiness is something outside and separate from ourselves. The key concern therefore is our mistaken sense that emptiness is somehow separate from ourselves or from the things that appear to us—that it is something we stick onto whatever appearance might be there.

Our view in meditation may be correct, but our understanding remains more coarse than subtle. Experiences do not arise as we continue meditating within that coarser understanding. Or we may have a little bit of experience and wish to discuss it with our teacher, who may or may not be fully qualified, and their explanation doesn't fully meet with our mind; that is, the experience you had does not seem to be addressed. Alas! We call this "falling off a cliff," which means that something vital for your understanding has not yet come. You have slipped regarding your understanding of the base.

It's also very important to understand your meditation in terms of the stages of the path. We need to aspire to fruition. But it can happen that we fall into hopelessness about the path. Such hopelessness is also a slippage.

Dzogchen meditation is the sustained continuity of our uncontrived nature. When we refer to this as our genuinely ordinary mind, we mean that nothing new is created. Any attempt to create a better mind is an error, a pitfall due to not understanding the path, which is narrow and difficult to navigate.

When afflictions such as desire, hatred, or jealousy arise, we bring their essence to the path. For Dzogchen practitioners, such afflictions dawn and are liberated. But if you engage antidotes as taught in the lower paths, you create a pitfall with respect to the antidote. If, for example, you try to prevent thoughts from arising, you are in a state of contrivance. This is a failure of understanding regarding the antidote. A pitfall.

Questions and Responses: Pitfalls Regarding Emptiness, Tantra, and Dzogchen

Question: What about the need to understand emptiness?

Response: It is important to realize that the nature of your mind is empty and free from all basis or foundation. Otherwise, you do not know your nature. When you find yourself thinking, "This is empty," you are involved in a thought that is contrived. The Dzogchen view is free from any such contrivance of the mistaken mind.

Or, you might have a little understanding of emptiness, as distinct from a vast meditation of emptiness. This is slippage in connection with the primordial. What is "a little understanding"? Using conventional metaphors here we can say that a teacup is like a little understanding and a house is like a big understanding. The point is that there is a great difference in profundity between a little and a vast understanding of emptiness. When we follow after thoughts, we are distracted from real recognition of them.

Thus, if you lack mindfulness and awareness, but nonetheless think that you have mindfulness, this is a pitfall that lands you in mental activity or conceptuality. You have not understood the actual state of your mind. As a result, you overlay something that does not exist onto the genuine abiding state.

Practitioners who do not know how to meditate correctly encounter these danger zones. Many mistaken understandings of meditation occurred in the past, and there is danger of more in the future. These errors mean that nothing comes of your meditation, no matter how much you apply yourself to it. Indeed, as we have said, it may even create conditions for a bad rebirth. Therefore, proceeding correctly is extremely important.

Some meditators arrive at a kind of nonconceptuality and think they have attained serene abiding when what they really have is a state of sloth, sunk in deluded obscuration. Others use reason and analysis to gain some conceptual ascertainment. They proudly conclude they have special seeing. Others develop an intense, tight style of perception and call this mindfulness. Or they mistake a neutral equanimity for the abiding state. If you start to feel that your everyday consciousness is the uncontrived and ongoing abiding state of your own mind, you have confused two very different states. Despite this latter being called "ordinary," it has a very special meaning. There is the everyday ordinary and the genuinely basic ordinary.

It may happen that, from within your meditative stabilization, you create attachment. Since you have no discomfort of any kind, since in fact your meditation is quite blissful, you conclude this is the supreme uncontaminated bliss. But it is not. It is a contaminated state.

The inexpressible unmistaken mind has no object and it is not directed toward any target. But unless you have gained unshakable certainty regarding this objectless state, you inevitably get involved with mistaken objects of consciousness.

Sheer awareness, the Great Completeness, is clear and unobstructed. To confuse our grasping at or attachment to objects with the unceasing self-clarity that is free from all such apprehension is a pitfall. Another pitfall is to confuse the unceasing clarity of sheer awareness with a deluded state of nonconceptuality, thinking this is timeless wisdom.

What can we do about such errors? The first important thing is to undertake the foundational practices, often called the preliminaries. These are grounded in the most profound quintessential instructions. Through engaging these practices, we accumulate the merit necessary for realization and purify the obstructions standing in its way.

By practicing the foundational practices well, it is possible to cleanse all causes and conditions contributing to obstructions that could otherwise overpower you. By connecting with the lama's blessings through these practices, you become a field capable of absorbing the unbroken rain of amrita that comes from the lama's blessings. Otherwise, you are like a field where the soil is hard and unbroken, ground that can neither absorb nutrients nor bring forth fruit.

In the actual practices of setting free and soaring forth, for example, you may err by either exaggerating or undervaluing. You work at it, but cannot gain certainty. This is the fault, or pitfall, of being influenced by many words but lacking experience.

As a result, understanding does not arise in your mindstream. In that case you are in the unfortunate situation of being neither a Dharma person nor a worldly person. You are stuck in the middle! Therefore it's really important to practice carefully.

QUESTION: What is meant by "contrived" in Dzogchen? Does it have to do with tantric practices of creation and completion?
RESPONSE: We don't use this term for the stages of creation and completion. "Creation-phase practice" means manifesting or creating yourself as an enlightened being, together with your pure land. "Completion-phase practice" involves dissolving this stage by stage to arrive at the view of reality. Since time immemorial we have been born as embodied beings, attached to our sense that our body is real. Tantric practice cuts such attachment at its root. This is how you give rise to yourself as an enlightened being. There are also practices in which the enlightened being is in front of you. Both such practices involve effort and mental activity.

In the Great Completeness we do not do gradual creation or completion practices. We just work with the view. Through the lama's kindness we receive Dzogchen teachings. From this perspective it is as if we are standing on the peak of a mountain, looking down the entire slope, the extent of other teachings.

In Tibet, proper teaching of Dzogchen means that students prepare for it by completing their foundational practices and engaging in creation practices, followed by learning the completion stage practices involving the winds and channels. Then we are ready for Dzogchen, the final view, the peak, including Dzogchen teachings of setting free and soaring forth. Now we have reversed this process. This is the teacher's fault. My fault. We are climbing this mountain from the top down. Once we're teaching from the very top like this, it may be difficult to go back down. I am being straightforward and honest with you. Please don't take offense.

In terms of Secret Mantra's triad of view, meditation, and conduct, when it comes to conduct, practitioners need facility with elaborate, simple, and very simple as well as secret conduct, in terms of their own behavior and also the conduct of their cohort.

Elaborate conduct involves extensive rituals done with real precision and elegance. Simple conduct is doing practice rituals with only the bare essentials. For example, alcohol, meat, and some measure of meditative stabilization are essential for the Feast (*tshogs*) practices. But other than that, you don't use special musical instruments or an elaborate setup as in the previous case. Your emphasis is on single-pointed concentration.

You wonder whether the tantric stages of creation and completion can support your practice of Dzogchen? Yes, definitely. Through deep practice of creation and completion, it becomes quite easy to understand Dzogchen. There's no better friend for Dzogchen than these.

In practice done very simply, you focus exclusively on your own practice. Someone looking from the outside might not notice anything, but you are centered in your practice and mindful of it.

When we speak about the training and reorientation that accords with sheer awareness, we mean that your conduct always accords with the view of Dzogchen, so that you are not governed by ordinary worldly concerns and considerations. Within this view, you are there for whatever arises.

Secret conduct means to practice so that no one even knows you are practicing. This was the custom of the great Indian siddhas. They lived in a time when approximately ninety out of a hundred practitioners were hearers or solitary realizers. Because this majority was likely to develop a wrong view if they learned about tantric practice, strict secrecy was maintained. It is also true that when you maintain secrecy the path is much quicker and easier. Indian tantrikas maintained secrecy very well.

In Tibet, on the other hand, everyone from the king down to the beggars was practicing tantra. The entire population got involved. The king's servants knew about the skull and other special objects necessary for practice, and they took an interest in it.

There was nobody in Tibet who had a thought for hearer practices alone. And in this way, very naturally, tantra spread everywhere in Tibet.

Prior to the ancient translation school of Nyingma, there was Bön. The numbers of Bön practitioners decreased, until by the time of Tritson Detsen there were relatively few and the country was by and large Buddhist.

After the Nyingmas were established, the new schools of Kadampa, Kagyu, Sakya, and Gelukpa developed. Every monastery had its own practices and specific rituals. Even though they were different in this regard, they were not different in terms of view, meditation, and conduct. So in that sense, there was no need for secrecy. Later, however, a kind of degeneration set in, and for that reason people started to put a great deal of emphasis on their identity as Geluk, Kagyu, and so forth. Still, it is really a matter of having different names. In view, meditation, and conduct, they are same.

Whether we are speaking of the old or new schools in Tibet, they all have a single source: the word of the Buddha. Everything they do is based on this, so whether one bears the name Nyingma or Kagyu and so on, the meaning, the view, is really the same.

The foundational practices are for cleansing our innumerable afflictions and defilements. Creation and completion practices train us in maintaining purity of vision and bringing suffering or happiness to the path. In Dzogchen we speak of form, sound, and mind actually being deity, mantra, and sheer awareness.

Our basic practice has to do with seeing everything known by our senses—forms, sounds, and thoughts—as genuinely pure. In this state, all externally appearing forms naturally arise as Buddhas and pure lands, all sounds as mantra, and all thoughts as the dynamism of the clear expanse. It is a rare practitioner who can practice this well, as these practices are difficult to accomplish. However, if you can actually accomplish your practice of this, you can very easily and naturally come into the Dzogchen view.

Yet, the way this has traditionally been done in Tibet is often different from how we approach this today in the West.

The Tibetan Context: Different Moves on the Mountain

In Tibet, practitioners in Dzogchen lineages move from the bottom to the top of the mountain; we here today are in an unusual circumstance, teaching from the top of the mountain. How did this come about? That Dzogchen has become such a famous teaching rests on the shoulders of both teachers and students. Students take great interest in it since they want what is exalted and renowned, and they really press on their teachers to receive it. Teachers want to please their students, so they teach it. Sometimes students who have read something about Dzogchen with other teachers come and ask me about it. But I always tell them, "Please do the foundational practices before you come to talk with me." Sometimes I tell them to learn Tibetan, too. They get upset, even angry, and leave. They leave and read some books, perhaps not even receiving teachings related with it, and such books become the basis of their understanding of Dzogchen.

My feeling is that unless one is a proper vessel, one is unlikely to understand the meaning of this teaching. My concern for your doing the foundational practices is to help you become a vessel for them. That is why I do not teach Dzogchen to anyone who asks. Please do not be put off by this. It's not that I am miserly or want to hold on to it. It's not that I don't want to teach. I just don't feel it helps to teach Dzogchen to someone who has not done foundational practices and some purification. Why not? Because anyone still possessed of the coarser afflictions simply will not understand. Many people are displeased with me nowadays because I do not teach to casual comers.

But it is not just some old-fashioned custom to cultivate the foundational practices and tantra before doing Dzogchen. This is not an old custom—it's *the* custom. If you call it an old custom, that already means you are throwing it away.

Stories of Great Practitioners

A Drikung Kagyu lama named Jigten Gonpo was greatly revered for his dedication to the foundational practices. He would say, "Other lamas find the central practice most meaningful. I find greatest meaning in the foundational practices." These practices are how we overcome strong obstructions and afflictions such as desire, hatred, ignorance, and pride. Usually we don't even recognize that we have these afflictions. Unless we soften and conquer them, it is very hard to understand this profoundly subtle view.

The great pundit Naropa was hit in the face by his teacher's shoe. He passed out. When he woke up from his swoon he had all the understandings of his teacher, Tilopa. His previous purifications made this possible. By the time the shoe struck him, he had fully purified all his afflictions. This made him instantaneously able to receive all of the realizations of a Buddha.

The great translator Marpa had his student Milarepa do many difficult things. Milarepa wound up with great sores all over his body. Yet this hard work purified his prior obstructions and afflictions. After that, all the good qualities of the creation and completion stages emerged in him instantaneously.[322]

As we have seen, Indian masters kept their practice entirely secret until they actually accomplished it and became genuine siddhas. Until then, no one knew they were practicing. For example, there was Kukuripa, whose name means "dog" in Hindi. He got this name because he spent his days with dogs near the ocean. During the day, nothing in his behavior gave the slightest indication to anyone that he was a practitioner. At night, the dogs manifested their real nature as dakinis when they encircled him as consorts. This is an exemplary way of understanding what it means to practice in secret: practicing where no one can see what you are doing, even keeping your mala beads hidden under your clothes where no one can see them, saying mantras so softly that no one can hear, all the while keeping your mind fully focused on practice and remaining completely silent about it until you are fully accomplished. Ordinary, worldly people do not get any wrong view then, or even notice that you are doing anything. This kind of practice is often done in hidden places, such as cemeteries, mountain places, or away from people. Such secrecy seems to speed up progress, so someone who can practice Secret Mantra in a hidden manner can accomplish it easily.

There was also a great yogi named Drilbupa. Possessed of excellent qualities and siddhis, he was such an outstanding practitioner that the king invited him to teach him the Dharma. He declined. The king was deeply displeased. Then a servant woman, who had a very beautiful daughter, said to the king, "Never mind. This is what we will do. We will send my daughter to the yogi and deceive him into falling from his monastic vows. He will be disgraced and we can unmask him. This will be his undoing." The king liked her idea and said, "Yes, let's do that. If she succeeds, we will reward her well."

The beautiful young woman went to the yogi, carrying much food, cloth, and other offerings. She stayed a long time. Finally he said, "Ah, soon it will be quite late. It is not good for a girl like you to travel alone at this time of night. You better leave quickly. So, go on!" She said, "Oh no! It is already late, and my home is very far away. I will die if I have to leave now." She stayed, he gave up his monkhood, and she became his wife. She gave birth to a boy and a girl.

The king told the girl's mother, "Aha, I see our plan has worked well." He issued an edict, not an invitation but an order, requiring that the yogi, the young woman, and their children come to the palace. Approaching the king's palace, the wife carried a large fragrant smoke offering, while the yogi led their son with one hand and their daughter with the other. The king addressed him immediately. "Once I invited you here to teach me the Dharma, and you refused. Now, you have fallen from your monkhood. You are a disgrace."

The king declared him unlawful, implying that great punishment would follow. The yogi simply answered, "I cannot follow your laws." Then, the yogi's daughter turned into a bell, the son turned into a dorje, while he and the old servant woman's daughter flew up into the sky.

This was how it was with the siddhas. Until they accomplished their full powers, nobody knew they were practitioners. In Tibet this very strict way of practicing Secret Mantra was not so widely spread. In particular, the kings and other Secret Mantra practitioners did not typically maintain such strict secrecy.

During Buddha's own time, practitioners would gather in Uddiyana, the land of the dakinis, perhaps somewhere in the area of Pakistan near the Indian border. In such group practice, sixteen, a hundred, or even thousands—as sometimes occurred in India—came together to practice. Practicing together in this way, all of them attained full and complete Buddhahood. Nowadays when practitioners come together, good signs indeed arise for them, though having everyone reaching Buddhahood is very rare.

The final category here, conduct in the manner of sheer awareness, characterizes someone who has fully completed realization as a siddha and is now a genuinely powerful and accomplished practitioner. In that case, whatever they do—walking, standing, sitting, lying down—is the activity of a siddha, not of an ordinary being.

For example, in days long past, a great accomplished practitioner, a genuine mahasiddha, walked across a bridge in India. The king approached, riding an elephant and preceded by his retinue. "Move aside!" they said. "The king is coming." The mahasiddha simply said *phat*, upon which the elephant, king, and his entire retinue were split in half. A spokesperson for the retinue approached the mahasiddha and said, "Please, we did not know who you were. Have compassion on us." This was accepted and the mahasiddha put everyone and everything back together again, something like rewinding a movie. The reconstituted king bowed down to the siddha and thanked him.

This is the kind of all-encompassing activity that siddhas can display, even though at other times they seem to be ordinary beings. In fact, all their behavior is the behavior of a siddha. They are victorious in every way, able to overcome anything. Their good qualities are always increasing. For most of us, however, who do not have this kind of power, it is best to follow the behavior known as the wholly excellent, or Samantabhadra behavior. We who cannot practice like mahasiddhas should sustain a practice in which our genuine and basic state flows freely and continuously, unimpinged upon by mind. This is how we begin.

Foundations of Dzogchen Practice

How can we sustain such conduct and practice? First we study well the four thoughts[323] that turn our mind to the path. We train well in them, developing a great open heart. Along with this superb method, we accumulate the foundational practices, thereby gathering the collections of merit and wisdom. In gathering merit, we have an object of focus; in gathering wisdom, we do not. Further, in order to quickly bring blessings within, we engage in Guru Yoga, the central practice for this purpose. Our practice doesn't come well while we remain contaminated with stains of the eight worldly activities. This means that all our aspirations center around these eight: happiness and unhappiness, gain and loss, praise and blame, help and harm.

To be a king of practice, we need to be free from even the slightest stain. We seek freedom from obstructions that are afflictions and also from more subtle obstructions that impede full expansion of our awareness into wisdom. If we harm or behave badly toward others, this brings suffering for ourselves. Therefore, it is important that as practitioners we cultivate an intention to bring only benefit to others and to conduct ourselves so that we never have to feel embarrassed about our actions. In this way, we bring pure practice and pure behavior to the path. This is the way of Samantabhadra, the wholly excellent. It is the first phase of our endeavor.

In the next phase, after completing foundational practices, we have core practices involving our special deity or yidam, and we take up the methods of creation and completion. Creation-phase practice, unique to tantra, means that we become embodiments of divinity. The wisdom stage of completion practice involves special precepts concerning the channels, winds, and luminous orbs. We need to sever completely all doubt about our practice and keep at it until our understanding is complete. Once you have settled into your own presence, you may find yourself thinking, "Oh, I'm done, I am complete. I am really doing well." If any such mind arises, push it back down as if you were hitting a nail square on the head.

In the final phase of our practice, we continue our wholly excellent conduct. Since the abiding state, the real nature of mind, suffuses everything, we need to be able to carry this understanding into all conventional activities. Conventional knowledge, which does not understand the ultimate, is of no help. Moreover, again, it is important to get past doubt. Unless we have clear certainty in our practice, it does not help. Once we know the real nature of our mind, which extends everywhere, we can say that knowing this one thing means everything is known. And in knowing all things, there is liberation into a single wholeness.

If our practice is not developing, we need to look even more carefully at the conduct associated with Samantabhadra. Therefore we will discuss this in a little more detail.

Our texts teach a wide range of practices. What is their real essence? A key point is to focus fully on our future lives and simply let go of this one. This is difficult. Yet, if we really want to succeed in practice, we need first to hear our teacher's teachings and advice. After that, we should go to an isolated place, whether forest or cave. We should be like a deer whose foot is caught in a trap and cannot move. This deer is unhappy day and night, filled with a yearning to go back where it came from. From the first light of dawn and through the dark of night, this deer thinks of nothing but how to get out of its trap. We likewise train to see cyclic existence as a trap we must escape. In a quiet, uninhabited place we focus entirely on our practice until we have fully understood the abiding nature of our own mind. It may seem challenging, but this is how we accomplish our purpose.

In doing so, we become like a lion. Lions can stay alone anywhere. This lionlike practitioner has no fear and doesn't become discouraged, no matter what. Such a practitioner just keeps going, and that very fact enhances their practice. We too need to persevere without a shred of attachment to any desirable goal; we engage wholeheartedly in practice yet are free from any desire for particular qualities and from any impetus to discard qualities that seem undesirable. Our behavior is like the wind that freely whisks about. It doesn't go to one place and say, "Oh, it's so nice here, I think I will stay." It moves freely through every situation, and this is how we should be.

This practitioner is completely free of the eight worldly concerns, these famous eight mundane attitudes that are ways of wanting what is good for oneself (seeking fame, for example) and not wanting what seems undesirable (ill repute). These do not tempt us at all. Even better is our taking joy when we meet with unpleasantness or suffering and have regret for our fortunate circumstances.

Being involved in the eight worldly behaviors means our practice will not go well. Rather, as practitioners, we give no thought to going after what seems pleasant or avoiding what seems unpleasant. In this we behave like a crazy person. No matter what is going on, we do not react in conventional ways to apparent happiness or suffering.

Yogis remain aware of whatever goes on in their mind. Good

or bad, it just appears and leaves. Whatever arises spontaneously in their mind, they proceed by simply doing that very thing. They follow their own code of conduct. They are not bound by the orders, suggestions, and ideas of other people, nor by the rope of holding to what others think they should be doing. They are like orbs spinning in space, without impediment of any kind.

Practitioners who have encountered the empty, clear nature of their own mind do not waiver from this for even a moment, so mistaken appearances do not arise for them. They sever completely the bonds of hope and fear. In this way they avoid obscuring thoughts such as "Hmm, my meditation is going well; I have studied with many great lamas; I seem to be getting some good signs," or, when doing yidam practice, "I seem to have accomplished it." This kind of thought obscures our face, the sheer essence dimension.

The very best kind of Samantabhadra or wholly excellent behavior is this: we simply remain in the stream of the view's own abiding state, the continuity of our wholly unfabricated base. We have no other thought.

There is nothing better than remaining continuously in the Dzogchen view, regardless of any difficult conditions that might occur. You may have a variety of problematic thoughts. You may have afflictions even greater than before. New sufferings arise. You might have fear or become physically ill, or feel you are about to die. All this could happen. In these circumstances, without relying on any other support, you stay with the continuity of the natural way things are. This is the most important thing for us to do. This is the king of all intentions and accomplishments.

A practitioner who stays with the continuity of their abiding state regardless of what else is happening has power over everything in cyclic existence and nirvana. Such a one is free from anything that could interfere with practice. These siddhas are like great waves in the ocean. And there are many such beings—you cannot stop them, they just keep coming. This is how we purify the darkness of both obstructions. Clairvoyance and magical activities arise and shine like the sun. This very famous Buddha is right within your own mind.

Even though great yogis can open earth treasures, sky treasures, and treasures of jewels, the yogi's own high realization is far more valuable than these. Realization is the focus for practitioners. They set aside these much less significant treasures to focus on the view. To do otherwise would be to act like a child who sees a rainbow and thinks, "Oh, it's so beautiful, I will go get it!" and chases after it. Yogis do not do that. For the yogi knows that to get distracted into thoughts about how to better this life is a life that has no essence at all. It is pointless because it only has to do with this one life.

Sixth Meditation

So, please settle into the view, a natural settling, and practice your meditation.

Questions and Responses: Furthering Meditation and Helping Others

Question: Can you say more about these meditative experiences that start like a flood down the mountainside and gradually become less overpowering?

Response: The greatest problem for meditators is when the three kinds of *nyam*, the meditative experiences of bliss, emptiness, and nonconceptuality, arise in sequence. Along with these may come clairvoyance; you start to know others' minds. This happens because your concentration is unbroken. You may have any of the five types of clairvoyance associated with the five senses. Then you tend to think, "I am doing very well. I can meditate day and night and know what others think." There is a lot of pride in this. Then, as we mentioned earlier, other people may also be impressed. Both the meditator and these others are deceived, and the meditator's pride increases even more. This is the worst and most deceptive place of error for a meditator. In fact you have only set up the causes for being born, for example, as a deity. You have in no way set up the causes for liberation. In order to move toward actual insight, you must have the wisdom that realizes emptiness. Without this, you are totally deluded regarding the status and benefit of your practice. If you don't have a root lama at this time who can check into your situation, it can be very difficult.

However, nowadays it is quite rare to have such experiences because everyone is so busy. There are so many discontinuities in our practice.

Practice requires perseverance. Once you are skilled in Dzogchen's view and have full experience of it, you can fulfill all the hopes of sentient beings. Dzogchen is the peak of the nine vehicles and through it you can complete all the grounds and the paths. It has a very special quality.

QUESTION: Can we be of benefit before then?
RESPONSE: Certainly. Long before then you can be a model for others by leaving aside worldly inclinations and helping to inspire those around you. Think carefully about this and see if it is so.

QUESTION: What about teaching children?
RESPONSE: Please do this with great care. The well-being of the world depends on giving children good training, on their learning well, and behaving well. This training of children depends on the teacher. So if you are that teacher, please be very careful and do your work well.

QUESTION: How can we help friends who are dying?
RESPONSE: There are very helpful things that almost anyone

can do, and there are other ways of helping if you know the practice of transference (powa).

First, it is very helpful if, prior to their death you can support them with a good mind, and with kindness; encourage them to pray according to their own faith and to connect with a deity or teacher for whom they have devotion. Anything you can offer conducive to their giving up attachment to this life and supporting them to focus on something that is positive and free of worldly attachment is excellent.

If you do not have the opportunity to work with them this way before they die, then once the consciousness has dissolved, that opportunity no longer remains. However, reciting mantra or refuge and so forth is also helpful to any living being. It plants a powerful seed that can ripen in a fortunate way in their next lifetime. For Buddhists, this means chanting, for example, "I bow to Buddha." The long recitation of all the various names of the Buddha is also a particularly powerful help.

Or you can simply recite mantras such as OM AH HUM or others.

OM embodies all of the bodies of the Buddhas; AH, the speech of all Buddhas; and HUM, the mind of all Buddhas. You can also say OM MANI PADME (*padme* rhymes with "may say") HUM, the mantra of Avalokiteshvara, or Guru Rinpoche's mantra, OM AH HUM BENZRA GURU PADMA SIDDHI HUM. In short, simply offer help with whatever mantras are familiar to you. They are all powerful and beneficial.

If you have received and been trained in powa[324] transmission, you can give this transmission and instruction to the dying person. What is not appropriate is for you to do powa—to transfer the consciousness—for someone else. Milarepa in general advises against this, lest things go awry. If someone who has this capacity puts a wealthy person in the exit turnstile in order to acquire their wealth, this is very vile.

In Tibet we say that we are all born with a god and a demon. Our positive mind is like a god, and our negative mind is like a demon. The god leads us toward positive actions. The demon opposes this, creating strife with respect to the good, trying to turn us away from it. Then the Lord of Death approaches to carry us off. On this occasion the activities of the god and the demon get weighed, and we proceed based on what is in ascendancy at that time.

Marpa emphasizes the importance of meditating on powa again and again. It's not sufficient to meditate and practice it once at the feet of the lama. You should be practicing it repeatedly. Then at the time of death, when you are overcome by a very powerful illness, you can instantly remember Amitabha and fly like an arrow to his pure land. This is very effective. But it is based on familiarity; you must continue to practice it. It is not something you simply do once. When friends die, the Dharma community definitely needs to do something for them. Therefore it's vital to keep the practice of powa fresh. Even if you have had the actual signs emerge in the past, but then let it go and don't keep up the practice, you might forget, and then it would be useless.

Marpa said, "If we practice, we all are Buddhas for sure. Even if we do not, we have Buddhahood." He was alluding to powa. The practice of powa is called "Buddhahood without meditation," because signs can emerge in just seven days of meditation. You are then assured of Buddhahood. It is not a matter of months and years.

QUESTION: Is Buddhism changing?
RESPONSE: Certainly. New customs are bound to arise in response to a cultural system already in place. Novelty, however, is just from the perspective of conventions. Ultimate nature is not something that can be improved. Buddha taught this and nothing new is going to replace it. This has been settled and peerlessly explained. Many good qualities are associated with such an ultimate view.

Guru Rinpoche gave many prophecies that the teachings of view, meditation, and conduct would in the future become diluted like milk with water. None of these changes affect the mind's true nature. Nothing new will happen there. We need to be constant and content with view, meditation, and conduct.

Regarding these three, His Holiness the Fourteenth Dalai Lama is unparalleled. There is no one like him in this world. He teaches peace; he is a great practitioner of sutra and tantra. Other people have pride in doing this or doing that, but anyone who observes carefully in terms of view, meditation, and conduct can understand His Holiness's good qualities. I do feel that if the teachings of His Holiness on the path of peace can spread in the world, war will decrease. A tremendous boon. These are all signs of His Holiness being a real bodhisattva.

QUESTION: How do we understand the difference between the supreme and the lesser common feats (siddhis)?

RESPONSE: The supreme feat is Buddhahood. The common, lesser feats can develop fairly quickly. They are helpful with the worldly activities of this life. As such, they are objects of attachment. They have nothing to do with the view. As practitioners, we shouldn't be hoping for or seeking them. The supreme siddhis, by contrast, erase problems that have their origins in beginningless time and are helpful forever into the future. The difference between these and the supreme feat of Buddhahood is like earth and sky. Excellent practitioners are satisfied with very little in terms of worldly things. They are always in touch with the view, and free of errors or pitfalls.

Thus, in terms of fruitional siddhis there is the supreme feat of Buddhahood and eight ordinary accomplishments. The first of these eight ordinary accomplishments is called "sky performance." Like the dakinis who live in the sky, one is able to remain in space for a long time without dying. The second involves a special sword with which one can conquer all enemies. The third is quick-footedness; it gets its name from a particular type of boot and is attained through accumulating a lot of mantra. With this siddhi one can instantaneously, just like that, reach the end of the ocean.

The fourth of the common siddhis involves a magical pot: you simply reach in and pull out what you need—food, clothing, whatever it might be. Fifth is the ability to fashion a pill that renders you invisible when you hold it in your hand and thus enables you, for example, to disappear from the sight of your enemies.

There is a class of being known as harmers, and the sixth common feat is to make them serve you, for a single such being can do the work of a hundred thousand humans. In that way, you can accomplish in one day whatever needs to be done. The seventh feat is the practice of extracting the essence of things into a very special elixir [so that eating normal food is not necessary].

There are other common feats as well. A certain type of tree fiber used to fill cushions in India is a metaphor for the lightness of body accomplished in one such feat. There is also the feat of using your practice to create an eye ointment that allows you to look into the earth and see what treasures are there.

The supreme feat, the sheer essence dimension, serves as the basis for both the emanation and richly resplendent dimensions. Both are for the sake of all sentient beings, but only tenth-stage bodhisattvas and above can take a resplendent dimension Buddha as their root lama. The rest of us don't have the fortunate karma to perceive such beings, even when they are present.

We who have ordinary eyes require another type of emanation. What we can experience are the emanation dimension beings. These, as we have said, arise in accordance with the karma, aspiration, and general disposition of the innumerable sentient beings interested in the teaching. Again we use the metaphor of the moon. There is only one moon. Its appearance is determined by the shape and size of the container whose water reflects it. The moon reflected in all these ways is the same, but appears differently because the vessels and other circumstances are different. If the container is triangular, circular, and so forth, the moon appears in accordance with that. Similarly, some emanation dimension beings write, some draw or paint, while others build statues and temples. In short, they do whatever is needed to help others ripen. It's not that everyone who engages in these crafts is an emanation dimension being, but those who engage in artistry to benefit others are one class of emanation.

Guru Rinpoche was an incarnation whose parents and other particulars were prophesied before his birth. Sometimes there is an accurate identification, sometimes there is not, but this is a particular type of emanation body.

The supreme emanation embodiment was Buddha's birth in India. This is supreme because Buddha overcame all obstacles, illustrating the twelve specific actions associated with his supreme type of emanation. Gautama Buddha was the fourth of the thousand Buddhas coming to our world during this fortunate aeon.

QUESTION: May a siddha engage in killing?
RESPONSE: Siddhas are not permitted to do any kind of killing unless they also have the power to bring back that life. Stories of all the siddhas are in the Tengyur, the literature that comments on the Buddha's teachings. I haven't seen any story where a siddha engages in vengeful killing. They are meant to behave beneficially at all times. If they are not helping other beings, they are breaking their pledges. Somebody who really has this power only acts for the good of others. Killing is just a common nonvirtue. There are stories of people who acquired power, including the capacity to bring death to others, and who didn't listen when their teachers told them they were not ready yet to display their power. They got into a lot of trouble, creating many obstacles for themselves and no doubt for others. But an actual siddha is someone who can, and always does, work in a way that is helpful to a person who is apparently being killed.

There is a tale about a young girl who had a large fruit orchard. Someone came by while she was picking fruit, and instead of picking fruit for himself, he said, "Fruit come here," and then ate the fruit that arrived in his hand. He was showing off his powers and, apparently, ate quite a lot of fruit. The girl, who was probably a dakini, spoke out. "Well, you're a fine siddha. You're taking my fruit! What are you doing? If you are really accomplished, then once you've eaten my fruit, you ought to be able to give it back!" This was very embarrassing for the would-be siddha. Her comment points to how a real siddha helps people and does not harm them. For example, Milarepa, prior to his full accomplishment of practice, engaged in a lot of harmful behavior and killed people. But once he had the power of a fully accomplished practitioner, he didn't kill or harm anyone.

QUESTION: How do we decide where to focus our practice?
RESPONSE: Decide what is central for your practice and stay focused on that. It is impossible to learn and practice all the different teachings and lineages that exist across the tradition.

We tend to have faith in what is appropriate for us, and it is entirely appropriate to make choices about what you will study, reflect on, and practice. Longchen Rabjam said that your head would split open if you tried to fit everything that exists into it!

At the same time, it is extremely important not to look down on other Buddhist practices and also to have a mind of equanimity with respect to non-Buddhists. Do not disparage them, even though you may be devoted to the teachings of your own path.

When someone becomes a Buddha, they recall what they did, whom they helped through what kinds of activities in their past lives, and if they were connected with Buddhism in those lives. You can find descriptions of this in the literature on the past lives of the Buddha, for example, and in other texts as well. A supreme emanation who exhibits specific deeds is clearly identified as a Buddha. Sometimes a being appears and engages in activities that help others. Such a person may or may not appear as a Buddha emanation.

It is important to be helpful, virtuous, and compassionate. Anyone who cultivates these qualities has a practice that is good and valuable, and they are gaining merit. But merit alone leads only to a higher rebirth, not to liberation.

QUESTION: What is meant by scriptural transmission?
RESPONSE: Scriptural transmission (*lung*) refers to hearing the words of a text through your ear consciousness. Your hearing it plants seeds for cultivating this teaching in the future. Moreover, when you attain a one-pointed concentration known as dharma stream samādhi, all the texts you have heard are understood, without any thought being required. For example, Tibetan practitioners listen to all texts of both the Kangyur, the complete collection of Buddha's teachings, and the Tengyur, the commentaries on it. Much time is spent on this. We do this so that when we achieve Dharma stream samādhi, we will understand all these just like that, naturally, without any explanation.

The first Dudjom Rinpoche was a great siddha, but not a scholar. Once he started looking at a book, then tossed it aside to give commentary on it. His words poured forth with no hesitation whatsoever. He had the inner vision to explain this text as a result of initiations and scriptural transmissions he had received in the past. Transmission from a Rinpoche is one element that allows you to do something like that. The next Dudjom reincarnation, Dudjom Jigdral Dorje, was an incredible scholar and writer.

Milarepa said that his stage of realization was such that he received teachings just through looking at trees or anything else in his sense field. He didn't need any other support for developing his understanding. Receiving transmission is a source for realization in which so much comes forth.

QUESTION: How can I diminish the afflictions that always seem to arise right during my meditation session? Especially as these relate to the practices of setting free and soaring forth?
RESPONSE: When you do these practices you will definitely have different kinds of meditative experience. As the text states, at first these are like water rushing down a mountainside. Then it is more like water on a flat plain, flowing here and there gently

and a bit randomly, but now you have some choice about where to move it. As we continue to make effort and to practice, as we continue to look into our own minds, our afflictions naturally diminish. The most important thing is to remain with the ongoing continuity of the abiding state that is your mind's own nature. The way your mind really is. This is how afflictions decrease. When clouds vanish, the sun and the moon really shine forth. In the same way, when obscurations such as desire, hatred, ignorance, pride, and jealousy decrease, the sun and moon of your mind's own real nature will shine forth. Once your afflictions are purified and dissolved in this way, your more subtle predispositions will also gradually be purified. This process continues until you reach the tenth bodhisattva ground. Therefore, if you carefully practice again and again and again, my hope is that this will occur, and that you will not forget what is said in the texts, but look into them carefully.

QUESTION: What about the afflictions that arise when I am at work or other daily activities. How do I deal with them?
RESPONSE: Afflictions can gradually be abandoned if we make effort. Buddha's last words were, "I have shown you the way and I have shown you the method. Now it depends on you." As we know, Buddha taught 84,000 antidotes for the 84,000 afflictions: 21,000 each for desire, hatred, ignorance, and a fourth set of 21,000 for the compounds of these. If we train in accordance with, for example, *The Root Text of the Seven Points of Training the Mind,* the famous compilation of Atisha's slogans by Chekawa Dorje,[325] we can overcome our afflictions. It all depends on whether we practice or not, whether we take things into our own hands or not.

For example, when afflictions arise, you can look at them and go along with them. You can fall completely under their power, like seeing someone you find attractive and thinking, "Ah, here's a good-looking person, I'll just ride with my feelings here." If you do, you have gone under the power of this desire. You can generalize from this to all other afflictions. When they take over, you no longer have power of your own. If, on the other hand, you think, "I have wasted so many lives with these desires and other afflictions. Again and again I get involved with them, following right after them, and again and again I end up suffering as a result." If you reflect deeply in this way, it is possible that at some point your afflictions will dissolve into space like a cloud into the deep blue sky. Instead of your being overpowered by them, they melt away as soon as they arise: as soons as one forms, it is liberated. This depends on training. And with all this, do not forget the tremendous importance of openhearted devotion and aspiration. If you have these, the path can come well. If you don't, it will not.

QUESTION: I am not sure if there is a custom for making this kind of request, but to amplify our own development and inspiration, we would very much like to hear from you anything about your story that you could tell us. I would find it especially helpful if you would speak about your practice.

RESPONSE: Method and wisdom are the root of developing openhearted devotion and reverence for our teacher. In order for this to come well, we need to accumulate appropriate actions and virtue for many, many lifetimes. Otherwise, it can be very difficult for genuine openheartedness and reverence to arise. On the other hand, when there is a lama with all kinds of clairvoyance and magical displays, faith arises rather naturally. But since I don't have any of these, it is likely difficult for you to have this kind of openhearted reverence or devotion.

Such devotion, which is really a state of openheartedness and receptivity, is very important. Its benefit is felt in this life and, even more importantly, in future lives. This quality develops best on the basis of hearing, reflecting, and meditation.

Since I am not much of a basis for your developing openhearted devotion, we can talk about this in terms of the blessings of my root lamas. Blessings come through such lamas like water pouring through a pipe. So long as the pipe is not clogged, the water flows easily. If there is an obstruction, it cannot. We need to be open to the blessings of the lineage. These blessings originate from Samantabhadra, the sheer essence dimension of enlightenment, and they descend through the entire lineage of teachers down to our own root lama. With meditative experience and realization, we can receive these very well.

The great qualities and blessings of the root lama are transmitted through a well-maintained lineage. Lineage becomes murky through the breaking of commitments, a very negative situation. It is important to maintain awareness of the pure pledges of your teachers and the entire lineage, and to know that the lineage teachers have not wavered from their own commitments. In that case, all is well. The tattering of such commitments is like wearing dirty clothes.

It's crucial that our lineage not degenerate and, as we have said, this relates to the pure maintenance of commitments. Dakinis and protectors of the lineages will protect day and night those who maintain the sacred commitments. Just as lamas must maintain commitments purely, students also need to maintain their pledges purely night and day. In this way, from the lama's lineage, beginning with the sheer essence dimension, or beginning with the Blessed One himself, the Buddha, Lord of All Sutras, or with the new transmission lineages that come through Dorje Chang, or with the Dzogchen lineages that arise through Samantabhadra, the blessings rain down on us like water through our own root lama. This is possible when the purity of the lineage has been maintained through maintaining sacred commitments.

In brief, there are three sources of blessing: Shakyamuni Buddha is the source for blessings through the sutra lineage, Dorje Chang the source for tantra, and Samantabhadra, the sheer essence dimension, the source for Dzogchen blessings. From these sources the blessings—waves of grace, waves of splendor—move through the various lineages, reaching you through your own root lama. It is rather like going to the kitchen and turning on the faucet. Your root lama is like the faucet from which you receive actual water in your own home. For the sake of your health and strength, it is important that the water coming through the tap is clean and good. Dirty water harms you. Food prepared with dirty water undermines your strength. A lineage polluted by sacred commitments that were broken is that kind of water.

Even when water itself is fresh and clean, if the tap it reaches is closed, it can't flow through. For practitioners, it is important to persevere in hearing, thinking, and meditation until you can completely open the faucet and receive the water of blessings flowing from this great reservoir. Whatever you can do in this regard is important. Otherwise, full reception of the water of blessings will not come. This is especially important in tantra, where maintaining sacred commitments is crucial.

If you knew there was water that significantly improved the health of anyone who drank it and that made food especially tasty, you would surely want some. This metaphor underscores that practicing sutra and tantra is how we access blessings. This means that with practice, good effects will come forth.

Of course, hearing this you may feel, "Well, Khetsun Sangpo is not really a very elegant person. But this is what he said." Yet when you actually experience the fruit of your practice, you will feel, "Ah, my teacher was really kind. There was no mistake in what he taught. The good effect is here." And when you come to die, you will have no worry. This is indeed the final fruit. This kind of experience is what really produces a devoted heart. Of course, if you don't practice, this cannot come about. But if you do actually practice, later you may feel, "Ah, this is really harmonious with me." When you say, "I seek refuge," you will have actual devotion, a truly open heart, not just some show of respect. Your devotion and conviction will be based on your own experience, on the fruit that you have tasted from your own practice. Infinite openheartedness will arise effortlessly. This is my hope.

Milarepa was petitioned by his students, led by Gampopa,

who said, "Ah, you are working for the welfare of sentient beings. We admire and have great faith in you, and we very much want some special advice from you." And Milarepa said, "Meet me where I sit." He was inviting them to his retreat dwelling near the border. This was a great distance from where they were and of course in those days, they didn't have trains or buses or airplanes but had to go by horse.

When the students arrived there they said, "We feel you are an actual Buddha, and what we most want to know is: What was the source of your Buddhahood? How did you do that? Please tell us." "All right, you come back tomorrow, and I'll tell you." So they left and then returned, saying, "Please! Now grant us the special precepts we have been waiting for."

Milarepa said, "Okay, this is my advice." He unswirled his robe and showed them . . . his bare backside. The skin on it was tough and hard like a horse's hoof, the result of all the effort he had put into sitting. The seat on which he sat was very hard. Milarepa said, "This is my special advice to you. If you can make this kind of effort, then you will become an actual Buddha. This will happen. It is real. It is true. That is my special advice."

Another story about deep devotion involves a mother and her son. As the boy was preparing to go to India on business, his mother said, "India is the land of Buddha. Please bring me a tooth of the Buddha." The son said, "Definitely, Ma, I will do it." But he forgot and returned from India empty-handed. His mother said, "Did you bring what I asked you to bring? Did you bring a tooth of the Buddha that I requested as support for my faith?" And he said, "Oh, no. I completely forgot. But next time I go, I will definitely bring it." When he set off for India a second time, his mother reminded him, "Please, this time do not forget. Remember that I am asking you, most earnestly, to bring me back a tooth of the Buddha. Please, remember what I have asked." The son said, "Don't worry, Ma, I won't forget. I will bring it." When he returned for the second time from India, his mother was very hopeful. She said, "I implored you so earnestly, surely you brought it this time?" And the son had to say, "No, I forgot it again."

The third time he headed for India, his mother said, "Do not return without something to support my prayers and my practice. If you return without this, I will die." Once more, the son went down to India, did his trading, and headed back home, having forgotten yet again. As he approached his mother's house, he remembered her words and thought, "Oh, I am lost, what can I do? I didn't bring her what she asked for. She will die!" Greatly distraught, he looked up and down, left and right. He saw a dead dog on the road. He took a tooth from that dog and wrapped it up beautifully. As he entered the house his mother said, "Well?" And he answered, "Yes, I have brought you a support for your prayers, and here it is: a tooth of the Buddha." She was very happy. She had enormous faith in it. She placed it in her house and all day long, whatever she was doing, she made obeisance to it. She bowed to it, she prayed to it, she constantly directed her faith and devotion toward it. When she died, there were many, many rainbows, and other amazing signs, an indication she had been liberated.

The blessings this woman received from this dog tooth were even greater than might have come from an actual tooth of the Buddha. The source was her own devotion. If you have devotion in your heart, amazing results are possible.

Another story: A monk named Karma, one of Buddha's cousins, had no faith in Buddha at all. Although he served the Buddha for twelve years, he did not during all that time notice anything he considered worthwhile. He heard Buddha teach the twelve divisions of sutras and found nothing useful in them. Without a sesame seed's worth of devotion, he decided Buddha had nothing meaningful to offer him and left. When you lack openhearted receptivity, even the presence of Buddha himself will not inspire you.

Then Ananda, another cousin of the Buddha, came to Buddha to ask "What can we do? My cousin has accumulated so much bad karma because of the way he treated you. What will happen to him in the future?" Buddha said, "There's nothing to be done. In seven days he will die and then he will be reborn as a hungry ghost with nine male and female organs all over his body."

Ananda was serving Buddha and accompanied him everywhere. He met with Karma. "You will have a terrible rebirth because of this. Buddha doesn't lie." "Sometimes he does." "Well, but sometimes he doesn't. This is in every likelihood exactly right." Ananda then proceeded to converse with his cousin so skillfully that Karma spent the next seven days in meditation. At the end of those seven days, his meditation was precise and correct. He became thirsty and took some water. The water was cold and as soon as it hit his stomach, he fell ill. This escalated into a severe seizure, and he died.

Ananda felt great pain at this. "Buddha was right, Karma died in seven days. Buddha is probably also right about his rebirth as a hungry ghost in a horrific body with nine different male and female organs." Ananda, his mind filled with pain at the suffering his cousin was likely undergoing, asked the Buddha what could now be done. Buddha said, "It is regrettable, but there is no way to avoid the ripening of our own karma. No one else can experience it for you."

Speaking again of the development of devotion, consider how, as years go by, you make effort at your practice. Although in your youth you had lots of friends, now at the end of your life you are rather alone, perhaps in an old-age home. Everyone you know has gone elsewhere. It is almost as if you were in prison. In fact you are quite helpless except for whatever practice you have developed. Because of your practice, you may be capable of patience. You may appreciate the teaching's inconceivable qualities. And you may reflect, "Well, I created certain interferences to my practice in the past." You may feel sad about this. And then you reflect further, "But then again, whatever I can do right now to build my practice will be very helpful." And then when you turn your mind to the teaching, you feel happy, as well as deeply and truly grateful for the teaching you have received. You feel how amazing this is. A very definite understanding arises. Along with it comes incommensurable and limitless openhearted devotion, real faith.

QUESTION: I usually begin my session with a prayer, and close with dedication, and do short sessions of different kinds of practice with some minutes in between. What do you suggest?
RESPONSE: Excellent. This is exactly how to proceed—prayer first, then meditation, and then a dedication. The reason for doing brief sessions is to prevent agitation and sleepiness from overcoming us. In general, we speak of four meditation sessions a day, and if we can manage six sessions daily that is quite good. The question of short session versus long session depends on your experience and capacity. If you develop the capacity, you can meditate all night and all day. You can get to a point where there is no difference between a meditative session and its aftermath. But that is challenging.

At the same time, by practicing as you describe, in short sessions, good qualities and understanding will arise. It is like a fire. If you keep feeding it, it is going to blaze up.

QUESTION: If there is no grasping or longing for the various meditative experiences that appear in meditation, is sheer awareness occurring?
RESPONSE: These meditative experiences arise as the mind habituates to practice. You will have experiences like pleasure in the body or clarity of the mind, or a sense of emptiness. These experiences arise and dissolve, adventitious occurrences. Neither the mistaken mind nor these experiences are capable of stability; they can only come and go. That is one thing distinguishing them from mindnature, which is always present in all circumstances. These meditative experiences are not what is important. What matters here is the wisdom that understands selflessness and leads to liberation. To have ongoing understanding is truly excellent.

QUESTION: We often hear about sheer awareness in terms of clarity and emptiness. Do the strengths of these vary? Is one stronger than the other?

RESPONSE: Unlike the meditative experiences we have been describing, these do not vary. They are always the same. Sheer awareness has a quality of intensity, or brilliance. Right with sheer awareness you have an understanding of selflessness. The three meditative experiences come mainly in connection with the cultivation of serene abiding rather than special seeing. Meditative experiences are like clouds. Stainless space is unchanging. Reality is the sheer essence dimension. It is the nature of sheer awareness to understand how things are and also the different kinds of things that there are. All good qualities are already present in sheer awareness. What identifies the nature is your actual understanding. This has a genuine quality of knowing. The quality of your serene abiding is stability, and only that. It does not have a quality of knowing or awareness.

Meditative experiences inevitably increase and decrease. The wisdom that realizes emptiness may seem to increase as we become accustomed to it, but it only looks that way because we are unfamiliar with such wisdom. As we gain familiarity, we may feel that our clarity is increasing. But from the perspective of the sheer essence dimension, reality itself, there is no change. Nor are there any obscurations. It's simply that we are getting more accustomed to the wisdom that recognizes this. Unlike fleeting meditative experiences, the sheer knowing of sheer awareness is not a sometime thing.

This is very important. With the base, we have sheer awareness. While we are on the path, its potency and dynamism develop. Then, in fruition, we have manifest all-suffusing sheer awareness, a union of the base sheer awareness and the sheer awareness of dynamism. The important thing to know that is that these are all the same. There is only one sheer awareness.

For example, perhaps you work in an office, first as a secretary, then as a treasurer, then you become a teacher in the organization. You remain the same person through all these different activities. It is not that sometimes serenity is mixed in with sheer awareness and sometimes not. Sheer awareness is always the same. Yet, we can speak of the sheer awareness of the base, the abiding state, the way things are. While on the path, we have path sheer awareness, meaning the dynamism of sheer awareness. When we manifest the fruit of our practice, we have the all-suffusing sheer awareness that is these two unified together.

QUESTION: Can you say more about the characteristics of tantra and Dzogchen?

RESPONSE: We have been discussing the special features of Secret Mantra—that is, of the sixth, seventh, and eighth vehicles. Beyond these, on the ninth vehicle, peak of all of paths, you rely on your own Dzogchen lama, on special instructions this lama gives, and on your practice based on these as well as on the compassionate motivation you are developing. All this plants seeds so that in the future you will come to a clear and definitive conclusion about your own mindnature.

Guru Rinpoche said, "The Dharma is without end. If you can recognize the sheer essence dimension of your own mind and dwell in its abiding state, you will find the root of all the hundreds and thousands of teachings." The abiding state of the mind—the sheer essence dimension that is the essence of all Dharma teaching—is limitless and goes on forever. So, he said, do not sever the root of the teaching. Sever the root of your mind. When you understand one thing, you understand everything.

If you do not cut the root of the teaching and instead cut the root of your mind, you understand everything. Just like that. Everything is liberated. If you do not cut the root of the mind, you won't understand anything.

THE THREE BUDDHA DIMENSIONS

What fruit does practice bring? What happens when you complete the wisdoms of hearing, thinking, and meditation?

Since time without beginning, the sheer essence dimension

has been with you. Now you awaken to it. In a real sense you become a Buddha once again. Your correct endeavoring brings this about. Yet, endeavoring without appropriate instruction will not bear this fruit. Nor will correct instructions unless they are followed by your own efforts. When you have both instruction and effort, your fruition is the three Buddha dimensions endowed with the five endless wisdoms and the circle of unending ornamentation (*mi zad rgyan byi 'khor lo*), the richly resplendent dimension. The virtues and features of this dimension are enumerated as the seven features of union and the eight lordly features. Please practice so that you can awaken to your actual Buddha dimensions and bring forth the resplendent and emanation dimensions.

The first of the seven features of union is the peak of all pure lands, the richly adorned Highest Pure Land. Spontaneously established, not constructed in any way, it is a vast realm of resplendence and enjoyment. This enjoyment is method. The second feature is union itself, meaning the union of the enjoyer and what is being enjoyed, as well as the union of method and wisdom. This union itself is wisdom. Thus, the first two features here are method and wisdom, respectively. The third is great bliss, and the fourth is the lack of any true nature.

A resplendent dimension being's heart is full of compassion. This supreme and continuous compassion is the fifth feature, and its uninterrupted continuity is the sixth. The seventh feature is that all six characteristics noted here are always and unceasingly present in the heart-mind of all resplendent dimension beings. Neither established nor negated, they are simply there. These are the seven aspects of union.

As for the eight lordly features, the first is being lord of the emanation dimension in the sense that one appears in whatever form is required to meet the needs of disciples.

In Buddha's retinue of disciples, there was one who was the poorest of the poor. Destitute and miserable, he was preparing to leave the community. Seeing this, Buddha emanated as someone even more destitute and went to visit this person. "You are even worse off than I am!" he exclaimed to Buddha. This encouraged him so much that he no longer felt a need to leave. Buddha began teaching him, and the formerly discouraged disciple achieved the state of a non-returner in the hearer lineage.

Emanations can appear in whatever manner best suits a disciple's need. If you are a king, there can be the manifestation of a king; if you are a minister, then an emanation appropriate to a minister; and if a translator, perhaps someone like Harvey!

The second of the eight is the lord of speech, uninterruptedly teaching the three wheels of dharma according to disciples' needs. Buddha's first teaching, the discourse on the four truths, was in accordance with those of lesser capacity. His middle wheel was on the lack of characteristics—namely, emptiness. The third wheel is the adorned teaching on how things actually are, a teaching for the most intelligent of disciples.

Third, the heart-mind lord, is compassion beyond conception, a compassion not based merely on reasoning or conceptuality. It is not limited by thought in any way.

Fourth is lord of magical emanation, an unimpeded state. The richly resplendent dimension means you are able to manifest unlimited magical emanations for the sake of disciples. This display's quality of unobstructedness is the magical emanation lord.

Fifth is lord of proceeding, meaning that you can proceed through all stages of the path to liberation. This refers specifically to manifest awareness of the single taste of all things in cyclic existence and nirvana. This lordship extends from the furthest depths of samsara all the way through to complete enlightenment.

Sixth is lord of desire. There are numerous amazingly attractive goddesses in the desire realm, yet due to the resplendent dimension, you have no attachment or attraction to them. Therefore, you are indeed a lord with dominion over desire.

Seventh is lord of arising in accord with disciples' wishes. This is even better than a wish-fulfilling jewel, which creates whatever you want. In this case, you are given in exact accordance with whatever you are seeking.

Eighth is lord of abiding, meaning that you are in the palace of the highest heaven. As such, you are also lord of the three realms. Because you are always and continuously teaching, you are lord over abiding.

This is a core enumeration of the main features associated with the resplendent dimension. In actuality, from the perspective of ordinary beings, there is no beginning or end to the features that we can enumerate regarding this richly resplendent dimension. I have given only a broad sketch of what this is all about.

Traditional Buddhism thinks about this world quite differently from how scientists understand it. When I was teaching at the University of Virginia, I was invited to join Professor Jeffrey Hopkins for a conversation with professors of Christianity from the Department of Religious Studies. The conversation turned to views on the structure of our world. I told them that Buddhists understand the world to be organized around Mount Meru at the center of four major continents in the four cardinal directions, with two islands flanking each of those continents. Thus there are twelve continents surrounding the vast mountain called Meru.

The professors asked whether the Himalayas, as the world's highest mountains, are identified as Mount Meru. I told them no, not at all, because the Himalayas are still part of what we call the southern continent, as is everything on this planet. Buddhist cosmology does not place Mount Meru anywhere on the southern continent, but in the middle of all four main continents.

Why, if such a great mountain exists, has no scientist observed it or any spacecraft recorded it? It is unlikely you would see this from a rocket because these are not things established by ordinary consciousness; they are quite beyond our common way of seeing things.

Buddha also said that to describe how many world systems

like ours exist, you multiply ten zeros by one hundred—a billion world systems. Each of these billion world systems has its own Mount Meru, four continents, and so forth. Shakyamuni arrives in all of these one billion world systems for the sake of sentient beings. This is why we say that the Buddha's activities are incredibly vast. We can never put a number on them; it is impossible to calculate the infinite number of emanation bodies in the cosmos.

Nor can we understand the Buddha's inconceivably vast activities from our ordinary perspective, and thus they are secret from us. These inconceivable and self-secret Buddha activities form a circle of adornment. Enlightened beings take form either as resplendent or emanation dimension beings, and in that guise explain the nine vehicles. Yet in terms of how things really exist, there is only oneness. If you were to condense all nine vehicles into their very essence, this would be the Great Completeness teachings, which include everything. Nothing is distant in relation to them, for there is nothing in all the world systems not included in or suffused by that essence. Everything arises from just this. In this way, a Buddha [as sheer essence dimension] is most concisely described as a majestic creator of everything.

Not a single one of the myriad things that appear in this vast world is truly established. There is nothing, anywhere, whether of the physical world or beings in it, not suffused by emptiness. The nature of reality, this emptiness, is not obstructive in the manner of external objects. Still, just as a large piece of cloth cannot pass through the eye of a needle, this vast view of the emptiness of all internal and external things cannot fit into the small mind of ordinary consciousness.

The sheer essence dimension is the abiding heart of all bodhisattvas and the essence of all phenomena. To enter enlightenment-mind is to enter the heart and essence of all things. When you enter the heart of all phenomena, there is neither subject nor object, apprehended or apprehender. You are beyond all that. The resplendent dimension arises from the sheer essence dimension, and when we abide in that resplendent dimension we possess the five unchanging characteristics associated with that state[326] and find only enjoyment in the five sense objects.

And what about the emanation dimension? When the time is right for any particular devoted disciple, it arises in accordance with the needs of that disciple. Thus, while the sheer essence, richly resplendent, and emanation dimensions are a unity, the various activities and actions of a Buddha are displayed according to the aspirations and the wishes of the disciples. *The Majestic Creator of Everything* describes the sheer essence dimension as birthlessly arising within a complete absence of conceptual thought. The richly resplendent dimension, replete with enjoyment of pleasures, arises from its essence. And then, through great compassion, the emanation dimension emerges to benefit beings.

I received many quintessential instructions from my excellent teachers and I took them all to heart. All four major orders of Buddhism in Tibet, although called by different names—Nyingma, Kagyu, Sakya, and Geluk—have the view. In every case, their view leads back to the teachings of the Buddha. None are other than the teachings of the Buddha. I have offered reflections on these teachings as they arose in our land of Tibet.

All Buddhas and their teachings are our Dharma friends. In that way we are part of the same extended family as Buddha's own students. His students are our more distant Dharma relatives. Then there is our closer-in Dharma family who have taken teachings from the same lama. And even closer are those who have been with the same lama in the same mandala and received the same the initiation together. These are our very close Dharma friends.

As students of the Buddha, we are like children of the same parent. Whenever you are within any of these circles—the extremely close, the close, or even the distant—negative speech of any kind can be very harmful to the teaching. It is for the sake of preventing and correcting this that I have written these words. Whatever practices or traditions you make central to your path is good. But do not look down upon other teachings. There is great benefit in all of them. Whatever I can do to help develop faith and prevent this kind of partisanship I have offered here.

Epilogue [to *Strand of Jewels*]

Now we come to the text's epilogue, a counterpart to its prologue. This is in verse and concludes the text:

> In disciples' Lotus Lake, by the power of karma and
>   prayer
> The unborn sheer essence dimension, pure as space;
>   and
> The unceasing rich and joyful dimension, astounding
>   in its splendor;
> Are continuously appearing like multitudes of stars,[327]
> To the eyes of persons with fortunate karma
> Who very precisely[328] see
> The real nature of all that can be known.
>
> Like a thousand shining lotus petals,
> Their excellent qualities of keen discernment and
> The renowned fruition of their accomplishment and
>   realization,
> Suffuses the three realms.[329]

Like space, the sheer essence dimension is unborn. The pure resplendent dimension arises endlessly in it, astonishing and radiant. This richly joyful dimension is endowed with two kinds of realization and compassion for others. Tenth stage bodhisattvas engage with resplendent dimension beings. For all disciples, based on their own prayers and karma, multifarious appearances arise like stars and planets in the sky, furthering all activities and teachings of the Buddha. These are the emanation dimension beings. Fortunate practitioners who come into contact with them will thereby understand the teachings.

Just as beautiful water lotuses bloom in many lovely colors and then produce even more flowers, so when we overcome all our afflictive obstructions and the obstructions to our potential for omniscience, when we achieve the fruits of realization based on teachings we have heard and practiced, our renown extends throughout the three realms.

Everything written here was composed by me, the old, unschooled, and ignorant Khetsun Sangpo. I wrote it in Dordogne, France, in a place surrounded by trees and forest. Hundreds practice meditation here. I completed this writing in 1993, in the eighth month on the sixth day. I pray that this will help myself and others. May it be fortunate for all.

Representations of Buddha's body, speech, and mind are offered to Rinpoche to sustain his own body, speech, and mind. The students express their wish that he live long and continue to offer the Dharma. Rinpoche answers, "I have to do that," amid much delight and laughter.

And he offers one more key teaching:

The commitment of our Dharma community is to be helpful to one another, to remain close and connected by kindness. This is my hope for you. All your commitments are included in that one.

Part Three

Khetsun Sangpo Rinpoche: Episodes from a Life of Practice

Khetsun Sangpo Rinpoche

A Life of Practice

KHETSUN SANGPO RINPOCHE (*mKhas btsun bzang po rin po che*) was born in the iron-bird year, 1921, in Barthang, part of the Yamdog area of Tibet, south of Lhasa. He founded the Nyingma Wish-Fulfilling Center for Study and Practice, now located in Sundarijal, Kathmandu, Nepal, and is widely renowned among the Tibetan scholarly community for his twelve-volume *Biographical Dictionary of Tibet and Tibetan Buddhism,*[330] with a thirteenth volume on Tibet's early history based on materials found at Dun-huang,[331] all published between 1973 and 1990. When the Dalai Lama encouraged religious leaders who fled Tibet to write about their lives in order to help preserve cultural memory, Rinpoche composed his own autobiography,[332] published in Dharamsala in 1973 (and later translated into Japanese), in which he discusses his life, his birth in southern Tibet, his religious training and work as a *ngagpa* and hail master as well as the development of his meditation practices. More recently, the Nyingma Wish-Fulfilling Center for Study and Practice published Rinpoche's commentary on *Wisdom's Sword* by Ju Mipham Rinpoche. His oral commentary on Mipham's *Mindnature in Three Cycles* has been translated into English, along with Mipham's written text, by Jeffrey Hopkins as *Fundamental Mind: The Nyingma View of the Great Completeness,* and his condensed commentary on Patrul Rinpoche's

Words of My Perfect Teacher was published by Snow Lion in 1986 as *Tantric Practice in Nyingma.*

While in Tibet, Rinpoche studied the texts of sutra and tantra for a twelve-year period beginning in 1937, when he was seventeen. After this, he trained in the art of hail protection from his father-in-law, a hereditary master who, by custom, could not pass this on because he had no sons, only daughters, one of whom, Chime Lhamo (*Chi med lha mo*) became Rinpoche's wife. In the years before leaving Tibet, Rinpoche became a successful hail master. Much later in life, Rinpoche commented that he'd had no wish to work as a hail master since it involved a kind of fight with the beings and forces that bring hail. He expressed gratitude that he always succeeded with peaceful methods and never had to resort to wrathful means that are also part of a hail protector's repertoire.[333] On the other hand, working as a hail protector meant spending the three summer months high in the mountains, essentially on retreat. This appealed to him very much.[334] He also took the opportunity to spend several months at Sera Monastery and also at the Gomang College of Drepung Monastery. Always the ready student, he made the most of this opportunity to learn more about Geluk presentations of the view, and to reflect on how this related to Nyingma positions. He did considerable writing on this topic at the time, but, alas, the work was left behind in Tibet and did not survive.

From a young age Rinpoche was profoundly oriented toward retreat, and between the years of 1949 and 1955 he mainly practiced in closed retreat, culminating in a dark retreat that was dramatically disrupted by a police search associated with the developing disturbances in Tibet. Unable to return to his home, now in Yade (*g.Yag sde*), Rinpoche was forced to flee over the border immediately, leaving behind his wife and three-week-old daughter.

His teachers were luminaries of the last great generation of twentieth-century masters teaching in traditional Tibet. From Jetsun Shugsep, he received the Heart Essence, Vast Expanse

(Longchen Nyingthig) transmission at Kangri Thogar, just above the Shugseb Dzogchen nunnery, where Longchenpa himself had practiced. Another important teacher was Kangyur Rinpoche, the great yogi famous for carrying out of Tibet and extensively teaching the Kangyur, who lived in exile in Darjeeling, and is best known to Western Buddhists for his magnificent commentary on Jigme Lingpa's *Treasury of Precious Qualities*. And Rinpoche always, in every way, expressed profound reverence for his teacher Dudjom Rinpoche, the first head of the Nyingma order in exile, whom he often described as a living Guru Rinpoche, and with whom he urged us to study whenever we had the chance. Khetsun Sangpo Rinpoche spoke also with admiring fervor of his great master Lama Gonpo, who spent his life in retreat, and about whom little else is currently known. Rinpoche revered him as the most exalted type of practitioner.

Rinpoche and Trulzhig Rinpoche were the two holders in their generation of the profoundly revered Essential Black cycle (Yangti Nagpo), which Rinpoche received from Drukpa Yongzin Rinpoche, who received it from its discoverer, or *terton*, the first Trulzhig Dongag Lingpa Rinpoche.

Khetsun Rinpoche conferred the full triad of that rare empowerment on a handful of students who then practiced the dark retreat (*mun tshams*) under his direct supervision. It was my incandescent good fortune to be one of them, receiving its initiations of guru, deva, and dakini twice in 1994, the first time alone and then again with Harvey Aronson and Tulku Jigme himself. Despite being in the middle of planning the new school, Rinpoche took the time to make the extensive preparations needed for this to occur.

In 1960, Dudjom Rinpoche asked Khetsun Rinpoche to represent him in Japan. With the encouragement also of His Holiness the Dalai Lama, Rinpoche spent ten years there, becoming fluent in Japanese and teaching at all the major Japanese universities. During this period he also worked extensively in Tokyo as a member of the Toyo Bunko, Japan's largest Asian Library. Upon his return in 1971, at the behest of Dudjom Rinpoche and the Dalai Lama, Rinpoche founded the Nyingma Wish-Fulfilling Center for Study and Practice in order to care for and train young Tibetans from the greater Himalayan region and beyond. Students came from Orissa, Ladakh, Mustang, Spiti, and other Tibetan refugee communities. Many were orphans or for other reasons impoverished, though several were identified tulkus. All received a first-class education, as well as food and shelter from childhood and well into early adulthood, made possible by Rinpoche's kindness and the personal support he garnered through sales of his books.

The school's early years were lean, with about twenty students sharing a very basic sleeping space in Dalhousie and then Mussoorie. Gradually, the number of students increased and better accommodations were found when Rinpoche designed and constructed a new building and settled the school in Sundarijal, in the northeast part of the Kathmandhu valley. From the early 1980s Rinpoche and his wife, Acha Migmar-la, were also raising his grandson, Kangyur Tulku Jigme Norbu Rinpoche. This boy, the son of the infant daughter left behind in Tibet, was recognized by Dudjom Rinpoche and His Holiness the Dalai Lama as the incarnation of none other than Rinpoche's teacher Kangyur Rinpoche. Today, Tulku Jigme continues the work of the school, providing a traditional shedra education to over fifty monks, and growing. Many of the center's earlier students now teach in their own centers or monasteries, including Lama Tenzin Samphel, who has lived and taught in France since 1987.

On returning from Japan in 1971, Rinpoche stopped in Sarnath, where Harvey Aronson struck up a conversation with him in a tea stall, and introduced me to him later that year. Professor Jeffrey Hopkins—one of the first in the United States to become fluent in Tibetan, thanks to the pioneering work of Geshe Ngawang Wangyal—met Rinpoche in Dharamsala that same year, and began to study Longchenpa's *Treasury of the Sublime Vehi-*

cle (Theg mchog mdzod) with him. Wanting to study further and share this opportunity with his students, Jeffrey invited Rinpoche to teach at the University of Virginia in 1974. A class of about 100 students, graduate and undergraduate, at that time the largest class ever in Religious Studies, listened to Rinpoche teach the not-yet translated *Words of My Perfect Teacher.* Those lectures, orally translated in real time by Jeffrey, became *Tantric Practice in Nyingma,* one of the very first, if not the first, detailed texts in English on the Foundational Practices. Rinpoche visited the University of Virginia several more times at Jeffrey's invitation, including in 1986 and 1991, when he also came to California and, in 1991, to Houston. His visits to the U.S.—Virginia, Texas, California, or Colorado—continued through the 1990s until 2006. He also visited France numerous times at Lama Tenzin Samphel's invitation and gave Essential Black empowerments and teachings there.

In addition, Khetsun Rinpoche was several times a visiting scholar at Rice University in Houston. During his stays in the United States, Rinpoche also taught in California, including at Jikoji Zen Center in Los Gatos and the Shambhala Center in Berkeley; (with kind assistance from students of the Rigpa Center); at Tara Mandala in Pagosa Springs, Colorado; at the Shambhala Center in Boulder, Colorado; and at the Margaret Austin Center outside Houston. He taught at Rice University's Glasscock School of Continuing Studies, and at Dawn Mountain Tibetan Buddhist Temple in Houston, which hosted several of Rinpoche's U.S. tours. On his last visit to North America he also taught in Toronto and Vancouver.

In the summer of 2009, the last summer of his life, Rinpoche planned and presided over a Great Accomplishing (*Drub chen*) of one hundred thousand offerings in the tradition of Essential Black. In early December, he left his body after bidding his students goodbye a few days before. His last words were a classic verse of poetry, "In one moment, every detail opens clear / in just one moment, a perfect Buddha is here."[335]

Khetsun Sangpo Rinpoche

A Brief History in His Own Words

During Rinpoche's third visit to the University of Virginia, a trip that also included teaching at Rice University and in California, Jeffrey Hopkins asked Rinpoche to speak about his life. The following is an excerpt from that conversation.[336]

PROFESSOR HOPKINS asked if I would speak a little bit about my life. Since he asked, I will comply. But this is not because I am well trained or have attained any high realization or great qualities. There is really not much of anything to tell except things that might embarrass me. But since Professor Jeffrey asked, I will tell some of my story, since, after all, this is my third visit here, and I enjoy being with you very much. I will speak without holding anything back.

I was born into a middle-class farming family. Around age eleven I began thinking that I would like to study in a monastery rather than remain a householder. When I approached my parents about this, they disagreed. In my family, the children stayed home; they were not sent away for education. But one day I took a leather pouch, loaded it up with one day's worth of *tsampa* (roasted barley), and ran away. I didn't have far to go, because there was a monastery, Norbu Choling, Khyam Gompa (*G.yag sde khyams rab brtan nor bu chos kling*) in Yade, on the other side of a pass from my house. I went there.[337]

Because I had run away from home, others at the monastery

looked down on me, and made me a servant of the other monks. This meant that I spent a lot of time carrying water from a long distance to different parts of the monastery. I spent my days getting water and my nights sweeping and cleaning the monks' quarters. There was an old monk there who taught me reading and writing in my spare time between chores. There isn't much to tell about this period of my life; I just spent it working.

Three months after my arrival at Norbu Choling, my father, having discovered where I was, brought me a few pieces of clothing and some food. He was concerned because I had never worked as a servant before and he thought this was inappropriate. He said to me, "Come home with me. You must." But I was determined to stay. I told him I was learning reading and writing, and that it seemed I would have more opportunity to study at the monastery, and that I would stay another year or two.

My father was still uneasy, so before he left he met with one of the monastery's leaders. He explained that I had never, at this young age, done much work and that I really didn't know very much. My father was worried about my well-being and asked this monastic official to be as kind to me as he could. This monk was a particularly frightening person who often beat the young monks. He told my father that young monks, myself included, were like cats crying "Meow, meow"—if you beat them they would at least pay attention. Still, since my father had requested I be shown some loving care, the monk would do what he could.

I remained in the monastery as a servant until I was fifteen. During this period I learned to read and write fairly well. I also memorized the monastery's prayers and learned to chant and play ritual music. I used to hide a book inside my robe. When no one was looking, I would stop work, take out my book, and study. When someone came along who would likely scold me for this, I put the book away and worked, but as soon as they were out of sight, I would take out the book and study again.

When I was fifteen, the monastery needed restoration and I was appointed the head of construction. I had some aptitude for this and learned how to do all the measurements and construction for building a monastery. Until I was eighteen, I worked on this restoration project. In those three years, the building progressed until only the murals remained to be painted on the inside walls, but because this work left me with even less time to study, I asked the monastery officials to give me some time off to focus on my books. But because I was efficient at restoration work, the monastery wouldn't give me any time off.

When I was eighteen, I told the monastery officials I wanted to go to Lhasa to attend the Great Prayer Festival. The officials gave me permission and I promised to return immediately afterward. I traveled with my friends Yingri and Tomé. As was the custom in Tibet, we carried on our backs everything we needed: our bedding, clothing, and food.

When I see people here in the United States with heavy bags of books on their backs I always recall, "Oh, that's what I did as a child." I remember it very well. I also look at the good circumstances you have for study here and I am amazed. In Tibet, you had to take everything on your back and seek out a teacher. If you were poor, you still had to gather something to give to your teacher, and this was a big worry. Here you have good facilities and I don't see your teachers beating you, so it must be impossible for you not to become great scholars. Or perhaps these good circumstances are too comfortable and it works against good study. It's probably better if you are a little uncomfortable.

Much later, after I left Tibet, I built a school in Nepal for about twenty students. It is a good place to stay and it has good food. Sometimes, when I observe the students who are not being very scholarly or skillful, I scold them, saying, "You have terrific circumstances compared to people of my time, and it is terrible to waste them."

My two friends and I went to Lhasa and attended the Great Prayer Festival. They returned to the monastery as soon as the festival ended, but I decided on another plan. Just over the pass from Lhasa is the Shugseb monastery, where there lived an old nun by the name of Lochen Rinpoche, also known as Jetsun Shugseb. I went to meet her and asked for three teachings. For many years I had heard about the practice of transference (powa) the cultivation of the winds (*rtsa rlung*), and severance (*gcod*). These are what I asked her to teach me.

Lochen Rinpoche was amazed at my request. "How could a boy your age have heard about these three?" I explained that I had been hearing of them for many years at the monastery. They were the reason I had come to her. But Lochen Rinpoche did not encourage me to stay at Shugseb. Instead, she said she would send me to study with Geshe Sogyal Rinpoche, who at that time was staying off in a corner room of the Sakya monastery, where he was one of the head instructors. His present incarnation is Nyingma but at that time he was Sakya. Geshe Sogyal Rinpoche was a student of Khenpo Thupten, whose own teacher was Dzogchen Khenpo Shenphen Chogyi Nangwa.[338]

Nonetheless, I remained at Shugseb for another week. Then Lochen Rinpoche told me, "This won't do. There are a lot of young nuns here, you'll begin spending time together and it won't work out." She said it would be better for me to live in the cave of Longchenpa nearby. Everyday at ten in the morning I was to visit her for instruction.

In the mornings I was very happy in this cave perched high on the mountain behind Shugseb. The sky was clear, the birds were full of song, and from the top of the mountain you could see almost as far away as the place where I was born. At night, when it was completely dark, I became quite sad. But then morning arrived and wiped away my fear of the night before. My mind became clear and happy and I was eager to study. I lived this way for about a year.

At that time, the chief official of that region was from the Lhalu (*Lha klu*) clan, and when Lord Lhalu learned that I had left my family and found my way to his area's monastery, he contacted my father. Soon thereafter, my family informed me that they were encountering various difficulties and I needed to return home immediately. So I returned home to my original monastery, where they were still working on the murals of the restored buildings. For about a year I stayed there, again working as a servant. But then I decided to leave and go to the far north of Tsang province.

I heard that Geshe Sogyal Rinpoche, whom Jetsun Shugseb had initially mentioned to me, had gone to India and returned to Sera Dropde (*gTsang Sera sgrub se*). I left my monastery to meet him there. The Tsang economy was very good at that time, and people made many offerings, including food, and they also sponsored many prayers. I stayed with Geshe Sogyal for a year and my studies went very well.

But Lord Lhalu found out where I was staying and sent me a very angry letter. He ordered me to return to my original monastery and study only Gelukpa texts, even though students in that monastery generally studied a variety of traditions—Geluk, Nyingma, and so forth. Lord Lhalu warned me that there was a monk who would report back to him if I studied anything else but Geluk texts. Nowadays, Lhalu is a leader in the Tibetan Autonomous Region.

I was born in a Nyingma family, and I felt a very strong affinity to Nyingma teachings. I showed my displeasure at Lord Lhalu and protested against his dictum by establishing a Nyingma organization in the monastery, holding prayers on the tenth day of the month [a Nyingma custom, as this is a day sacred to Guru Rinpoche]. I spent a year in this kind of rebellion, and finally Lord Lhalu ordered me before him and said, "I told you to study only Geluk doctrines, and here you are working for the Nyingma teachings. According to law you should be badly punished for your disobedience, but since you are a religious person, I can't do that." Instead he decided to send me to Sera, the great Geluk monastery in Lhasa, to study with Pabongkha, who would be giving lectures on the stages of the path. Lord Lhalu provisioned me for the journey and sent me to Lhasa. I was the only Nyingma there, but since there were many scholars visiting and gathering, my studies went really well. But after a year and a half, I contracted chicken pox and was no longer able to study, so I traveled back to the monastery near my home village.

Because I had so much training, I became the senior teacher at my home monastery. Lord Lhalu, knowing that I had studied with the Gelukpas, thought that I would teach and refute the doctrine of the Nyingma but as soon as I returned, I revitalized our practice of Nyingma prayers. Lord Lhalu finally told me, "Either you give up this Nyingma business, or get out of here." Since I wasn't going to give up my Nyingma practice, I moved to a nearby tantric ritual temple.

One of their main practices was stopping hail. It was my karma that when I arrived at the temple, I met an elderly practitioner and his wife who had several daughters but no sons.[339] Women were not trained as hail masters and therefore, having no sons, the practitioner had no one to whom he could to pass on the transmission of stopping hail; I became regarded as the person who could fulfill this role. The hail master I studied with was known as Nyenteng Ngagpa, because his family or house lineage was called Nyan Teng (*gnyan steng*). His monastery was known as "The Place Where Mantra Overpowers Demons" (*bDud brtul drag snag gling*). In winter, we spent three months in retreat preparing for the hail-protection rituals and in the summer we stayed high in the mountains. You could see the hail coming from there, so if we saw a hail storm approaching we performed the rituals. Otherwise there was nothing to do except stay in retreat and meditate.

In spring and fall there was no danger of hail, so during these times I would visit Drukpa Yongzin Rinpoche,[340] whose previous incarnation had been a tutor of the Fifth Dalai Lama. He was therefore called a grand holder of the teachings, or Yongzin, in all of his subsequent reincarnations. This lama was the student of a terton, and I received the full transmission of revealed teachings, which included instructions on the dark retreat, a meditation practiced in total darkness. The benefit of this type of practice is that if you can do it properly for seven days, you can attain buddhahood.

Near Drukpa Yongzin was the hermitage of Lama Gonpo (*mGon po*) Rinpoche, a reincarnation of Dodrupchen Rinpoche from the Golok area of Amdo, whose teacher had been Lama Tsultrim Rangdrol from Kham Sharlung (*Khams sharlung*). I met Lama Gonpo Rinpoche in the Copper Cave of Crystal Village (*Shel grong zangs yag brag*) and received numerous Dzogchen instructions from him, and in particular instructions from the famous *Yeshe Lama* of Jigme Lingpa.[341]

Lama Gonpa was a great yogi, always staying in hermitages, moving from one sacred place to another, attended by some of the many monks and nuns who were his disciples. He never had a fixed residence. Since he was an outstanding person and teacher, I asked for the teaching of the Longchen Nyingthig. He refused. When I begged and cried, he commented, "Nowadays everybody wants sudden enlightenment. I am the only one who's doing gradual practice, working extremely hard." Finally, he agreed to teach me, and every day he would do a little bit of the text with me. As we moved from place to place, he always emphasized the importance of a good foundation, starting with the four thoughts that help turn the mind away from the ordinary concerns of samsara. In this way I became familiar with some of the central works of the Longchen Nyingthig. When it came to Dzogchen, Gonpo Rinpoche did not rely on texts; he gave instructions that laid bare the teachings (*dmar khrid*), and instructions that came from his own long experience (*myong khrid*). In time, he told me stories of his own studies: how he received Dzogchen from Lama Tsultrim Rangdrol Rinpoche (*bLama Tshul khrims rang grol*), including how he received teachings on Jigme Lingpa's masterpiece, *Yeshe Lama*, from him. Then he gave me instructions and transmission of *Yeshe Lama*.[342]

Lama Gonpo Rinpoche wanted to go on a pilgrimage to Samye, and since his knees were in very bad shape from so much time in meditative posture, he asked me to help and accompany him. We traveled together, taking the old Tibetan-style boat, a leather coracle, down the Tsangpo River to Samye. At Samye, Gonpo Rinpoche offered all his possessions and announced he was going to Samye's Cave of White Light (*bSam yas 'od dkar brag*), in Lhokha. The cave gets its name because this is where the dakini Yeshe Tsogyal attained a rainbow body. Incredible things happened in this place, and I would run out of time if I told them all to you. Here, though, is a brief story from our time there.

When we arrived at this place, we heard fantastic music and wondered how the three people staying in this hermitage could make such a grand sound. Those three resident hermits in turn thought the visiting lama must be causing this amazing symphonic display. In fact, this was probably a sign that Gonpo Rinpoche was going to die in this place.

We arrived on the twenty-fourth day of the tenth lunar month. On the twenty-fifth day, Gonpo Rinpoche announced that he had some important teachings for us and that we should call his chief patron so that she could also hear them. Her name was Sangye Drolma (*Sangs rgyas sgrol ma*), and she lived at Tshering Jong, where Jigme Lingpa had founded a nunnery and lived out the last years of his life. She arrived at noon the next day. Gonpo Rinpoche told her that this would be the last day she would be able to meet with him, so she should ask any and all of her questions on meditation now. She had none, because she was so concerned that this was the last day of his life.

Lama Gonpo said, "If you don't have anything to ask, all of you leave. Close up this place. Nobody come in here for seven days." When we left him in the cave, Lama Gonpo, who was a large person, was wearing heavy clothes because of the cold. His main attendant became uneasy, and so after six days he decided to look into the cave. He saw only clothing inside, no body. The attendant started to gather the clothing, but then the lama appeared, yet much smaller than he was when we last saw him, with a tremendous brilliance of light, and emitting rainbows.

Gonpo Rinpoche had explained before going into this final

retreat that he would reduce the size of his body and turn it into a rainbow body, but that if this were not successful, we were to cremate his body. The attendant wanted to cremate what remained of his body, but two other reincarnated lamas there wanted to bring the remains to their monastery. Everyone began arguing. Lama Gonpo's students felt that the proper thing to do was to obey Lama Gonpo's wishes and cremate his remains. So we did this, and many absolutely extraordinary things occurred. Rainbows and relics of different kinds appeared in the ashes. We divided the relics and sent half to the monastery of Dodrupchen; the remainder we divided to place in two or three stupas (reliquaries).

After this, I continued working as a hail master, living comfortably and doing my rituals until the Chinese invaded. If I told you about my escape from Tibet and the difficulties involved in that, you would be moved to great sorrow, but it is late in the day. And, if I told you about those events and my time in retreats, that would also take a lot of time, so I think I've said enough today. Still we can have some questions.

Questions and Responses: Rinpoche on Monasticism and Meditation

Question: It's a simple question. Was the name Khetsun Sangpo given by your parents?

Response: The name that my parents gave me was Karma Wangpo. At the monastery the abbot gives each monk a name, and everyone wonders what name they're going to get. You receive part of the abbot's name and the other part you wonder about. I was given the name Khetsun Sangpo. I didn't change my name after that. I didn't have to.

Question: Would Rinpoche tell us more about his meditative experiences?

RESPONSE: Anyone conducting a meditation retreat according to the tantric system has unusual experiences. It just goes with the territory. But it's part of the tantric system to keep these secret, so I will keep it secret in accordance with the way it's supposed to be. When you light a fire, you'll necessarily get some heat. Just so, if you receive initiation and oral transmission of a particular practice, as well as instructions on how to do it, and then you actually engage in that practice, it pretty much couldn't happen that you wouldn't get some fantastic experience from it. When a practice is done properly you definitely will get results. When it isn't, then there's no certainty. I'm talking about practice conducted properly. Many people come and tell me that even though they are engaging in such-and-such practice, they feel full of desire and hatred, even more than before. I explain that's not the fault of system, it's just that they're doing the practice wrong.

QUESTION: At any point did you decide to quit the monastery, especially when you had to do all the drudge work without being able to study?
RESPONSE: I never thought to give up Dharma practice. Once you start, you can see that day by day you're getting closer to the time of your own death and thus your enthusiasm and heartfelt effort get stronger and stronger. So I never thought to leave.

ན་མོ་གུ་རུ། །

རྒྱལ་ཀུན་གསུང་གི་རྡོ་རྗེ་འོད་དཔག་མེད། །
པདྨའི་རིགས་འཛིན་པདྨ་ལས་འཁྲུངས་ཤིང་། །
པདྨ་ཐོད་ཕྲེང་རྩལ་དུ་གྲགས་འབར་བ། །
སྐྱབས་ཀྱི་མཆོག་ཏུ་བསྟེན་ནོ་བྱིན་གྱིས་རློབས། །

མགོན་པོ་གང་གི་ཕྲིན་ལས་སྤྲེལ་བ་ལ། །
མཁ༷ས་པའི་གཏན་ཚིགས་རིགས་ལམ་དཔལ་རྣོན་པོས། །
ལོག་པར་རྟོག་པའི་དྲྭ་བ་འདྲལ་མཛད་ཅིང་། །
ཡང་དག་ལྷ་ལ་བཙུན་པའི་རིགས་སྔགས་འཆང་། །

མཁ༷ས་བཙུ༷ན་བཟ༷ང་པོ༷འི་ཡོན་ཏན་དཔལ་ལྡན་པ། །
གང་ཕྱོད་ཞིང་འདིར་མཛད་པ་བརྟུལ་བ་ལས། །
བདག་ཅག་དུཿཁས་མནར་བ་འདི་དགོངས་ལ། །
གཟུགས་སྐུའི་བཀོད་པ་མྱུར་བར་བསྟན་པར་གསོལ། །

འཁོར་འདས་ཆོས་ལ་འཛིགས་པ་མེད་པའི་གནས། །
སྒྲིབ་བྲལ་ཆོས་སྐུའི་དབྱིངས་ལས་མ་གཡོས་བཞིན། །
འཁོར་འདས་ངོ་མཚར་ཡོན་ཏན་བསམ་ཡས་པ། །
ལྷུན་གྱིས་གྲུབ་པའི་བཀོད་པ་བསྒྱུར་བར་གསོལ། །

Prayer for Khetsun Sangpo Rinpoche's Swift Return

H. E. DUNGSE THINLEY NORBU RINPOCHE

IN RESPONSE to a request accompanied by the offering of a white scarf from Tulku Jigme, grandson of the Supreme Being and head of Shedrub Dorje Ling, the Nyingmapa Wish-Fulfilling Center for Study and Practice, as well as the assembly of pupils there, this prayer was made by Thinley Norbu, skillfully playing on the name Khetsun Sangpo (*khey-tsun-sangpo*) and on the name of his grandson, Jigme.

Victors' vajra speech, Amitabha,
Lotus lineage holder, Lotus-born,
Widely known as Pema Thö Dreng Sel,
Bless us, supreme refuge, sole support.

To increase our protector's great deeds
With skilled (*khey*) proofs, reasoning's sharp blade,
You strike through our web of wrong ideas,
Mantra holder of bright (*tshun*) right views.

Glorious: wise (*khey*), bright (*tshun*), and kind (*sang*),
Now that your work here has subsided,
Please think of our pained sad suffering.
We pray you quickly take form again.

ཇི་ལྟར་དགོས་འབྱུང་ཡིད་བཞིན་ནོར་བུ་ལ། །
གསོལ་བ་བཏབ་པས་དགོས་རྒྱུ་འབྱུང་བ་ལྟར། །
བདག་ཅག་ཁྱེད་ལ་དད་པའི་རྗེས་འཇུག་རྣམས། །
གསོལ་བཏབ་སྨོན་པའི་འབྲས་བུ་འགྲུབ་གྱུར་ཅིག །

ཅེས་དམ་པ་དེ་ཉིད་ཀྱི་སྐུ་ཚ་བོ་སྤྲུལ་སྐུ་འཛིགས་མེད་ཀྱིས་དབུ་བཞུགས་པའི་བཤད་སྒྲུབ་འདོད་འཇོ་གླིང་གི་འདུས་སྡེ་ནས་ལྷ་རིག་ཧེན་དང་བཅས་ཏེ་བསྐུལ་མ་གནང་ངོར་ཕྲིན་ལས་ནོར་བུས་གསོལ་བ་བཏབ

You, fearless (*jigme*) in swirl and peace,
Not stirring from true form's stainless realm,
Please with ease show your most amazing
Great traits, beyond mind, in swirl and peace.

Just as a wish-granting jewel bestows
All that is needed, please grant to us
What we faithful followers request.
May our deep prayer to you bear fruit.

Notes

1. Longchen Rabjam, *The Precious Treasury of Philosophical Systems,* trans. Richard Barron (Junction City, Calif.: Padma, 2007), 360.
2. Longchen Rabjam, *Precious Treasury,* 360. See Maitreya, *Buddha Nature,* trans. Rosemarie Fuchs (Ithaca, N.Y.: Snow Lion Publications, 2000).
3. "In three real jewels, three root Blissful Ones / Channels, winds, bright orbs this bodhi-mind / Essence, nature, heart-move mandala / Until full bodhi I seek refuge." See Anne C. Klein, *Heart Essence of the Vast Expanse* (Ithaca, N.Y.: Snow Lion, 2009), 35, 65.
4. The passage is from Maitreya's *Commentary on the Sublime Continuum (Uttaratantra Shastra, Mahāyāna-uttaratantra-śāstra),* in *Buddha Nature,* 168. The first two qualities prefigure the emptiness and luminosity of sheer awareness in Longchenpa and Jigme Lingpa.
5. *Thog ma med pa nas gnas pa'i rigs* and *rgyas 'gyur gyi rigs.*
6. Longchenpa cites Maitreya, chapter 1, line 40, in *Precious Treasury,* 155; Tibetan, 85a. (Hereafter, Tibetan numbers follow page numbers in brackets.)
7. *Precious Treasury of Philosophical Systems,* 149 [81a]. Longchenpa cites Maitreya, chapter l verse 62. While other epithets are also important, the quality of stainlessness stands out: hence the translation here of *chos dbyings* as "stainless" This space is also the place of arising, or basis, of everything, as Longchenpa emphasizes in the first chapter of *The Precious Treasury of Basic Space (Chos dbyings mdzod),* translated by Richard Barron in *A Treasure Trove of Scriptural Transmission* (Junction City, Calif.: Padma Publishing, 2001). Indeed, this basic, stainless, and originary space is fundamental to the arising of everything. It is also inseparable from primordial knowing (*ye shes*). In the introduction to his commentary on *The Precious Treasury of Basic Space,* Longchenpa describes this space as "primordial knowing, totally pure in nature, and as mindnature, and ultimate truth." Later he writes that "stainless space and primordial knowing are inseparable in their total purity" (*Precious Treasury of Basic Space,* 133). This purity is an important portal for how everything can be experienced as the mandala of Buddhahood and why

everything is always complete and perfect, no matter what—an essential insight in the practice of both sutra and tantra (*Precious Treasury of Basic Space,* 134).

8. *Buddha Nature,* 174. Longchenpa cites in the context of describing the bodhisattva approach.
9. *Buddha Nature,* 302 [163a]. Longchenpa also emphasizes purity as an epithet of *chos dbyings/dharmadhātu* in the Dzogchen context at *Buddha Nature,* 340 [182b], and 302 [163a]. At *Buddha Nature,* 326 [191b], Longchenpa again points to base, path, and fruition's relation to stainless space in Dzogchen.
10. TEXT EDIT: Possibly *gnas pa ngar med steng ngo bo* should be *gnas pa ngar med stong nge ba*, in which case the line could read, "Your unclear stability, an empty essence." Otherwise the line reads, "That which rests on unclear stability."
11. Although the teaching is widely known in English as "Heart Essence of the Vast Expanse," our translation of it as "Heart Essence, Vast Expanse" draws from Jigme Lingpa's equation of this transmission with the heart, or innermost essence, of all the teachings. He calls these Dzogchen teachings "the essence (*thig*) of the great heart (*snying*) *which is also* the space of the vast expanse (*long chen*)" (italics added by translator). See Tulku Thondup, *Masters of Meditation and Miracles* (Boston: Shambhala South Asia Editions, 2002), 41. The expanse itself is the essential heart of all teachings. Also, Jigme Lingpa writes of the yellow scrolls that he receives at Boudhanath and later reveals as Heart Essence, Vast Expanse: "Wonderful! I am entrusting into the hands of the sacred protectors the yellow scrolls, which are like the essence of the great heart of space, the pupil of [its] eye, and the very essence of the Seven Treasures (*kLong chen sNying thig,* vol. hum, 551 [12a.6]) in Jigme Lingpa, *Collected Works* (Paro, Bhutan: Dilgo Khyentse edition, 1972).
12. His autobiography has been published in Tibetan by the Nyingmapa Wish-Fulfilling Center for Study and Practice and in Japanese by his Japanese student Shinichi Nagatsawa, but it is not yet available in English.
13. Because of his responsibilities at the school, Khetsun Rinpoche declined an invitation to teach in California for an extended period of time. He recommended Lama Gonpo Tsayden of Amdo come instead, and Lama Gonpo spent several fruitful years teaching Longche Nyingthig texts to a broad range of students. Those same students came to study with Khetsun Rinpoche when he visited California after Lama Gonpo's departure.
14. In the first, very private, retreat, Rinpoche taught two texts included in the backmatter to Jigme Lingpa's *Yeshe Lama:* the *Lion's Roar*, which provides crucial identification on sidetracking and slipping (*gol shor*), and *White Lotus* (*Pad ma dKar po*). The second retreat is where Rin-

poche taught *Strand of Jewels*. Although initially Rinpoche had no intention of seeing that teaching published, much less translated into English, in time he came to wish for this to occur.

15. TEXT EDIT: *ched* corrected to *ches* by Lama Tenzin.
16. The two truths, conventional and ultimate; the two collections, wisdom and merit; the two enlightened or Buddha dimensions (Tib., *sku*; Skt., *kāya*) refer to (1) the formless essential dimension (*dharmakāya*) and (2) the form expressions, the emanation and richly resplendent dimensions.
17. In Mahamudra, the teacher identifies and introduces the student to base, path, and fruition in the context of bestowing a consecration or initiation (*dbang*). This is done through relying on signs (*rtags*) and words (*tshigs*) as well as on objects associated with the consecration. In this sense, consecration is a special method in Mahamudra. Initiation is also important in Dzogchen, and a lama may make an identification of base, path, and fruition, during, for example, an initiation into the dynamism of sheer awareness (*rig pa'i rtsal dbang*). By and large, however, Dzogchen lamas do not emphasize making such identifications part of a formal initiation. What is important is that the identification occur when the student is in a state of sheer awareness.
18. The name "primordial knowing" can be applied to the genuine state of the base (*gzhi'i gnas lugs*) and to the unchanging base (*'gyur ba med pa'i gzhi*), according to Lama Tenzin Samphel (Houston, April 2010).
19. The well-known phrases *gzhi dus* and *lam dus* are often, and most literally, translated as "at the time of the base" or "at the time of the path." Here, however, temporality is mostly metaphorical; lest we think that there is some initial, prior, time when there is only base, the phrase is here rendered less literally as "at" or "in," meaning "in the context of" the base. After a discussion with Lama Tenzin, I am glossing *dus* here as *gnas skabs*, which could also be translated "context."
20. Lama Tenzin Samphel notes that the name "primordial knowing" can be applied to the genuine state of the base (*gzhi'i gnas lugs*) and to the unchanging base (*gyur ba med pa'i gzhi*) (Houston, April 2010).
21. TEXT EDIT: *rnam grang* corrected to *rnam grangs*.
22. TEXT EDIT: *blag tu rol par* corrected to *blag tu rtogs par*.
23. The Tibetan word *sku* (Skt., *kāya*) is translated as "Buddha dimension" when referring to the fruitional state of Buddha manifestations—the form dimensions and so forth, and as "dimension of enlightenment" when referring, as here, to aspects of one's mind at the time of the base or the path, or of Buddha manifestation in a more abstract sense.
24. Khetsun Sangpo Rinpoche likened this insubstantiality to the insubstantiality of the ocean's glittering. (Reported by Harvey Aronson from conversation with Rinpoche at the Nyingmapa Wish-Fulfilling Monastery, Sunderijal, Nepal, March 2009.)

25. TEXT EDIT: *gzhis dngos* corrected to *gzhi dngos.*
26. This work is central to tantric studies in Nyingma, a portal to understanding many of the most vital topics in the Tibetan tantric tradition. Commentaries on it have been written by such luminaries as Vimalamitra , Rongzon Pandita, Longchen Rabjam, Jamgon Kongtrul, Mipham Rinpoche, Dodrupchen Chen III (Jigme Denpa Nyima) and others.
27. *Guhyagarbha*, cited in *Collected Works of Longchen Rabjam* (*gsung 'bum, dri med 'od zer, sde dge par ma*, TBRC W00EGS1016299, 33 folios; 519–584). *Rgyud gsang pa snying po'i rtsa ba.* (Exact location of quote unknown.)
28. See also *The Tantra without Letters*, cited by Longchen Rabjam in his *Precious Treasury*, 341: "All beings of the three realms stray from the ground of being, / Which is not anything at all, into every possible state of confusion."
29. *The Unimpeded-State Tantra (dGongs pa zang thal gyi rgyu/Kun bzang dgongs pa zang thal las rdzogs pa chen po chos nyid mngon sum zhi khro lhun grub kyi phrin las),* by the terton rGod kyi ldem 'phru can (1337–1408), vol. 1 (Bylakuppe, Karnataka: Ngagyur Nyingma Institute, 2002), 464 ff. TBRC W10160. The verse Rinpoche cited, taken from the *Kun bzang smon lam (Prayer of All Goodness)*, is contained in the *Unimpeded-State Tantra.* It is cited in *Chos spyod kyi rim pa rnam par grol ba'i lam gyi shing rta zhes bya ba zhugs so,* by Dudjom Rinpoche (Dudjom Jigdral Yeshe Dorjee, 1904–1988). The verse begins at page 324 in the Tibetan text. The third line cited here starts at 324.2, because Khetsun Sangpo Rinpoche has skipped the verses in between to create his own emphasis. The entire passage in Tibetan reads (cited lines in bold): ***gzhi gcig lam gnyis 'bras bu gnyis / rig dang ma rig tsho 'phrul te*** */ kun tu bzang po'i smon lam gyis / thams cad chos dbyings pho brang du/mngon par rdzogs te 'tshang rgya shog / kun gyi gzhi ni 'dus ma byas / rang byung klong yangs brjod du med / 'hor 'as gnyis ka'i ming med do /* ***de nyid rig na sang rgyas te/ ma rig sems can 'khor bar 'byams.***
30. TEXT EDIT: *tsho 'phrul gyisi* [5a4] corrected to *tsho 'phrul de.*
31. TEXT EDIT: *zhes* [5a5] corrected to *zhes dang.* Note that the next lines, also apparently quoted from the same text, the *Gong pa Zang Thal,* do not directly follow this quotation. This quote is from the ninth chapter of the *Kun bzang smon Lam,* 519.6–520.2. The missing lines are

    kun tu bzang po'i smon lam gyis / thams cad chos dbyangs pho brang du / mngon par rdzogs te 'tshang rgya shog / kun gyi gzhi ni 'dus ma byas / rang byung klong yangs brjod du med / 'khor 'das gnyis ka'i ming med do.

    Kun bzang smon lam [rtsa gsum gter bdag gling pa. "chos spyod ngag 'don nyer mkho 'dod 'byung sa brtol ljon bzang /." In gter chos/_rtsa gsum gling pa/.

Source: TBRC W4CZ1042. vol. 1: 17–814. Pharphing, Kathmandu, Nepal: *bka' gter sri zhu ewam dpe skrun khang*, 2002–2010.

32. TEXT EDIT: *mya ngan 'das 'gro bas* [5a.6] corrected to *mya nan 'das 'phro.* The quotation is found in *Do ha mdzod kyi snying po don gyi glu'i 'grel pa*, in *bsTan 'gyur* (sDe dge). TBRC W23703, 154.6–7.
33. This assertion, "one entity with different ways of appearing" (*ngo bo gcig la snang tshul tha dad*), recalls but differs from the classic Madhyamaka description of the relation between two truths as "one entity with different isolates [different for thought]" (*ngo bo cig ldog pa tha dad*).
34. Khetsun Sangpo Rinpoche to Harvey Aronson, Nyingmapa Wish-Fulfilling Monastery (April 2009).
35. TEXT EDIT: *gnas la 'di la* corrected to *gnas pa 'di la.*
36. TEXT EDIT: *yongs grub cis* corrected to *yongs grub ces.*
37. TEXT EDIT: *kun gzhi ni mang tshig* corrected to *kun ni mang tshig.*
38. Khetsun Sangpo Rinpoche observes that this is so named not because it itself is a consciousness, but because it can *give rise* to a consciousness; more specifically, it can give rise to a naturally luminous consciousness. It also gets the name "allground consciousness" because the karmic winds give rise to consciousness like wind gives rise to waves (conversation with Harvey Aronson at Nyingmapa Wish-Fulfilling Monastery, March 2009). Lama Tenzin Samphel adds, "The karmic wind arises from the allground, which contains both good and bad predispositions (*bag chags*). In dependence on this wind, the allground consciousness (*kun gzhi rnam shes*) arises. The allground and the allground consciousness are one entity (*ngo bog gcig*)."
39. That is, the single allground is the point of departure for samsara and nirvana. Samsara arises based on a knowing consciousness, which is naturally clear, a mind (*sems*) that is knowing (*rig pa*). This mind's knowing, however, is completely different from the sheer awareness (*rig pa*) of Dzogchen. Based on this sheer awareness, there is nirvana.
40. TEXT EDIT: the text's *rig bya* is a misprint for *rig cha.*
41. The allground is as beginningless as samsara. It differs from the primordial base, as well as from the factor of primordial knowing, whose essence is empty and whose nature is clear. The seeds for a Buddha's qualities and the seeds for sentient beings' afflictions are both present in the allground. However, a Buddha's good qualities do not come from those seeds; they arise from primordial knowing. Another way to say this is that the seeds of the Buddha qualities are present while one is a sentient being, but obstructed. This is discussed in Jigme Lingpa's *rDzogpa chen po'i gnad gsum shan 'byed* (vol. na [that is, 12], 99–102, a *siddhanta* type of text (TBRC W7477-6070-101-104-any). The text at 99.3–4 reads, *Kun gzhi 'khor 'das kun gyi gzhi yin te / rnyog ma can gyi chu dang khyad par med / bag la nyal gyi gti mug mgo rmongs nas / ye shes rang rig pa'i dangs chu lkog tu gyur.* In English:

The allgound grounds the whole of cyclic existence and
nirvana
No different from water mixed with some other substance
Within the obscuring bewildered tendencies (*bag la nyal*)
Is hidden the pure water of self-knowing primordial
knowing (*ye shes rang rig*).

42. Khetsun Sangpo Rinpoche clarification (conversation at Nyingmapa Wish-Fulfilling Monastery, April, 2009). This is identical with the single allground mentioned above, from which both samsara and nirvana proceed. But it is different from the allground consciousness (*kun gzhi rnam shes*) of Chittamātra.
43. TEXT EDIT: *byung bas nas* corrected to *byung bas na*.
44. Buddha nature pervades all beings; therefore the mind of ordinary sentient beings is suffused with Buddha nature, also known as the essence of wisdom. This and many other names are simply different designations for it (Lama Tenzin Samphel). The quote in the text is at 170.5–6 in *Byang sems kun byed rgyal po in bka' 'gyur* (sDe dge par phud) (TBRC W22084. 97: 3–173).
45. Lama Tenzin Samphel notes that other important synonyms include "the perfection of wisdom," "Buddha nature," "sheer essence dimension," or "sheer awareness" (Septvaux, France, May 2011).
46. TEXT EDIT: *ngo spros* corrected to *ngo spro*.
47. TEXT EDIT: *rang ngo rang gi cha las rang ngo rang gis ma rig* should be *rang ngo rang gis ma rig*.
48. TEXT EDIT: omit *cha las rang ngo rang gis* (scribe mistakenly repeated from previous line).
49. Lama Tenzin Samphel singled out the term *mun chen* as unique, noting he had never seen it either in the writings of Dudjom Rinpoche or Dodrupchen Rinpoche.
50. *Sems nyid ngal gsor 'grel chen* [in Shing rta chen mo] on page 333.2 in *The Great Commentary on Resting in Mindnature,* vol. 4, by Longchen Rabjam (TBRC W00EGS1016299). (We have not yet located the quote itself.)
51. Khetsun Sangpo Rinpoche notes that this inborn unawareness has the characteristic of adhering to self (conversation with Harvey Aronson, Nyingmapa Wish-Fulfilling Monastery, April 2009).
52. TEXT EDIT: *gzhi la ma rig ma shar* is corrected to *gzhi la rig ma shar*. Khetsun Sangpo Rinpoche commented that this means there is ignorance, unawareness in the base (conversation with Harvey Aronson at Nyingmapa Wish-Fulfilling Monastery).
53. Cited in Dudjom, *Chos spyod* (The Practice of Dharma) op. cit., 325.4 (Xeroxed edition, n.p., n.d.).
54. TEXT EDIT: *'rjes ngas* corrected to *brjed ngas* (per Khetsun Sangpo Rinpoche).

55. *Lamp Distilling the Practices: A Commentary on the Meaning of the Five Stages [of the Guhyasamaja Completion Stage]* (*Caryamelapakapradipa; sPyod bsdus sgron ma*).
56. Middling desire is defined as a mind that is equal parts desire and hatred. See Lati Rinbochay and Hopkins, trans. 1979:41. *Spyod bsdus sgron ma (dbu med bris ma)* TBRC WIKG10776. 60.3.
57. TEXT EDIT: *brjed ngas* corrected to *brjed nges.*
58. In his oral commentary, Rinpoche points out that this term is used by *vaibhāṣikas* in the sense of "attainer" and thus, implicitly, is not to be confused with the "mind of near attainment" at the time of death.
59. In the context of meditation, such "natural appearance"—or, literally, "self appearance" (*rang snang*)—refers specifically to your own perceptions, which come from you but that you may misperceive as arising from something or somewhere else (Khetsun Sangpo Rinpoche, personal conversation with translator, Sundarijal, Nepal, n.d.).
60. Khetsun Sangpo Rinpoche points out that mental consciousness (*yid*) is a stronger term than "mind" (*sems*). Mind precedes the mental activity of identifying I and mine (conversation at Nyingma Wish-Fulfilling Monastery, March 2009). This accords also with Jigme Lingpa's discussion of perception in his Wisdom Chat #71.
61. Lama Tenzin Samphel notes that they arise from desire in the sense that desire makes us more likely to do these things. The thoughts arising from desire have the nature of method (personal conversation, fall 2012). These forty are elsewhere said to be associated with the mind of red increase, *mched pa*, in the dissolutions of death (Lati Rinbochay and Hopkins, 38ff).
62. Yangchen Gawe Lodro lists these items from the forty thoughts arising from desire as great engagement in hardship, middling engagement in hardship, small engagement in hardship, and vehemence. *sPyod bsdus sgron ma.* TBRC WIKG10776. 59.6–60.2.

    Lama Tenzin also notes that these forty arise from desire yet have the nature of wisdom in the sense that bliss, associated with desire, is method, while knowing emptiness is wisdom (personal conversation, fall 2012).
63. I rely here on Jeffrey Hopkins for the translation of *'gyogs pa.*
64. TEXT EDIT: *nang gsel gzhi* corrected to *nang bses bzhi.*
65. TEXT EDIT: *shin tu dka' ba* corrected to *shin tu dga' ba.*
66. Yangchen Gawe Lodro gives this as "non-taking up" in *Death, Intermediate State, and Rebirth,* 1979:41. There are other differences between his and Aryadeva's lists of the forty thoughts arisen from desire as well, especially in the last half of this list.
67. This bears no connection with the more esoteric use of the term *thabs lam* (Lama Tenzin Samphel, Houston, August 2009).
68. Lama Tenzin Samphel, Houston, May 2011.

69. Lama Tenzin Samphel glosses this as "completely established" (*yongs su grub pa*) and "established in every part" (*cha tshang ma grub pa*) (Houston, August 2009).
70. TEXT EDIT: *gzhon pa* corrected to *zhon pa.*
71. TEXT EDIT: *srog gis* corrected to *srog 'dzin gyis.*
72. TEXT EDIT: *mi mnyam* (unequal) should read *me mnyam* (fiery).
73. In general, the main work of the male wind is connected with the breath. Urination and so forth is the work of the female wind. In wind-channel practices, the female red from one's mother creates heat and melts the white element from one's father, which descends as liquid light, causing bliss (Lama Tenzin Samphel).
74. TEXT EDIT: *mchod pa'i rten byed* corrected to *mched pa'i rten byed.*

    This does not mean primordial knowing is an effect. Perhaps Khetsun Sangpo Rinpoche is thinking of Longchenpa's statements in *Treasury of Philosophical Tenets* (159) that Buddhahood (like primordial knowing) is not achieved through a causal process that involves something being developed, even though it may seem that way, but through a causal process that involves disengagement, like removing clouds so that the sun shines. The point is that primordial knowing is, like Buddha nature, intrinsic to every living being. The path allows us to access this, but does not cause it.
75. TEXT EDIT: *mi mnyam* corrected to *me mnyam.*
76. Lama Tenzin Samphel notes that, similarly, the arch of the foot itself is shaped like a bow and its color is green, the color of wind. This is discussed in *Secret Visions of the Fifth Dalai Lama,* by the Fifth Dalai Lama, trans. Samten Karmay (London: Serindia Publications, 1991).
77. TEXT EDIT: *mchod pa'i rten byed* is corrected to *mched pa'i rten byed.*
78. Khetsun Sangpo Rinpoche notes that the "meditative stabilization of cessation" occurs when one contemplates only emptiness, the abiding state, and not appearances such as color, shape, and so forth. Just emptiness and nothing else. Through such contemplation, all mistaken appearances and all error cease. Once all defilements have been extinguished, they provide the basis for the maintenance of the five pure primordial knowings. It then becomes possible to manifest magical displays (conversation at Nyingmapa Wish-Fulfilling Monastery, March 2009).
79. In *Seven Spiritual Trainings (Sems sbyongs bdun),* TBRC W12827-2061, pp. 329–338, Longchenpa points out that since space is ever-present, meditating on the wind-current, or energy associated with it, is always appropriate.
80. Lama Tenzin Samphel notes that this is indicated by the *ma* feminine ending (*gsum skor ma*) (Houston, April 2010).
81. This is seen as a spiral that winds out from itself.
82. This term, *gtum mo* in Tibetan, is most literally translated as "female

wrath." It may be that "wrathful" was the term's original meaning, but the fame of the Six Yogas of Naropa have made its meaning as "heat" more familiar. (Thanks to Michele Martin for this observation.)

83. For a good overview of the winds and other central features of Tibetan medicine, see Dr. Yeshi Dhonden, *Health through Balance* (Boston: Snow Lion, 2012), and Yangchen Gawe Lodro, *Death, Intermediate State, and Rebirth,* trans. Jeffrey Hopkins (Ithaca, N.Y.: Snow Lion, 1981).
84. *Lamrim Yeshe Nyingpo, Oral Instructions in the Gradual Path of the Wisdom Essence* by Chog Gyur gLingpa, trans. Erik Pema Kunzang in *Light of Wisdom,* vol. 1 (Rangjung Yeshe Publications, 1999). Tibetan text by Choggyur Lingpa (1829–1870), who was active in Derge and collaborated with Kongtrul Lodro Taye and Khyentse Wangpo in editing these treasures. The text itself is *mChog gyur bde chen gling pa yi zab gter yid bzhin nor bu'i chos mdzod chen mo.* Source: TBRC W22642 Vol. 31, 358.3–4, *Yeshe Nyingpo 'grel ba bla ma thug sgrub rdo rje drag rtsal las zhal gdams lam rim ye shes snying po'i 'grel ba ye shes snang ba rab tu rgyas pa* 358.3–4. This is the 338-page root text, *Chogling Terma—Lama'i thugs sgrub rdorje grags rtsal.* We have not located the commentary.
85. Rinpoche's mention here of *gZhi rten dang yul* emphasizes that all appearances from the base and appearances to the mind are erroneous.
86. Aryadeva, *sPyod bsdus sgron me* (TBRC WIKG10776), 59.1–5.
87. These eighty arise naturally in dependence on the allground.
88. Because it is the mind that holds onto objects, we can say that the uninterrupted error, the very nature of cyclic existence, unfolds based on subject and object. This is not saying desire arises from hatred but simply identifying the different types of minds. Lama Tenzin Samphel notes that another significant textual source for discussion of the thirty-three types of hatred is the *Collection of Secrets Tantra* (*Zang ba 'dus pa; Guhyasamāja*).
89. Aryadeva, *sPyod bsdus sgron me* (TBRC W1KG10776), 61.1.
90. Lama Tenzin Samphel notes that this comes because bliss is itself a method (personal conversation, Houston, Tex., spring 2013).
91. Dri med 'od zer (another name for Longchen Rabjam), *sGyu ma ngal gso'i 'grel chen shing rta bzang po.* However we found the quote in Longchenpa's *rDzogs pa chen po sems nyid ngal gso'i 'grel pa shing rta chen po (glegs bam phyi ma)* in *rDzogs pa chen po ngal gso skor gsum dang rang grol skor gsum bcas pod gsum* (TBRC W23760), vol. 2, 611.5–612.3.
92. Khetsun Sangpo Rinpoche added the interpolation "to true existence" in commenting on this line of his text, and added, "Having overcome holding to true existence, one's experience of objects is greatly changed. That is, once you gain some understanding of how everything lacks true existence, which is what it means to lack 'self,' then you see all

conventional appearances as fluctuating and so forth. But, until full enlightenment, you do not see them this way consistently. Still, to the extent that they appear evanescent, you have the sense that they are utterly bereft of an existence that is true."

93. TEXT EDIT: *sang se* corrected to *sang seng.*
94. *Fine Chariot: A Commentary on Putting Illusions to Rest* (*sGyuma Ngal gSo*), and the *Pure Chariot* (*Shing rta rnam dag*), commenting on *At Ease in Meditation* (*gsam rten ngal gso*). In *rDzogs pa chen po sems nyid ngal gso'i 'grel pa shing rta chen po* (*glegs bam phyi ma*). In *rDzogs pa chen po ngal gso skor gsum dang rang grol skor gsum bcas pod gsum* (TBRC W23760), vol. 2, 611.5–612.3.
95. TEXT EDIT: *rkyen gyi* corrected to *rkyen gyis* (to parallel previous line's construction).
96. TEXT EDIT: *mi long* corrected to *me long.*
97. TEXT EDIT: *skye 'dzig* corrected to *skye 'jigs.*
98. Khetsun Sangpo Rinpoche further observed here that we can speak of appearances from both a perspective of error and of being free from error, which is wisdom.
99. Khetsun Sangpo Rinpoche notes that this text is not a Nyingma tantra, it is from the later transmission, most likely found in the Tangyur. However, there are many sources that have not survived, except for quotations from them that are still in use (Sunderijal, Nepal, March 2009).
100. TEXT EDIT: *stag gnyis* corrected to *brtag gnyis.*
101. TEXT EDIT: *bzhugs tsam na* corrected to *bzhugs tsa na.*
102. For, if you realize this essence, you are Samantabhadra.
103. *The Majestic Creator of Everything* (*Kun byed rgyal po*) (TBRC W21521), 92.6–7.
104. TEXT EDIT: *blo bur* corrected to *glo bur.*
105. TEXT EDIT: *dbyen pa chos nyid* corrected to *dben pa chos nyid.*
106. The term *dran snang* can refer to anything that appears or is recalled. Here, however, Khetsun Sangpo Rinpoche glossed *dran snang* as "recall and appearances" in order to point out that among all appearances and recollections only the appearance of reality (*chos nyid snang*) is unchanging. In this context *dran snang* refers to remaining in unmistaken open awareness and not getting involved with thinking about mistaken appearances. At that time, the impure mistaken mind is not wandering and it has no power, whereas open awareness is powerful and unwavering. Lama Tenzin Samphel adds that for beginners, such "recall and appearances" depend on mindfulness, the use of consciousness, as the method. Gradually the practitioner arrives at realization, at wisdom, and the recalling, or memory; and the appearance of reality is an extraordinary method, with wisdom as its fruit, the final attainment.
107. Here Guru Rinpoche identifies appearance of reality as a method for achieving wisdom. He notes that the wisdom-factor (*shes rab gyi*

cha) is the knowing of non-true existence. Appearance and emptiness each arise in dependence on the other; method and wisdom, however, are one essence (*ngo bag cig*). So we can distinguish between appearance from a mistaken perspective, which is unawareness, and from an unmistaken perspective, which is wisdom. Khetsun Sangpo Rinpoche also noted that wisdom is the factor of a non–truly established knowing (*rang zhin bden pa ma grub pa shes rab gyi cha*) (conversation in Boudhanath, Nepal, August 2009).

108. Lama Tenzin Samphel suggests this quote is from one of Guru Rinpoche's *gTer*, but we have not been able to ascertain the specific text.

109. Here "method path" (*thabs lam*) refers to the completion stage of, for example, *rtsa rlung* practice. *Thabs lam* is very important at this stage.

110. Khetsun Sangpo Rinpoche's main point here is that "emptiness" is the same in all these traditions (conversation at Nyingmapa Wish-Fulfilling Monastery, March 2009).

111. Usually referred to as the *Reliquary of Simultaneously Arisen Union* (*lHan cig skyes sbyor gyi ga'u ma*). Khetsun Sangpo Rinpoche further observed that this work is a major source for the Mahamudra teaching. The practice referred to in the title of this text signifies that right when thought arises, it is in union with clarity. This practice is very powerfully and precisely developed within the Drukpa lineage, and is similar to the method-path (*thabs lam*) of Nyingma. It is connected with completion stage (*rdzogs rim*) practices, such as practices of the winds and channels as well as consort practices.

112. Probably the same person known as Chen Ngawa Chökyi Dragpa (*Spyan snga chos kyi grags pa*), the Fourth Shamar Rinpoche (1453–1524), a disciple of the Seventh Karmapa, Chögyi Dragpa Gyatso.

113. We do not know the name of this text.

114. The "father" here is the omniscient Lingre Pema Dorje, a twelfth-century lama of the Drukpa Kagyu from dbU gTsang, and the "son" is Ras btshang pa gyare.

115. rGod tshang pa gonpo dorje, known earlier in life as Dondrub Sengge (Don grub seng ge). In later life he initiated the tradition of the Drukpa Kagyu known as Upper Druk (*stod 'brug*). Among his main disciples the best known are Yang Gonpa (*Yang dgon pa*), Orgyenpa Rinchen Pal (*O rgyan pa rin chen dpal*), Madunpa (*Ma bdun pa*), and Bari Chilkarwa (*Ba ri spyil dkar ba*).

116. This refers to another branch of Kagyu, the Tsalway Kagyu (*Tshal ba'i bka' rgyud*), originated by Shang Yudragpa Tsondru Dragpa (*Zhang g.yu brag pa brtson 'grus grags pa*), who is also known as Shang Rinpoche (*Zhang rin po che*). Lama Shang was a disciple of Dakpo Gomtsül (*Dwags po sgom tshul*, 1116–1169), also known as Öngom Tsültrim Nyingpo (*sGom po tshul khrims snying po*), who was himself a nephew of Gampopa.

117. The Drikung Kagyu (*'Bri-gung bKa'-brgyud*) school of Tibetan

Buddhism was founded at Drikung in Central Tibet by the Drikung Rinpoche Jigten Gonpo ('Bri-gung Rin-po-che 'Jig-rten-mgon-po, 1143–1217).

118. Kun dga' rgyal mtshan, *sDom gsum Rab tu dbye ba,* Vol. 12 in *Sa skya bka' 'bum*, TBRC W00EGS1017151, 52.3–52.4.
119. The stages of creation and completion.
120. School of Padampa Sangye.
121. TEXT EDIT: *mang yang* corrected to *mang na yang.*
122. TEXT EDIT: *thugs rgyud* corrected to *thugs rgyus.*
123. Khetsun Sangpo Rinpoche (Nyingmapa Wish-Fulfilling Monastery, March 2009).
124. *Phyag chen zhal gdams* (by Guru Rinpoche). We have not been able to find this quotation.
125. Khetsun Sangpo Rinpoche glossed *sems* here as *sems nyid* (Sundarijal, March 2009).
126. TEXT EDIT: *rang ngo she* corrected to *rang ngo shes.*
127. Here the original Tibetan, *rol rtsal,* simply means *rol ba.* Dynamism, display, and ornamentation (*rtsal, rol, rgyan*) while one is on the path, are respectively the three Buddha dimensions: the essential, rich, and emanation dimensions.
128. Khetsun Sangpo Rinoche noted this realization is root and agent of the thirty-seven branches of enlightenment (*sum cu rtsa bdun byang chub chos*) (Sundarijal, March 2009).
129. If you understand well that our nature is unbounded wholeness, you understand everything. All doubt is eliminated, everything is clear. This is what "cutting the root" actually means. As Rinpoche notes, all the grounds and paths are encompassed by our understanding of unbounded wholeness (*thigle nyag gcig*) (Lama Tenzin Samphel, conversation, Houston, April 2011).
130. TEXT EDIT: *zhagi med* corrected to *gzhig med.*
131. This also means that one is knowingly present, *rig,* to the nature of one's mind: *sems kyi ngo bo* (Khetsun Sangpo Rinpoche, March 2009).
132. *Doha mDzod* (Skt: *Doha Kośa*), TBRC W23702, 49: 380–384. Tibet: [snar thang 17ff.]. This is a collection of spontaneous vajra songs by the Indian masters of the Mahamudra lineage.
133. Everything depends on realizing mindnature. And nothing goes beyond that realization.
134. TEXT EDIT: *sus kyang she* corrected to *sus kyang shes*. The point here is that nothing exists or can be known that is beyond the mind. Realizing mindnature is an all-encompassing realization.
135. TEXT EDIT: *sku ru ming btags* corrected to *ku ru ming yang btags.*
136. *Kun byed rgyal po* TBRC W21521 170.6-171.
137. Lama Tenzin Samphel notes that, at least in this context, *chos dbyings, chos nyid gyi dbyings*, and *dbyings* are identical in meaning. Also, that

dbyings means, and is sometime defined as, "the empty" (*stong po*) (Houston, fall 2013).

138. The defining characteristic of mind, its [conventional] essence or *ngo bo,* is that it is mistaken. Yet, as with all phenomena, the nature of mind is light, a union of appearance and emptiness. The capacity or power (*nus pa*) of the fruitional mind is what develops on the path: for example, knowing, kindness, and capacity (*khyen rtse nus gsum*) are all part of the fruitional power that the path brings forth.
139. Lama Tenzin Samphel glosses "homeground" (*gshis*) here as "essence" (*ngo bo*). This is the genuine, unmistaken essence, whereas the conventional essence, like the conventional mind it defines, is mistaken.
140. Lama Tenzin Samphel notes that, although sometimes their meanings vary, in this context *gdangs,* here translated as "radiance," is not different from the meaning of *mdangs*, which can be translated as "radiance," "tone," "glow," or "complexion."
141. *Guhyasmaāja, gSang 'dus.* Could not locate quotation.
142. 'Jigs med gling pa, *rNam mkhyen shing rta / Yon tan rin po che'i mdzod las bras bu'i theg pa'i rgya cher 'grel rnam mkhyen shing rta* Volume 2, 7–882. TBRC W1KG10193.
143. We were not able to locate this quote. This is also vol. *kha* (3) of Longchenpa's *gSung 'bum.*
144. TEXT EDIT: *yang de las* changed to *gsang ba.*
145. TEXT EDIT: *yid shes* corrected to *ye shes.*
146. Lama Tenzin Samphel notes that path sheer awareness is described as free of crassness because such presence is very clean and clear; it is an awareness of path itself (*lam rig pa*). When the basic *rig pa* meets path *rig pa*, one has the all-suffusing *rig pa* (*khyab brtal rig pa*). This is the fruitional sheer awareness of Dzogchen, that knower for which reality is manifestly evident. Rinpoche's main point here is that when the base and path *rig pa* come together, you have fruitional *rig pa*. To put this another way, the path sheer awareness (*lam rig*) understands the way things are (*gnas lugs*). When basic sheer awareness and path presence are united, this is the all-pervasive sheer awareness of Dzogchen, also known as the fruitional open awareness (*'bras bu'i rig*). (From a conversation in Houston, fall 2013).
147. Lama Tenzin Samphel glossed the original *snang ba mched pa* here as *snang ba yongs*; hence it is translated as "all" in this context.
148. TEXT EDIT: *mchod pa'i snang ba* corrected to *mched pa'i snang ba.*
149. Mental functioning is conceptual. The mental consciousness is not; it is the basis for the ability of each sense faculty to know its own object. A mental consciousness can be either an afflictive obstruction or an obstruction to omniscience. In this context, Lama Tenzin notes, it is the former.
150. While Dzogchen often emphasizes that the fruitional primordial

knowing is not a mind, not a consciousness, the wisdoms of hearing and thinking are indeed consciousnesses.

151. TEXT EDIT: *rnam shes dang yid shes* corrected to *rnam shes dang ye shes.*

152. As Khetsun Sangpo Rinpoche notes, this refers to the six types of consciousnesses.

Translator's observation: To be perfectly consistent, this dyad should either be consciousness and primordial consciousness (wisdom), or knowers and primordial knowers. However, I went with the nominalized "consciousness" to indicate ordinary, reifying (and reified) knowing, and the verbal form, "knowing," to indicate the sheer quality of *ye shes*. For the same reason, in the previous dyad, *shes rab* is rendered sublime (*rab*) knowing (*shes*).

153. TEXT EDIT: *sang ba mchod* corrected to *snang ba mched.*

154. To take what appears to our senses as real is to be involved with the karmic winds, because the "holding as real" itself (*dngo por 'dzin pa*) arises in dependence on the winds of karma. Generally speaking, explains Lama Tenzin Samphel, our ordinary consciousness depends on the karmic wind that is its mount. Its grasping depends on the consciousness that rides on, or depends upon, its karmic wind. In this way, we are involved in ongoing recognition and grasping of objects.

155. Buddha being all-knowing means that Buddhas also see impure things—karma and defilements—because they know what ordinary beings see. Therefore, seeing things as they are, *and* seeing the varieties, can refer not only to emptiness but also to perceptions arising through ordinary beings' karma and afflictions. The view perceiving these varieties is a way of seeing; the view of how they exist is a way of knowing.

156. Lama Tenzin Samphel points out: the understander of this is sheer awareness (*rig pa*) (Houston, fall 2013).

157. TEXT EDIT: *byung med na* corrected to *byung na 'ang.*

158. *dKon mchog sprin gyi mdo.* In *bKa' 'gyur* (sDe dge par phud). TBRC W22084 Vol. 64, p. 184.1.

159. TEXT EDIT: *so sor rtog pa* corrected to *so sor rtogs pa.*

160. TEXT EDIT: *gzhi gnas kyi* corrected to *gzhi gnas kyis.*

161. TEXT EDIT: *zhe gzungs* corrected to *zhes gzungs.*

162. *Samdhinirmocana Sutra, mDo dgongs pa nges 'grel.* In *bKa' 'gyur* (stog pho brang bris ma). TBRC W22083. 63: Leh: sMan rtsis Shes rig dPem zod, 1975–1980.

163. All the Buddha's sutra teachings, as classified by the *Samdhinirmocana sutra,* are included in the classification of the twelve sets of sutra (*gsungs rab yan lag bcu gnyis*).

164. Thus we see that there is implicit wisdom in such stillness, which itself reveals how the mind actually is. As Lama Tenzin Samphel notes, no antidote is engaged; there is simply a natural process of easeful settling.

165. For example, terms such as non-distraction (*ma g.yengs*) or non-meditation (*mi bsgom*).

166. TEXT EDIT: *mi yong gi dgos pa* [25a.5] corrected to *mi yong gi dogs pa.*
167. TEXT EDIT: *gsum pa rim du* corrected to *gsum pa rim pa bzhin du.*
168. In this context, Lama Tenzin Samphel says, glossing *theng re tsam*, "very occasionally" means that thoughts may come once or twice in the course of an hour.
169. TEXT EDIT: *slar yang rnam yengs* corrected to *slar yang rnam g.yeng.*
170. TEXT EDIT: Possibly *gnas pa ngar med steng ngo bo* should be *gnas pa ngar med stong nge ba,* in which case the line could read, "Your unclear stability, an empty essence." Otherwise the line reads, "That which rests on unclear stability."
171. TEXT EDIT: *yod yin min* corrected to *yod med yin min.*
172. Lama Tenzin Samphel commented on these lines in Rinpoche's text: "Even though we call this special seeing, it has been with you from the first. Even as ordinary beings we are never for a moment separate from that nature. However, insofar as we lack blessings and merit, we do not recognize it. The same is true for the whole time we are on the path, thinking that this is meditation and this is not when actually all of it—the observing, the wondering—is nothing other than sheer awareness itself" (Houston, April 2012).
173. TEXT EDIT: *nyid dngos po* corrected to *'di nyid dang po.*
174. rGyal ba Lorepa, a great master of the Drukpa Kagyü school, 1187–1250.
175. TEXT EDIT: *rtogs bsam sgom chen* corrected to *rtogs sam sgom chen.*
176. We could not locate this text in his collected works, *rGyal ba lo ras pa'i gsung 'bum.*
177. "Movement" *('rgyu)* can, as here, refer to the movement of conceptuality, says Lama Tenzin Samphel. However, when *rig pa* abides, whatever is moving is its own dynamic display (*rtsal*), not conceptual thought.
178. TEXT EDIT: *rol pa 'das ma 'das* corrected to *rol pa las ma 'das.*
179. Thus, special seeing has the quality of recognizing itself, as well as being qualified by serene abiding.
180. That is, although objects appear unceasingly and clearly, there is no attraction to or fixation on them, therefore this is special seeing.
181. TEXT EDIT: *lhangs* corrected to *lhongs.*
182. TEXT EDIT: *gzung 'jug yang* corrected to *gzung 'jug tshang.* That is, even though there are thoughts, stillness and superb seeing are complete (comment from Lama Tenzin on October 24, 2011).
183. TEXT EDIT: *zhes* has been excised as it does not signify the close of an identifiable quotation [29b2].
184. Abu Hralpo, *Rdogs chen pa a bu hral po'i snying gtsam.* TBRC W2CZ5981 (No scans). Quotation found in folio-version of text in possession of translator, p.3.2–6.4 n.p. n.d.
185. Dudjom Rinpoche ('Jigs bral ye she's rdo rje), *Rdzogs chen ngo sprod skal ldan snying po* inside "*Zhal gdams bslab bya phyogs bsdebs nang gses le tshan zhe dgu*" in the *gsung 'bum* of *'Jigs bral ye shes rdo rje.*

TBRC W20869. Vol. 25, 336.5–337.5. Kalimpong: Dupjung Lama, 1979–1985.

Lines from this segment *not* cited in *Strand* are: *rig pa dang po bla mas ngo sprod pas rang ngo rang gis shes nas ngo rang thog tu 'phrod / 'khor 'das kyi chos ji ltar snang yang rig pa rang gi rtsal las ma 'das par shes pa.*

186. TEXT EDIT: *nam rtog 'di mi dran* corrected to *rnam rtog 'dis mi dran.*
187. Lama Tenzin Samphel glossed "it" (*kho*) here as "thought" (*rnam rtog*).
188. *rDzogs chen ngo sprod skal ldan snying nor yod*, TBRC W20869 Vol. 25, 336–342. This work contained inside another work, *Zhal gdams bslab bya phyogs bsdebs nang gses le tshan zhe dgu*, 336. 5–337.5
189. So called because Guru Rinpoche is said to have written this for an elderly woman, according to Khetsun Sangpo Rinpoche. So far we have been unable to locate this text.
190. TEXT EDIT: *spyi gzungs* corrected to *spyi gzung.*
191. Lama Tenzin Samphel notes: "Subject and object, no longer apart, meet together due to your understanding. In that meeting place there is clear light. Just *chos nyid* itself. The appearance (*snang ba*) of reality's clear light only occurs when, in this sense, there is an object. This is different from the *dbying,* or spacious matrix (which could also be translated as 'infinite womb,' following Ngawang Sangpo [Hugh Thompson] in that this latter is simply empty."
192. TEXT EDIT: The citation from Guru Rinpoche continues. The Tibetan text should have *tersar*—marks indicating that this is revealed *terma*—indicators on these lines as well.
193. Lama Tenzin Samphel notes that they are pure insofar as you need not refute or cease the object, you need only dissolve grasping (Houston, Fallfall, 2012).
194. Jigme Lingpa makes a similar point in commenting on *The Praise of Mother Wisdom,* noting that the unborn (ungraspable) nature of things is always present, even as they are "born" and present to the senses.
195. TEXT EDIT: *rkyen gyi* corrected to *skyen gyis.*
196. TEXT EDIT: *gdug* corrected to *'dug.*
197. Lama Tenzin Samphel notes that once one recognizes that there is no place of arising, abiding or ceasing, there is clear simpicity. Recognizing this, you recognize your own consciousness.
198. 'Jigs bral ye shes rdo rje. *Zhal gdams bslab bya phyogs bsdebs nang gses le tshan zhe dgu*. In *gsung 'bum* of *'jigs bral ye shes rdo rje.* TBRC W20869 Vol. 25: 295–346. Scanned from Kalimpong: Dupjung Lama, 1979–1985. Quotation 337.5–340.3.

Note on the Tibetan text: *ces gsung so* appears to end the quotation from *rgan mo mdzub bdzugs* that begins on 32a.3. There is a break at 33b.6, then the quotation picks up again, until 34a.6, but without tersar marks. These segments are all taken from *For an Old Woman* (*rGan mo*), as indicated by Rinpoche's ending the quotation at 33b.6. This quote appears in the *rDzogs chen skal ldan snyig nor* [photocopy, no bibliograpical info, except that it is taken from the *Dudjom gZung 'bum*].

TEXT EDIT: *rang ngo shes dus* corrected to *d'o na rang ngo shes dus.* This quote within a quote (ending with *gcig shes kun grol rang rig rang ngo*) is from Dudjom Rinpoche's *Mountain Dharma* (*Ri Chos).* Published as *Alchemy of Accomplishment: Instructions of Mountain Dharma,* trans. Tony Duff (n.p.: Padma Karpo Translation Committee, 2011).

199. TEXT EDIT: *bzhag co na* corrected to *bzhag tsa na.*
200. TEXT EDIT: *thog tu bcad* corrected to *thog tu bca'.* The three phrases here are almost identical to the famous *Three Statements of Garab Dorje:* (1) *Ngo rang thog tu sprad*; (2) *thag gcig thog dug cad;* and (3) *gDengs grol thog du 'cha'.*
201. TEXT EDIT: *tsam gyi* corrected to *tsam gyis.*
202. This is cited by Jigme Lingpa in *sGom phyogs dris lan* TBRC W7477 521.6. It is also cited in *bDud 'joms rinpoche gsung 'bum* Vol. 25, pp. 337.5–340.
203. According to Lama Tenzin Samphel, this means that the very essence (*ngo bo*) of basic mindfulness (*gnyug dran*) is naturally and of its own accord wholly settled down. This is what is sustained. This basic mindfulness is a very relaxed, easy kind of mindfulness, not strained or effortful in any way (Houston, fall 2012).
204. This statement is apparently from Patrul Rinpoche's *mThar thug rdzogs pa chen po'i sang rgyas pa'i thabs dgongs pa rang 'grel zhes bya ba,* 16 folios, 31 pages. n.p. n.d., 8.4–6. We could not locate it in any TBRC volume.
205. Patrul Rinpoche (rDza spal sprul, 1808–1887), on *bTha' spyod smon lam, sNying thig gi sngon 'gro'i khrid yig kun bzang bla ma'i zhal lung* Vol. *ja* [7]. Also, Vol. 8, *snying thig ya bzhi* Tārā mantra ritual of Patrul Rinpoche in the *Gsung 'bum* of Orgyan 'jigs med chos kyi dbang po. TBRC W2CZ5981 (no scans). This quote was found in photocopy version (no publisher) of *Mthar thug rdzog pa chen po'i sangs rgyas pa'i thabs zab mo dgongs pa rang grol zhes bya ba bzhugs so,* 9.4ff.
206. This tradition is connected with Padampa Sangye and the Severance (*gCod*) tradition of Machig Labdron.
207. TEXT EDIT: *steng* corrected to *stong.* For, during serene abiding, all the senses, coarse and subtle, have ceased, and some people think this itself is meditation. But this is just an empty serenity.
208. Khetsun Sangpo Rinpoche notes: This is an error because it implies you experience meditation as episodic. This impairs its continuity. Such disruption occurs because you are looking to focus specifically on the in-between of thoughts. The mistake referred to here is in thinking that [only] this in-between space is your meditation. It wrongly suggests discontinuity (Sundarijal, Nepal, n.d.).
209. That is, in the process of seeing that phenomena are like space, untrue,

illusory, and so on, they fall into thinking. This thinking is an extreme of analysis. It means you are working with the conceptual, effortful mind, and this is not correct. If you are analyzing, and if you lack an actual identification of mind nature, you are just in ordinary mistaken mind.

210. Lama Tenzin Samphel notes that whatever is occurring, there is no need to either fix or undo (Houston, fall 2012).
211. We have not been able to locate this quote in *Phyag rdzogs man ngag* TBRC W1KG4338, even though passages exist there that engage similar material, or in *rTse la sha tshogs rang grol gyi gsung gdams zab*.
212. TEXT EDIT: *chos po* corrected to *chen po*.
213. It is possible that "the three" here might mean "arising, abiding, and ceasing." Longchenpa's phrase *'ol 'gyu 'phreng gsum* can also be read as indicating "three types of thought in connection with *rig pa*. In that case, *'ol* is clearly appearing thought; *'gyu* is the movement of thought; and *'phreng* is "fixed" or "fastened." Each of these imperils practice because if you do not recognize it, you will fall into error. Khetsun Sangpo Rinpoche notes that there are really three obstacles: a failure to be aware of the true nature of the arising, abiding, and cessation of subtle conceptions while at the same time thinking one is free from all proliferations. Therefore if you recognize this as your own mind, this is sufficient. See oral commentary for further elaboration on this point.

    Rinpoche's citation is from Longchenpa, *Yid bzhin mdzod kyi 'grel pa*, TBRC W0658 Vol. *vam,* pp. 1470–74.
214. That is, they count the number of times a thought arises and ceases. "Here is one arising, there is one ceasing." This is mistaken.
215. See also *Yid bzhin mdzod* root text Chap. 20, pp. 125.5ff. From *Zang thal,* cited in Rinpoche's text 38b.2–to 38b.3 *phyin ci log.* (Here he is drawing from the root text, athough not putting it in quotation marks.)
216. This suggests they misunderstand such a gap, which they think of as their genuine nature, to be something other than whatever is dawning.
217. The wording here, *skad cig yud tsam . . . spang bar bya,* is a citation from the root text of Longchenpa's *Yin gzhin mdzod* (n.p. n.d., TBRC W00KG02660) 126.1–2. Lama Tenzin Samphel suggests, and the translator agrees, that Rinpoche here is drawing from the root text and inserting his own commentary among cited lines, forming a cohesive whole, rather than clearly distinguishing root text and commentary (Houston, October 2011). We could not locate this at this time in TBRC.
218. These people are describing a mentally fabricated practice, whereas the brilliancy and vivid awareness of genuine primordial knowing cannot be contrived.
219. TEXT EDIT: The cited text says *sor bzhugs,* but Lama Tenzin Samphel suggests that Rinpoche's *sor bzhag* seems more correct.
220. TEXT EDIT: *ngang bskyangs* corrected to *ngang la bskyangs.*

221. There are two states of mind: emanating (*spros*) and still (*gnas*). The claim here is that in both of these states, the best practitioner lets dynamism (*rtsal*) be; the middling is not distracted by it; and even the least distinguished can discriminate abiding from movement. (Adapted from comments by Lama Tenzin Samphel.)
222. The wording "profoundly ordinary" (*tha mal*) distinguishes this meaning from the *merely* ordinary, or mistaken, mind, says Lama Tenzin Samphel. The reference here is not to the mistaken mind.
223. Being in place is a reference to sheer awareness, which is already there. "Placing" is a method for setting open awareness in place. Thus, these are mutually contradictory.
224. We understand the quotation to be from Longchenpa, as the first line was locatable under his name. However, we have not discerned which of his works it is from.
225. These are the four concentrations (*dhyāna, bsam gtan*) of the form realm, the four absorptions *(samāpatti; snyoms'jug)* of the formless realm, and serene abiding. For a classic (Geluk) presentation of these nine, see Leah Zahler, et al., *Meditative States in Tibetan Buddhism: The Concentrations and Formless Absorptions* (Boston: Wisdom Publications, 1984).
226. There are four states of meditative absorption associated with the formless realm, four states of concentration associated with the form realm, and the desire realm itself, making nine levels of cyclic existence.
227. TEXT EDIT: *mi rtog par* corrected to *mi rtogs par*. This accords with Rinpoche's oral commentary on the four primordial pitfalls (*ye shor*) and the four danger zones of slippage (*phrang shor*) regarding base, path, emptiness, and antidote. He thus uses slightly different terms, but essentially parallels the four pairs of pitfalls, or strayings, listed in the glossary to *Lamp of Mahamudra*, by Tsele Natsok Rangdrol, trans. Erik Pema Kunsang (Boulder, Colo.: Shambhala, 1989), 78, 104.

    Basic sidetracks: slipping from the essence of emptiness, *stong nyid gshis shor;* from the path, *lam gyi gshis shor;* from the antidote or remedy, *gnyen po gshis shor;* and into a generalized emptiness, *stong nyid rgyas 'debs su gshis shor.*

    Temporary pitfalls: falling from the essence, *gshis kyi 'phral shor*; from the path, *lam gyi 'phal shor*; from the antidote, *gnyen gyi 'phral shor*; and into generalizing, *rgyas 'debs 'phral shor.*
228. TEXT EDIT: *pha* seems to be a scribal error and is omitted here.
229. Khetsun Sangpo Rinpoche glossed this as "a slipping away of something that has great value" (Nyingmapa Wish-Fulfilling Monastery, March 2009). Lama Tenzin Samphel also notes that the home ground is the original base; it is your nature, which means that nothing further is needed, and you are always there. Therefore, taking the path as a way to get to the primordial base, or to make it arise, is an error.
230. TEXT EDIT: *ye shos* corrected to *ye shor.*

231. Lama Tenzin (Houston, fall 2012) has observed that unless you recognize your own mind nature as utterly without root and unfettered, you have not understood the nature of mind as it actually is. Rather, you have contrived and deviated into a very minimal type of emptiness.
232. TEXT EDIT: *nyin yod* corrected to *nyen yod.*
233. We cannot find this exact quotation in the *sGyu ma mkhan bzang po lung bstan pa'i mdo*. The text itself is found in *bKa' 'gyur* (*sTog pho brang bris ma,* Leh, Ladakh, TBRC W22083. Vol. 39. TBRC has another edition as well, though we could not locate the quote there either. It is in *Chos kyi 'byung gnas sa'i snying po 'khor lo bcu pa'i mdo* in *bKa' 'gyur* (sDe dge par phud). TBRC W22084. Vol. 65 (Delhi: Karmapae chodhey gyalwae sungrab partun khang, 1976–1979), pp. 201–484.
234. TEXT EDIT: *yang yang* corrected to *mang yang*. This refers to the non-normative activities of a genuine siddha, such as drinking and so on.
235. Khetsun Sangpo Rinpoche further glossed such activities as "free from [mistaken] mind and ongoing."
236. Khetsun Sangpo Rinpoche in private conversation with translator (Nyingmapa Wish-Fulfilling Monastery, April 2009).
237. Lama Tenzin Samphel to translator in personal conversation (n.p., n.d.).
238. Lama Tenzin Samphel notes that reification, a type of superimposition, is the cause of doubt.
239. Khetsun Sangpo Rinpoche to translator (Nyingmapa Wish-Fulfilling Monastery, April 2009).
240. From *bDud 'joms bsung 'bum*, TBRC W20869 Vol. 25, 336.
241. The seven aspects of supreme union (in Tibetan, *kha sbyor yan lag bdun*) are (1) *longs spyod rdzogs pa* (complete enjoyment); (2) *kha sbyor* (union); (3) *bde ba chen po* (great bliss); (4) *rang bzhin med pa* (no self-nature); (5) *snying rjes yongs su gang ba* (completely filled with compassion); (6) *rgyun mi chad pa* (uninterrupted); and (7) *'gog pa med pa* (unceasing). The full Tibetan passage reads: *sangs rgyas longs spyod rdzogs pa'i sku'i rang bzhin ni kha sbyor yan lag bdun dang ldan pa ste, longs spyod rdzogs pa'i yan lag dang, kha sbyor gyi yan lagbde ba chen po'i yan lag rang bzhin med pa'i yan lag snyingrjes yongs su gang ba'i yan lag rgyun mi 'chad pa'i yan lag'gog pa med pa'i yan lag rnams so.*
242. There is nothing really to see, because this is neither a material object nor something possessed of particularizing characteristics.
243. *Kun byed rgyal po* TBRC W21521, pp. 16.1–4.
244. TEXT EDIT: *bstan* corrected to *brtan.*
245. TBRC *kun byed rgyal po* W21521, pp. 92.6–93.3.
246. TBRC W21521 *kun byed rgyal po*, pp. 51.1.
247. TEXT EDIT: *sgar* [48b.2] corrected to *skar.*
248. TEXT EDIT: *rnam gcod* [48b.2] corrected to *rnam dpyod.*

249. Above (where dakinis reside), upon, and beneath the earth.
250. All the main headings from part 1 appear here in part 2, the commentary. The commentary contains additional subheadings indicating material that is touched on without elaboration in *Strand* itself and is here given greater attention and elaboration.
251. Lama Tenzin Samphel notes that in general when we speak of the dharmakāya we are referring to this, *gzhi'i chos sku,* the dharmakāya of the base.
252. Khetsun Sangpo Rinpoche added the qualifer about freedom from stains. He also noted that the *gzhi snang,* or "basis of appearance," is the same as the "base at the time of the base" (*gzhi'i dus gyi gzhi*) (March 2009).
253. In other contexts, however, the actual appearances themselves can be referred to as *rtsal.*
254. Lama Tenzin Samphel notes (personal conversation, 2012) that this description and naming of the allground is in contrast to the primordial actual allground (*thog med'i kun gzhi*).
255. Khetsun Sangpo Rinpoche's oral commentary (Sundarijal, April 2009).
256. Discussion of the allground consciousness is from a conversation with Khetsun Sangpo Rinpoche at the Nyingmapa Wish-Fulfilling Monastery (March 2009).
257. In some presentations, such as Jigme Lingpa's *Wisdom Chat* #71, it is *yid,* mental functioning, which comes first, and mind, *sems,* is said to arise from that.

    Lama Tenzin Samphel thinks Rinpoche's discussion here reflects the same point—that there is a generic awareness that precedes an awareness which clearly identifies its object; it is just a matter of applying different terms to the generic and specific functions. Thus, in talking about the eight collections of consciousness, the order of presentation is reversed, but the meaning is the same. Generally speaking, this is a discussion related to the topic of mind and mind-arisen factors (*sems* and *sems 'byung*) A related term, *yid la byed pa,* can be glossed as "mentation," as well as "mindfulness" or, sometimes, "remembering" (*dran pa*).
258. In Tibetan, *sems 'di kun gzhi rnam shes yin.*
259. See, for example, Lati Rinbochay and Elizabeth Napper, *Mind in Tibetan Buddhism* (Ithaca, N.Y.: Snow Lion, 1979).
260. *Strand* [5.3].
261. This is one of Longchenpa's three "Chariot" texts: the *Great Chariot* (*Shing rta chen mo*), which comments on *At Ease in Mind Nature* (*Semnyid Ngal gso*); the *Fine Chariot* (*Shing rta gZangpo*), commenting on *Putting Illusion to Rest* (*sGyuma Ngal gSo*), and the *Pure Chariot*

(*Shing rta rnam dag*), commenting on *At Ease in Meditation* (*gsam rten ngal gso*). In *rDzogs pa chen po ngal gso skor gsum dang rang grol skor gsum bcas pod gsum*. TBRC W23760. Vol. 2, 611.5–612.3.

For a full listing of Longchenpa's works, see Tulku Thondup, *The Practice of Dzogchen* (Ithaca, N.Y.: Snow Lion, 2002), 156.

262. *Strand* [10.5].
263. TEXT EDIT: *rkyen gyi* corrected to *rkyen gyis.*
264. *Strand* [5.6].
265. TEXT EDIT: *gzhi la ma rig ma shar* [7a.5–6] is corrected to *gzhi la rig ma* shar. Khetsun Sangpo Rinpoche commented that this means there is ignorance, unawareness in the base (conversation with Harvey Aronson, Nyingmapa Wish-Fulfilling Monastery, April 2009).
266. Cited in Dudjom, *chos spyod* op. cit., 325.4 [Xeroxed edition, n.p., n.d.]. (We could not locate in TBRC catalog.)
267. *A Lamp Distilling the Practices: A Commentary on the Meaning of the Five Stages* [*of the Guhyasamaja Complete Stage*] (*Caryamelapakapradipa; sPyod-bsdus*), TBRC W1KG10776.
268 This is likewise the advice Longchenpa gives in the seventh of his *Seven Trainings (sems sbyongs bdun),* TBRC W12827-2061, pp. 329–38. Longchenpa notes that "the wind of space, being present at all times, is [always] appropriate."
269. *Strand* [7.14].
270. *Lam Rim Yeshe Nying po*, TBRC W22642 Vol. 31, 358.3.
271. *Strand* [4.15].
272. *Strand* [10.5].
273. *Strand* [5.18].
274. *Strand* [11.10].
275. The Tibetan, *rDza rgyud brtag gnyis pa,* is a reference to the *Hevajra Root Tantra*. Khetsun Sangpo Rinpoche noted (conversation at the Nyingmapa Wish-Fulfilling Monastery, March 2009) that this text is not a Nyingma tantra; it is from the later transmission. It is included in the Tangyur.
276. *Strand* [11.17].
277. *Strand* [11.17].
278. TEXT EDIT: *bzhugs tsam na* corrected to *bzhugs tsa na.*
279. For, if you realize this essence, you are Samantabhadra.
280. TBRC *Kun byed rgyal po*, W21521, pp. 92.6–7.
281. Lama Tenzin Samphel reflects: Clouds arise *in* the sky, not *from* the sky. In this way, all phenomena arise in the sky of reality (*chos nyid*). We don't say that reality is the place from which they arise, but that the essence of what they are is reality (personal conversation, undated).
282. Lama Tenzin Samphel notes that the afflictions, consisting of different habitual tendencies, are piled one on top of the other; since they are different from one another, they are not seamlessly connected. Thus,

there are spaces in between. In this case, space is not an ultimate, not Buddha nature, but simply marks a boundary (personal conversation, undated).

283. As noted above, Garwang Chögyi Dragpa is probably the same person known as Chen Nga Chökyi Dragpa Gyatso (sPyan snga chos kyi grags pa rgya mtsho), the Fourth Shamar Rinpoche. See Erik Pema Kunsang, *Rang-jung Yeshe Tibetan-English Dictionary of Buddhist Culture* (www.dharmadictionary.net).

284. Gonpo Dorje (rGod tshang pa, 1189–1258) was known earlier in life as Dondrub Senge (Don grub seng ge). In later life he initiated the tradition of the Drukpa Kagyu known as Upper Druk (sTod 'brug). Among his main disciples the best known are Yang Gonpo (Yang dgon pa), Orgyenpa Rinchen Pal (O rgyan pa rin chen dpal), Madunpa (Ma bdun pa), and Bari Chilkarwa (Ba ri spyil dkar ba).

285. The Drikung Kagyu ('Bri-gung bKa'-brgyud) school of Tibetan Buddhism was founded at Drikung in Central Tibet by the Drikung Rinpoche Jigten Gonpo ('Bri-gung Rin-po-che 'Jig-rten-mgon-po, 1143–1217).

286. Tibetan, *sDom gsum Rab dBye.* In *Strand* [12.21].

287. Blo-bzang Chos-kyi Rgyal-mtshan, 1570–1662.

288. Tibetan, *Phyag chen rtsa ba.* In *Strand* [13.5].

289. School of Padampa Sangye.

290. TEXT EDIT: *mang yang* corrected to *mang na yang.*

291. *Strand* [13.11].

292. This paragraph was taken from another talk by Rinpoche, date and location unknown.

293. *Strand* [14.1].

294. This paragraph was taken from another talk by Rinpoche, date and location unknown.

295. That is, once we really understand the Dzogchen view, we are not dependent on other views. However it can be very helpful, and in fact traditional, to study other views in order to truly appreciate the unique qualities of Dzogchen. We can do this, for example, by studying Longchenpa's *Precious Treasury* or his *Resting in Mindnature,* or Jigme Lingpa's *Treasury of Precious Qualities.*

296. Lama Tenzin Samphel notes that both ignorance and sheer awreness arise from the base. However the dynamism of the basis (*gzhi'i rtsal*) refers to sheer awareness, not to ignorance (Houston, April, 2011).

297. This paragraph is from Lama Tenzin Samphel's conversational response to questions from the translator (Houston, April, 2011). Lama Tenzin further notes: "Whenever you have mental functioning, you have longing, grasping, duality, a sense of external objects and appearing objects (*zhen pa, 'dzin pa, gnyis 'zin, phyi'i yul, snang yul*). So long as subject and object have not truly been seen as empty, there is bound

to be subtle dualism; even though subject and object are coarsely distinguished. Appearances (*snang ba*) and appearing objects (*snang yul*) occur only in the presence of mental functioning."

298. Clarification thanks to Lama Tenzin Samphel.
299. Thus, as Lama Tenzin Samphel clarifies, there is no *rnam shes* when there is *ye shes*. When ordinary consciousnesses ceases, there is wisdom.
300. *Strand* [14], second line from bottom.
301. Everything depends on realizing mindnature. And nothing goes beyond that realization.
302. TEXT EDIT: *sus kyang she* [19b.6] corrected to *sus kyang shes*. The point here is that nothing exists or can be known that is beyond the mind. Realizing mind's nature is an all-encompassing realization.
303. *Strand* [14], last line.
304. *Strand* [15.19].
305. Lama Tenzin Samphel (Houston, fall 2013).
306. *Strand* [16.1]. We found this quote in *Secret Essence* (chap. 12, 16.6 in TBRC volume W00EGS1016299-I1CZ5003 521–586); we were not able to locate the quote in *Great Chariot,* though possibly Jigme Lingpa cites it there. See note 147.
307. TEXT EDIT: *yang de las* changed to *gsang ba snying po'i rtsa ba*. Vol. *kha* of Longchenpa *gSung 'bum*. See note above.
308. Khetsun Sangpo Rinpoche (Nyingmapa Wish-Fulfilling Monastery, March 2009).
309. *mNgon rtogs rkyan, Abhisamayālaṅkāra* by Maitreyanatha. See *Golden Garland of Eloquence,* trans. Gareth Sparham, Vols 1–4 (n.p.: Jain Pub, Co., 2001–2013). This translation features Tsongkhapa's famous commentary on the text, *Golden Garland of Eloquence (Legs bshad gser phreng)* as well as the commentaries (*Vṛtti* and *Aloka*) by Vimuktisena and Haribhadra.
310. Discussed in *Strand* [16.3ff]. Here we see that while Dzogchen often emphasizes that the fruitional primordial knowing is not a mind, not a consciousness, the wisdoms of hearing and thinking are indeed consciousnesses.
311. The Tibetan remains the same, *gzhi gnas,* often translated as "calm abiding." However, since the point of this text is partly to distinguish how these practices function in Dzogchen, we use a different English term when explicitly and exclusively discussing the Dzogchen description of the calm state.
312. Khetsun Sangpo Rinpoche mentioned here that Machig Labdron's *Quintessential Instructions* are very helpful in dealing with distraction. He did not elaborate.
313. "Geshe" became part of his name after he spent time at a Geluk monastery early in his ordained life. He likely did not have a geshe degree and he was, in any case, a Nyingma teacher.

314. *Strand* [21.17].
315. That is, although objects appear uncesasingly and clearly, there is no attraction to or fixation on them; therefore this is special seeing.
316. TEXT EDIT: *lhangs* corrected to *lhongs.*
317. TEXT EDIT: *gzung 'jug yang* corrected to *gzung 'jug tshang.* That is, even though there are thoughts, stillness and special seeing are complete. Lama Tenzin commented on this October 24, 2011.
318. *Strand* [24.10].
319. Lama Tenzin's further observations here (from Houston, fall 2012): So long as we recognize our own mind's nature as free of elaborations, there is no fault, even when thoughts arise. As great as the difference between earth and sky, however, is the difference between something appearing to one who understands their nature and to one who does not, even if both are free of elaborations. Therefore, to say that simply because your mind is free of elaborations everything that appears to you is pure, or is just mind, is a great error.
320. *Strand* [25], end of last line.
321. The elephant is, in this context, a symbol of arrogance.
322. Rinpoche also told the translator: "When I was young, I very much hoped and believed I would do much difficult service for lamas. I did, and it was in fact challenging. So this is the advice I offer to you" (Sundarijal, April 2009). He did not explain. However his life story is indeed a tale of devotion and hard work, especially founding a school and monastery at the request of His Holiness Dudjom Rinpoche and His Holiness the Dalai Lama. After enduring very difficult times in Mussoorie and various places in the Kathmandu Valley, the school is now flourishing in Sundarijal, Nepal (about thirty minutes past Boudhanath), and since the passing of Khetsun Sangpo Rinpoche at the end of 2009 it has been under the guidance of his grandson, Kangyur Tulku Jigme Norbu.
323. Briefly, these are (1) our good fortune to have a human rebirth; (2) the impermanence of our lives; (3) karmic cause and effect; and (4) the woes of cyclic existence. These constitute the outer, or ordinary, stages of the foundational practices and are classically discussed in texts such as Patrul Rinpoche's *The Words of My Perfect Teacher,* as well as the commentary on it by Khetsun Sangpo Rinpoche, *Tantric Practice in Nyingma.* They are also discussed in famous works of other Tibetan traditions such as Tsongkhapa's *Great Treatise.*
324. Transference—the practice for sending one's consciousness to a pure land as one is dying.
325. In Jamgön Kongtrül's commentary on Atisha's slogans, see *Entering the Path to Enlightenment,* trans. Ken McLeod (Boston: Shambhala, 1987).
326. Teacher, time, retinue, teaching, and pure land.

327. TEXT EDIT: *sgar* [48b.2] corrected to *skar.*
328. TEXT EDIT: *rnam gcod* [48b.2] corrected to *rnam dpyod.*
329. Above (where dakinis reside), upon, and beneath the earth.
330. See the list of Khetsun Sangpo Rinpoche's texts in the Bibliography.
331. *Nectar for the Ear: An Early History of Tibet Edited from Findings Unearthed at the Duhuang Caves* (*Bod kyi rgyal rabs sa 'og nas brñed pa'i dum bsgrigs rna ba'i bdud rtsi*) (Dharamsala: Library of Tibetan Works and Archives, 1986).
332. *Rang gi rtogs pa brjod a gzu bo'i rna rgyan mdzas pa'i ratna* (Dharamsala: Library of Tibetan Works and Archives, 1973).
333. Conversation with Khetsun Sangpo while preparing lectures on hail protection for Rice University's Scientia group (fall 1990).
334. His description of these practices is written up in "Hail Protection," by Anne C. Klein with Khetsun Sangpo Rinpoche, in *Religions of Tibet in Practice*, ed. Donald Lopez (Princeton, N.J.: Princeton University Press, 1997) and in "Divining Hail: Deities, Energies, and Tantra on the Tibetan Plateau," in *Mantic Knowledge in World Views and Life-Worlds in East Asia,* ed. Michael Lackner (Leiden: Brill, forthcoming.)
335. *Skad cig thams cad bye brag phyed / skad cig gcig gis rdzogs sang rgyas.*
336. Transcript of Professor Hopkins' oral translation, edited by Elizabeth Wallett.
337. For more description of this area, see the Nyingma Wish-Fulfilling Center's edition of Rinpoche's autobiography, *mKhas btshun rtogs brjod, mKhas btshun rtogs brjod* [Autobiography of Khetsun Sangpo Rinpoche], TBRC W00KG09699 (Dharamsala: Library of Tibetan Works and Archives, 1973), 79–80.
338. This information about Geshe Sogyal Rinpoche's teachers was provided by Khetsun Rinpoche's son, Kangyur Tulku Jigme Norbu, who notes that Khetsun Sangpo Rinpoche traveled to meet with Geshe Sogyal Rinpoche whenever he taught in Central Tibet, in places such as at Sedrag Drupde (*Se dbrag sgrub sde*), Drakmar (*Brag dmar*), Minkyi monastery (*sMin kyi dgon pa*), Khyungtse monastery (Khyung rtse dGon pa), and elsewhere.
339. My memory is that Rinpoche spoke of his wife's family as consisting of seven daughters, but I could not confirm this.
340. He had been a disciple of the Fourth Drukpa Pema Garpo.
341. The information about Lama Gonpo in this paragraph and the next comes from Tulku Jigme Rinpoche. He did not include it in the talk he gave at the University of Virginia, although, after one of my own retreats, he spoke to me very movingly about his veneration for this lama. A description of Rinpoche's studies with Lama Gonpo can also be found in the Nyingmapa Wish-Fulfilling Center's edition of his autobiography, *mKhas btsun rgan po' 'bel gtam kun gsal me long bzhugs so, dpal snga 'gyur bshad sgrub 'dod 'zo gling* (esp. 49 and 191). The auto-

biography (189–193) also includes a catalog of the texts Rinpoche studied with him (*Thob yig rag rim*).

342. This brief description of Lama Gonpo and his teachings to Khetsun Sangpo Rinpoche, pointed out to me by Rinpoche's long-time student and my friend of many years, Dr. Yukari Sueyasu, appears in the 2002 edition of Rinpoche's autobiography, *mKhas btsun rgan po' 'bel gtam kun gsal me long bzhugs so, dpal snga 'gyur bshad sgrub 'dod 'zo gling,* 49–51.

English-Tibetan Glossary

Sanskrit equivalents are included here for core philosophical terms only. Many of the most central terms of this work are not translations from Sanskrit but emic Tibetan terms, thus they have no Sanskrit equivalent.

abiding serenity (Dzogchen), calm	gzhi gnas
abiding state	gnas tshul
abiding state/way things are	gnas lugs
abyss	gcong rong
actions	las (Skt. karma)
affliction	nyon mongs (Skt. kleśa)
afflictive obstruction	nyon sgrib (Skt. kleśāvaraṇa)
ageless	gra ma myam
all	thams cad
all-embracing, all-suffusing	khyab brdal
allground	kun gzhi (Skt. ālayavijñāna)
always	rtag tu
animal	dud 'gro
appearances (to the senses)	snang ba (Skt. avabhāsa)
arrogance	khengs pa

artificial unawareness	kun tu btags (Skt. parikalpita)
atom	phra rab (Skt. paramānu)
attentive introspection	shes bzhin (Skt. saṃprajanya)
attraction, yearning, orienting	zhen
authentic sheer awareness	rig pa'i tshad ma
awareness holder	rig 'dzin (Skt. vidyadhara)
barbarian	kla klo
base/ground	gzhi (Skt. ālaya)
basic sheer awareness/sheer awareness of the base	gzhi'i rig
basic stainless purity	gzhi'i chos dbyings
basis	rten (Skt. āśraya)
bed	mal
behavior	spyod pa (Skt. caryā, bhoga)
beholder	gzigs
being, nature	rang bzhin (Skt. svabhāva)
beyond	pha rol (Skt. para)
blessing	byin rlabs
bliss and emptiness	bde stong
blizzard	bu yug
bodhi-mind	byang chub sems
body-cherishing	lus gces
body, speech, and mind	sku gsung thugs
boundlessness	tshad med
bow (i.e., with arrow)	gzhu
Brahma	Tshangs pa

brilliancy	sa le
buddha	sangs rgyas
Buddha and Buddha's heirs	rgyal ba sras bcas
buddha dimension, dimension of enlightenment	sku
bustle	'du 'dzi
catastrophe	mtshang
ceaselessly	rgyun mi chad par
center	dbus
central land	yul dbus
channels, winds, and bright orbs	rtsa, rlung, thig le (Skt. prāṇa, nāḍi, bindu)
chant	bzlas
child of good family	rigs kyi bu
cleanse	byang
clear opening	zang kha
clear presence	gsal rig pa'i cha
compassion, compassionate condition	rkyen
consciousness	rnams shes (Skt. jñāna/vijñāna)
contrary	'gal zla
conviction	thag ma chod
Copper Mount	Zang mdog dpal ri
crass practice	chos dred
critical point, eruption	lhongs
crown	spyi bo
crude	rtsub

cry out	'o dod
curved knife	gri gug
dakini	mkha' 'gro (Skt. *ḍākinī*)
danger zone, perilous situation	'phrang
dark	mun pa
dark prison	khri mun
death	'chi ba
defilement	sgrib (Skt. avaraṇa)
degenerated	nyams
delight	dgyes
demon	bdud
desire	'dod sred
desire and hate	chags sdang
desire king	'dod pa'i rgyal po
deviant path	lam gol
deviation, sidetracking	gol ba
dharma	chos
dharma platitudes	kha chos
dharma wheel	chos kyi 'khor lo
Diamond Being	rDo rje sems
difficult lot	skal ba ngan ba
dimension, Buddha dimension	sku (Skt. kāya)
disappearing	sane seng
display	rol pa
doing nothing	bzo med
domain, constituent	khams (Skt. dhātu)
door	sgo

dumb	lkugs pa
dynamic display, dynamism	rtsal
dynamic playfulness	rol rtsal
easeful equilibrium	mnyam par bzhag
eight impingements	mi khom brgyad
emaciated	rid
emanation dimension	sprul sku (Skt. nirmāṇakāya)
embrace	khyud pa
encircled	bskor
endless	mtha' med pa, mtha' yas
endowment	'byor ba
enjoyment	longs spyod (Skt. saṃbhoga)
enlightened dimension	sku (Skt. kāya)
enlightened state	dgongs
enlightenment mind	byang chub sems (Skt. bodhicitta)
enmity	shes 'gras
enter	zhugs
environment and essence	snod bcud
erring view	log lta can
error and deludedness	nor 'khrul
error base, basis of error	'khrul gzhi
eruption, critical point	lhongs
essence	dwangs bcud; ngo bo (Skt. svabhāva, vastu)
established, set up, ensured	grub (Skt. siddhi)
ethics	khrims (Skt. śīla)
evanescent	ban bun

evident, manifest	mngon sum (Skt. pratyakṣa)
exhausted	nyam thag
exhilaration	rab tu mgu ba
expanse	klong
factor of knowingness	mkhyen cha
failing	nyon mongs (Skt. kleśa)
faith, receptivity, openhearted presence	dad pa (Skt. śraddhā)
falling off a cliff	gshis phrang shor
false forms	sgyu lus
father-mother	yab yum
fault	nyes
fear	'jigs pa
feat	dngos grub (Skt. siddhi)
feet	rkang pa
field of razors	spu gri'i thang
find	rnyed
fixated	a 'thas
fleshy wound	sha'u
flirting	sgeg pa
fluctuating	phyad phyol
focus (lit. roll, condense)	dril ba
follow	'brang
food and drink	bza' btung
Forder	Mu stegs pa (Skt. Tīrthika)
forest of swords	ral gri'i tshal
form body	gzugs sku

four boundless states	tshad med bzhi
four consecrations	dbang bzhi
fourfold	bzhi yi ngang
fox	wa
free	bsgral; thar ba (Skt. mokśa)
free rein	kha yan du
freedom, well-favored life	dal 'byor
freshness, naturalness	so ma
full enlightenment	byang chub snying po
full essence dimension	ngo bo nyid kyi sku (Skt. svabhāvikakāya)
gain	thob pa (Skt. prāpti)
gasp	shugs ring
general base	spyi gzhi
god-fiend	lha bdud
good	bzang (Skt. bhadra)
good rebirth	bde 'gro
great bliss	bde chen (Skt. mahasukha)
grow weary	skyo shas
hammer	tho lum
hard to bear	brnag par dka' ba
harmful spirit	gdon
hateful	zhe sdang
hear	thos (Skt. śrāvana)
heart center	snying dbus
heart-movement (Dzogchen)	thugs rje (Skt. karuṇā)
heartfelt confidence	dad pa

heartfelt contrition	'gyod sems
helter skelter	zang zing
high and low	mchog thun
highest, supreme (path)	anu (Skt. anu)
holder of presence	rig 'dzin (Skt. vidhyādhara)
holder of the vajra	rdo rje 'dzin pa
holy word, commitment	dam tshig (Skt. samaya)
home, abode	gnas
homeground	gzhis
hot ash	thal tshan
I, self	bdag (Skt. ātman)
ignorance, obscuration	gti mug (Skt. moha)
ignorance, unawareness	ma rig pa (Skt. avidyā)
ills, harm, faults and blocks	nad gdon sdig sgrib
illusion	rdzun ris
immediacy	thog dus
immense expanse	klong yangs chen
immense purity	yongs dag chen
impoverished	phongs
in the future	phyis nas
inborn authenticity	gnyug, gnyug ma lhan skyes
independence	rang dbang (Skt. svatantra)
infraction	ltung (Skt. patati)
infuse	bsres
intellectual understanding	go yul
intention	kun slong
intrinsic condition	gshis

iron cell	lcags khyim
jewel	nor
jeweled island	rin chen gling
key instruction	gnad (Skt. marma, nāḍi)
knowing that accords how it is	ji lta ba bzhin du shes pa
laced with holes	'al 'ol
lack	bral
lasso	zhags pa
lay bare (confess)	mthol lo bshags
laziness	le lo
let be	sor bzhag
letting be	rang 'gros
level	rim pa (Skt. krama)
life	srog (Skt. jīva)
light	'od
likewise	de bzhin
limpid	seng nge
liquid	skom
little	chung
living being	sems can (Skt. sattva)
Lokesh Lord	'Jig rten dbang phyug
long-lived god	tshe ring lha
loveliness	sdug pa
luminous	gsal ba
magic net	sgyu 'phrul dra ba
Mahayana	Theg chen (Skt. Mahāyāna)
main practice	dngos gzhi

maintain	skyong
maliciousness	mi srun pa
mandala	dkyil 'khor (Skt. maṇḍala)
manifest sheer awareness	rig pa'i mngon sum
manifold	sna tshogs
mantra	sngags
me-sense	bdag 'dzin (Skt. ātmagrāha)
meandering, meandering onslaughts	'byams
meaning	don (Skt. artha)
meaningful	don yod (Skt. amoghu)
meditation	sgom (Skt. bhāvayati)
meditative experience	nyams
meet	mjal
melt	zhu
mental consciousness	yid shes (Skt. manojñāna)
mental functioning, mentation	yid/yid la byed pa (Skt. manaskāra)
merit	bsod nams (Skt. punya)
me-sense	bdag 'dzin (Skt. ātmagrāha)
Middle Way	dbU ma (Skt. Madhyamaka)
mind	blo, sems (Skt. buddhi, mati, citta)
mind holding	sems 'dzin
mind which is reality	chos nyid kyi sems
mind-muse	yid 'phrog
mind's real nature of mind	sems kyi chos nyid
mindful presence	dran rig (Skt. smṛti)

mindfulness	dran pa (Skt. smṛti)
mindnature	sems nyid
minds and knowers	blo rig
mindstream	sems kyi rgyud, rgyud
mirror	me long
misdeed, wrong	sdig pa
miserliness	ser sna
moan and wail	sme sngags
modification	bcas bco
molten bronze	khro chu
moon-heart	thugs ka'i zla dkyil
mortal	mi rtag
most basic mind	gnyug sems
most fundamental base	gnyug ma'i bzhi
mud	'dam
mudra	phyag rgya (Skt. mudra)
my mindstream	rang rgyud
my vision	rang snang
natural radiance	rang mdangs
naturally dawning presence	rig pa rang shar
nature, being	rang bzhin (Skt. svabhāva)
nectar	bdud rtsi (Skt. amṛta)
nourishment	zas
obscured/murky	rmugs pa
obstruction	sgrib pa (Skt. āvaraṇa)
obstructions to omniscience	shes sgrib (Skt. jñeyāvaraṇa)
obtainer	thob pa (Skt. prāpti)

omniscience, kindness, and power	mkhyen brtse nus gsum
omniscience, omniscient knowing	mkhyen
originally pure, primordially pure	gzod pa'i dag pa
orient toward, yearn for, adhere to	zhen
ornament/ornamentation	rgyan
overstate, exaggerate	sgro 'dogs (Skt. samāropa)
own display	rang snang
pain	sdug bsngal
path	lam (Skt. mārga)
playful emergence	rol ba
pleasure-playing	bde rol
pledge, commitment	dam tshig (Skt. samaya)
precise alertness	hrig gis
predispositions	bag chags (Skt. vāsanā)
preparatory allground	sbyor gzhi
presence to everything	kun rig
primordial knowing	ye shes (Skt. jñāna)
primordial slippage/pitfall	ye shor
primordially	ye nas
primordially pure, originally pure	ka dag (ka nas dag pa)
pristinely pure, limpid	sang nge
probe	bsnun
profoundly ordinary	tha mal
proliferation, iteration, ripple	spros pa
protect	skyob
protector	mgon po
pure	rnam dag

purify defilements	sdig pa sbyong
putrefied corpse	ro myags
quintessential instruction	man ngag
racing	tshab tshub
rapture	rangs pa
reality, real nature	chos nyid
realizer	rtogs mkhyen
red light	'od dmar
reflection	gzugs brnyan
refuge ocean	skyabs gnas rgya mtsho
reject	nges 'byung
release	dbyung
richly resplendent dimension	longs sku (Skt. saṃbogakāya)
right (direction)	g.yas
right (virtue)	dge
rigid	rengs
ripen	rnam smin
rise forth	yar la bzhengs
rope	thag pa
saw	sog le
seed	sa bon
seen and empty	snang stong
self-arisen, naturally arisen primordial knowing	rang 'byung ye shes
self-luminous sheer awareness	rig pa rang gsal
sense faculty, sense power, senses	dbang po
senseless	tho co

sensory sources	skye mched
serene abiding	gzhi gnas (Skt. śamatha)
set up, established	grub
settled ease, natural settling	rang babs
Seven Treasuries	Rin chen sna bdun
sheer awareness	rig pa (Skt. vidyā, vedana)
sheer awareness of the base	gzhi'i rig
sheer awareness of the path	lam rig
sheer awareness to/of reality	chos nyid kyi rig pa
sheer essence dimension, essential dimension	chos sku
sheer self awareness	rang rig (Skt. svasaṃvedana)
shine forth	snang
siddhi	dngos grub
sidetracking, deviation	gol ba
significance	don
skin	pags pa
slash	bcad gtubs
slave	bran g.yog
slide, slippage	shor
smile	'dzum
sole refuge	skyabs gcig
solitary realizer	rang sangs rgyas (Skt. pratyekabuddha)
solitude	dben pa
source of all refuge	skyabs gnas kun 'dus
space	dbyings
spacious immensity	yangs khrol le

spear	gsal shing
special seeing	lhag mthong (Skt. vipaśyanā)
speech-blocks	ngag sgrib
spiritual counsel	gtams ngag
spiritual friend	bshes gnyen (Skt. kalyāna-mitra)
spontaneously complete	lhun rdzogs
spontaneously occurring	lhun grub
stainless basic space	gzhi'i chos dbyings
stainless space	dbyings/chos dbyings (Skt. dharma-dhātu)
stand	ldang pa
star	skar ma
state, way of being	yin lugs
status	yin tshul
steadfast nature	bzhugs tshul
steady, ongoing	a 'thad
stove	thab
strength	zungs
strong	drag po
sublime knowing, wisdom	shes rab (Skt. prajñā)
suffering	sdug bsngal
suits	phrod
sunlight	nyin mo
superimpose	sgro 'dogs (Skt. samāropa)
supreme desire	'dod rgu'i mchog
supreme way of being	mchog tshul
sustained continuity	rgyun bskyangs

swift sprung	thol skye
swiftly	myur du
swirl	'khor ba
thick	stug po
three real jewels	dkon mchog gsum dngos
three realms	khams gsum
three root Blissful Ones	bDe gshegs rtsa bag sum
three roots	rtsa gsum
three worlds	srid gsum
throw off	bor ba
tight mindfulness	'jur dran
tomorrow	nangs pa
tongue	lce dbang
tormented	gzer ba
training and reorientation	'dul shugs
training method	'dul byed
transform	bsgyur
tri-spoked vajra	rdo rje rtse gsum
true form	chos sku (Skt. dharma-kāya)
trust	gdeng, gdengs
unawareness, ignorance	ma rig pa (Skt. avidyā)
unbearable	bzod med
unbounded wholeness	thig le nyag gcig
underplay, undervalue, detract	skur 'debs
unfettered	rtsa bral
unfortunate realms in hard rebirths	ngan song ngan 'gro
unimpeded transparency	zang tha

uninhibited	rgya yan
unknown	mi grags par
unpleasant	nyams mi dga' ba
unstable	nges pa med
until	bar du
use	bkol zhing spyod pa
utterly vivid emptiness	stong sang nge
vajra form	rdo rje sku
Vajrasattva	rDo rje sems dpa'
Vajrayogini	rDo rje rnal 'byor ma
vase	bum pa
vehicle, practice vehicle	theg pa (Skt. yāna)
very being, own nature	rang bzhin (Skt. svabhāva)
very foul mind	byur po che yi sems
vigor	brtson
violate	nyams
virtue	dge (Skt. kusala)
vital point	mtshang rig
vivid	sa le
vivid clarity	sa le hrig ge
vows	sdom pa
vulture	bya rgod
wander	'khyams
wealth	nor, longs spyod (Skt. saṃbhoga)
weapon	mtshon
white lotus	pad dkar

wholeness that is self-knowing presence	rang rig nyag gcig
wide awake	hrig ge
wild	reg
wind	rlung (Skt. prāṇa)
wood	shing
world	'jig rten
world and peace	'khor 'das
wrong(s), misdeeds	sdig
year	lo
your own unfolding	rang grol
youthful	gzhon nu

Tibetan-English Glossary

ka dag	pure at the source/ primordial purity
kun tu btags pa'i ma rig pa	artificial unawareness
kun rig	presence to everything
kun slong	intention
kun gzhi	allground
kla klo	barbarian
klong	expanse
klong yangs chen	immense expanse
dkon mchog gsum dngos	three real jewels
dkyil 'khor	mandala
bkol zhing spyod pa	use
rkang pa	feet
rkyen	condition
lkugs pa	dumb
skal ba ngan ba	difficult lot
skar ma	star
sku	enlightened dimension
sku gsung thugs	body, speech, and mind
skur 'debs	underplay, undervalue, detract

skom	liquid
skyabs gcig	sole refuge
skyabs gnas kun 'dus	source of all refuge
skyabs gnas rgya mtsho	refuge ocean
skyo shas	grow weary
skyong	maintain
skyob	protect
skye mched	sensory sources
bskor	encircled
kha chos	dharma platitudes
kha yan du	free rein
khams	domain, constituent
khams gsum	three realms
khengs pa	arrogance
khyab brdal	all-suffusing, all-embracing
khyud pa	embrace
khri mun	dark prison
khrims	ethics
khro chu	molten bronze
mkha' 'gro	dakini
mkhyen	omniscient knowing, omniscience
mkhyen cha	factor of knowingness
mkhyen brtse nus gsum	omniscience, kindness, and power
'khor ba	cyclic existence, swirl
'khor 'das	cyclic existence and nirvana, swirl and peace

'khyams	wander
'khrul gzhi	basis of error
go yul	intellectual understanding
gol ba	deviation, sidetracking
gra ma myam	ageless
gri gug	curved knife
grub	established, set up
dge	right, virtue
dgongs	enlightened state
dgyes	delight
mgon po	protector
'gal zla	contrary
'gyod sems	heart-felt contrition
rgya yan	uninhibited
rgyan	ornament/ornamentation
rgyal ba sras bcas	Buddha and Buddha's heirs
rgyun bskyangs	sustained continuity
rgyun mi chad par	ceaselessly
sgeg pa	flirting
sgo	door
sgom pa	meditation
sgyu lus	false forms
sgyu 'phrul dra ba	magic net
sgyur	transform
sgrib	obstruction
sgro 'dogs	superimpose
bsgral	free

bsgro 'dogs	overlay, overstate, excess
ngag sgrib	speech-blocks
ngan song ngan 'gro	unfortunate realms in hard rebirths
nges pa med	unstable
nges 'byung	reject
ngo bo	essence
ngo bo nyid kyi sku	full essence dimension
dngos grub	feat
dngos gzhi	main practice
mngon sum	evident, manifest
sngags	mantra
gcong rong	abyss
bcad gtubs	slash
bcas bco	modification
lce dbang	tongue
lcags khyim	iron cell
chags sdang	desire and hate
chung	little
chos	Dharma
chos kyi 'khor lo	Dharma wheel
chos sku	sheer essence dimension
chos dred	crass practice
chos nyid	reality, real nature
chos nyid kyi dbyings	stainless space
chos nyid kyi rig pa	sheer awareness of reality
chos nyid kyi sems	mind which is reality

mchog thun	high and low
mchog tshul	supreme way of being
'chi ba	death
ji lta ba bzhin du shes pa	knowing that accords with how it is
mjal	meet
'jig rten	world
'Jig rten dbang phyug	Lokesh Lord
'jigs pa	fear
'jur dran	tight mindfulness
nyam thag	exhausted
nyams	degenerated; violate; meditative experience
nyams mi dga' ba	unpleasant
nyin mo	sunlight
nyes	fault
nyon sgrib	afflictive obstructions
nyon mongs	affliction, failing
gnyug	basic
gnyug ma lhan skyes	inborn basic mind
gnyug ma'i gzhi	most fundamental base
gnyug sems	most basic mind
mnyam par gzhag	equilibrium, easeful equilibrium
rnyed	find
snying dbus	heart center
gti mug	ignorance
rtag tu	always

rten	basis
rtogs mkhyen	realizer
ltung	infraction
stug po	thick
stong sang nge	utterly vivid emptiness
tha mal	profoundly ordinary
thag pa	rope
thag ma chod	conviction
thab	stove
thams cad	all
thar ba	free
thal tshan	hot ash
thig le nyag gcig	unbounded wholeness
thugs ka'i zla dkyil	moon-heart
thugs rje	compassionate heart-movement
Theg chen	Mahāyāna
theg pa	vehicle, practice vehicle
tho co	senseless
tho lum	hammer
thog dus	immediacy
thob pa	gain; obtainer
thol skye	swift sprung
thos	hear
mtha' yas	endless
mthol lo bshags	lay bare (confess)
dad pa	faith, heartfelt confidence

dam tshig	pledge, holy word
dal 'byor	freedom
dug lnga	five poisons
dud 'gro	all-suffusing animal
de bzhin	likewise
don	meaning, significance
don yod	meaningful
dwangs bcud	essence
drag po	strong
dranpa	mindfulness
dran rig	mindful presence
dril ba	focus, wrap (lit. roll, condense)
gdams ngag	spiritual counsel
gdung ba	pain
gdeng, gdengs	trust
gdon	harmful spirit
bdag	I, self
bdag 'dzin	me-sense
bdud	demon
bdud rtsi	nectar
bde 'gro	good rebirth
bde chen	great bliss
bde stong	bliss and emptiness
bde ldan	great bliss
bde rol	pleasure-playing
bDe gshegs rtsa bag sum	three root Blissful Ones

'dam	mud
'du 'dzi	bustle
'dul byed	training method
'dul shugs	training and reorientation
'dod rgu'i mchog	supreme desire
'dod pa'i rgyal po	desire king
'dod sred	desire
rdo rje sku	vajra form
rDo rje rnal 'byor ma	Vajrayogini
rdo rje rtse gsum	tri-spoked vajra
rdo rje 'dzin pa	holder of the vajra
rDo rje sems dpa	Diamond Being, Vajrasattva
ldang pa	stand
sdig pa	misdeed
sdig pa sbyong	purify defilements
sdig sgrib	defilement
sdug pa	loveliness
sdug bsngal	pain, suffering
sdom pa	vows
nangs pa	tomorrow
nad gdon sdig sgrib	ills, harm, faults and blocks
nor	jewel; wealth
nor 'phrul	error and deludedness
gnad	key instruction
gnas	home
gnas skor	pilgrimage
gnas tsul	abiding state

gnas lugs	abiding state, the way things are
rnam dag	pure
rnam smin	ripen
rnams shes	consciousness
sna tshogs	manifold
snang	appear, shine forth
snang stong	seen and empty
snang ba	(sensory) appearances
snod bcud	environment and essence beings
brnag par dka' ba	hard to bear
bsnun	probe
pags pa	skin
pad dkar	white lotus
spu gri'i thang	a field of razors
spyi bo	crown
spyi gzhi	general base
spyob pa	protect
spyod pa	behavior
sprul sku	emanation dimension
spros pa	proliferation, iteration, extrapolation
sbyor gzhi	preparatory allground
pha mtha' med pa	endless
pha rol	beyond
phongs	impoverished
phyag rgya	mudra

phyad phyol	fluctuating
phyis nas	in the future
phra rab	atom
phrod	suit
'phrang	danger zone, perilous situation
bag chags	predispositions
ban bun	evanescent
bar du	until
bu yug	blizzard
bum pa	vase
bor ba	throw off
bya rgod	vulture
byang	cleanse
byang chub snying po	full enlightenment
byang chub sems	enlightenment mind, bodhi-mind
byin rlabs	blessing
byur po che yi sems	a very foul mind
bran g.yog	slave
bral	lack
blo	mind
blo rig	minds and knowers
dbang po	senses; sense faculty; sense power
dbang bzhi	four consecrations
dbang mdzad	power-wielding
dbu ma	middle way

dbus	center
dben pa	solitude
dbyings	stainless space
dbyung	release
'byams	meandering, meandering onslaughts
'byor ba	endowment
'brang	follow
ma rig pa	unawareness, ignorance
man ngag	quintessential instruction
mal	bed
mi khom brgyad	eight impingements
mi grags par	unknown
mi rtag	mortal
mi srun pa	maliciousness
mun pa	dark
me long	mirror
myur du	swiftly
rmugs pa	obscured, murky
sme sngags	moan and wail
rtsa ba gsum	three roots
rtsa bral	unfettered
rtsa rlung thig le	channels, winds, and bright orbs
rtsa gsum	three roots
rtsal	dynamic display, dynamism
rtsub	crude
brtson	vigor

Tshangs pa	Brahma
tshad med	boundlessness
tshad med bzhi	four boundless states
tshab tshub	racing
tshe ring lha	long-lived god
mtshang	catastrophe
mtshang rig	vital point
mtshon	weapon
'dzum	smile
rdzun ris	illusion
wa	fox
zhags pa	lasso
zhu	melt
zhugs	enter
zhe sdang	hateful
zhen	attraction, yearning; v. orient toward, yearn for, adhere to
gzhi	base, ground
gzhi gnas	serene abiding
bzhi yi ngang	fourfold
gzhi'i dbyings chos dbyings	basic stainless purity
gzhi'i rig pa	basic sheer awareness, sheer awareness of the base
gzhis	homeground
gzhu	bow (i.e., with arrow)
bzhugs tshul	steadfast nature
gzhon nu	youthful
zang kha	clear opening

Zang mdog dpal ri	Copper Mount
zang thal	unimpeded transparency
zang zing	helter skelter
zas	nourishment
zungs	strength
zla	month
gzigs	beholder
gzugs sku	form dimension
gzugs brnyan	reflection
gzer ba	tormented
gzod pa'i dag pa	originally pure
bzang	good
bza' btung	food and drink
bzo med	doing nothing
bzod med	unbearable
bzlas	chant
'al 'ol	laced with holes
'o dod	cry out
'od	light
'od dmar	red light
yangs khrol le	spacious immensity
yab yum	father-mother
yar la bzhengs	rise forth
g.yas	right
yid 'phrog	mind-muse
yid/yid la byed pa	mental functioning, mentation

yid shes	mental consciousness
yin tshul	status
yin lugs	state, way of being
yul dbus	central land
ye nas	primordially
ye shes	primordial knowing, primordial wisdom
ye shor	primordial slippag, pitfall
yongs dag chen	immense purity
rang grol	your own unfolding
rang 'gros	letting be
rang rgyud	my mindstream
rang mdangs	natural radiance
rang snang	my vision; own display
rang babs	settled ease, natural settling
rang dbang	independence
rang 'byung ye shes	naturally arisen, self-arisen primordial knowing
rang bzhin	very being, own nature
rang rig	self-aware sheer awareness
rang rig nyag gcig	wholeness that is self-knowing presence
rang sangs rgyas	solitary realizer
rangs pa	rapture
rab tu mgu ba	exhilaration
rab med	endless
ral gri'i tshal	a forest of swords
rig pa	sheer awareness presence

rig pa rang shar	naturally dawning presence
rig pa rang gsal	self-luminous sheer awareness
rig pa'i mngon sum	manifest sheer awareness
rig pa'i tshad ma	authentic sheer awareness
rig 'dzin	awareness holder, holder of presence
rigs kyi bu	child of good family
rid	emaciated
Rin chen sna bdun	Seven Treasuries
rin chen gling	jeweled island
rim pa	level
reg	wild
rengs	rigid
ro myags	putrefied corpse
rol ba	playful emergence
rol tsal	dynamic playfulness
lam	path
lam gol	deviant path
lam rig	path sheer awareness
las	action
lus gces	body-cherishing
le lo	laziness
lo	year
log lta can	erring view
longs spyod	wealth, enjoyment
rlung	wind
sha'u	fleshy wound

shing	wood
shes 'gras	enmity
shes sgrib	obstructions to omniscience
shes bzhin	attentive introspection
shes rab	sublime knowing, wisdom
shugs ring	gasp
shor	slide, slippage
gshis	intrinsic condition, homeground
gshis phrang shor	falling off a cliff
bshes gnyen	spiritual friend
sa bon	seed
sa la	brilliancy
Sangs rgyas	Buddha
sa le	vivid
sa le hrig ge	vivid clarity
seng nge	limpid, pristinely pure
sems	mind
sems kyi rgyud, rgyud	mindstream
sems kyi chos nyid	mind's real nature of mind
sems can	living being
sems nyid	mindnature
sems 'dzin	mind holding
so ma	freshness, naturalness
sog le	saw
sor bzhag	let be
srid gsum	three worlds

srog	life
gsal ba	luminous, clarity
gsal rig pa'i cha	clear presence
gsal shing	spear
bsod nams	merit
bsres	infuse
hrig gis	precise alertness
hrig ge	wide awake
lha bdud	god-fiend
lhag mthong	special seeing
lhun grub	spontaneously occurring
lhun rdzogs	spontaneously complete
lhongs	critical point, eruption
a 'thad	steady, ongoing
a 'thas	fixated
a nu	highest, supreme (path)

Bibliography of Works Cited

TBRC: Tibetan Buddhist Resource Center

Unattributed Texts

Anuttara Tantra
rGyud bla ma
TBRC W00KG02837

Cloud of Jewels
Ratnamegha
dKon mchog sprin *in* bKa' 'gyur (sDe dge par phud)
TBRC W22084, 64

Collection of Secrets
Guhyasamāja
gSangs ba'dus pa
TBRC W4CZ7445, pp. 289-441

Definitive Commentary on the "Enlightened State Sutra"
Saṃdhinirmocana Sūtra
mDo dgongs pa nges 'grel *in* bKa' 'gyur (sTog pho brang bris ma)
TBRC W22083, 63. Leh: Smanrtsis Shesrig Dpemzod, 1975–1980

Enlightened Mind, Majestic Creator of Everything
Byang sems kun byed rgyal po *in* bKa' 'gyur (sDe dge par phud)
TBRC W22084, 97: 3–173. Delhi: Delhi Karmapae Chodhey Gyalwae Sungrab Partun Khang, 1976–1979.

Majestic Creator of Everything
Kun byed rgyal po *in* rNying ma rgyud 'bum (mTshams brag dgon pa'i bris ma)
TBRC W21521, 1: 2–192. Thimphu: National Library, Royal Government of Bhutan, 1982.

Self-Dawning Tantra
Rig pa rang shar/Rig pa rang shar chen po'i rgyud
TBRC W1KG11703, 2: 3–470 234 ff. (pp. 1–468)
A'dzom chos sgar, 2000[?] [dKar mdzes bod rigs rang skyong khul, dPal yul rdzong]

Sutra of the Ten Essential Teachings
sNying po 'khor lo bcu pa'i mdo/Sa'i snying po 'khor lo bcu pa'i mdo *in* bKa' 'gyur
(sDe dge par phud)
TBRC W22084, 65: 201–484. Delhi: Delhi Karmapae Chodhey Gyalwae Sungrab Partun Khang, 1976–1979.

Sutra on the Questions of Bhadra the Magician
sGyu ma mkhan bzang po lung bstan pa'i mdo *in* bKa' 'gyur (sDe dge par phud)
TBRC W22084, 43: 36–73. Delhi: Delhi Karmapae Chodhey Gyalwae Sungrab Partun Khang, 1976–1979.

The Tantra Without Letters
Yi ge med pa; Yi ge med pa'i rgyud; Yi ge med pa'i rgyud chen po zhes bya ba rin po che'i rgyal mtshan gyi rgyud rgyal po'i gdud rgyud rgyal po'i gdud rgyud lta ba nam mkha'i dang mnyam pa'i rgyud chen po. N.p.: n.p., n.d.

The Tiger [Hevajra] Root Tantra
rTsa rgyud brtag gnyis kyi 'gyur
TBRC W11577, 2: 225. Dehra Dun: Sakya Center.

AUTHORED TEXTS

Āryadeva (Arya de ba, c. 150–250 C.E.)
Lamp Distilling the Practices: A Commentary on the Meaning of the Five Stages [of the Guhyasamaja Completion Stage]
Caryāmelāpaka-pradīpa
sPyod bsdus/sPyod bsdus sgron me
TBRC W1KG10776

Candrakīrti (Zla bag rags pa)
Entrance to [Nāgārjuna's] 'Stanzas on the Middle Way'
Madhyamkāvatāra (dbU ma la 'jug pa)
TBRC W1KG3871 and W19458

Chogyur Lingpa (mChog gyur bde chen gling pa, 1829–1870)
Commentary on the Heart of Primordial Knowing, Stages of the Path

bLa ma'i thugs sgrub rdo rje drag rtsal las zhal gdams lam rim ye shes snying po'i 'grel ba ye shes snang ba rab tu rgyas pa *in* mChog gling gter gsar
TBRC W22642, 32: 71–524. Paro: Lama Pema Tashi, 1982–1986.

Great Treasure of Wishfulfilling Jewels: A Profound Revelation
mChog gyur bde chen gling pa yi zab gter yid bzhin nor bu'i chos mdzod chen mo
TBRC W22642, 39. Paro: Lama Pema Tashi, 1982–1986.

Oral Instructions in the Gradual Path of the Wisdom Essence in *Light of Wisdom*
Lam rim ye shes snying po/bLa ma'i thugs sgrub rdo rje drag rtsal las zhal gdams
Lam rim ye shes snying po *in* mChog gling gter gsar
TBRC W22642, 32: 5–70. Paro: Lama Pema Tashi, 1982–1986.

Dudjom Rinpoche Jigdral Yeshe Dorje (bDud 'joms 'jigs bral ye shes rdo rje, 1904–1984)
Chariot of the Path: Practices on the Path to Liberation
Chos spyod kyi rim pa rnam par grol ba'i lam gyi shing rta
TBRC W20869, 18: 7–414. Kalimpong: Dupjung Lama, 1979–1985.

Introducing Dzogchen, A Heart Jewel for the Fortunate
rDzogs skal ldan snying nor/Ngo sprod
rDzogs chen ngo sprod skal ldan snying po *in* Zhal gdams bslab bya phyogs bsdebs nang gses le tshan zhe dgu
TBRC W20869, 25: 336.5–337.5. Kalimpong: Dupjung Lama, 1979–1985.

Mountain Retreat: A Simple Explanation of the Quintessence of Practice: The Alchemy of Accomplishment
Ri chos bslab bya nyams len dmar khrid go bder brjod pa grub pa'i bcud len
TBRC W20869, 13: 451–476. Kalimpong: Dupjung Lama, 1979–1985.

Dorje Lingpa (rDo rje gling pa, 1346–1405)
Prayer of All Goodness
Kun bzang smon lam/bZang spyod smon lam gyi 'don thams kun bzang 'dzum zhal
TBRC W1KG2118, 1: 535–542. Kathmandu: Khenpo Shedup Tenzin and Lama Thinley Namgyal, 2009.
Also in: gSung 'bum, bLo bzang bstan 'dzin dpal 'byor. TBRC W23880: 690–705. Delhi: Don-'grub-rdo-rje, 1977.

Gampopa (Gampopa, Dwags po lha rje, 1059–1153)
Simultaneously Arisen Union
Lhan cig skyes sbyor bskyang thabs shin tu zab mo
W8039, 8 ff. (pp. 922–37). [s.n.], [lha sa]. [2004]. Edited by karma bde legs.

Gyelba Lorepa (Rgyal ba lo ras pa grags pa dbang phyug, 1187–1250)
Essential Instructions on the Great Seal
Phyag chen man ngag *in* gSung 'bum *of* Grags pa dbang phyug
TBRC W23440. Kathmandu: Khenpo S. Tenzin, 2002.

Kunga Gyaltsan (Kun dga' rgyal mtshan, 1182–1251)
Discriminating the Three Vows
sDom gsum rab tu dbye ba *in* Sa skya bka' 'bum
TBRC W00EGS1017151, 12: 11–113. Kathmandu: Sachen International, 2006.

Jigme Lingpa (Kun mkhyen 'jigs med gling pa, 1729/1730–1798)
Chariot of Omniscience
rNam mkhyen shing rta
Yon tan rin po che'i mdzod las bras bu'i theg pa'i rgya cher 'grel rnam mkhyen shing rta *in* gSung 'bum *of* 'Jigs med gling pa
W1KG10193, 440 ff. (pp.1–880). Gangtok: Sonam T. Kazi, 1970–1975.

A Collection of Instructions and Replies to Various Queries on Buddhist Meditation and Practice
sGom phyogs dris lan
kLong chen nam mkha'i rnal 'byor gyi gsung thor bu phyogs bsdebs *in* gSung bum *of* 'Jigs med gling pa (A 'dzom par ma/'Brug spa gro la bskyar par brgyab pa)
TBRC W7477, 4: 503–754. [Chengdu, 1999?]

Longchen Rabjam (kLong chen rab 'jam pa dri med 'od zer, 1308–1364)
A Treasure Trove of Sublime Scriptural Transmission, A Commentary on the "Treasury of Stainless Space"
Chos dbyings rin po che'i mdzod kyi 'grel pa lung gi gter mdzod
TBRC W1CZ2550. A'dzom chos sgar. Skar mdzes bo rig rang skyong khul, dpal yul rdzong. 199?
Translated by Richard Barron as *A Treasure Trove of Scriptural Transmission*. Junction City, Calif.: Padma Publishing, 2001.

Distinguishing Three Essential Elements of the Great Completeness
rDzogs pa chen po'i gnad gsum shan 'byed/('u) *in* gSung 'bum *of* 'Jigs med gling pa
(A 'dzom par ma/'brug spa gro la bskyar par brgyab pa)

TBRC W7477, 12: 101–104. [Chengdu, 1999?]

Fine Chariot, Great Commentary on Putting Illusions to Rest
rDzogs pa chen po sgyu ma ngal gso'i 'grel pa shing rta bzang po *in* rDzogs pa chen po
ngal gso skor gsum dang rang grol skor gsum bcas pod gsum
TBRC W23760, 2: 597–765. 1999.

Great Chariot
Shing rta chen mo/rDzogs pa chen po sems nyid ngal gso'i 'grel pa shing rta chen po/Sems nyid ngal gso 'grel chen
Sems nyid ngal gso'i 'grel pa *in* gSung 'bum *of* Dri med 'od zer (sDe dge par ma)
TBRC W00EGS1016299, 4: 83–781. Derge: sDe dge par khang chen mo, 2000.

The Great Commentary on Resting in Mindnature
Sems nyid ngal gso 'grel chen *in* gSung 'bum *of* Dri med 'od zer (sDe dge par khang)
TBRC W00EGS1016299, 4: 83–781. Derge: sDe dge par khang chen mo, 2000.

Root of the Wish Fulfilling Treasure
Yid bzhin mdzod kyi rtsa ba *in* gSung 'bum *of* Dri med 'od zer (sDe dge par ma)
TBRC W00EGS1016299, 1. Derge: sDe dge par khang chen mo, 2000.

Sevenfold Foundational Mind Training Instructions
sNgon 'gro sems sbyong bdun gyi don khrid, *in* sNying thig ya bzhi.
TBRC W12827, 1: 329–338. Delhi: Sherab Gyaltsen Lama, 1975.

Ngorchen Kunga Zangpo (1382–1456)
Treasury of Songs
Doha mdzod *in* bsTan 'gyur (gSer gyi lag bris ma)
TBRC W23702, 49: 380–384. Tibet: sNar thang.

Padmasambhava (Padma 'byung gnas, 8 C.E.)
Great Seal of Heartfelt Advice
Phyag chen zhal gdams
TBRC W1KG8321, 3 ff. (pp. 229–34)
Quintessential Advice of Simplified Pointing Out Instructions, as for an Old Woman
rGan mo mdzub btsugs kyi gdams ngag
TBRC W2CZ6597 p. 57

Panchen Losang Chogyel (Pan chen blo bzang chos rgyal, 1570–1662)
Root of the Great Seal
Phyag chen rtsa ba

Patrul Rinpoche (A bu hral po/O rgyan 'jigs med chos kyi dbang po, 1808–1887)
Heartfelt Instructions
sNying gtam/A bu hral po'i snying gtam tshig su bkod pa'i ko'i ko
mThar thug rdzog pa chen po'i sangs rgyas pa'i thabs zab mo dgongs pa rang grol zhes bya ba
TBRC W2CZ5981

The Words of My Perfect Teacher
sNying tig gi sngon 'gro'i khrid yig kun bzang bla ma'i zhal lung *in* gSung 'bum *of* Orgyan 'jigs med chos kyi dbang po
TBRC W24829, 7: 23–616. Chengdu: Si khron mi rigs dpe skrun khang, 2003

Terton Gokyi Demtru Chen (rGod kyi ldem 'phru can, 1337–1408)
Unimpeded Enlightened State Tantra
dGongs pa bzang thal gyi rgyud
Kun bzang dgongs pa zang thal las rdzogs pa chen po chos nyid mngon sum zhi khro lhun grub kyi phrin las
TBRC W10160, 1. Bylakuppe: Ngagyur Nyingma Institute, 2002.

Tsele Natsok Rangdrol (Rtse le sna tshogs rang grol, 1608–?)
Quintessentials of Mahamudra and Dzogchen
Phyag rdzogs man ngag
rTse le sna tshogs rang grol gyi gsung gdams zab phyogs sgrig
TBRC W1KG4338. Kathmandu: Khenpo Shedup Tenzin and Lama Thinley Namgyal, 2007.

Tsultrim Rinchen (Tshul khrims rin chen, 1697–1774)
Treasury of Praise
Do ha mdzod *in* bsTan 'gyur (sDe dge)
TBRC W23703, 52: 269–273. Delhi: Delhi Karmapae Choedhey, Gyalwae Sungrab Partun Khang, 1982–1985.

Vasubandhu (dbYig gnyen)
Abhidharmakośakārika
TBRC W19720

English-Language Sources

Asanga/Maitreya. *Commentary on the Sublime Continuum* (*Uttaratantra Shastra, Mahāyāna-uttaratantra-śāstra*). Translated by Rosemarie Fuchs. Ithaca, N.Y.: Snow Lion Publications, 2000.

Klein, Anne C., *Heart Essence, the Vast Expanse: A Story of Transmission.* Ithaca, N.Y.: Snow Lion Publications, 2009.

———. *Meeting the Great Bliss Queen.* Ithaca, N.Y.: Snow Lion Publications, 2009.

———. "Story and Symbolism of Yeshey Tsogyal, the Great Bliss Queen." In *Buddhism in Practice.* Edited by Donald Lopez. Princeton: Princeton University Press, 1995. pp. 139–169.

Klein, Anne C. with Geshe Tenzin Wangyal Rinpoche. *Unbounded Wholeness: Dzogchen, Bön, and the Logic of the Nonconceptual.* Oxford: Oxford University Press, 2006.

Klein, Anne C. and Khetsun Sangpo Rinpoche. "Divining Hail: Deities, Energies, and Tantra on the Tibetan Plateau." In *Mantic Knowledge in World Views and Life-worlds in East Asia.* Edited by Michael Lackner. Leiden: Brill Publishers, 2015.

Klein, Anne C, with Khetsun Sangpo Rinpoche "Hail Protection." In *Religions of Tibet in Practice.* Edited by Donald Lopez. Princeton: Princeton University Press, 1997.

Lati Rinbochay and Jeffrey Hopkins. *Death, Intermediate State and Rebirth in Tibetan Buddhism.* Ithaca, N.Y.: Snow Lion Publications, 1981.

Longchenpa. *Kindly Bent to Ease Us.* Translated by Herbert V. Guenther. Emeryville, Calif.: Dharma Publishing, 1975.

———. *The Precious Treasury of Philosophical Systems* (*Grub mtha' mdzod*). Translated by Richard Barron. Junction City, Calif.: Padma Publishing, 2007.

Rangdrol, Tsele Natsog. *Lamp of Mahamudra.* Translated by Erik Pema Kunsang. Boulder, Colo.: Shambhala Publications, 1989.

Sangpo, Khetsun. *Fundamental Mind: The Nyingma View of the Great Completeness.* Translated and edited by Jeffrey Hopkins. Ithaca, N.Y.: Snow Lion Publications, 2006.

———. *Luminosity and Emptiness: Analysis of Fundamental Mind,* with oral commentary. Translated and edited by Jeffrey Hopkins. http://uma-tibet.org/edu/gomang/gomang_first.php

———. *Tantric Practice in Nyingma.* Translated by Jeffrey Hopkins. Edited by Anne C. Klein. Ithaca, N.Y.: Snow Lion Publications, 1996.

Tarthung Tulku. *Gesture of Balance: A Guide to Self-Healing and Meditation.* Emeryville, Calif.: Dharma Publishing, 1977.

Zahler, Leah, ed. and annot. *Meditative States in Tibetan Buddhism: The Concentrations and Formless Absorptions.* With Lati Rinbochay, Denma Lochö Rinbochay, and Jeffrey Hopkins. Boston: Wisdom Publications, 1983, 1997.

Bibliography of Tibetan-Language Works by Khetsun Sangpo Rinpoche

(mKhas btsun bzang po rin po che), 1920–2009

mKhas btsun rgan po' 'bel gtam kun gsal me long. Sunderjal: Nyingmapa Wish-Fulfilling Center for Study and Practice, 2002.

Biographical Dictionary of Tibet and Tibetan Buddhism. rGya bod mkhas grub rim byon gyi rnam thar phyogs bsgrigs. Compiled by Khetsun Sangpo. 12 vols. Dharamsala, H.P.: Library of Tibetan Works and Archives, Headquarters of H.H. the Dalai Lama: 1973–1990. TBRC W1KG10294.

Vol. 1. The Arhats, Siddhas, and Panditas of India. *bDag cag rnams kyi ston mchog don kun grub pa dang de'i rjes 'jug rgya gar paN grub mang po'i rnam par thar pa ngo mtshar pad mo'i 'dzum zhal gsar du bzhad pa.*

Vol. 2. The Sixteen Sthaviravadins. *'Phags pa gnas brtan chen po bcu drug gi rtogs brjod pa gdung sel nor bu'i 'od snang.*

Vol. 3. The Nyingma Tradition I. *Bod du sgrub brgyud shing rta chen po mched brgyad las/snga 'gyur gsang chen rnying ma pa'i bla ma brgyud pa rjes 'brangs dang bcas pa'i rnam thar ngo mtshar rgya mtsho (stod cha).*

Vol. 4. The Nyingma Tradition II. *sNga 'gyur gsang chen rnying ma pa'i bla ma brgyud pa rjes 'brangs dang bcas pa'i rnam thar ngo mtshar rgya mtsho (smad cha).*

Vol. 5. The Kadampa Tradition I. *bKa' gdams gsar rnying gi rjes 'brangs dang bcas pa'i bla ma brgyud pa'i rnam par thar pa kun btus nor bu'i do shal (stod cha).*

Vol. 6. The Kadampa Tradition II. *bKa' gdams gsar rnying gi rjes 'brangs dang bcas pa'i bla ma brgyud pa'i rnam par thar pa kun btus nor bu'i do shal (smad cha).*

Vol. 7. The Kagyupa Tradition I (Karma Kagyupa). *bKa' brgyud bla ma brgyud pa rjes 'drangs dang bcas pa'i rnam thar sgrub brgyud rin chen phreng ba.*

Vol. 8. The Kagyupa Tradition II (Dugpa Kagyupa). *'Brug pa bka' brgyud pa'i rnam thar bsgrub brgyud rin chen phreng ba.*

Vol. 9. The Kagyupa Tradition III (Drigyu Kagyupa). *'Bri stag bla ma brgyud pa'i rnam thar sgrub brgyud zin chen phreng ba.*

Vol. 10. The Sakyapa Tradition I. *Lam 'bras dang bcas pa'i rnam thar phyogs btus mkhas pa'i yid 'phrog (stod cha).*

Vol. 11. The Sakyapa Tradition II. *Bod du sgrub brgyud shing rta chen po mched brgyud pa rjes 'brangs dang bcas pa'i rnam thar phyogs btus mkhas pa'i yid 'phrog (smad cha).*

Vol. 12. The Kagyupa Tradition IV (Shangpa Kagyupa). *Shangs pa bka' brgyud/zhi gcod/sbyor drug rdor bzlas bcas kyi bla ma brgyud pa'i rnam thar.*

mKhas btshun rtogs brjod [Autobiography of Khetsun Sangpo Rinpoche]. Dharamsala: Library of Tibetan Works and Archives, 1973. TBRC W00KG09699.

Don rnam nges shes rab ral gri'i 'grel mchan bzhugs so [Commentary on (Mipam Rinpoche's) Sword of Wisdom]. Sunderjal: Nyingmapa Wish-Fulfilling Center for Study and Practice. N.p.: n.p., n.d.

Proverbs and Lyric Poems

Bod kyi rgyal rabs sa 'og nas brnyes pa'i dum bsgrigs rna ba'i bdud rtsi [Nectar for the Ear: An Early History of Tibet edited from findings unearthed at the Duhuang Caves]. Sunderjal: Nyingmapa Wish-Fulfilling Center for Study and Practice, 1986. TBRC W00KG09696.

gTam dpe sna tshogs dang gzhas tshig sna tshogs. Dharamsala: Library of Tibetan Works and Archives, 1973–1990. TBRC W1KG10294.

Extensive Calendrical and Other Charts

Lo rtsis re'u mig mkhyen byed gter gyi tha ram. N.p.: n.p., n.d.

Credits

Photographs

Page 2: Khetsun Sangpo Rinpoche's first visit to the United States, in March 1972, Falls Church, Virginia. Photo by John Buescher. Used with permission.

Page xl: This photograph was taken during Khetsung Sangpo Rinpoche's teaching of *Strand of Jewels* at Pema Osel Ling, Santa Cruz, California, July 1996. Photo by Carol Faust. Used with permission.

Page 114: This photograph was taken during the Buddha Month of Sagadawa, Boudha, Kathmandu, in June 2009, at the time of Khetsung Sangpo Rinpoche's Great Accomplishment (Drubchen) of the *Yangti Nakpo* (Golden Syllable of the Essential Black), which was the practice of a rare dark-retreat lineage he carried. Photo by Sheila Hunt. Used with permission.

Page 240: This photograph was taken during Khetsung Sangpo Rinpoche's visit to Houston, Texas, 2002. Photo by Anne C. Klein.

Line Drawings

Page 341: Ekajati. Drawing by Konchok Lhadrepa.
Page 341: Rahula. Woodblock by Gomchen Ulekshé.
Page 342: Damchen Dorje Lekpa. Woodblock by Gomchen Ulekshé.
Page 342: Tseringma. From the Chöling Collection.

Index

Abiding, Movement, and Awareness (Ju Mipham), xxxvi
Acha Migmar-la (second wife), 246
afflictions
carrying to path, 188, 199
conceptions and, 130–31
in daily activities, 222–23
foundational practices for, 206
limitation of calming practices on, 95
during meditation, 221–22
network of, 144, 286n282
purifying, 174
severing, 119
See also defilements, adventitious; five poisons
allground (*kun gzhi*), 11, 269nn38–39, 269n41
"actual preparatory," 13, 270n42
as beginningless, 171
as "error base," 124
mistaken mind and, 160, 191
neutrality of, 125, 169, 170
predispositions in, 11, 13, 23, 29
and sheer essence dimension, distinguished from, 57, 125, 163–64, 169, 170–71
allground consciousness, 11, 125, 269n38, 285n256
Amitabha, 216, 261
analysis, limits of, 167
Ananda, 227–28
antidotes
in balancing winds, 21, 132
to illusion, 21, 129
in path-vehicles, 109, 170
as pitfalls, 61, 97, 176, 179, 199
sheer awareness as, 125
appearances
arising of, 123
and emptiness, unity of, 151, 152, 154, 198, 235
as illusory, 25, 27, 29
mental consciousness and, 55
mistaken, 29, 130, 131, 132, 133, 143
not grasping as real, 77, 126
recall and, 33, 274n106
as self-appearing and self-liberating, 187–89
understanding through meditation, 176
Aronson, Harvey B., xvii, xxii–xxiii, xxxiii, xxxv, 245, 246
arrogance, elephantine, 93, 196
Aryadeva, 130
Condensed Trainings, 136
Lamp Distilling the Practices, xxvii, 15, 17, 21, 23, 127, 131
Asanga, xxv

aspiration, 141, 184, 218, 223, 236
Ati, 117
  See also Great Completeness
attachment, 126–27
  to common feats, 217
  cutting, 202
  to meditative experiences, 193, 198, 201
  mind and, 15, 160
  overcoming, 152, 177, 182, 189
  at time of death, 215
attainers, 271n58
Avalokiteshvara, mantra of, 215

bardo. *See* intermediate state (bardo)
base, xxvi, 7, 11, 166
  abiding state of (*gzhi'i gnas lugs*), 160
  and fruition, indivisibility of, 5
  great completeness, 45
  as great empty, 9
  ignorance in, 286n265, 287n296
  three Buddha dimensions in, xxiv, xxv, 3, 5, 122–23, 124
blessings, xxix–xxx, 41, 67, 150, 156, 201, 209, 223–24, 224–25
bliss
  desire and, 15, 271n62
  and emptiness as Great Seal, 35
  meditative experience of, 67, 69, 79, 89, 95, 177, 181, 182, 193, 198
  misunderstanding, 99, 201
  of sheer awareness, 75
Blissful Ones, 5, 13, 31, 37, 55, 123–24, 135, 147, 168
  See also Buddhas
bodhicitta. *See* enlightenment mind (bodhicitta)
bodhisattva grounds, 163, 191, 222
bodhisattvas, 140, 183–84, 218, 237
body, 17, 29, 45, 63, 118, 162, 163, 177, 202
  See also posture; subtle body
Bön, 204
bowing, 119
"Buddha again," xxv, 105, 232
Buddha dimension, fourth, 151, 156
Buddha dimensions, three, 237
  appearing according to need, 111, 113
  base, path, fruition of, xxiv–xxv, 5, 122–24, 231–34
  as great empty, 9
  inseparability of, 166
  mindnature and, 45, 47, 49, 142
  relationship of, 235–36
  sentient beings as inseparable, 31
  single essence of, 11
  spiritual accomplishments and, 105, 107, 109
  supreme feat and, 218
  usage of term, 267n23
  See also enlightenment, three dimensions
Buddha dimensions, two, 3, 109, 267n16
Buddha nature, xxv, 270nn44–45, 272n74
Buddha qualities, 43, 151, 156, 269n41
Buddhahood, xxv
  aspiration toward, 119, 120
  mistaken views of, 187
  as one's own mind, 105, 135, 165
  powa and, 216
  as sheer essence dimension, 122
  as supreme feat, 217
Buddhas
  allground seeds of, 269n41
  as all-knowing, 278n155
  ancestor of, 43
  arising from emptiness, 134–35

emanations of, 220
as illusory, 27, 128–29
mind and, 43, 49
not seeking elsewhere, 51, 81, 167–68
in one moment, 247
ordinary sentient beings and, 9, 11, 33, 67, 121, 122, 135, 232
See also Blissful Ones
Buddhism
changes in, 216–17
science and, 234–35
Budon (*Buston*), 37, 147

Candrakirti, *Entrance to the Middle Way,* 165
Cave of White Light, 256
Chakrasamvara Tantra, 138
channels, 138–39
See also winds
Chariot of Omniscience (Jigme Lingpa), xxi, xxvi, 49, 51, 167
Chekawa Dorje, *Root Text of the Seven Points of Training the Mind,* 222
children, training, 214
Chime Lhamo (first wife), 244
Chog Gyur Lingpa, *Commentary on the Heart of Primordial Knowing, Stages of the Path,* 21
clairvoyance, 177–78, 212–13, 223
clarity, 124, 152, 181
limpid, 91, 161
meditative experience of, 67, 69, 79, 89, 95, 177, 181, 193, 198, 213
mistaken understandings of, 91, 190–91, 194–95
in special seeing, 178
and thought, union of, 275n111
two types, 156–57
Clear Lamp Commentary, 23, 25
clear light, 35, 79, 156, 280n191
Cloud of Jewels Sutra, 59, 174
Collection of Secrets Tantra (*Guhyasamaja Tantra*), 49, 139, 140
collections, two, 3, 267n16
Commentary on the Heart of Primordial Knowing, Stages of the Path (Chog Gyur Lingpa), 21
compassion, 183–85, 232, 233, 236, 237
compassionate responsiveness, xxiv, xxv, 3, 5, 41, 122, 150–51, 157, 183–84
completion stage (*rdzogs rim*), 35, 138, 275n109, 275n111
See also creation and completion stages
conceptual thoughts, 83, 160
forty arising from desire, 15, 17, 25, 127, 136–37, 271nn61–62
freedom from, 168
in meditation, 75, 85, 97, 177, 194
in serene abiding, 63, 67, 69
seven associated with obscuration, 130–31
subtle, 190, 289n319
thirty-three arising from hatred, 21, 23, 25, 127
See also eighty conceptions
Condensed Trainings (Aryadeva), 136
conduct, 103, 202–3, 208, 210–13, 216–17
consciousness, 55, 99, 132, 138–39, 162–63, 278n152, 288n299
consecration, 37, 146, 180, 267n17
continuity, xxix, 85, 89, 97, 134, 137, 141, 174, 176, 179, 191–92, 196–97, 199, 212–13, 222
cosmology, 234–35
courage, 105

creation and completion stages, xxxi, 37, 101, 139, 146, 202, 203, 206, 210
cyclic existence
allground and, 11, 13, 169, 269n39
arising in mindnature, 47, 49, 149–50, 151
base of, 9, 57
emptiness of, 154
as illusion, 27, 133–34
seeds of, 29, 129
three Buddha dimensions and, 164–65

Dagpo Hlaje (*Dwags po lha rje*). *See* Gampopa
dakinis, 71, 138, 206, 208, 217, 219–20, 224
Dalai Lama. *See* Tenzin Gyatso, H. H. Dalai Lama XIV
dark retreat (*mun tshams*), xxxiv, 244, 245, 254–55
dawn/dawning, 9, 61, 69, 73, 131, 146, 187
of appearances, 25, 43, 71
of meditation, 93
of primordial knowing, 156
of sheer awareness, 35, 181
of thoughts, 15, 17, 83, 85, 89, 91, 189
Dawn Mountain Tibetan Buddhist Temple, xix, xxxv, xxxviii, 247
death and dying, 214–16, 256–57
defilements, adventitious, xxvi, 5, 31, 33, 122, 142, 143–44, 170
Definitive Commentary on the Enlightened State Sutra, 59, 174
delusion, 5, 9, 15, 23, 128–31
desire, 23
forty thoughts arising from, 15, 17, 25, 127, 136–37, 271nn61–62
middling, 15, 131, 271n56
devotion, 67, 185, 223–24, 225, 226–29, 289n322
dharma, meaning of term, 119
Dharma friends, 236–37
dharmakāya. See sheer essence
Discriminating the Three Vows, 37
Dorje Chang, 224
doubt, 65, 103, 169, 284n238
dreams, 25, 27, 29, 57, 126, 129, 130, 133, 169
Drikung Kagyu, 35, 145, 206, 275n117, 287n285
Drilbupa, a great yogi, 207–8
Drukpa Kagyu, 145, 275n111, 275n114, 287n284
Drukpa Lama Gotsangpa (rGod tshang pa), 35, 275n115
Drukpa Yongzin Rinpoche, 245, 254
Dudjom Rinpoche (first), 221
Dudjom Rinpoche (second). *See* Jigdral Yeshe Dorje, H. H. Dudjom Rinpoche
dynamic playfulness (*rol rtsal*), 71
dynamism, xxv, 17, 41, 93, 123, 156, 160, 276n127, 283n221, 287n296
Dzogchen, xxii, xxiii
as both easy and difficult, 117, 139–41
characteristics of, 231
conduct in, 203
creation and completion stages, importance of in, xxxi
discriminations in, xxix
experience, importance of in, 157, 159
meditation in, 61, 65, 79, 87, 95 (*See also* serene abiding: special seeing)

path and fruition as one taste in, 123
supreme practice of, 194
use of different postures in, 138–39
view, xxvi–xxvii, 7, 9, 11, 13, 15, 124–27, 153, 164–68, 191, 200, 287n295
See also Great Completeness

easeful equilibrium/equipoise, 63, 85, 95, 192, 198
three methods of, 59, 61, 278n164
effort, xxix, xxx
in creation and completion, 202
devotion and, 228
in Dzogchen practices, 65, 174, 176–77, 191
fruition of, 232
that muddies things up, 188
eighty conceptions, xxvi–xxvii, xxviii, 15, 17, 19, 21, 23, 25, 127–30, 131–34, 273n87
emanation dimension (*nirmāṇakāya*), xxiv, 81, 121
arising in accordance with need, 236
base, path, fruition of, xxiv
compassionate responsiveness and, 183–84
in context of base, 3, 123
mindnature in, 41
perception of beings in, 218
spiritual accomplishments in, 107, 109
emanations, categories of, 109, 232–34
empowerment, 181, 183, 245, 247
emptiness, xxv, 35, 81, 134, 275n110
and clarity, union of, 45, 149–50, 189–90
coarse understanding of, 199
free of elaborations, 183, 289n319
in Great Seal, 145
importance of understanding, 199–200
primordial slippages into, 95, 97, 284n231
special seeing recognizing, 67, 75
unconditioned, 123
view of, 167, 235
empty essence. *See* emptiness
enlightenment, 69, 233
instantaneous, 140, 174, 255
thirty-seven elements of, 43, 152, 276n128
enlightenment, three dimensions, 121
base, path, fruition in, 122–23
as mindnature, 150–51, 153
as one's own mind, 165
relationship between, 155–56
usage of term, 267n23
enlightenment mind (bodhicitta), 47, 81, 111, 141, 143, 164, 184–85
Entrance to the Middle Way (Candrakirti), 165
equipoise. *See* easeful equilibrium/equipoise
errors, 190, 289n319
appearance and, 274n98
chain of, 129
holding, 21
in meditation (*See under* meditation)
overstating and undervaluing, xiii, 45, 135, 154, 201–2
of perception, xxvi–xxvii, 27, 129
uninterrupted, 273n88
See also sidetracking and slipping

Essential Black cycle (Yangti Nagpo), xxxiv, xxxvi, xxxvii, 245, 247
evanescence (*khral khrol*), 25
Exemplifiers (*Vaibhāṣika*), 130
extremes, three, 9

faith, 220, 223, 227
familiarization, 85, 150, 174, 192, 194, 230, 281n203
feats, supreme and common, 105, 107, 217–19
Fine Chariot (Longchenpa), 25, 27, 128, 135, 283n261
five poisons, 19, 77–78, 131, 190
five primordial knowings, 47, 105, 143, 153, 164
  three Buddha dimensions and, 45, 105, 135
  and winds, relationship to, 19, 21, 272n78
flickering (*phyal phyol*), 25
flimsiness (*al 'ol*), 25
foundational practices (*sngon 'gro*), xxx, xxxi, xxxiv, 99, 101, 201, 202, 204, 205, 206, 209
four thoughts, 209, 255, 289n323
fruition, 3, 7
  as five primordial knowings, 153
  great completeness, 45, 124
  indivisibility with base, 5
  phenomena in, 49, 277n138
  of practice, 166–68, 225
  three Buddha dimensions at, 122, 123, 124, 231–34
full essence dimension (*ngo bo nyid sku; svabhāvikakāya*), 41, 43, 151

Gampopa, 35, 225–26
  Simultaneously Arisen Union, 35, 275n111
Gandenpa tradition. *See* Geluk tradition
Garab Dorje, 119
Garwang Chögyi Dragpa, 35, 145, 275n112
Gautama Buddha. *See* Shakyamuni Buddha
gaze, sheer essence dimension, 137
Geluk tradition, xxviii, 37, 39, 147, 148, 204, 253–54
genuine state (*gnas lugs*), 3, 267n18
Gonpo Dorje (aka Gotsangpa), 35, 145, 275n115, 287n284
  See also Garwang Chögyi Dragpa
Gotsangpa (*rGod tshang pa*), 35, 145, 275n115, 287n284
grasping, 15, 77, 125–27
  at appearance, 132, 133
  at clarity, 157
  freedom from, 83, 85, 153
  liberation in its own place, 188–90
  in meditation, 65, 67, 69, 77, 79, 89, 91, 99, 194
  at self, 143
  yearning and, 189
  See also attachment
Great Chariot (Longchenpa), 13, 127
Great Completeness, 7
  abiding state of, 124
  base, path, fruition in, 3, 5, 7
  as essence of nine vehicles, 231, 235
  experience, importance of in, 53
  initiation in, 267n17
  mistaken understandings of, 191, 201
  practice from peak of mountain, 202, 205
Great Seal, 275n111
  consecration in, 3, 267n17
  in Geluk tradition, 147, 148

in Indian tradition, 144–45
in Kagyu tradition, 35, 145–46
meditation of, 63, 85, 177, 193
as method and wisdom, indivisible, 151
mindnature as, xxviii, 149–51
in Nyingma tradition, 41, 43
in Sakya tradition, 37
Great Seal of Heartfelt Advice (Guru Rinpoche), 41, 43, 45, 149, 151, 152
Guru Rinpoche, 144, 178, 192, 219
on Dharma, 231
mantra of, 215
on meditation, 65
on method and wisdom indivisible, 33, 274n107
prophecies of, 216–17
on sheer awareness, xxix
on three phases of key instructions, 75, 77, 79, 81
Gyalwa Lorepa (*rGyal ba Lorepa*), xxx, 69, 187, 279n174

hail protection, 244, 254
hatred, thirty-three thoughts arising from, 21, 23, 25, 127
haziness (*ban bun*), 25
Heart Essence, Vast Expanse (Longchen Nyingthig), xxiii, xxxiv, 244–45, 255, 266n11
heartfelt and straightforward, xxi, xxii, 118
Heartfelt Instructions (Patrul Rinpoche), 71, 72
Highest Tantra (*rGyud bla ma*), 31, 142
Highest Yoga Tantra, 145
homeground 9, 49, 93, 95, 97, 103, 277n139, 283n229
Hopkins, Jeffrey, xviii, xxxiii, xxxiv, 234, 243, 246–47, 249
ignorance, 13, 15, 130–31, 160, 286n265, 287n296
acquired, 137
in allground, 169
inborn, 143
illusions, 27, 29, 89, 128–29
See also dreams
inborn unawareness. *See under* unawareness
India, 206–7, 208
Indrabhuti, 139–41, 174
initiation, 117, 138, 141, 146, 174, 236, 258, 267n17
instructions, key (*gnad*) , 77, 79, 81, 99
intellect, xxix
intention, 209–10, 212
intermediate state (bardo), 79, 163
Introducing Dzogchen, a Heart Jewel for the Fortunate (Dudjom Rinpoche), 73, 75
introduction to mind, xxvii, xxviii, 124–25, 141, 187, 196

Jamgön Kontrul Lodro Thaye, xxiii
Jamyang Khyense Wangpo, xxiii
Jetsun Shugsep, xxxiv, 244–45, 252, 253
Jigdral Yeshe Dorje, H. H. Dudjom Rinpoche, 221, 245, 246
Introducing Dzogchen, a Heart Jewel for the Fortunate, 73, 75
prayer by, xiii–xv
on severing root of mind, 105
Jigme Lingpa
Chariot of Omniscience, xxi, xxvi, 49, 51, 167
nonsectarianism of, xxiii
refuge prayer of, xxiv–xxv, 265n3
Yeshe Lama, 255, 266n14

Jigten Gonpo, 145, 206
Jonagpa tradition, 147
Ju Mipham Rinpoche
  Abiding, Movement, and Awareness, xxxvi
  Three Cycles of the Fundamental Mind, xxxvi

Kagyu lineage, xxviii, 33, 35, 187, 204
Kamtshangpa Kagyu, 35, 146
Kangyur Rinpoche, xxxiii, 245, 246
Kangyur Rinpoche Tulku Jigme Norbu, xxxiii, 245, 246, 261, 263, 289n322
karma, 99, 128, 155, 162, 169, 228
karmic winds, 17, 55, 57, 137, 138–39, 278n154
Kaydrub Trodragpa (*Khas grub kro brag pa*), 37, 146
Khetsun Sangpo Rinpoche, xiii, xvii, 289n322
  Acha Migmar-la (second wife), 246
  autobiography of, 243, 266n12
  birth of, 243
  Chime Lhamo (first wife), 244
  Dzogchen, approach to, xxii, xxxv
  on hail protection, 254, 257
  on having to study Geluk texts, 253–54
  on his monastic life, 249–51, 258
  in Japan, xxxiii, 245–46
  on Jetsun Shugsep, 252
  name of, 257
  nonsectarian vision of, xxiii–xxiv, xxviii, 244
  parinirvana of, xxxviii, 247
  on practice, 257–58
  prayers for, xiii–xv, 261, 263
  studies and training of, xxxiv, 244–45
  on time with Lama Gonpo, 255–57
  traditional teaching style of, xxii, 205–6
  in the West, xxi, xxxiii–xxxv, xxxv–xxxvii, 247, 266nn13–14
  works of, xxii, xxxiii–xxxiv, 243–44
Khetsun Sangpo Rinpoche, teachers associated with
  Drukpa Yongzin, 254, 290n340
  Jetsun Shugsep, xxxiv, 244–45, 252, 253
  Kangyur Rinpoche, xxxiii, 245, 246
  Lama Gonpo (aka Lama Gonpo Tsayden), xxxiv, 245, 255–57, 266n13
  See also Jigdral Yeshe Dorje, H. H. Dudjom Rinpoche
killing, 219–20
kindness, 5, 118, 119, 123, 157, 215
Kukuripa, 206–7

Lama Gonpo Tsayden (aka Lama Gonpo Tsayden), xxxiv, 245, 255, 266n13
  death of, 256–57
Lama Tharchen, xxii
lamas
  homage to, 119–20
  identifying nature for student, xxviii, 124–25, 141, 187, 196
  meaning of term, 118–19
  role of, 150, 156, 178, 183, 201, 224–25
  two kinds of splendor, 118
  See also spiritual teachers
Lamp Distilling the Practices (Aryadeva), xxvii, 15, 17, 21, 23, 127, 131
letting be, 89, 91, 93

Lhalu (*Lha klu*) clan official, 252, 253–54
liberation
and dawning, simultaneous, 187–88
three doors, xxviii, 61, 63, 65, 179
lineage, xxiv, xxv, 119
blessings of, 67, 180–81, 224–25
Dzogchen, 205
of Great Seal, 35, 144–45
naturally abiding, 187
Lingre Pema Dorje, 275n114
lion and monkey story, 136
Lochen Rinpoche. *See* Jetsun Shugsep
Longchen Nyingthig. *See* Heart Essence, Vast Expanse (Longchen Nyingthig)
Longchen Rabjam, xxiii, 220
on errors in meditation, 89, 91, 93, 195
on familiarity, 83, 85, 194
Fine Chariot, 25, 27, 128, 135, 285n261
Great Chariot, 13, 127
posture of, 137
Precious Treasury of Philosophical Systems, xxiv
on stainless space, xxv–xxvi, 265n7
Treasury of Philosophical Tenets, xxiv–xxv
long-life prayers, xiii
Lord of Death, 216
Lord Shvari (Rithro Wangchug), 35, 145
lordly features, eight, 232–34
Losang Chogyal, *Root of the Great Seal,* 37, 39, 147
Losang Chogyi Gyaltsen, 147, 148
Lotus Lake, 113, 237
luminosity, mother and child, 190
Machig Labdron, 37, 147
Madhyamaka, 163, 183, 198
Mahāmudra. *See* Great Seal
Maitreya, xxv
on dhatu, xxvi
five books of, xxv
Ornament of Clear Realization, 173, 179
Sublime Continuum, xxv–xxvi
Maitripa, 35, 145
Majestic Creator of Everything, 13, 31, 47, 109, 111, 134, 135, 142–43, 164, 236
mantra, 215
Marpa, 35, 145, 206, 216
masterly qualities, eight, 105, 107
Maudgalayana, 27, 129, 140
meditation
beginners, guidance for, 177
distinctions in types, 57, 59, 173–74, 193
Dzogchen view of, 61, 65, 79, 124, 125, 182–83, 199
errors in, 87, 89, 91, 93, 178, 190–92, 281n208, 289n319
importance of, 83, 133–34, 156, 181
mistaken understandings of, 200–202
practice and scholarship, comparison for, 148
prophecies about, 216–17
purpose of, 152–54, 185
sleepiness in, 183
specific instructions (exercises), 134, 137, 154, 168, 182, 213
thieves of, 85
for working with seasonal energies, 132
See also practice
meditative experiences, 63, 177–78, 221–22, 229, 230
attachment to, 193

meditative experiences (*continued*)
of bliss, clarity, nonconceptuality (*nyam*), 67, 69, 79, 89, 95, 177, 181, 198, 213
meditative stabilization, 89, 91
of cessation/extinguishment, 131, 132, 272n78
three methods of, 175–76
memory, 172
mental analysis, 89, 281n209
mental consciousness (*yid*), 15, 17, 55, 137, 271n60, 277n149
mental functioning (*yid byed*), xxvii, 55, 125, 160, 161–62, 167, 168, 277n149, 287n297
merit, 209, 220
Meru, Mount, 107, 234
metaphors
blissful cushion, 63
dry leaves when root is cut, 69
dumb person's dream, 83
fresh water, 225
helter-skelter arrow of maliciousness, 75
lotuses, 237
mirrors, 11, 77, 128, 188
monkey, 75
moon, 109, 155, 218
ocean, 154, 267n24
rust on gold, 33, 143, 190
seeing one's own eyes, 181
small child in battlefield, 85
snooty elephant, 93, 196
unmoving ocean, 63
water rushing down mountain, 63, 177, 181, 221–22
water wheel, 29
waves, 83
woven cloth, clothing, 144, 235
method, path of, 35, 275n109
method and wisdom, 33, 43, 144, 145, 151, 223, 274n107
Middle Way, 3
Milarepa, 35, 145, 206, 215, 220, 221, 225–26
mind
abiding state of, 121
afflicted, 21, 132
as ancestor of all Buddhas, 43
apprehending objects, 23, 273n88
defining characteristic of, 47, 277n138
emanating and still, 283n221
gods and demons in, 215–16
investigating, 65, 179–80
lacking grasping, 77, 79
lama's introduction to, xxvii, xxviii, 124–25, 141, 187, 196
luminosity of, 69
names for, 71, 73
in serene abiding, 63
severing root of, 105, 231
and sheer awareness, distinguishing, 53, 159, 160–61, 168
subtle, 161, 162, 191
three doors to liberation and, 61
See also mistaken mind
mind (*sems*) and mental function (*yid byed*), xxvii, 125, 161, 285n257
Mind Only school, 125, 163
mindful presence (*dran rig*), 61, 79, 97
mindfulness (*gnyug dran*), 85, 89, 99, 152–53, 171–72, 191, 200, 281n203
mind-holding, 191
mindnature (*sems nyid*)
as base, 9, 53
as Buddha, xxi, 51, 156
as free of birth, cessation, abiding, 45
as Great Seal, xxviii, 41, 149–50, 149–51

homeground of, 49, 277n139
names for, 47
purity and spontaneity of, 31, 33, 45, 153
realization of, 159, 160–61
recognizing, 81, 166
as seed, xxv
as self-risen, 45
of sentient beings and Buddhas, 142–43
special seeing of, 69, 71
as unborn, 151, 166
mistaken mind, 184–85
allground and, 191
Dzogchen view and, 200
in meditation, 152–53, 159–60, 180, 197, 229
positive qualities of, 165, 171–72
and unborn mind, differentiated, 141, 151, 157, 165–66
monkey and lion story, 136
"Mother," 134
Mother Perfection of Wisdom Sutra, 27, 29, 129

Nāgārjuna, xxv, 33, 144, 165
naming, 171
Naropa, 35, 145, 206
Ngawang Wangyal, Geshe, 246
nine vehicles, 117, 231, 235
nirmāṇakāya. See emanation dimension
nirvana
arising in mindnature, 150, 151
base of, 9
causes of, 174
emptiness of, 154
illusory phenomena of, 27
names for phenomena of, 13, 270n45
radiating from allground, 11, 13, 269m39
seeds of, 29, 129
three Buddha dimensions as, 165
nondistraction, 141
non-holding, 25
non-meditation, 61, 79, 189
nonsectarianism (Rimé), xxiii–xxiv, 204, 236–37
Norbu Choling, Khyam Gompa, 249–51
Nyingma school
nine vehicles of, 117
two purities in, 122
Nyingma tradition, xxv, xxviii, 117, 122, 149, 204, 245, 253–54
Nyingma Wish-Fulfilling Center for Study and Practice, xiii, xv, xxxv, 243, 246, 251

obscurations, seven conceptions associated with, 130–31
obstructions, two, 142, 144, 172–73, 209
"obtainer," 130
omniscience, two kinds, 147, 168
one taste, 5, 122, 123, 233
Open Presence Naturally Dawning, 129
oral commentary, xxi
ordinary beings
arising from emptiness, 134–35
intrinsic luminous alertness of, 67
mistaken path of, 127
perceptions of, xxvi
original face, 7, 13, 15, 47, 67, 71, 77, 79, 81, 83, 121, 135, 137, 150, 280n197
Ornament of Clear Realization (Maitreya), 173, 179
ornamentation (*rgyan*), xxv, 5, 105, 109, 122, 123, 232, 276n127

overstating and undervaluing, xiii, 45, 135, 154, 201–2

Pacification (also Pacifiers), 37, 87, 147, 193
Padampa Sangye, 147, 276n120, 281n206
Panchen Losang Chogyal, 37, 39
Parting Questions for Guru Rinpoche (Yeshe Tsogyal), xxxvi–xxxvii
path, 3, 7
  and fruition as one taste, 123
  great completeness, 45
  mistaken mind on, 165
  phenomena of, 47, 49
  sheer awareness, 161
  three buddha dimensions of, 5, 122
Patrul Rinpoche (*rDza spal sprul*), 192
  Heartfelt Instructions, 71, 72
  on mind, 85
  Words of My Perfect Teacher, xxxiv, 243–44, 247
Pearl Garland Tantra, xxiv
Pema Osel Ling, xxii
perception, xxvi–xxvii, 129, 162–63
perfection of wisdom, 134
permanence, 126–27
phenomena
  arising from mindnature, 41, 43, 149–51, 166
  illusory, 27, 129
  proper recognition of, 89, 190, 281n209
Piburn, Sidney, xix
playful expression/emergence, xxv, 5, 123, 157
pointing, 126
pointing-out instruction, 77, 79, 81
posture, 137–39
  sheer essence dimension, 137
powa. *See* transference (powa)
practice, 144
  complexity of, xxx–xxxi
  as contrived, meaning of, 202
  devotion in, 228–29
  essence of, 210–11
  fruition of, 166–68, 231–34
  investigating appearances, 133–34
  lifelong commitment to, xxii
  perseverance in, 214
  sessions of, 229
  view of purity in, 204–5
  See also conduct; meditation
practitioners
  blessings, importance of to, 225
  capacity of, 57, 59, 87, 117
  dangers to, 178, 193, 200–202, 214
  excellent, qualities of, 217
  experience, importance of, 148
  faults of, 89, 91, 93, 99, 101, 193–98
  focus for, 203, 213, 220
  intention, importance of, 209–10
  like deer and lion, 103, 211
  stories of great, 206–9
  threefold typology, falseness of, 91, 93, 196–97
  Western, xxi
  See also trainees, three categories of
Prāsangikas, 163–64
prayers, 229
Precious Treasury of Philosophical Systems (Longchenpa), xxiv
Precisely Discriminating the Three Vows (Sakya Pandita), 146
predispositions, 83
  in allground, 11, 13, 23, 29, 129, 130
  as dynamic display, 17

mental functioning and, xxvii
subtle, 191, 222
pride, 65, 87, 119, 178, 193, 213, 217
primordial knowing (*ye shes*), 3, 265n7, 267n18, 272n74
and consciousness, distinguished, 55, 162–63, 168, 278n152
enumerations of, 47, 164 (*See also* five primordial knowings)
inborn unawareness and, 13, 127
in Kagyu tradition, 33, 35
as method, 144
misunderstanding, 91, 282n216
in Sakya tradition, 37
sublime knowing and, 159–60, 162–63, 168
threefold nature of, 5
as unity of clarity and emptiness, 149–50
primordial wisdom, xxvi, xxix
pure appearances, 189
purities, two, 5, 122–23, 124
purity, xxvi, 45, 143, 153, 190, 204

reality, 55, 286n281
clear and mistaken, distinguished, 171
in Kagyu tradition, 33
recognizing sheer awareness as, 79, 190
spiritual accomplishment and, 105
ultimate, 129, 155–56
unchanging, 142
rebirth, 95, 99, 128, 198, 200, 220, 228
recall and appearances, 33, 274n106
Rechungpa, 35, 145
refuge, 119–20, 225, 265n3
Rice University, xxxvi, 247
richly resplendent dimension (*sambhogakāya*), xxiv, 121
base, path, fruition of, xxiv
beings of, 232
in context of base, 3, 123
mindnature in, 41
spiritual accomplishments in, 107
Rinchen Sangpo, 149
rituals, 203
Root of the Great Seal (Losang Chogyal), 37, 39, 147
Root Text of the Seven Points of Training the Mind (Chekawa Dorje), 222

sacred commitments, 224, 225, 238
Sakya Pandita, *Precisely Discriminating the Three Vows,* 146
Sakya tradition, xxviii, 37, 146, 204
Samantabhadra
activity/conduct of, 101, 103, 105, 209, 210
as enlightenment mind, 143
homage to, 119
literal meaning of, 143
as mindnature, 111
as source of blessings, 224–25
sambhogakāya. See richly resplendent dimension
sameness, 55, 111, 168
samsara. *See* cyclic existence
Samye monastery, 255–56
sangha, as illusory, 27, 129
Saraha, xxv, 9, 35, 61, 63, 145, 176
scriptural transmission (*lung*), 221
Second Tiger Root Tantra (*Hevajra Root Tantra*), 141–42, 286n275
secrecy, 121, 203, 204, 206–7, 208, 258
Secret Essence Tantra, 9, 268n26
Secret Mantra, xxx, 5, 67, 101, 103, 202–4, 208

seeds (in allground), 29, 129, 269n41
Self-Dawning Tantra, 11, 23
sense powers, five, 132, 133
sense-doors, five, 21, 126
sentient beings
  adventitious defilements and, 5
  allground seeds of, 269n41
  as Buddhas, 142, 144, 165, 166
  as mind, 49
  perception of emanation beings, 218–19
  realization to be called Buddha, 9, 11, 33, 121, 122
serene abiding, xxix, xxx, 71, 124
  clarity in, 157
  deviations in, 87
  Dzogchen view of, 65, 95, 173, 174–75, 288n311
  faults and good qualities distinguished, 57, 59
  limits of, 181–82
  middle phase of, 67
  mistaken understandings of, 99, 200
  and sheer awareness, distinguishing, 178–79, 230
  and special seeing, relationship of, 182–83
  three phases of, 63, 65
  See also under special seeing
Seventeen Tantras, xxiii
Severance (also Severers), 37, 87, 147, 193
Shakyamuni Buddha, 219
  emanation of, 235
  Indrabhuti and, 139–41
  last words of, 222
  as source of blessings, 224
  stories about, 227–28, 232–33
Shariputra, 27, 129, 140
sheer awareness (*rig pa*)
  allground and, 13, 125
  associated with base (*gzhi'i rig pa*), 122–23, 160–61
  continuity of, 195–96
  essence of (*rip pa'i ngo bo*), 31, 160
  experiencing beyond thought, 67, 279n172
  freeing grasping mind into, 77, 79
  fruitional, 55, 277n146, 277n150
  intrinsic dynamism of, xxix
  playful display of, 188
  recognizing, 79, 81, 83
  self-recognition, 41
  tantric understanding of, 159–60
  three qualities of, xxv, 230, 265n4
  threefold division of, 53, 161, 230–31, 277n146
  as triply free, 89, 282n213
  unchanging, 181
sheer awareness holders (*rigzin*), 5, 121
sheer essence dimension (*dharmakāya*), xxiv, 121
  and allground, distinguishing, 57, 125, 163–64, 169, 170–71
  base, path, fruition of, xxiv
  as beyond mind, 171–72
  in context of base, 3, 122–23, 285n251
  heart and essence of all, 235–36
  mindnature in, 41
  names for, 71, 73
  as unborn, 166
  unchanging, 143–44, 151, 165
Shri Singha, 119
siddhas, 212–13, 219–20, 221
  mistaken, 65
  stories of, 206–9
siddhis. *See* feats, supreme and common

sidetracking and slipping, 87, 89, 91, 93, 95, 99, 101, 193–99, 200–202
slippage, eight places of, 95, 97
Simultaneously Arisen Union (Gampopa), 35, 275n111
sitting, advice on, 137–38
six realms, 27, 29, 126, 127, 128, 129
Soaring Path (*thögel*), 126–27, 138
Sogyal Rinpoche, Geshe, 185, 252, 253, 290n338
sound, importance of, 133
space, stainless, 230
special seeing, xxx, 124, 174
arisen from wisdom, 175
in Dzogchen, 65, 66, 67, 176–79, 181–82, 188, 279n172, 289n316
faults and good qualities distinguished, 57, 59
fixation-free stillness in, 71, 279n180
mistaken understandings of, 99, 200
serene abiding and, xxix, 67, 69, 70, 71, 182–83, 187, 188, 279n179
sheer essence dimension in, 71, 73, 75
spiritual teachers
homage to, 3
and students, relationship between, xxvii–xxviii, xxix, 206, 223
See also lamas
stainless space (*dharma dhatu*), 9, 47, 57, 79, 146, 155, 164, 169, 189, 190, 230
three aspects of, xxv–xxvi, 265n4, 265nn7–9
stories
Buddha's tooth/dog tooth, 226–27
destitute disciple of Buddha, 232–33
girl in orchard, 219–20
great yogi Drilbupa, 207–8
Karma, Buddha's cousin, 227–28
of Kukuripa, 206–7
lion and monkey, 136
mahasiddha crossing bridge, 208–9
Marpa and Milarepa, 206
Milarepa and Gampopa, 225–26
Naropa and Tilopa, 206
Strand of Jewels, purpose of, xxii, 117–18
striving. *See* effort
subject and object
freedom from, 111
meeting in clear light, 280n191
perception of, 136, 137
transcending, 83
Sublime Continuum (Maitreya), xxv–xxvi
sublime knowing (*shes rab*), 35
of the basis (*gzhi shes rab*), 161
distinctions in sutra and tantra, 159
threefold, 55
as unborn nature, 33
subtle body, 17, 19, 21, 138–39
suffering, 29, 103, 105, 127–28
Sutra on the Questions of Bhadra the Magician, 27, 29, 128, 135
sutras, twelve sets of, 59, 278n163

tantra, xxxi, 159, 170, 203, 224, 225, 231
Tantric Practice in Nyingma (Khetsun Rinpoche), xxxiv
Taranatha, 37, 147
Tenzin Gyatso, H. H. Dalai Lama XIV, xiii, xxxv, 217, 243, 245, 246, 289n322

Tenzin Samphel, Lama, xxxv, 246
Thinley Norbu Rinpoche, H. E. Dungse, xxxviii, 261
Three Cycles of the Fundamental Mind (Ju Mipham), xxxvi
Tibet, xxiii–xxiv, 202, 203–4, 205, 208, 244, 251
Tilopa, 35, 144, 145, 206
times, four, 167–68
trainees, three categories of, 109, 111
transference (powa), 215–16, 289n324
Treasury of Philosophical Tenets (Longchenpa), xxiv–xxv
Treasury of Praise, 47, 164, 276n132
true existence, holding to, 25, 273n92
Trulzhig Dongag Lingpa Rinpoche, 245
Trulzhig Rinpoche, xxxiv, 245
trust, xxvii, xxix
Tsalway Kagyu, 275n116
Tsele Natsok Rangdrol, 89, 95, 198
Tshering Jong, 256
Tsultrim Rangdrol, Lama, 255
Tulku Jigme. *See* Kangyur Rinpoche Tulku Jigme Norbu
two stages. *See* creation and completion stages
two truths, 3, 267n16

Uddiyana, 139, 208
ultimate truth, xxvi, 265n7
unawareness, 169, 274–75n107
  inborn, 13, 15, 33, 127, 130, 270n51
  learned, 15, 271n60
  unbounded wholeness (*thigle nyag gcig*), 45, 109, 152, 171, 276n129
Unimpeded-State Tantra, 9, 13, 15, 130, 268n29
union, seven aspects of complete, 105, 232, 284n241
University of Virginia, xxxiii, xxxiv, xxxv, 247
Uttara Tantra. See *Sublime Continuum* (Maitreya)

vajra vehicle, 5
Vajrasattva, 119
vanishing, mistlike (*sang seng*), 25
views, 7, 9, 11, 13, 15, 124–27
  arising of wrong, 130
  ascertaining, 181
  limits of conceptual, 166
  meditation and, 57, 67
  mistaken, 197–98, 199
  prophecies about, 216–17
  realizing, 45, 47, 49, 164
  two kinds of, 167

weakness, internal, 103
White Lotus, 266n14
winds
  channels and, 138–39
  five root, 17, 19, 21
  five secondary, 17, 21, 132–33
  function of, 19, 21
  internal, 19
  life-bearing, 19
  male and female, 19, 21, 272n73
  neutral, 19
  seasonal energies and, 21, 131–33
  See also karmic winds
wisdom, threefold, 173, 288n310
wisdom wind, 137, 138–39
Words of My perfect Teacher (Patrul Rinpoche), xxxiv, 243–44, 247
world systems, 234–35
worldly concerns, eight, 209, 211

Yade (*g.Yag sde*), 244, 249
Yeshe Lama (Jigme Lingpa), 255, 266n14
Yeshe Tsogyal
  cave of, 256
  Parting Questions for Guru Rinpoche, xxxvi–xxxvii
yogis, 13, 37, 39, 73, 103, 105, 147, 211–13

Zhang Tshal, 35, 275n116

About the Author

Khetsun Sangpo Rinpoche (d. 2009) was born in Central Tibet to farming parents who did not support his monastic training. At the age of eleven he ran away to a local monastery, and then later pursued serious study with several renowned teachers in Central Tibet, including Jetsun Shugseb and the hermit Gonpo Rinpoche. He eventually became a mantrika (ngagpa) in the Nyingma tradition, and a skilled hail-protection master. For ten years, he served as His Holiness Dudjom Rinpoche's representative in Japan, becoming fluent in Japanese. Later, at the request of Dudjom Rinpoche and His Holiness the Dalai Lama, he founded the Nyingma Wish-Fulfilling Center, a school for young monks. Until his death at the age of ninety he remained committed to traditional teaching methods, while at the same time developing a style that Western students could assimilate.

He has published thirteen volumes on Tibetan cultural history. His works in English are *Tantric Practice in Nyingma* and *Fundamental Mind.*

About the Translator

Anne Carolyn Klein, PhD, also known as Rigzin Drolma, is a professor in the department of religion at Rice University and a lama in the Nyingma tradition. She is cofounder, with Harvey Aronson, of Dawn Mountain Tibetan Buddhist Center in Houston, Texas (www.dawnmountain.org). She has studied, practiced, and translated in the Geluk, Nyingma, and Bon textual and oral traditions. Her work has received support from Fulbright, NEH, Ford Foundation, and Fetzer Institute. Her books include *Heart Essence of the Vast Expanse*, *Meeting the Great Bliss Queen*, *Knowledge and Liberation*, *Path to the Middle*, and *Unbounded Wholeness* (with Geshe Tenzin Wangyal Rinpoche).

Ekajati

Rahula

Dorje Lekpa

Shenpa Marnak